BOLLINGEN SERIES LXXXIV

MYTH, RELIGION,

AND MOTHER RIGHT

Selected Writings of

J. J. Bachofen

TRANSLATED FROM THE GERMAN BY
RALPH MANHEIM

WITH A PREFACE BY GEORGE BOAS
AND AN INTRODUCTION BY JOSEPH CAMPBELL

BOLLINGEN SERIES LXXXIV

PRINCETON UNIVERSITY PRESS

THIS IS THE EIGHTY-FOURTH
IN A SERIES OF WORKS SPONSORED BY BOLLINGEN FOUNDATION

First Princeton/Bollingen Paperback Printing, 1973

Translated and adapted from *Johann Jakob Bachofen: Mutterrecht und Urreligion*, a selection edited by Rudolf Marx. Enlarged edition, copyright 1954, Alfred Kröner Verlag, Stuttgart (Kröners Taschenausgabe, Vol. 52).

Library of Congress Catalogue Card No. 67–22343

ISBN 0–691–01797–2 (paperback edn.)
ISBN 0–691–09799–2 (hardcover edn.)

MANUFACTURED IN THE UNITED STATES OF AMERICA
DESIGNED BY ANDOR BRAUN

Editorial Note

THIS VOLUME is a translation of *Mutterrecht und Urreligion,* a selection of the writings of J. J. Bachofen edited by Rudolf Marx and first published in 1926 by Alfred Kröner Verlag, Stuttgart. Grateful acknowledgment is made to Schwabe & Co., Basel, for permission to draw on the scholarship of *Johann Jakob Bachofen: Gesammelte Werke,* edited by Karl Meuli, for clarification and additional information. We are also indebted to Schwabe & Co. for permission to reproduce Plates I, III, and V from Volume 4 of their edition, and to Harcourt, Brace & World, Inc., for permission to quote Robert Fitzgerald's translation of Sophocles' *Oedipus at Colonus.*

Bachofen wrote at a time when the Greek and Roman gods and heroes were identified with one another more closely than they are today, and generally speaking, he used Latin forms even where we would find the Greek more appropriate. The editors felt, however, that to modify his usage in this respect would be intrusive. The reader will find the necessary equivalents in the glossarial index.

Special thanks are due to Ernest Nash for information on the location and condition of the works of art depicted in Plates I, III, and V. The late A. S. B. Glover was responsible for the compilation of the bibliography and the glossarial index, and for valuable editorial advice on the text.

Contents

CONTENTS

From The Myth of Tanaquil

List of Plates

Preface

THE NAME of Johann Jakob Bachofen, if mentioned at all in books of reference, is attached to a theory of social development which maintains that the first period of human history was matriarchal. And if any discussion of the theory is added, it will be to the effect that it is almost universally discredited. As a matter of fact this is only a small part of Bachofen's contribution to social philosophy, and it would be perhaps more appropriate, if labels are required, to list him among the philosophers of history rather than among either ethnologists or sociologists. For, as the studies in this volume will show, his attitude toward cultural history was not that of the empirical anthropologist or that of the annalist. His focus of interest was the inner life of human beings rather than what he called the externals of human development. He was more concerned with literature, language, architecture, and the other arts than with economic factors, military adventures, territorial expansion, the succession of rulers, population growth, and revolutions, whether in isolation from one another or all in a grand hodgepodge. His purpose in the three sets of essays which make up this volume was to discover, if possible, the universal law of history.

It is clear that the success of such a purpose depends upon certain premises about human nature being true of all human beings and not merely of Europeans. All philosophers of history require such premises, for without them they would be left with a diversified group of data whose homogeneity they would never find. A Marxist, for instance, takes as his main premise the economic determination of all social regimes; the Augustinian, the basic dependence of man's fate upon his obedience or disobedience to the laws of God. In short, if there is a single universal law covering any collection of facts, it is intrinsic that it describe what is common to the whole collection. But since there is always the possibility of finding several common properties, the philosopher has to decide which is of the greatest importance. His decision in turn will determine the type of law—materialistic, logical, ethical, or even aesthetic—that he will uncover. And this in turn will determine the kind of fact he will seek and, naturally, the kind of interpretation he will provide for his readers.

Now if one thing is certain about all human beings, it is that they communicate their inner life in symbolic terms. No one who admits that we have an inner life believes that it is open to the scrutiny of anyone other than the person to whom it belongs. Even the naïve realist, if such a being exists outside of textbooks, grants that he cannot feel what another person is feeling, cannot dream another person's dreams, cannot put himself, as he might say, into the mind of anyone else. Our inner life is a complex of religious aspirations, fears, struggles to survive in an environment which at times is hostile and at others friendly, illusions, images, and fictions. But we do not merely worship in silence: we express our adoration of the superhuman powers in ritual and we elaborate myths to be narrated by each generation to its successor, myths that sound like explanations of natural events—such as the round of the seasons or the sudden occurrence of an earthquake or flood —or myths that are simply pictorial, allegorical, or gestures of veneration. In general these myths take the form of concrete emblems in which events or constellations of natural objects are invested with human traits. This tendency survives in what John Ruskin called the pathetic fallacy, but it may also be found in those vestiges of mythography which crop up in scientific writings when their author, taken off his guard, speaks of the simplicity of Nature or the attraction of positive and negative charges of electricity or of a cause which produced its effect. In Bachofen's time, the first half of the nineteenth century, this type of speech was deprecated, but it was part of his originality to ask what it was about human beings that led them to think, and hence to talk, in this fashion.

His answer was the ineradicable religious nature of mankind. He made a sharp contrast between what he called ideas and facts. "What cannot have happened was nonetheless thought," he said.* And he was more interested in what men have thought than in those material circumstances which gave rise to their thinking. For if we remove from history the inner life of the people about whom we are writing, we have but a small part of the story. It is undeniable that people have to eat, find or build shelters for themselves, propagate their kind, rear their children, and dispose of their dead. But if we simply observe the physical behavior of the human race in such situations, we shall have no idea of what is going on. We see a man killing game, skinning it, roasting it, and eating it, and we say that he is hungry and is trying to alleviate his hunger. But the act may not follow from any hunger at all: it may be a piece of religious ritual, a sacrifice to some god unknown to the observer. Who from a non-Christian culture would be able to understand the actions of a priest celebrating his daily Mass? So if we were to observe a bird building her nest and knew nothing about birds and their customs, we should have no more understanding of the process as a part of the biological regimen of the animal than if, knowing nothing about games, we were to watch two men who sat at opposite sides of a checker board and moved red and black disks from time to time.

Bachofen was one of those men who see a problem in what is generally accepted as unproblematic. He was a jurist and a historian of Roman law. He therefore knew that a set of symbols invested an idea which was not overtly present in them. But he encountered colleagues who were not aware of what might seem obvious. In all symbolic communication there is both the visible sign and the significance of the sign. To write the history of the law simply as a series of verbal changes would be absurd. It would be akin to listing all the appearances of the Cross and maintaining that it always meant the same thing. The history of almost any legal concept, such as homicide, reveals profound changes in man's appraisal of human life, of shifts in social organization, of reinterpretations of social classes, of—in this case—growing egalitarianism, of the emancipation of women, of modifications of

* See p. 214.

technology. But all this is taken for granted. To Bachofen it was important to discover, if possible, what accounts for these changes. What induced men to believe that it was just as serious to kill a peasant as an earl? What happened to induce men to think that it was more serious to kill a man as part of a premeditated plan than to kill him accidentally? The outer fact is that one person killed another. Somehow we have grown to take into account such vague ideas as motivation and the sanctity of all human life, but these things cannot be observed directly. One cannot *see* sanctity or the desire for revenge.

After studying what can be observed, Bachofen came to certain conclusions as to its meaning, that is, as to its congruence with religious, ethical, and aesthetic beliefs. First among his conclusions was that as society advances it liberates the human spirit from "the paralyzing fetters of a cosmic-physical view of life." † That is, man always is engaged in a struggle with physical nature, a struggle in which he may win or lose. But from the very beginnings of human society there has been a steady increase in our victories over "natural necessity." ** These optimistic words were printed in 1870. There was little then or for the next quarter century to make them seem unreasonable. Yet even if he had foreseen the calamities of our own time, or the ironical subservience to natural necessity that we have imposed upon ourselves, he would have argued that this period was simply one of those times of retrogression out of which we would emerge into greater freedom.

To pursue his search then for the meaning of history, Bachofen turned to the only documents which gave any hint of what men might have believed in the distant past. And he found them first in the tombstones of the ancient Mediterranean culture. Just as almost all the pre-Socratic philosophers saw the universe as an interplay of opposing forces, so these documents represent death as being bound up with life. We all know that both the Greeks and the Egyptians represented dying as a passage into another life, sometimes naïvely, as when they furnished the dead with artifacts that are needed on earth, or sometimes metaphorically, as when they depicted scenes of farewell. One does not say good-by to the inanimate; one throws it away when it is worn out. The fundamen-

† See p. 236.   ** See p. 238.

tal duality of existence was observed in the opposition of male and female, of the active and the passive (reflected even in grammar), of heaven and earth, of the sun and the moon. Such duality could not be left unresolved. Otherwise the cosmos would break in two, and that was unthinkable if there actually was a cosmos. To emerge from this dilemma one can deny the reality of one or the other of the conflicting beings, find some third thing which will be the source of them both, or see their connection as phases of a single process which is more real than either.

It was the last of these possibilities that Bachofen found to be the belief of the ancients. At a time when abstract science was not yet formulated, men had to express their ideas in symbols which were clear to them, as the symbols of mathematics are clear to us. And such symbols remain in the form of myths. Pliny describes a picture by Socrates the painter, in which Ocnus is shown twisting a rope while, behind his back, an ass gnaws off the end which he has just twisted.†† This has been interpreted both as an allegory of sloth and of the vanity of human labor. But when it is assimilated to other symbols that are also paradoxical in what they represent, the conclusion seems to be that they all signify rather the passage from one state of being to its opposite. Creation then is but one end of destruction, destruction the beginning of creation. So in the famous fragment of Heraclitus, "The way up and the way down is one and the same." It is the process itself which is one; its stages are of course various.

When we have grasped this, we have a clue to the philosophy of Bachofen. Thus we must always envision oppositions in cultural history as the poles of a single process of transformation. The process itself has a single purpose, but its communication can be accomplished only by whatever material means are available. The beauty of myth and symbol lies in their synthetic power; they can combine in one presentation disparate elements which would be self-contradictory if put into a declarative sentence. In the picture of Ocnus both the beginning and the end are seen in a single glance as united. To be sure, as a picture it is composed of discrete elements, the man, the rope, the ass, and their relative positions. But as a symbol it is unified by its meaning. To put the meaning

†† See p. 54, n. 4.

PREFACE

into words is possible, if one has the words to utilize, but the story of Ocnus as a narrative will again be subject to the necessity of telling one incident after another. The symbol presents them all at once, and the work of interpretation goes on in the mind of the spectator.

Bachofen was fully aware of his difference from other historians. The idea of granting to religion first rank among the creative forces "which mold man's whole existence" is considered, he says, "indicative . . . of narrow-minded incompetence." *
And yet he clung to the hypothesis, for he maintained that it alone is capable of giving us an understanding of why men struggle to free themselves from the bonds of earth, of why they have not been content to settle down and relax. At the time this was written, a few years before 1860, little if anything was known of tribes which did cease to struggle and which died rather than meet the challenge of time and change. But Bachofen was always ready to admit diversities so long as they were not basic, and there is nothing in his theory that denies that where religion has lost its power, the pace of history will slacken. Change, he agreed, is always gradual; it has its ups and downs.† We find, moreover, cycles in history in which the end of the cycle returns to its beginning. We find people all over the world who are in different stages of history, so that we cannot take a cross section of humanity at any one date and expect to find all human beings at the same developmental point.

The whole question of human development has been reexamined in recent years since the vogue of evolutionism has waned. It is no longer the fashion to think of North American Indians, Polynesians, Africans, and Eskimos as primitive in the older sense of representing a stage through which all men passed at the beginning of human history. Hence it is no refutation of Bachofen to point out that as of 1966 no people can be found which has the myths and the same symbols that have been utilized by him, though we are not asserting that this is the actual fact. The reflection is introduced here simply to point out that when anthropologists say that they can find no tribe in which there is sexual promiscuity or matriarchy, but that both are mixed up with marriage taboos and patriarchal customs, this in no way proves

* See pp. 84f.   † See p. 94.

xvi

that in the history of such tribes there was no period in which promiscuity was practiced and women were predominant.

In fact, it might well be argued that if sexual relations are regulated by law and promiscuity prohibited, it is because they had previously been unregulated and promiscuity had prevailed. For one does not forbid something which no one wants to do. The elaborate incest taboos would not have been necessary if no one had the inclination to be incestuous. One could with some reason conclude that if sexual relations are regulated by law, it is because they were once unregulated. Bachofen's reason for asserting primitive promiscuity, aside from the empirical evidence among the "lower orders" and the polygamous tendencies of most males, is that the emphasis on sexual decorum in matriarchal societies can be explained only as a reaction against a state of affairs which had become intolerable. He had at his disposal a large sheaf of myths and accounts of cults which honored a predominant mother-goddess such as Demeter. By the time they were described by historians, they had already become obsolete or had been meta-morphosed into secret rites of which only the initiates were cognizant. It is unlikely that anyone would deny the priority in time of such religious themes. For such emblems as the Cosmic Egg and the Earth Mother not only occur very early in cultural history but were known to be early by the ancient mythographers. In fact, their antiquity may have been their charm.

If, then, promiscuity is denied, there would be little reason for prohibiting it. And if it is prohibited, then something must replace it. What replaced it, according to Bachofen, was a society in which the mother was the dominant figure not only in the family, but also in society and the pantheon. Names passed from mothers to children and property from mothers to daughters. In an extreme form this state of affairs was called by Bachofen Amazonism. According to legend the Amazons were a people from whose society all males were excluded. If there is any historical basis for such a legend, it was, Bachofen thought, a matriarchal society in which the race was continued under the strict supervision of women. That this is not unreasonable, even though the documen-tary evidence is legend, is shown by the simple fact that babies survive only because of maternal care and that thus the fundamental element of any society must be a mother and her children. There are still in existence, as everyone knows, societies in which descent is traced from the mother rather than from the father, and, it has been argued, that is because, whereas paternity is frequently a matter of dispute, maternity is a matter of direct observation.

Bachofen's theory of a matriarchal society out of which modern patriarchal societies evolved was accepted pretty generally among sociologists until about the beginning of the twentieth century. It was the classic pattern for historians to follow. In his *History of Human Marriage* Westermarck attacked it as early as 1891, citing Bachofen as the principal sponsor of the thesis. But Westermarck, like his modern colleagues, looked to modern nonliterates as exemplars of what primitive societies must have been like, though this is obviously an assumption which prejudices the whole argument. Bachofen preferred to see evidence of a historical situation in legend, on the ground that legend preserves the collective memory. Since we can observe for ourselves the retention of ideas rejected by empirical science in both art and religion, we cannot in an a priori fashion deny the cogency of such reasoning, even though it is admittedly an intellectual reconstruction rather than an observed fact. But what else could it be? One can no more observe the primordial past in human institutions than one can in one's own life. One relies on memory—admittedly faulty—in the latter case and on the collective memory in the former.

The theory of the passage from hetaerism, as Bachofen called the state of sexual promiscuity, in the sense of external history, to matriarchy is perhaps not so important for an understanding of Bachofen as the evidence of man's nostalgia for the rule of women. In Western Europe at least we know that the position of women in the Homeric legends was much higher than it was in historical Athens, if by "higher" we mean more dignified, respected, authoritative. The Homeric goddesses are not all subservient to Zeus by any means, and the stories in the *Odyssey* give us such figures as Nausicaä, Circe, Calypso, and Penelope, who, though both good and evil, are not women cloistered in the inner chambers of the palace. We know furthermore that in Republican Rome, and of course later, too, wives gained more and more prominence in family and public affairs. Christianity made its way partly because of the influence of women. And by the epoch of chivalry women were raised to a position of eminence equaled only by that of the Virgin Mary. We have often marked the level of a society by the freedom from male domination which has been gained by women, and the word "gained" is deliberate. To refuse to see this is to refuse to admit that social changes are initiated by human desires.

Whether Bachofen was stimulated by Hegel's theory of development through dialectical evolution or not—and the question must remain open in view of the prevalence of analogous ideas in his time—he agrees with Hegel that abuse leads to social development.** The insistence upon any exclusive right leads to its nullification. Thus when women were the prey of any man who wanted them, the situation was intolerable and led over to the rule of women, the abandonment of communal property and of communal parentage. Marriage was then instituted as a regulative principle. But when women took over the rule of society as well as the exclusive ownership of children and property, this gave rise to an equally intolerable situation, for especially in time of war defense required a body of warriors who could not both exercise the duties of mothers and governors and at the same time engage in warfare. The reasoning here is analogous to that of such philosophers as Hobbes, Locke, and Rousseau, who argued on the basis of natural rights which they substantiated by assuming a state of nature as an intellectual model which would make a transition to a higher stage comprehensible. The higher stage in Bachofen's system was of course patriarchy. The three stages according to this schema are first the tellurian, in which there is motherhood without marriage, no agriculture, and apparently nothing resembling a state; then the lunar, in which there is conjugal motherhood and authentic or legitimate birth and in which agriculture is practiced in settled communities; and lastly the solar period, in which there is conjugal father right, a division of labor, and individual ownership. The mythical names which Bachofen gave to these periods will seem strange and perhaps even

** See p. 150.

superstitious to the modern reader, but they all correspond to religious beliefs, still flourishing today—if not overtly expressed in verbal formulas, at least to be found in our emotions, our art, and our symbols. But the point is that where one finds tellurian ideas, man's dependence on the earth is reflected in sexual and parental relations, in the gathering of food, and in a belief in the chthonic. Similar correspondences will be found when women are predominant between agriculture, the moon, and deities who protect and express fertility. And analogous data will be discoverable for the third, or solar, period. But none of this is intended to deny the existence of survivals, of vestiges of earlier times in subsequent times.

There are certain themes in Bachofen which have a strong similarity to those of Nietzsche. Though Bachofen's name does not appear in any of the indexes to any of Nietzsche's works, Nietzsche was a great admirer of Bachofen's colleague, Jakob Burckhardt, and Burckhardt himself was an admirer of Bachofen. Both Nietzsche and Bachofen see in struggle the source of all greatness, and both agree that every nation has a character of its own which expresses itself in its desire for power. In the mature Nietzsche the power sought is largely power over oneself, and in the words of Zarathustra, the eagle's eye is above the bull's neck. According to myth the eagle could look at the sun without blinking, and Bachofen's modern man struggling to liberate himself from the fetters of the material world had no other reason for doing so than his love of independence. It is to be noted also that in his early *Birth of Tragedy* Nietzsche took over Bachofen's terms, the Dionysiac and the Apollonian, for two types of will, the creative and the contemplative, and that he also maintained that they were fused into one in the Greek tragedy before the time of Euripides. At this period of life, when he was under the influence of Schopenhauer, he had little regard for the value of individuality, for individuality was thought of as an expression of the will to live.

But later, after *The Birth of Tragedy* and his repudiation of Schopenhauer, a great difference appears in Nietzsche's philosophy and that of Bachofen. There was then a revulsion against the notion of collective souls and a disgust with any theory that would deny the individual his rights as against those of society. Now the wills of man were seen as either masterful or servile, and of the two previous types of will the Dionysiac became preferable to the Apollonian. Freedom for the individual could never be given by society, but must be achieved in rebellion against society. At this period in his career, influenced it is generally believed by Gobineau, he turned to the Italian Renaissance for his ideal and saw a model in the figure of Cesare Borgia. Now it is the individual will, not the collective, which creates good and evil by fiat. Though the desire for power is common to both Nietzsche's and Bachofen's human being, Nietzsche is more inclined to accentuate man in combat with society rather than society as molding the man.

In spite of this important difference between the theories of Bachofen and Nietzsche, there remains an element of identity in the role assigned by both to myth. To Bachofen myth was the "exegesis of the symbol." †† Similarly in *The Birth of Tragedy* (section 10) we find that myth has for its domain the whole area of "Dionysian truth." Dionysian truth is that truth which is intuitive and as such has to be nonverbal. But just as in Bachofen the symbols of our intuitions are explicated in myth which then evolves into philosophic knowledge, so in Nietzsche myth expresses itself in tragedy and music. That is, both men realize that the human mind refuses to stop short of communication, but whereas Nietzsche with his hatred for society refuses to allow the public to contemplate the tragedy as a spectator, Bachofen sees in the gradual transformation of myth into communicable symbols the fulfillment of its potentialities. In short, for Bachofen communication is the very essence of knowledge. Knowledge is the link which binds men together. But the link is binding not merely as cognition but as religious cognition.

The individualism of the mature Nietzsche undoubtedly came from Burckhardt. He read him, he said, constantly. Burckhardt, as is well known, saw in the Italian Renaissance the rise of powerful individuals who recognized no law above their own will. Such a human condition was the highest to which man could attain. It was this which he called "culture," as opposed to those situations in

†† See p. 48.

which the state and then religion were the dominant forces. The periods preceding culture were such that the freedom of the individual was inevitably restricted and, if the individual asserted himself, he had to do so against the social order. But the tendency to anarchy inherent in any individualism was mitigated by the highly developed sense of honor, a mixture of conscience and egotism which, as Burckhardt says,* often survives after man "has lost, whether by his own fault or not, faith, love, and hope." But a sense of honor resides within an individual, and by its very nature as a mixture of egotism and conscience it cannot be conferred upon one by any external power as if it were a military decoration. Moreover, as in Hegel the "eternal man" embodies all the aspirations and ideals of a society, so for Burckhardt philosophers, poets, and statesmen become aware of the dim problems of the masses while poets express them in luminous symbols. This function of the poet unites Bachofen, Burckhardt, and Nietzsche, for all three were aware of the power of the nonscientific or, if one prefers, the nonrationalistic insights which mold a culture and transmit to its members their deepest feelings.

We have become accustomed to think of a society either as a loose collection of men and women engaged in various pursuits or, on the other hand, as an overindividual soul which in some mysterious way directs the lives of its individual components. For Bachofen neither concept is valid. He sees the human mind as thinking or feeling in certain general patterns which it is impelled to articulate. These patterns are expressed first in symbolic form and are then in turn transformed into myths. The myths in their turn are expressed in rationalistic language and become the various sciences. But as this process is going on, there remain in every society men and women who express new insight in new symbols which will someday become rationalistic systems of a novel type. Nevertheless the primordial insights and intuitions recur, though their symbolic vestments may be novel. It is one of the tasks of the philosopher, he maintains, to recapture these in their original form.

Such a point of view is clearly analogous to that of Carl Jung in

* Jakob Burckhardt, *The Civilization of the Renaissance in Italy*, tr. by S. G. C. Middlemore (New York and London, 1944), p. 263.

his theory of archetypes. If we take literally expositions of this theory which attribute the archetypes to pre-uterine memories, then it is true that it becomes absurd. For there are no individuals capable of remembering anything whatsoever until conception. But if we interpret it in the sense that all human beings have fundamentally the same aspirations, fears, ways of thinking, in short, the same kind of psychic life, then the symbols and myths which they elaborate take on more significance than kinship tables, basketry and pottery, basic foods and customs of producing them, and types of shelter. For if we could find something that was common to all men, it could not be denied that we should have acquired a wisdom which would lead to greater understanding of our fellow men and their problems. It would alleviate our provincialism and strengthen our compassion. But this group of three philosophers and their followers do recognize, in spite of their differences, that below the surface of sensory experience and beyond the generalizations based upon its phenomena, there lies an area in which the sources of a culture can be found. These sources, since they are below the surface, cannot be directly observed, but their character can be inferred from their expression in art and religion. No one yet has explained, for instance, so common an event as personal loyalty, to say nothing of our fear of gods, our hopes for a future life, or our desire for order. We may attribute them to certain socially useful ends. But we then overlook the existence of their opposites which are sometimes more powerful. It is the nature of an individualized experience to be incapable of direct communication in rational terms. This is merely elementary logic. But the endless series of narratives both in verse and prose, paralleled by the equally endless series of dramas, paintings, sculptures—all illustrative of incidents which seem precious to men and women—demonstrates the hard fact that mankind wants more than statistical tables and physical theorems if life is to be complete. Men want at a minimum the incorporation of rational knowledge in concrete form, and it is precisely this which Bachofen illuminated. The details of his interpretations may be viewed skeptically—he would have been the last to set himself up as a dogmatist. But the standpoint from which he made his investigations still must be assumed by anyone who wants more than a superficial view of human history. The situation may be simplified as follows: Does human action spring entirely from reactions to external phenomena or does our inner life determine our vital programs?

George Boas

Introduction

I

IT IS FITTING that the works of Johann Jacob Bachofen (1815–1887) should have been rediscovered for our century, not by historians or anthropologists, but by a circle of creative artists, psychologists, and literary men: a young group around the poet Stefan George, in Munich, in the twenties. For Bachofen has a great deal to say to artists, writers, searchers of the psyche, and, in fact, anyone aware of the enigmatic influence of symbols in the structuring and moving of lives: the lives of individuals, nations, and those larger constellations of destiny, the civilizations that have come and gone, as Bachofen saw, like dreams—unfolding, each, from the seed force of its own primary symbol, or, as he termed such supporting images, "basic insights" (*Grundanschauungen*) or "fundamental thoughts" (*Grundgedanken*). And he himself had such an easy, graceful skill in his interpretation of symbols, unshelling flashes of illumination from all sorts of mythological forms, that many of his most dazzling passages remind one of nothing so much as a marksman exploding with infallible ease little clay figures in a gallery. Read, for example, the brief chapter on the symbolism of the egg! * From any page of this passage one can learn more about the grammar of mythology than from a year's study of such an author as, say, Thomas Bulfinch, whose *Age of Fable* appeared just four years before Bachofen's *Mortuary Symbolism*.

Comparing the approach of these two mid nineteenth-century

* Below, pp. 22–39.

students of classical mythology, one immediately remarks that, whereas the interest of Bulfinch lay in the anecdotal aspect of his subject, summarizing plots, Bachofen's concern was to go past plots to their symbolized sense, by grouping analogous figures and then reading these as metaphors of a common informing idea. He describes the method in his section on India:

> We must distinguish between the form of the tale and its content or idea. The form lies in the fiction of a single definite event, which takes its course and moves toward its conclusion through a concatenation of circumstances and the intervention of a number of persons. This formal element must be discarded as a fabrication, a fable, a fairy tale, or whatever we may term such products of the free fancy, and excluded from the realm of historical truth. But in respect to the guiding thought, we must apply a different standard. This retains its significance even though the garment in which it is shrouded may merit little regard. In fact, when dissociated from this single incident, it takes on the greater dimension of a general historicity, not bound by specific localities or persons. †

We are on the way, here, to Carl G. Jung's "collective unconscious." And it was this informed recognition of an implicit psychological, moral import in all mythology that chiefly recommended Bachofen to the poets.

In his introduction to *Mother Right* Bachofen explains his science further:

> It has been said that myth, like quicksand, can never provide a firm foothold. This reproach applies not to myth itself, but only to the way in which it has been handled. Multiform and shifting in its outward manifestation, myth nevertheless follows fixed laws, and can provide as definite and secure results as any other source of historical knowledge. Product of a cultural period in which life had not yet broken away from the harmony of nature, it shares with nature that unconscious lawfulness which is always lacking in the works of free reflection. Everywhere there is system, everywhere cohesion; in every detail the expression of a great fundamental law whose abundant manifestations demonstrate its inner truth and natural necessity.**

† Below, pp. 199f.   ** Below, p. 76.

Moreover, since, according to this view, mythologies arise from and are governed by the same psychological laws that control our own profoundest sentiments, the surest way to interpret them is not through intellectual ratiocination but the exercise of our psychologically cognate imagination. As Bachofen declared in the retrospective autobiographical sketch that he wrote in 1854 at the request of his former teacher, the great jurist and historian, Friedrich Karl von Savigny:

> There are two roads to knowledge—the longer, slower, more arduous road of rational combination and the shorter path of the imagination, traversed with the force and swiftness of electricity. Aroused by direct contact with the ancient remains, the imagination [*Phantasie*] grasps the truth at one stroke, without intermediary links. The knowledge acquired in this second way is infinitely more living and colorful than the products of the understanding [*Verstand*]. ††

To read mythology in this way, however, it is necessary to cast aside one's contemporary, historically conditioned manner of thought and even of life. "It is one of my profoundest convictions," Bachofen told his old preceptor, "that without a thorough transformation of our whole being, without a return to ancient simplicity and health of soul, one cannot gain even the merest intimation of the greatness of those ancient times and their thinking, of those days when the human race had not yet, as it has today, departed from its harmony with creation and the transcendent creator." *

One can see why the academicians shuddered—and the poets were delighted. Rainer Maria Rilke was touched; Hugo von Hofmannsthal as well. But there was far more to the reach of Bachofen's work than a poet's grammar of the symbolizing imagination. Implicit in this grammar, and developed in his ample volumes, is the idea of a morphology of history—first, of classical antiquity, but then, by extension, of mankind: an idea of the course and moving principles of our destiny that is becoming, in a most interesting way, increasingly corroborated as archaeologists throughout the world lift forth from the earth, for all to see, the

†† Below, pp. 11f.   * Below, p. 16.

tangible forms that his intangible mythoanalytic method of invisible excavation (pursued at home in his library) had anticipated.

2

One has to keep reminding oneself, when reading this perceptive scholar, that in his day the sites of Helen's Troy and Pasiphaë's Crete had not yet been excavated—nor any of those early neolithic villages that have yielded the multitudes of ceramic naked-goddess figurines now filling museum cabinets. Bachofen himself was impressed by the novelty of his findings. "An unknown world," he wrote, "opens before our eyes, and the more we learn of it, the stranger it seems." † Indeed, in his student years he had already passed beyond the learning of his century when he noticed that there were customs recognized in Roman law that could never have originated in a patriarchal society; and on his first visit to Rome, with his father in 1842, his intuition of a second pattern of custom was reinforced by his reading of the symbols that he found there on certain tombs.

Inspired, then, by what today would be called an "organic," "holistic," or "functional" theory of culture—believing, that is to say, that whether great or small, sacred or profane, every element of a cultural aggregate must be expressive, ultimately, of the "informing idea" (*Grundanschauung*) of the culture from which it took its rise—the young Bachofen realized that the anomalous features recognized in the Roman legacy would have to be explained either as imports from some alien province or as vestiges of a no less alien period of native Italic culture, antecedent to the classical; and, as he tells in his work on mother right, it was in Herodotus' account of the customs of the Lycians that he found his leading clue. "The Lycians," he read, "take their names from their mother, not from their father"; from which he reasoned that, since a child's derivation from its mother is immediately apparent, but from its father remote, primitive mankind may not have understood the relation of sexual intercourse to birth.

† Below, p. 69.

xxviii

Descent from the mother would then have been the only recognized foundation of biological kinship, the men of the tribe representing, on the other hand, a social, moral, and spiritual order into which the child would later be *adopted*, as in primitive puberty rites.

There is an interesting confirmation of this bold hypothesis in the writings of one of the leading anthropologists of our own century, namely Bronislaw Malinowski, whose volume *The Sexual Life of Savages* (based on notes from a four-year expedition to New Guinea, 1914–18) has the following to say of the natives of the Trobriand Islands:

> We find in the Trobriands a matrilineal society, in which descent, kinship, and every social relationship are legally reckoned through the mother only, and in which women have a considerable share in tribal life, even to the taking of a leading part in economic, ceremonial, and magical activities—a fact which very deeply influences all the customs of erotic life as well as the institutions of marriage. . . .
>
> The idea that it is solely and exclusively the mother who builds up the child's body, the man in no way contributing to this formation, is the most important factor in the legal system of the Trobrianders. Their views on the process of procreation, coupled with certain mythological and animistic beliefs, affirm, without doubt or reserve, that the child is of the same substance as its mother, and that between the father and the child there is no bond of physical union whatsoever. . . .
>
> These natives have a well-established institution of marriage, and yet are quite ignorant of the man's share in the begetting of children. At the same time, the term "father" has, for the Trobriander, a clear, though exclusively social definition: it signifies the man married to the mother, who lives in the same house with her and forms part of the household. The father, in all discussions about relationship, was pointedly described to me as *tomakava*, a "stranger," or even more correctly, an "outsider." . . . What does the word *tama* (father) express to the native? "Husband of my mother" would be the answer first given by an intelligent informant. He would go on to say that his *tama* is the man in whose loving and protecting company he has grown up . . . the child learns that he is not of the same clan as his *tama*, that his totemic appellation is different, and that it is identi-

cal with that of his mother. At the same time he learns that all
sorts of duties, restrictions, and concerns for personal pride unite
him to his mother and separate him from his father.**

Now, as we know today, it is extremely risky to reason from
the circumstances of a contemporary tribe back to earliest mankind: we have learned too much in the past few years concerning
the antiquity of our species, which is today being reckoned
(largely on the basis of the finds of L. S. B. Leakey in the Olduvai
Gorge in Tanganyika) as far back as to circa 1,800,000 B.C. In
Bachofen's day the absurdly recent Biblical date for the creation
not only of mankind but of the world (3760 B.C., according to one
manner of reckoning; 4004 by another) was still, in most
quarters, accepted as about correct. Adam Sedgwick, Darwin's
geology teacher, set down, for example, that "man has been but a
few years' dweller on the earth. He was called into being a few
thousand years of the days in which we live by a provident
contriving power." †† And so it was that, like most others of his
generation, Bachofen could believe that in dealing with the
ancients he was searching a tradition "going back," as he more
than once averred, "almost to the beginning of things." And his
romantic sense of the holiness of his task derived, in part at least,
from this illusion.

Bachofen recognized and described two distinct orders of
mother right, associating the first with the absolutely primitive,
nomadic, hunting and foraging states of human existence, and the
second with the settled agricultural. However, unfortunately for
the cogency of his argument, when looking for examples of an
absolutely primitive condition, he made the mistake of naming a
wild lot of horse and cattle nomads who were not primitive at all
(they were barbarous enough, but not primitive); namely, the
Massagetae, Nasamones, Garamantes, etc., whom classical historians had described as using their women in common and
copulating publicly, without shame. Bachofen termed the primitive socioreligious order that he deduced from this uncertain

** Bronislaw Malinowski, *The Sexual Life of Savages* (New York, 1929),
  pp. 3–7.
†† Quoted from Loren Eiseley, *The Firmament of Time* (New York, 1962),
  p. 93.

evidence the premarital "hetaerist-aphroditic," representing it as
governed by the natural law (*ius naturale*) of sex motivated by
lust, and with no understanding of the relationship of intercourse
to conception. The classical goddess symbolic of such a way of life
was Aphrodite; its vegetal symbol for the Greeks and Romans had
been the wild, rank vegetation of swamps, in contrast to the
ordered vegetation of the planted field; and its animal symbol was
the bitch. Its brutal order of justice was the justice of the balance,
eye for an eye and tooth for a tooth, retaliation; yet with the
mitigating, softening, humanizing principle already at work of
mother love.

"Raising her young," Bachofen observed, "the woman learns
earlier than the man to extend her loving care beyond the limits of
the ego to another creature, and to direct whatever gift of
invention she possesses to the preservation and improvement of
this other's existence. Woman at this stage is the repository of all
culture, of all benevolence, of all devotion, of all concern for the
living and grief for the dead." *

The second stage in Bachofen's reconstruction, which he
associated with agriculture, is better attested by far than the first,
and is, in fact, acknowledged by many anthropologists today
pretty much as Bachofen described it—though, of course, with
greater definition of detail and emphasis on the local variations.
Professor W. H. R. Rivers, for example, states in a detailed article
on mother right in James Hastings' *Encyclopaedia of Religion and
Ethics* (in which, by the way, the name of Bachofen does not
occur), both that "there is reason to connect mother-right with a
high development of the art of agriculture," and that "it is almost
certain that by far the most frequent process throughout the world
has been a transition from mother- to father-right." †

In Bachofen's usage the term mother right—which Malinowski
and Rivers also employ—does not require that the woman should
hold political sway; in fact, according to his theory of stages, the
normal head of a primitive hetaerist-aphroditic horde would have
been a powerful male tyrant, who through main strength would
have been able to make use of whatever women he chose. The
force of the principle of mother right would even then have been

* Below, p. 79.   † Vol. 8, pp. 859 and 858 respectively.

evident, however, in the family concepts and emotions of kinship and concern, as well as in magic and religion wherever the properly female powers of fruitfulness and nourishment were concerned.

But in reaction to the sexual abuses to which females, under such primitive circumstances, would have been subjected, revolts must have ensued, Bachofen reasoned; and he thought he could point to a number of instances in classical history and legend: the various tribes of the Amazons in both Africa and Asia, and, in particular, the notorious deed of the women of Lemnos.** Such revolts and the conditions following them would have been, he believed, transitional, leading away from the earlier communal usages to the later settled, monogamous state of life. And another influence, perhaps equally conducive to monogamy, he supposed, would have been the acceptance by the male of his proper domestic role when, finally, the inevitable recognition of the physical similarities between fathers and their own children would have led to both an understanding of, and a pride in, the relationship of parent and child.

However, the main transforming force Bachofen identified with the rise of agriculture and the coming into being, therewith, of a comparatively gentle, settled mode of existence, favorable to the female. Furthermore, since woman is the living counterpart of the tilled and holy earth, the female acquired new importance in the ritualistic magico-religious sphere wherever agriculture flourished. Bachofen therefore named this second, higher stage of mother right the "matrimonial-demetrian," or "-cereal," for the Greek agricultural goddess Demeter and her Roman counterpart Ceres; and the greatest part of his lifework was devoted to researches in the mysteries of this higher, nobler transformation of the *ius naturale.*

Like the lower, it was supported by the force and majesty of sex; but now with desire for progeny, not merely the urge of lust. Furthermore, the analogy of begetting and birth to the sowing and harvest of the tilled fields gave rise to those great poetic mythologies of the earth goddess and her spouse that have been everywhere the support of the basic rites and mysteries of civilization.

** Below, pp. 173–77.

Bachofen has filled his pages with the most eloquent celebrations of the beauty and power of these mighty mythologies, the systems of analogy on which they are founded, and the contribution they have made to the humanization of mankind; and no matter what one's final judgment may be as to the value of his reconstruction of the stages of the evolution of society, there can be no doubt concerning the force and value of his readings of that great heritage of mythic symbols which is basic not only to the civilizations of the Occident but to those of the Orient as well—and was even echoed in pre-Columbian America among the Aztecs, the Pawnee, the Zuñi, and the Sioux.

In fact, when it comes to considering the larger, world-historical as opposed to the merely classical, application of Bachofen's theories of the stages of mother right, it is relevant to note that the first field anthropologist to recognize an order of matrilineal descent among primitive peoples—and even to have associated this order with Herodotus' account of the Lycians—was an eighteenth-century missionary among the Indians of Canada, the Reverend Joseph François Lafitau, S. J. (1671–1746); in his *Mœurs des sauvages Amériquains comparées aux mœurs des premiers temps* (Paris, 1724), at times he launches into eulogies of the spiritual, social, and practical *supériorité des femmes* that even rival those of Bachofen himself.

C'est dans les femmes que consiste proprement la Nation, la noblesse du sang, l'arbre généalogique, l'ordre des générations et de la conservation des familles. C'est en elles que réside toute l'autorité réelle. . . . Les hommes au contraire sont entièrement isolés et bornés a eux-mêmes, leurs enfants leurs sont étrangers, avec eux tout périt. . . . ††

Moreover, one of the very first to acknowledge the importance for science of Bachofen's researches and to write to him in appreciation was an American anthropologist, the jurist and ethnologist Lewis Henry Morgan, whose pioneering study of the Iroquois had prepared him to recognize the value and universal reach of Bachofen's revelation.

†† Vol. 1, p. 71.

3

Bachofen's instinctive response to those silent signals from the lost world of "the mothers" that captured his imagination in youth and held him fascinated throughout life has been attributed, possibly with reason, to a lifelong devotion to his own young and beautiful mother. Daughter of a distinguished patrician family of Basel, née Valeria Merian, she was hardly twenty when he was born, in 1815. He remained a bachelor until her death in 1856 and for nearly a decade thereafter, when he married, in 1865, the young and beautiful Louise Elizabeth Burckhardt, who was the age his mother had been when he was born.

Among the bachelors of scholarship, however, there have been many devoted sons, yet none with quite Bachofen's gift; and the awakening—or let us say, rather, in Bachofen's own terms, the fathering and fostering of that gift—must be ascribed to the masters of the great romantic school of historical research with whom he studied, the most influential of whom was the distinguished jurisprudent Friedrich Karl von Savigny, whose lectures he attended and friendship he enjoyed at the University of Berlin from 1835 to 1837. This was the same inspiring professor of the history of law who, thirty years before, had launched the brothers Grimm on their world-celebrated pioneering careers in Germanic philology, mythology, and folklore.

Bachofen was born December 22, 1815, in Basel, where both his father's family and his mother's had been established and respected since the sixteenth and seventeenth centuries. Burgomasters and city counselors were numbered among his ancestors; art collectors and geologists. Johann Jacob, however, seems to have been the first historian of either line. As a youngster he first attended a private "house school," together with his younger brother Carl, where little Jakob Burckhardt, three years younger than himself, also arrived as a pupil. Then came his boyhood grammar-school years, from which he graduated with honors in 1831. He attended the fine high school in which Nietzsche was later to be a teacher; and after two years there and two semesters at the University of Basel, he went on to Berlin to study law—and to encounter the great man who would become the master of his destiny and mystagogue of his way to wisdom.

Von Savigny was an imposing, gracious scholar with an eye for the genius of a student. As the leading mind of Germany's new "historical school" of jurists, he had himself been a major contributor to the unfolding of that country's romantic thought in its golden age, and something of the atmosphere of those enchanted days must still have hung about him. The family of his wife, Kunigunde Brentano, had been intimates of the Goethe household: her father, a companion of Goethe's youth; and her younger sister, Bettina, that same pretty little elf, who, in 1807, threw herself in worship before Goethe's feet in a gesture of such charm that he allowed her to continue to be a cherished nuisance in his life until 1811—when a violent scene between his young admirer and Christiane, his wife, put an end to the whole affair. Clemens Brentano, the colorful brother of these two attractive sisters, had been a member, in those days, of the Heidelberg group of romantics, and in collaboration with Ludwig Achim von Arnim (who was later to marry Bettina) had edited the famous ballad collection *Des Knaben Wunderhorn* (1805–08), to which the young Grimms, still in their teens, also were contributors.

Kunigunde and Friedrich Karl were married in 1804, and though he then was a youth of but twenty-five, his formidable treatise on *The Law of Property* had already appeared the year before and been recognized as introducing a new approach to the interpretation of law—an organic, holistic, ethnological-historical approach, it might be called today; and in view of its undoubted influence on both the Grimm brothers and Bachofen at the critical, formative moments of their careers, it must be counted among the most influential seminal writings of its time. Briefly, the proposition argued was that, since the laws of a people are part and parcel of their national life, law codes cannot be imposed arbitrarily on alien populations without regard for their past history or present state of civilization: law and language, religious and secular custom, are of a piece.

In 1804, at the time this argument made its impact on the Grimms, it carried for young Germans a special patriotic appeal. The French, who had been ravaging Europe since March 1796 (when Napoleon, addressing the ragged army of a destitute Republic, had issued his famous proclamation: "You are badly fed and all but naked. . . . I am about to lead you into the most fertile plains of the world. Before you are great cities and rich provinces; there we shall find honor, glory, and riches"), were now the absolute masters of Europe, and on the first day of spring, March 21, 1804, their Code civil des Français, later known as the Code Napoléon, had come automatically into force throughout the Empire, without any regard whatsoever either for the past history or for the present state of civilization of any of the numerous peoples involved. Von Savigny's ethnological-historical thesis, consequently, inspired the brothers Grimm to dedicate their learning and their lives to a reconstruction of the old Germanic backgrounds and ideals of their national cultural heritage. Bachofen's case was different: he was not German but Swiss, and in his day the Napoleonic terror was already a nightmare of the past.

Yet inherent in Bachofen's work, as well as in that of the brothers Grimm, was an intense social motivation and a passionate interest in learning that contributed a sense of timeliness and even urgency to his otherwise rather recondite researches. For the period in which he matured was one rather of social and class confusion than of international strife; and, as he viewed the scene from his Alpine vantage point, the whole fabric of European civilization was being torn asunder in the name of principles that were misconceived and by means that could lead, in the end, only to ruin. As he tells in his retrospective sketch, he made his second trip to Rome at the very peak of the fateful year of 1848, and the second day after his arrival, the honorable and admirable Count Pellegrino Rossi, whose lectures he had attended at the University of Paris, was murdered on the steps of the Roman House of Assembly. "The storming of the Quirinal, the flight of the Pope, the Constituent Assembly, the proclamation of the Republic," he writes, "followed in quick succession. . . . And with the arrival of Garibaldi's band and the various patriotic legions from all over Italy, things became even more fantastic." *

"It is a mistake of the Progressives to imagine that they will never be surpassed," he wrote twenty years later to his friend the

* Below, p. 14.

classical historian Heinrich Meyer-Ochsner of Zurich. "Before they know it, they are to be ousted by the 'More-Enlightened.' They have still, as Athens once had too, schoolmasters for their bosses; but at last there will come the porters and the criminals. . . . When every scoundrel counts for as much as an orderly citizen, it's all out with rational government. . . . I begin to believe that for the historians of the twentieth century there will be nothing to write about but America and Russia." †

In contrast, therefore, to the young Grimms, for whom the great cause of the hour had been the rescue of the German soul, the cause for the Swiss scholar Bachofen, from his earliest years to the end, was the rescue of all of Europe. "The supreme aim of archaeology," he wrote in his *Mortuary Symbolism*, ". . . consists, I believe, in communicating the sublimely beautiful ideas of the past to an age that is very much in need of regeneration." **
And so it was that, whereas von Savigny's learned inspiration had sent his sensitive earlier students searching, for the rescue of their heritage, into its spiritual backgrounds in the northern Indo-Germanic past, so now, one generation later, it sent the young Swiss, Bachofen, off to Rome, to Greece, and beyond, to the realm of "the mothers" of Goethe's *Faust*.

4

Bachofen's dates, 1815–1887, significantly match those of Charles Darwin (1809–1882), and his first important publication, *An Essay on Ancient Mortuary Symbolism*, even appeared in the same year as Darwin's *Origin of Species*—1859. The significance of these coincidences appears when it is remarked that both men were pursuing independent researches, one in fields of physical, the other of spiritual investigation, just when the scientific concept of a natural evolution of forms was only beginning to supplant the old Biblical doctrines of a special creation of fixed species, with man above and apart, and a special revelation of God's law to but

† From a letter to Heinrich Meyer-Ochsner, May 25, 1869, quoted by Rudolf Marx in his introduction (p. xxvi) to the volume of selections of which the present is a translation.
** Below, p. 23.

one chosen people. Bachofen, like Darwin, was a pioneer, therefore, in the formulation of a scientific approach to a very tender subject, and, like his contemporary in the biological field, he took as the first principles of his thinking two methodological axioms: (1) phenomena are governed by discoverable natural laws; and (2) these laws are continuously operative, uninterrupted by miraculous intervention.

Observing, therefore, that within the field of his concern there was an apparent graduation of forms, from the simpler to the more complex, the less conscious to the more, Bachofen assumed that these must represent the stages of a general course of cultural evolution. And again as in the biological field, so in this of cultural evolution, the representatives of the various periods of development lay scattered over the earth, having undergone in the various provinces of diffusion local adjustments to environment and independent secondary developments and regressions. To reconstruct the master pattern of the general development, consequently, the first requirement had to be a diligent collection of specimens from all quarters; next, meticulous comparison and classification; and finally, imaginative interpretation—proceeding step by step to ever more inclusive insights. In *The Myth of Tanaquil*, published 1870, Bachofen is explicit in this regard:

> The scientific approach to history recognizes the stratifications of the spiritual modes that have gradually made their appearance, assigns to each stratum the phenomena that pertain to it, and traces the genesis of ideas. Proceeding thus through all the stages of reality, it leads us to realize what this spirit of ours once was, through the passage of the ages, but is today no more. ††

Specifically, Bachofen's procedure was, first, to saturate his sight and mind with the primary documents of his subject: Roman legal texts, Etruscan tombs, ceramic wares, etc., regarding each specimen of antiquity as a biologist would a bug, casting from his mind presuppositions, viewing it from all sides, considering its environment, and comparing it with others.

"A historical investigation which must be the first to gather,

†† Below, p. 246.

verify, and collate all its material," he states in one of his most important passages, "must everywhere stress the particular and only gradually progress to comprehensive ideas." *

In the biological sciences, specimens gathered from all quarters of the earth are compared, clustered, and classified according to categories of broader and broader scope: variety, species, genus, family, order, class, phylum, and finally, kingdom. So also, in Bachofen's spiritual science:

> Our understanding will grow in the course of investigation; gaps will be filled in; initial observations will be confirmed, modified, or amplified by others; our knowledge will gradually be rounded out and gain inner cohesion; higher and higher perspectives will result; and finally they will all be joined in the unity of one supreme idea. †

And so we find that, just as in his elucidation of legends he pressed past the anecdotes, so likewise in his interpretation of cultures: religious beliefs, laws and customs, family structures, political practices, philosophies, sciences, crafts and economics, are all viewed as related manifestations of implicit informing ideas, and it is to the recognition and naming of these that his attention is addressed.

Wherever identical, or essentially comparable, constellations of myth and custom are discovered, Bachofen assumes a relationship. "Agreement in idea and form between the mythologies of countries far removed from one another discloses a cultural connection which can be explained only by migration," he declares, for instance, in his study of the myth of Tanaquil; ** which is a principle, of course, that would be accepted without question by any botanist or zoologist. And since, within the various provinces of a distribution of this kind, all sorts of secondary variations will have occurred—local progressions, regressions, transpositions of emphasis, etc.—the dual task of the researcher, after gathering his specimens and arranging them according to province, will have to be, first, to identify the source and interpret the informing idea of the earliest examples of

* Below, p. 119.   † Below, p. 120.   ** Below, p. 213.

xxxix

each complex, and then, to isolate and interpret severally the observed variants.

All attempts at interpretation, however, according to Bachofen's view, must concur with the realization that the mainsprings of mythological thought are not those of a modern rational ideology. Mythological symbols derive from the centers rather of dream than of waking consciousness, and their sense, consequently, cannot be guessed through conscious ratiocination. The meaning of a myth resounds in its evoked associations, and if the scholar is to become aware of these, he must allow their counterparts to arise within himself from those regions of his own nature that he shares still with early man. "If it is true, as Aristotle says," Bachofen wrote in his retrospective sketch, "that like can be grasped only by like, then the divine can be apprehended only by a divine mind, and not by the rationalistic self-conceit that sets itself above history. Abundance of information is not everything, it is not even the essential." ††

Now of course there is romanticism in this kind of thinking, romanticism and religion: but so had there been romanticism in the sages, prophets, and visionaries who brought forth the early symbols. And it was through his acquiescence in the modes of their experience, thought, and communication that this modern gentleman was enabled to recognize in their messages, collected in his fine patrician home, the accents of a prehistoric world and way of life that was remoter and darker by centuries than the classical civilizations of Rome and Athens: from a deeper vein of the soul, as well as of time, than the classical scholarship of his day had yet suspected to exist. And he was mercilessly massacred, consequently, in the academic journals. One of the learned reviewers of his work on mortuary symbols wrote: "408 closely printed pages, full of the queerest, most adventurous dreams—dreams that in their profundity pass, at times, into realms even of consummate imbecility." * The work on mother right, two years later, received more of the same ruthless treatment—and at this point Bachofen seems to have decided that he had had enough. Some twenty years

†† Below, p. 16.

* *Literarisches Zentralblatt*, Nr. 27, 1860; cited in Carl Albrecht Bernoulli, ed., J. J. Bachofen, *Versuch über die Gräbersymbolik der Alten* (Basel, 2d edn., 1925), p. vi.

before he had had to endure an earlier round of public humiliation, when a school of newspaper sharks of the political left had
taken it upon themselves to protest both his appointment to a
professorship in Roman law at the University of Basel and his
elevation to a place on the City Council, attributing both honors to
family influence. At that time, after waiting a decent interval for
the hue and cry to abate, he had quietly resigned both posts; and
now, again, he simply walked away. His beloved mother had died
five years before, and now his zeal for his career died as well. He
packed and took a trip to Spain.

But as fate and his destiny would have it, in his luggage he had
brought along for leisure reading Theodor Mommsen's recently
published *History of Rome* (1854–56), and as he made his way
through its three volumes, this greatly celebrated work of truly
massive scholarship seemed to him to epitomize precisely that
"rationalistic self-conceit that sets itself above history" which he
despised from the depth of his soul. It so aroused his ire that he
determined, then and there, to refute it by presenting in a work of
his own a fundamental problem in classical culture history that
could not be handled—and, indeed, would not even have been
recognized—from such a materialistic, political-economic point of
view. Returning to Basel, therefore, he set himself to work, and
eight years later gave forth the final major harvest volume of his
learning, *The Myth of Tanaquil*.

5

It is in this last of Bachofen's major works, *The Myth of Tanaquil*,
which appeared in the year 1870, that his view can best be studied
of the inward force of spiritual principles—*Grundanschauungen,
Grundgedanken*, as opposed to merely economic and political,
rationally determinable laws—in the shaping of the destinies of
historic civilizations. The profound contrast of the Orient and the
Occident also is confronted here, and in terms, specifically, of a
contrast in the motivating spiritual modes of mother and father
right.

Both Bachofen's critics and his admirers have frequently remarked his tolerance of both the pagan-Oriental and the Christian-Occidental—archaic matriarchal and progressive patriarchal—strains in our compound modern heritage. His much shorter-lived Danish contemporary, Sören Kierkegaard (1813–1855), had found it necessary in the name of spiritual integrity to reject the pagan from his soul in favor of the Christian strain, while his young friend Friedrich Nietzsche (1844–1900), likewise finding the two together intolerable, had rejected with a vocabulary of moral exaltation no less elevated than Kierkegaard's, not the pagan, but the Christian. The genial, somewhat portly, comfortably long-lived Swiss patrician Bachofen, on the other hand, seems to have found no difficulty whatsoever in remaining a solid Protestant, wholly committed in his own way of life to what good Protestants take to be the basic Christian virtues, while yet becoming, with every fiber of his being, the most inspired interpreter and protagonist in his century of the moral orders—Aphroditic as well as Demetrian—of the goddess.

It is true that in the past Hegel and Goethe, Petrarch, Erasmus, and many other Christian humanists had managed to live with both traditions. "Zwei Seelen wohnen, ach! in meiner Brust," mused Goethe's hero, Faust. However, the classical soul had been for them largely of the Apollonian, patriarchal order, while the supernatural claims of the Biblical revelation had not yet been discredited by nineteenth-century scholarship and science. They did not have to abjure their reason in order to be Christians, nor their Christianity to be scions of the Greeks. Hegel had regarded the two orders, respectively, as the *thesis* and *antithesis* of a single spiritual process, of which his own philosophy announced the *synthesis*. Goethe contrived to wed the two in his marriage of Helen and Faust. But in Bachofen's peaceful soul there seems to have been no sense of disaccord whatsoever. With a perfectly calm, scientific eye—good biologist of the spirit that he was!—he regarded with equal understanding every stage of what he took to be an orderly evolution of human ideals from the early earthbound modes of the Aphroditic and Demetrian, nomadic and early agricultural, stages, to the more elevated and illuminated modes of the higher civilizations: Athenian, Roman, medieval, and humanistic-modern. For him there was alive at the heart of each of these orders of life the vital force of an informing insight, *Grundan-schauung, Grundgedanke,* which it was the aim of his science of symbols to identify and elucidate. And what he rejected with whole heart—as Nietzsche rejected Christian "yonder-worldlings" and Kierkegaard, the dialecticians of *this* world—was the sealing away of these wellsprings of inspiration with a pavement of economic and political modern thought—of which violation of the creative spirit Mommsen had become for him the prime example.

However, even the most patient and well-disposed modern reader may feel, on turning to *The Myth of Tanaquil,* that its almost aggressively *un*modern, moralizing vocabulary so colors the argument as to violate the very principle of objectivity that the author intended to illustrate; and indeed, that his projection of the sentiments of a romantically inclined Swiss Protestant patrician into the institutions of Rome was an impropriety even less acceptable to modern taste than Mommsen's projection of the psychology of a nineteenth-century history professor.

For we have learned, these days, from a school of romantics of our own, not to evaluate cultures in terms even of "low" and "high," let alone "basely sensuous" and "spiritually pure"; and especially to eschew all such phraseology in relation to the cultural contrasts of Orient and Occident, Africa, Asia, and Europe. The late Professor Robert H. Lowie, of the University of California, evaluating in 1937 the ethnological theories of his nineteenth-century predecessors, wrote, "In his chronology, Bachofen is a typical evolutionist of the old school. Once more a belief in progressive stages appears. . . ." † And in the same vein, Professor R. R. Marett, of Exeter College, Oxford, censured not only Bachofen but also his contemporaries, Lewis H. Morgan and J. F. McLennan. "Every one of these great thinkers must plead guilty to the charge," he declared, ". . . of definitely committing themselves to a treatment involving the fallacious notion of a unilineal evolution." ** Yet even as these anti-evolutionary judgments were being pronounced with all the confidence of a young science, the excavations of the archaeologists (from a different department,

---

† Lowie, *History of Ethnological Theory* (New York, 1937), p. 41.
** Marett, *Tylor* (London, 1936), pp. 180–1.

however, of the university system) were beginning to reveal that there had indeed been a stage-by-stage evolution of human culture from low to high, and even from what, in terms of a nineteenth-century point of view, might well have been described as "basely sensuous" to "spiritually pure."

The essential epoch-making cultural mutations, it now was being shown, had occurred in specific, identifiable centers, from which the effects then had gone out to the ends of the earth, like ripples on a pond from a tossed stone. And wherever those expanding waves had reached, they had combined variously with waves from earlier centers of mutation, so that all sorts of interesting configurations were discoverable for anthropological monographs. To make the point, one need mention only the epochal invention of the food-producing arts of agriculture and stock-breeding, about the ninth millennium B.C., in the Near East (Asia Minor, Syria, Palestine, northern Iraq, and Iran). From this center a new style of human living spread westward and eastward to the Atlantic and Pacific. Next, a galaxy of small agriculturally based cities (the earliest in the world) appeared in the Tigris–Euphrates valley about 3500 B.C., and within these, writing and mathematics were invented, as well as an astronomically calculated calendar, monumental architecture, kingship, and all the other basic elements of archaic civilizations. The combination then appeared in Egypt c. 2850 B.C., Crete and India c. 2600, China c. 1500, and Middle America between about 1200 and 800. Next, the mastery of the horse, 1800 B.C. or so, in the grasslands of Southeast Europe and Southwest Asia, was followed by the irresistible incursions of the patriarchal, horse-and-cattle-herding, chariot-driving Aryans into the tilled lands of India and the Near East, Greece, Italy, and Western Europe. At about the same time the Hebrews entered Canaan, bringing a unique brand of patriarchal monotheism from which the world-conquering, missionizing civilizations of Christianity and Islam arose. And finally there evolved in Rome (first pagan, then Christian) the concept and corpus of civilizing law that in time became the root and stock from which not only every modern constitution derived, but also the universal charter of the United Nations—not to mention those further contributions of Europe to the world, the scientific method of research and the power-driven machine, from which innovations the great sky and ocean liners have emerged that today are bearing from every corner of the earth to the corridors of that same U.N. those graduates of Oxford, Cambridge, Paris, Harvard, and Columbia who bring back to Alma Mater the recirculating spiritual "winds of change" of this amazing twentieth century of ours.

Are we not to name all this an "evolution," "unilinear" and in "progressive stages"?

Moreover, it is difficult to pretend not to notice that all the main creative centers of this development were situated in a zone between 25 and 60 degrees north of the equator, 10 degrees west and 50 east of Greenwich.

This stage by stage evolution, which in broad outline Bachofen discerned (though with no idea, of course, of the great length of its backward reach in time), he did not regard as the consequence of a merely physical accumulation of inventions, but treated as a function of psychological mutations: a graded maturation of the mind. And he saw this growth epitomized, stage by stage, in relevant symbolic images, hypostasizing the founding insights (*Grundanschauungen*) of each of the several degrees. Every system of mythology, he states, is the exegesis of such a nuclear symbol: "It unfolds in a series of outwardly connected actions what the symbol embodies in a unity." †† And the message of the symbol is not a mere thought or idea, but a way of *experience* which can be understood only by responding to its summons.

"The symbol awakens intimations," Bachofen writes; "speech can only explain. The symbol plucks all the strings of the human spirit at once; speech is compelled to take up a single thought at a time. The symbol strikes its roots in the most secret depths of the soul; language skims over the surface of the understanding like a soft breeze. The symbol aims inward; language outward." * And in accord with the inward sense of its commanding symbol, Bachofen held, the civilization of each mounting stage brought forth the mythology and creative deeds of its unique destiny—as did Gothic Europe in response to its symbol of the Crucified Redeemer, Israel to the Covenant, Athens to its sky of Apollonian light, and the Lycians to the female earth.

Bachofen envisioned the course of the spiritual maturation of

†† Below, p. 48.   * Below, pp. 49f.

humanity in five capital stages. Two, as we have seen, were dominated by the female point of view; three, thereafter, were dominated by the male. Within the geographic range of his purview, he identified Africa and Asia as the chief seats of development of the earlier stages of this sequence, and Europe— specifically Greece and Rome—of the later.

From the Near East, according to his reading of the evidence (and we now can be reasonably certain that his reading was correct), there came the earliest agricultural village communities of Greece, and of Italy as well. They were characterized, according to his theory, by the religiously enforced moral order of the second stage of mother right, the agricultural telluric-Demetrian. Their mythologies and associated symbolic customs were of a profoundly poetic beauty—recognizing in every significant phase of life the mystery of the female power, symbolized in the mother goddess Earth and present in every wife and mother. It was a world, as he tells, held in form by "that mysterious power which equally permeates all earthly creatures," † the love of mothers for their young; and the blood kinship of the matrilineal family was the fundamental structuring principle of the social order.

It is pertinent to remark at this point that in Bachofen's nineteenth century the Hegelian concept of a dialectic of statement and counterstatement, thesis and antithesis, in the rolling tide of history was a commonly accepted thought, inflected variously, however, by the numerous vigorous theorists of that really great period of creative historical thinkers. Karl Marx, for instance (whose dates, 1818–1883, match very closely those of our author), saw, wherever he looked, the economic-political conflict of exploiter and exploited. Nietzsche, who came to Basel in 1869 as a young professor of classical philology and for the next half decade was a frequent guest in Bachofen's home (spending Sundays, however, with his idol Richard Wagner in Lucerne, whose dates, 1813– 1883, again approximately match Bachofen's span of years), saw the dialectic of history, and of individual biography as well, in terms of an unrelenting conflict between the forces of disease, weakness, and life-resentment, on the one hand, and, on the other, courage and determination to build life forward toward a realiza-

† Below, p. 79.

tion of potentials. Bachofen, far more learned in the matter of antiquity than either of these celebrated thinkers, and indeed than Hegel himself, saw the dialectic as of the mothering, feminine, earth-oriented, and the masculine, mastering, idea-and-heaven oriented powers. In his masterwork *Mother Right* he had already written:

> The progress from the maternal to the paternal conception of man forms the most important turning point in the history of the relations between the sexes. The Demetrian and the Aphroditean-hetaeric stages both hold to the primacy of generative motherhood, and it is only the greater or lesser purity of its interpretation that distinguishes the two forms of existence. . . . Maternity pertains to the physical side of man, the only thing he shares with the animals: the paternal-spiritual principle belongs to him alone. Here he breaks through the bonds of tellurism and lifts his eyes to the higher regions of the cosmos. †

The first stage in the rise of the masculine principle to supremacy is symbolized, according to Bachofen's view, in the figure of the solar child, the solar hero, born without earthly father from the virgin-mother Dawn: the mythic personification of the rising sun. Here the masculine principle is still subordinated to the female.

The second stage he terms the Dionysian. Its mythologies are of the sun god at the zenith, equidistant from its rising and setting hours, masterfully fertilizing the earth as the phallic power. However, there is a dangerous regressive trend potential in this situation. "The Dionysian father," Bachofen writes, "forever seeks receptive matter in order to arouse it to life." ** Thus the masculine principle has not yet broken free to the independent sphere of its own *ius naturale*, while, as exciter of the female, Bacchus-Dionysus, the god of women and the wine of life, tends to reactivate the primary passions of physical lust, and so to precipitate a regression from the marital-Demetrian to the hetaerist-Aphroditic stage of sexuality. And this, he declares, is the way things went and have remained in Africa and Asia, where "the original matriarchy underwent the most thorough Dionysian transformation." ††

† Below, pp. 109f.   ** Below, p. 114.   †† Below, p. 103.

In Greece the long struggle against the earlier telluric mother-nature powers is documented in the myths and legends of such heroes as Bellerophon, Heracles, Theseus and Perseus, Oedipus and Orestes. There is marked in these an advance to the sky-bright Apollonian stage of masculine spirituality. However, the advance was only temporary; for in the end it was Dionysus and his maenads who again gained the day in Greece. Only in Rome did an essentially masculine spiritual order become effectively established and confirmed—in the tenets and world legacy of Roman civil law.

It is therefore the great argument of Bachofen's *Myth of Tanaquil* that the effort of European man to achieve the proprietorship and rational control of his own destiny, releasing himself from the dominion of cosmic-physical forces and a primitive philosophy of existence, must be recognized as having gained its first enduring victory as the dominant driving force and creative principle of the history of Rome. And it was a victory gained only at the cost of a ruthless suppression and subordination of the claims and allures of the natural world—the more cruel and ruthless, the greater the allure.

"It is no paradox," he states, "but a great truth borne out by all history that human culture advances only through the clash of opposites." * And in the case of Rome, the clash was between the Oriental principle represented in the Aphroditic, Demetrian, and Dionysian legacies of the Sabines and Etruscans, Hellenistic Carthage and, finally, Cleopatra's Hellenistic Egypt, and, on the other hand, the austerity of a race inspired to create, under the sign of reason, a world empire of illuminated law.

Bachofen interpreted both Rome's terrible annihilation of Carthage and Virgil's sympathy with that violent work, displayed in the Aeneid, as expressions, respectively, in act and in sentiment, of the inward necessity of this spiritual clash; and in demonstration of the fact that it was indeed a clash primarily of *Grundanschauungen,* spiritual ideals, and not of merely economic and political interests, he analyzed the transformation of the elements of the legend of Queen Tanaquil as they passed from their seat of origin in the Asiatic Near East to European Rome.

* Below, p. 227.

xlviii

They had been the elements there of an obscene fertility festival, an orgy of the type described in Frazer's *Golden Bough*, "to make the crops to grow." The festival queen had been a temple prostitute in the character of the Great Goddess, and her temporary spouse, with whom she was publicly united in accordance with the primal *ius naturale*, was a young lusty in the role of the god, who, following his service, was sacrificed on a pyre; while for a period of five days and nights a general orgy rendered appropriate veneration to the hetaeric divinity of the occasion.

Folk festivals of this sort arrived in Italy from Asia and were particularly evident in the traditions of the Sabines and Etruscans —of which Bachofen cites numerous examples; and Tanaquil's legend was one of these. She was represented as the queenly throne-giver of the last three kings of the Roman Etruscan line: Tarquinius Priscus (the legendary fifth king of Rome, r. 616–578 B.C.), of whom she was supposed to have been the consort and adviser; Servius Tullius (the sixth legendary king, r. 578–534), the son of a slave woman who married Tanaquil's daughter and by the contrivance of his mother-in-law succeeded to the throne; and finally, Tarquinius Superbus (the seventh and last legendary king of this line, r. 534–510 B.C.), who was supposed to have been Tanaquil's son or, according to other accounts, her spouse. But such a female donor and patroness of royal rule and power is not a properly Roman but an Asiatic figure, derived, along with the concept of kingship itself, from Asia, and of the same symbolic context as the Asiatic goddesses and heroines of legend, Anahita and Mylitta, Dido and Cleopatra. Bachofen's great point is that in Rome her entire character was transformed, and that neither economics nor politics but a spiritual ideal was the force responsible for the change. She lost her "basely sensuous" Aphroditic-venereal traits and became the model matronly patroness of the rights of women in the Roman state, an example of the nobility of the dutiful Roman wife, and a champion of the humanizing principle of love and mercy in a society governed otherwise by sheerly masculine ideals of statecraft. And this transformation accorded, furthermore, with the whole spirit of Roman as opposed to Oriental culture, whether in its religious, economic, political, or aesthetic aspect: for these are all of a piece. They do not derive one from another, but are expressions equally of a common *Grundgedanke*, manifest in the various departments of life; and to read them otherwise is to flatten the whole structure and thus to lose sight of the problem of history itself.

Furthermore, not only was Tanaquil transformed from a goddess of hetaeric type to one of "spiritual purity," but in the course of time a second development ensued, when she was conceived not as a goddess but as a historic queen. Bachofen concludes this remarkable, inexhaustibly suggestive discussion by saying:

> We might be tempted to regard this subordination of the divine to a human idea as the last stage in a process of degeneration from an earlier, more sublime standpoint. And indeed, who will deny that beside the cosmic world-spanning ideas of the Bel-Heracles religion, which gave rise to the notion of a woman commanding over life and throne, the humanized Tanaquil of the Roman tradition, adapted as she is to everyday life, seems an impoverished figure, scarcely comparable to the colossal Oriental conception. And yet this regression contains the germ of a very important advance. For every step that liberates our spirit from the paralyzing fetters of a cosmic-physical view of life must be so regarded. . . . Rome's central idea . . . the idea underlying its historical state and its law, is wholly independent of matter; it is an eminently ethical achievement, the most spiritual of antiquity's bequests to the ensuing age. And here again it is clear that our Western life truly begins with Rome. Roman is the idea through which European mankind prepared to set its own imprint on the entire globe, namely, the idea that no material law but only the free activity of the spirit determines the destinies of peoples.†

6

Johann Jacob Bachofen's career falls into three clearly marked stages. The first, his period of preparation, extends to 1851, the year of an inspiring horseback pilgrimage that he took through Greece. The following decade, 1852–61, was the period of labor on his major works. The manuscript of his *Greek Journey* was

† Below, pp. 236, 237.

finished in 1852, but remained unpublished until its rescue, in 1927, by the Munich group. In 1854 he composed his retrospective sketch, in 1859 published the work on *Mortuary Symbolism*, and in 1861, *Mother Right*; after which, as already remarked, he left Basel for a change of air in Spain.

The final period of his career began with the eight years of leisurely, peaceful labor on *The Myth of Tanaquil*, while a new and pleasantly fulfilling transformation of life and home took place around him. In 1865 he married and traveled with his young bride to Rome, the magical mother-city of his learning, from which he had returned in youth with "a new seriousness of soul" and "a more living, positive background" for his studies.** A son was born the next year, 1866; and Bachofen retired, then, from a judgeship he had held since 1842. The arrival in Basel, three years later, of Nietzsche brought a new brilliance to the Bachofen domestic circle, and it was about that time that signs began to appear, as well, of a new, significant, and rapidly increasing scientific appreciation of his published works—not, indeed, from the classical circles of academic hardshelled crabs to which he had turned, at first, in vain; but from the unforeseen quarter of a new science, anthropology.

For during the year of Nietzsche's arrival there came into Bachofen's hands a copy of John F. McLennan's *Primitive Marriage* (published in London, 1865), and there he found that his own work not only had been decently recognized, but also was furnishing the basis for an entirely new approach to a totally new scientific topic: the prehistory of marriage. The next year, 1870, Alexis Giraud-Teulon, a young scholar from Geneva, came to Bachofen's door, full of admiration for the great man who had opened to science the world age of mother right; and it was in that same year that Bachofen's interest in his own career was suddenly renewed.

"My task," he wrote on November 10 to his old friend Meyer-Ochsner, "is now to assemble the evidences of the maternal system from all peoples of the earth, to prepare, on the basis of this amplified material, for a second edition of *Mother Right*. . . . Sources of such information are the works of travel. . . . And I

** Below, p. 13.

am enjoying from these the great advantage of becoming familiar with a world that expands my horizon immensely and brings me into spiritual rapport, moreover, with new peoples, new individuals, and a truly heroic race of voyagers, missionaries and bravely adventurous hunters. We have been·brought up in just too limited a classical way. . . ." ††

And it was very much as though his readings in the expanded field were sending out telepathic calls; for almost immediately letters of encouraging admiration arrived, on the one hand, from that greatest anthropological traveler of all, Professor Adolf Bastian of the University of Berlin, President of the Berlin Anthropological Society, and on the other, from the leading American ethnologist of the period, Lewis Henry Morgan, whose *League of the Iroquois* had appeared some twenty years before (1851). On Christmas Day in 1871 this honorary member of the Hawk clan of the Seneca nation of the Iroquois sat down at his desk in Rochester, New York, and wrote to the distant outcast in the Alps: "My first notice of your investigations was in Prof. Curtius' *History of Greece.** I there found that you were examining a class of facts closely allied to those upon which I had been for some time engaged. I have now your Mother-right. . . ." † The correspondence that ensued endured until the year of Morgan's death in 1881, and during the course of it, there appeared one day at Bachofen's door, in further testimony of the regard in which he was held across the sea, a shipment of publications on the aborigines of America, which had been sent to him from Washington, D.C., with the compliments of the Government of the United States.

Ironically, Lewis H. Morgan's widely read treatise on the prehistoric stage-by-stage evolution of culture, *Ancient Society*, published 1877, in which Bachofen's achievement is accorded both recognition and due praise,** caught the eyes and imagination of Karl Marx and Friedrich Engels, into whose vision of an early communal order of civilization its hypotheses seemed to fit;

†† From a letter quoted by Rudolf Marx, p. xxvii (cf. above, p. xxxvii, note).
 * Ernst Curtius, *The History of Greece*, tr. by A. W. Ward (New York, 1871). 3 vols.
 † Quoted from Morgan MSS by Leslie A. White, ed. of Lewis H. Morgan, *Ancient Society* (Cambridge, Mass., 1964), p. 297, n. 5.
** Ibid., pp. 297–8.

and so the works of the two learned jurists, respectively of Rochester, N. Y., and of Basel, were admitted to the canon of permitted Marxist readings. In fact, in Engels's own treatise on *The Origin of the Family, Private Property, and the State* (1884), Bachofen's view of the evolution of culture is accorded respectful approbation—though with correction, of course, of the romantic bourgeois thought of a basically spiritual instead of economic-political-exploitational motivation of the procession.

Bachofen did not live to complete or even to initiate the publication of his proposed revised and enlarged version of *Mother Right*. In 1880 and 1886 he produced two volumes of shorter pieces, entitled *Antiquarian Letters, Dealing Chiefly with the Earliest Concepts of the Family*. However, on November 27, 1887, he suffered a stroke and died. His widow and son brought out a posthumous work, *The Lamps of Roman Tombs*, in 1890; it carried an introduction by Alexis Giraud-Teulon, the loyal spiritual son who had been the first to render Bachofen the satisfaction of a gesture of recognition. Giraud-Teulon's own treatise, *Les Origines de la famille, questions sur les antecédents des sociétés patriarchales*, had greeted the master's eyes in 1874. By the time of his death a considerable harvest was beginning to be gathered from those diligent gardens of Academia which Heine, in his *Harzreise*, amusingly describes as consisting of beds of little sticks set up in rows, each bearing a bit of paper with a notation from some book—the work then consisting in transferring notations from older beds to new, in ever-changing arrangement. However, this fame itself became largely responsible, in the end, for the fading of Bachofen's name, when, at the turn of the twentieth century, there was a trend in anthropology away from theoretical reconstructions of the earliest state of man.

For Bachofen's name had finally become associated almost exclusively with the one aspect of his writing that was most open to question—that namely, which the Marxists had picked up, of the primal Aphroditic-hetaerist stage of communal sexuality. A formidable attack on this view of primitive life appeared in 1902 in a work by the anthropologist Heinrich Schurtz, *Altersklassen und Männerbünde*, where it is argued that "marriage in its beginning goes back as far as the evidences of human society can be followed," and furthermore, that "the alleged vestiges and evidences of a period of sexual promiscuity are nothing but manifestations of the sexual license of the mature but still unmarried young."††

We have remarked already the anti-evolutionary schools of social science that arose in the United States and England. On the Continent, also, grandiose total views lost favor as new ethnological information came pouring, in great variety, from all quarters of the earth, and as the great remoteness in time of the earliest paleolithic, and even prepaleolithic past became increasingly apparent and impressive. Bachofen's reputation foundered, along with the reputations of a number of other interesting nineteenth-century pioneers who, in the frame of the brief prehistoric prospect of their period, had supposed themselves to be working closer to the flaming sword of the archangel at the gate of the garden of Eden than was the case.

Ironically again, however, the other aspects of Bachofen's thought were meanwhile becoming increasingly accepted—but over other scholars' names. For example, in Sir James G. Frazer's *The Golden Bough*, which first appeared in 1890 (the year of Bachofen's posthumous *Lamps of Roman Tombs*) and was then reissued in twelve massive volumes between 1907 and 1915, the central problem under investigation is of a piece with those by which Bachofen's interest had been aroused. This was a Roman custom that could not be explained in normal classical terms: the reported tradition of the goddess Diana's sacred grove at Nemi, where the priest—regarded as the husband of an oak tree—gained his office by murdering his predecessor and would lose it when he himself, in turn, was slain. The great British scholar, in his own way, actually completed in this mighty work the last task that Bachofen had set himself, "to assemble the evidences of the maternal system from all peoples of the earth"; and he arrived, as had his predecessor—apparently independently—at the recognition of an age of mother right antecedent to that of the Greek and Roman patriarchal systems.*

Following Frazer's work, and in acknowledged dependence

---

†† Schurtz, *Altersklassen und Männerbünde* (Berlin, 1902), pp. iv–v.
 * James G. Frazer, *The Golden Bough* (New York, 1-vol. edn., 1922), Chap. XIV, "The Succession to the Kingdom in Ancient Latium," pp. 152–8.

upon it, there appeared in 1903 Jane Harrison's richly documented *Prolegomena to the Study of Greek Religion*, which, if Bachofen's name were mentioned anywhere in its pages, might be read from beginning to end as an intentional celebration and verification of his views. In the twenties Sir Arthur Evans excavated the ruins of Cretan Knossos, and in the fifties the young genius Michael Ventris deciphered some of the writings discovered there: and the prominence in this pre-Hellenic treasure trove, both of the Great Goddess and of her son and consort Poseidon (whose name, *Posei-dās,* means "Lord of the Earth"),† has now confirmed irrefutably not only Bachofen's intuition of an age of mother right preceding the patriarchal ages, but also his recognition of Syria and Asia Minor as the proximate Asiatic provinces from which the agriculturally based mother right culture complex came to the isles and peninsulas of Greece and Rome.

Furthermore, it may be noted that Bachofen's methodological idea of the *Kulturkreis* as an organically coherent culture province generated and sustained by the force and phenomenology of an informing *Grundanschauung* became the leading inspiration of a number of extremely influential independent ethnological researchers: Leo Frobenius and Adolf Jensen, for instance, and Fathers Wilhelm Schmidt and Wilhelm Koppers.

However, the most important aspect of Bachofen's contribution is not his mere anticipation of archaeological finds nor even his influence on ethnologists who have developed and applied his ideas, but the profundity and lucidity of his reading of mythological symbols—specifically the symbols of the great creative pre-Homeric, pre-Mosaic "age of fable" that now lies open to our eyes. For that was the age from which the founding themes and images of both our classical and our Biblical mythologies were derived; which is to say, the *Grundanschauungen,* the grounding themes and images of an essential part of our cultural heritage and, thereby, of our own culturally conditioned psychology: the creative period, as we now know, of those agriculturally based mother-right symbologies that Sigmund Freud, in *Totem and Taboo,* confessed he was unable to explain. "I cannot suggest," Freud

† Leonard R. Palmer, *Mycenaeans and Minoans* (New York, 1962), pp. 119–31, "The Mycenaean Religion."

wrote in 1912, "at what point in this process of development a place is to be found for the great mother-goddesses, who may perhaps in general have preceded the father-gods." **

Bachofen's concentration of his whole mind and being for some fifty years of his life on the reading of the pictorial script of precisely that system of religious imagery—stemming from an age of mythopoetic thought immediately antecedent to both the Biblical and the classical patriarchal formations—opened in a magical way a deeper view than any patriarchal mythology or its analysis, not only into our cultural past, but also into our culturally structured souls. That is why the psychologist Ludwig Klages, who was the first member of the Munich circle to be struck by the force of these perceptions, wrote in a statement published in 1925 that Bachofen had been "the greatest literary experience" of his life, determining the whole course of his career.

"In Bachofen," he declared, "we have to recognize perhaps the greatest interpreter of that primordial mentality, in comparison with the cultic and mythic manifestations of which, all later religious beliefs and doctrines appear as mere reductions and distortions." ††

Leo Frobenius termed the same period of mythopoetic creativity to which Bachofen's whole genius had been dedicated, the period at "the apogee of the mythological curve." Before it extend the millenniums of primitive, pre-agricultural hunting and foraging cultures. After it come the flowerings of the great monumental civilizations of Mesopotamia and Egypt, Greece and Rome, India, China, and across the Pacific, Mexico and Peru—the symbologies and mythologies of which are as like to each other as so many descendants of a single house. Sir James G. Frazer likewise points back to that age as the ultimate source of those magical rites and myths "to make the crops to grow" that survive in modified, reinterpreted, and distorted forms in many of our own basic religious practices and beliefs. Bachofen, at that source, was thus indeed at the "time of the beginning"—not of mankind, as he believed, in the short terms of early nineteenth-century science,

** *Totem and Taboo*, in the Standard Edition, tr. James Strachey (London, 1955), Vol. XIII, p. 149.

†† Ludwig Klages, Introduction to J. J. Bachofen, *Versuch über die Gräber-symbolik der Alten* (Basel, 1925), pp. x–xi.

but of civilization. And so it is that, through the extraordinary ability of his own alert humanity to interpret the mythic forms of that germinal time, we are introduced to the psychological ground of our entire cultural heritage. Nietzsche, as we have said, had to reject the Christian strain of our mixed heritage; Kierkegaard, the pagan. Wise, deep-seeing, sagely Bachofen, on the other hand, could with equal eye regard the whole sweep of what he saw to be an orderly progression in which his own mode of consciousness participated as a member. And it was to this realization of an ultimately unitary *ius naturale* of spiritual existence, made manifest throughout the range of human faith and works, that his life vocation ultimately called him.

"A time inevitably comes," he wrote to his Berlin master, Von Savigny, "when the scholar seriously examines his studies for their relation to the supreme truths. He becomes aware of a desire, an urgent need, to come a little closer to the eternal meaning of things. The husk no longer suffices. The thought of having struggled so long with mere worthless forms becomes a torment. And then one is saved by the realization that even in these things one may discover 'the eternal footprint.' . . . I see more and more that *one* law governs all things." *

Joseph Campbell

* Below, pp. 15, 16.

Myth, Religion,
and Mother Right

My Life in Retrospect

Bachofen wrote this autobiographical sketch at the
suggestion of his former teacher Friedrich Carl von
Savigny, professor of Roman law at the University
of Berlin. It was found among Bachofen's papers in
1916, in an envelope addressed and sealed by Savigny.

A REVIEW of my work over the last fifteen years is not to be undertaken lightly. The recollection of past occupations carries one back
to the life one was leading at the time, and awakens memories that
seemed to be buried forever. For inner and outward life are
indivisible, and every literary endeavor inevitably takes its place in
the general picture of one's past activities and state of mind. Inner
experience and purely outward circumstances join to shape our
work. It is impossible to think of one without the other. Consequently, when I began to think back on my work in this early
period, images of my whole past life rose to mind, and the paper
your Excellency asked me to write grew from a mere literary
inventory to a kind of autobiography. I must own that it fills me
with the sort of malaise that a man experiences at the sight of his
own portrait—and there is no doubt that at many points it will call
for the reader's indulgence and patience.

I was drawn to the study of law by philology. It is here that I
started and hither that my legal studies led me back. In this respect
my attitude toward my field has always remained unchanged.
Roman law has always struck me as a branch of classical and
particularly of Latin philology, hence as part of a vast field
encompassing the whole of classical antiquity. What interested me
was the ancient world itself and not the applicability of its lessons
to present-day needs; it was ancient and not modern Roman law
that I really wanted to study. With these attitudes taken over from
philology, I often found myself in a painful opposition to the

instructors and books I had chosen as my guides. More and more I came to disregard the modern point of view and subordinate it to ancient criteria. I felt an increasing distaste for all modern systems. I wanted to see the material in its original form, and looked on all attempts to adjust it to modern conceptions as mere misrepresentation of a sort that was bound to frustrate any true understanding of ancient life. It struck me as an unwarranted dogmatization that could only result in error and perplexity. I was also dissatisfied with the current method of resolving controversies, which struck me as no better than Justinian's dream of a jurisprudence free from doubt and contradiction. It seemed to me much more fruitful to investigate the profound reasons why equally distinguished jurists could come to entirely different conclusions. For strange as it may seem, it is perfectly true that in questions of jurisprudence opposite views can often be equally justified. I was glad that Justinian had not succeeded in effacing every trace of these disputes that always arise where there is freedom of thought. I myself was convinced that the golden age of Roman law must have brought forth the most abundant deviations and conflicts in all its branches. With this in mind, I derived the greatest pleasure from reading our legal sources, and if it had been up to me, I should have given the explanation of Pandect titles precedence over all systematic lectures with their dogmatic principles and the so-called proofs so painstakingly collected in support of them.

But this notion of mine had one great drawback, as I was soon to discover. I memorized very few of the positive rules of jurisprudence and was always at a loss when called upon to recite rules and exceptions. From an intellectual point of view it seemed to me that I had not lost much. But my method of study had not been calculated with a view to examinations. Of this I was well aware. And in order to make good the deficiency, I was compelled to abandon the source materials and memorize from textbooks for a year. A *privatissimum* in Göttingen drilled me thoroughly, and a few months in Basel completed the work. There was a brief period in which I knew Mühlenbruch's *Doctrina* almost word for word, and could have opened the tattered old tomes to any desired paragraph even in the dark. The ideal candidate for the doctorate was held to be one who could find any reference in any book without either a light or an index. My work was not in vain. I came through both preliminary and final examinations with flying colors and received the highest grades. Once again I was able to exchange my textbooks for the *corpus juris*, the classics, and Cujacius. It was high time. For the breath of antiquity that I drew from its literary works was as refreshing to me as the Alpine air of the Engadin that I visited recently. I found Gaius and Cicero infinitely more enjoyable than Mühlenbruch, and my dissertation * gave me several months of the most delightful and satisfying association with the sources. This work completed, I thought of devoting a small book to explaining the difference between *res mancipi* and *res nec mancipi*.† I abandoned the idea, partly because the reading of the significant literature made the subject utterly distasteful to me, and partly because the work would have delayed my departure for Paris, planned for the winter of 1839–40. The prospect of visiting a French university after those of Switzerland and Germany was very attractive to me, and although there was little to be learned about the classics in Paris, I spent a whole year at the École de droit. I had no objection to the subordinate position occupied by Roman law in France. I had always regarded it as a part of ancient rather than modern life, a fragment of classical philology, a product of conditions that had long sunk into oblivion, an outgrowth of ideas that had very little relation to those of the Christian Germanic peoples.

Hitherto I had been preoccupied with ancient law, totally disregarding its modern adaptation. Now for the first time I came into close contact with one of the most celebrated and widespread bodies of modern legislation and with the literature and jurisprudence based on it. Even though it did not give me the same intellectual pleasure as the study of Roman antiquity, I thoroughly enjoyed this introduction to a purely practical field and was glad to immerse myself in the juridical life of our time to the exclusion of ancient learning. From this period dates my belief that such a

---

* *De Romanorum iudiciis civilibus, de legis actionibus, de formulis et de condictione dissertatio historico-dogmatica* (Göttingen, 1840).

† *Res mancipi* are things in which, under Roman law, property was transferred by a formal process of seizing or taking in hand (mancipium); *res nec mancipi* are things in which property passed by simple delivery.

separation between the ancient and the modern in legal studies is far preferable to the fusion of the two then prevailing in Germany. If the classical and modern eras are each accorded their own independent rights, we shall have the most thorough scholars as well as the most capable practitioners. There are two means by which jurisprudence can preserve or recover its freshness; by direct association with the old wisdom and by occupying itself with practical life. Even if Paris does nothing for the appreciation of classical law, it is superior to the German schools when it comes to inculcating efficiency in modern legal practice. Thus I may say that Germany disclosed the ancient world to me, while France gave me access to that of modern law.

It was at this time that I met Pardessus, Count Pellegrino Rossi, and the aged Count Pastoret, then Chancellor of France, men who have all made significant contributions to our field, though in different branches. Rossi and Pastoret had preserved grateful memories of Switzerland from their early years, and it is perhaps to this circumstance that I owed my friendly reception in their homes. At this time Rossi enjoyed high favor among the students, who had thrown stones at him some years earlier. The two gendarmes who had escorted him for a long time had long since become superfluous. His often adroit and assuredly insincere pronouncements in favor of trial by jury, the constitutional charter, freedom of the press, Polish independence, and similar catchwords of the revolutionary journalism of the time had brought about this shift of mood. Otherwise his personality was unchanged. He had about him an insulting, Italian sort of arrogance which increased, or at least became more blatant, with the brilliance of his situation, and which was one of the reasons for his unexpected downfall in Rome. I believe that in his heart he particularly despised those qualities of the French people which he most warmly praised in public. He held the British nation in far higher esteem, and it is certain that the admiration for its great political qualities that he expressed on every possible occasion was no concession to the public mood in the most brilliant days of the July monarchy,** but rather the expression of a deep-seated

** The Orléanist regime in France under Louis Philippe, lasting from July 1830 till 1848.

conviction and an expressly chosen means of holding up a mirror to French vanity.

It was these frequent glances at England that chiefly decided me to spend some time in London after my stay in Paris. Blackstone and several French works had given me a general knowledge of English political and juridical institutions, and this added to my curiosity. My plan was carried out. No year in my life has been so rich in work, instruction, and enjoyment as the one spent in England. It is seldom that one can fully estimate the value of such periods of life. The flexibility of youth makes one equally receptive to all manner of learning and the study of so many different fields gives one the sensation of a continuous triumphal march. When I established myself in London, I was still uncertain as to what I had particularly come to look for. Everything, I thought, or at least a little bit of everything, material and ideas for the future. I was at an age when everything still belonged to me, when even this everything was not enough, and I had no idea in what corner of this vast field my spirit would ultimately settle down. I was fascinated by the life of the law courts with all their patriarchal pomp, but there was also the British Museum with its treasures. Might it not be possible to combine the two aspects, to cultivate them both, side by side? My experience showed that far from being incompatible, the two occupations were mutually helpful.

I wrote nothing about English law. When I think of it now, I am amazed that I was able to gain even a general view of the most important material. Amid all these occupations the end of the winter approached, slowly, slowly, like old age. I wished to be gone out of the fog, the hustle and bustle of the big city. A quiet abode of the Muses—that was what I needed in order to glance back over all that I had experienced and learned, and translate it into ideas. Oxford did not live up to my expectations. Its glacial air of aristocracy, the hollow splendor, the immobility that lay over everything, the countryside, the people, and particularly men's minds, drove me away after a few days. I went to Cambridge and there found what I was looking for: scholarly activity, pleasant companionship, and above all peace and quiet. With a great sense of well-being I now continued my search for medieval processualists in the public library and in those of some of the colleges. The good people of Cambridge could not see what interest there could be in such works nowadays.

England's schools aim to educate the upper classes of the country, not to form scholars or officials. And scholarship is only a small part of education, particularly when it comes to teaching a British subject how to exercise the rights and duties which constitution and custom accord the privileged classes represented at the universities. This higher purpose would not be achieved by courses of lectures, and still less by leaving the student to his own resources, giving him full independence in the choice of his studies or of his extracurricular activities. In England, consequently, the young man is assigned a tutor. He lives in the tutor's college, and the association between them extends even to vacation periods and the customary tours of the Continent.

In those days I was so close to my German student's life that the contrast with the English system made a strong impression on me. What is the situation of a twenty-year-old boy in Berlin or in Paris when his parents have trustingly sent him off to the university? The question surely deserves the most thorough consideration. I have given it a good deal of thought in connection with Basel, for in order to take a practical view of matters, one must live in the midst of them. And I have not abandoned the hope that something of the sort will come into existence here. The form, after all, is indifferent provided that the aim is achieved: general education on a foundation of humane sciences in place of mere specialized instruction. Besides, if present materialistic trends become dominant, learning is likely to become once more a priesthood which will lack state support, and must have recourse to private funds and private activity of all sorts. Only then will it be possible to realize the ideal of which I have spoken and to eradicate the literary proletariat with all its evil consequences. My visit to Cambridge marked my last protracted stay in England.

On my return home I took the words "Thy lot is Sparta" ††

†† *Spartam nactus es:* the first part of a proverb quoted by Cicero (*Letters to Atticus* 4.6.2), meaning roughly, "Sparta is the place fate has chosen for you; be an ornament to it."

8

very much to heart. In exchanging the broad perspectives of Paris and London for the petty circumstances that now surrounded me, I really had great need of this philosophical consolation. Yet even here I was soon to find not a little that was good and estimable. It is only in one's own native land that one can be firmly rooted. It is only here that one can know life's great experiences, for the destinies of families and states are fulfilled not in one life, but in the chain of successive generations.

Here, in Switzerland, no one who has studied can decline to take part in public affairs, least of all one who has acquired a doctorate in law and, as the shopkeepers say, has nothing to do. Study for the mere sake of study is something that is not understood by a people whose character is chiefly distinguished by practical concern. But my plans were sharply opposed to the public opinion of my native land. After all my digressions in France and England, I wished to settle down quietly in my intellectual homeland, the field of philology and jurisprudence. At this time I resumed my work on the Voconian law * and another on the ancient Roman law of debt,† both of which youthful ventures were published. I began my course on the history of Roman law with a lecture on "Natural Law and Historical Law," printed in manuscript form.** This lecture offended the philosophers by its recognition of all manner of historical phenomena and the political scientists by its emphasis on a higher origin of legal systems, independent of human will. And yet my superiors did not despair of me. Perhaps it would do no harm to try me out. At all events I did not seem to be of a revolutionary nature, perhaps on the contrary, too close to Savigny. In short, at the next vacancy the Grand Council appointed me a regular member of the Basel criminal court, and a short time later I was advanced to the position of *Statthalter*, i.e., vice-president.

My hope of undivided scholarly activity had again been shattered. Yet, even so, I found considerable free time. I began to

---

* *Die lex Voconia und die mit ihr zusammenhängenden Rechtsinstitute* (Basel, 1843). *The lex Voconia* (169 B.C.) forbade women to inherit property.
† *Das nexum, die nexi und die lex Petillia* (Basel, 1843).
** *Das Naturrecht und das geschichtliche Recht in ihren Gegensätzen* (Basel, 1841).

carry out my plan of reading through all the classics, legal and nonlegal, at least once, and in addition I studied the principal works of the modern [juridical] literature.

My literary studies were limited to two works, Blume's *Iter Italicum* and Winckelmann's *History of Art* with Fernow's notes. From the former I gained a few learned notations which were later useful to me in the libraries of Milan, Turin, and Rome. But to my reading of Winckelmann's works I owe an enjoyment of a far higher order—indeed, one of the greatest pleasures of my whole life. Since then I have dwelt much in the regions that it opened, especially at times when everything else seemed to lose interest for me. Ancient art draws our heart to classical antiquity, and jurisprudence our mind. Only together do the two confer a harmonious enjoyment and satisfy both halves of man's spirit. Philology without concern for the works of art remains a lifeless skeleton. The *id quod decet* (that which is fitting) that Cicero's Archias †† declared to be the supreme element in all art and something that cannot be taught or learned—this is what one acquires from association with ancient art, a sense of the measure and fullness in all things, the supreme human harmony. The magic of Winckelmann's history of art lies in these perfections, in the noble classical grace, unrelated to that of the modern dancing master, that is diffused throughout the work. One cannot help seeing that it was written beneath the warmer sun of Italy, where one feels everything more deeply, pain and joy and the true meaning of things; it is no product of our smoky study rooms, with their rancid smell of tallow candles and oil lamps.

In my wanderings through the museums of Italy my attention was soon attracted to one aspect of all their vast treasures, namely mortuary art, a field in which antiquity shows us some of its greatest beauties. When I consider the profound feeling, the human warmth that distinguishes this realm of ancient life, I am ashamed of the poverty and barrenness of the modern world. The ancient tombs have given us a well-nigh inexhaustible wealth. At

†† Bachofen's reference to Archias seems to be a slip. He probably had in mind Cicero's reference to the actor Roscius in *De oratore* (tr. Sutton and Rackham, Vol. 1, p. 93): "the great Roscius himself whom I often hear affirming that the chief thing in art is to observe good taste [*id quod decet*]."

first we may regard the study of tombs as a specialized field of archaeology, but ultimately we find ourselves in the midst of a truly universal [religious] doctrine.

All the treasures that fill our museums of ancient art were taken from tombs, and in general human civilization owes them more than is usually supposed. In nomadic societies the tomb was the first and only stable edifice. Building was done more readily for the dead than for the living; perishable wood was held to be sufficient for the life span allotted to the living, but the eternity of man's ultimate dwelling place demanded the solid stone of the earth. In all essential things the earliest men thought soundly and correctly, as we may expect of those who were still so close to their eternal origin. The oldest cult is bound up with the stone that designates the burial place; the earliest temples were related to the burial site, while art and ornament originated in the decoration of tombs. It was the tombstone that gave rise to the concept of the *sanctum*, of the immovable and immutable. This concept also applies to boundary posts and walls, which along with tombstones constitute the *res sanctae*.* In them ancient man saw an image of the primordial power which dwells in the earth, and consequently all three bear its symbol. The earth sends forth tombstones, boundary posts, and walls as though from its womb, where, as Plato says, they previously slumbered; the phallus is its mark. The altar cult is also related to the tomb, itself an altar among the most ancient peoples as well as in the Christian catacombs: sacrifices to the giver of life were made over the resting place of the corpse. The symbol came into being in the tombs and there it was longest preserved. The thoughts, feelings, silent prayers conceived over the tomb cannot be expressed in words, only intimated by the symbol with its eternally unchanging earnestness. Antiquity made full use of the symbolic, most enduringly and profoundly in its art.

Ought I, by way of explaining my interest in the ancient tombs, to speak of epigraphy and epigrammatics and many other related fields? I prefer to think of the enjoyment I have derived from my visits to tombs. There are two roads to knowledge—the longer, slower, more arduous road of rational combination and the shorter path of the imagination, traversed with the force and swiftness of

* See pp. 40ff.

electricity. Aroused by direct contact with the ancient remains, the imagination grasps the truth at one stroke, without intermediary links. The knowledge acquired in this second way is infinitely more living and colorful than the products of the understanding.

The cemeteries of southern Etruria are close to the great military highway leading from Florence to Rome, and yet are little visited. Castel d'Asso, Vorchia, Bieda, Toscanella, Corneto † do not awaken depressing thoughts as do modern monuments to human transience. Like the ruins of Rome they suggest only that a necessary end is appointed to all things human. No painful feelings disturb our contemplation of the natural course of development, and these ruins recall the strength rather than the weakness of mankind. I love the peoples and the ages that do not work for the day, but have eternity in mind in all their activity. They deserve to have their tombs standing as they stood on the day they were built. We find no fault with the root which has burst through the ceiling like an artificial wedge or split off a fragment of the portal and cast it into the depths. The stillness of nature is the most worthy setting for an eternal home. When all else has forsaken man, the earth with its vegetation still tenderly embraces his stone dwelling place. For the ancient mind this is no mere image but a truth. All those necropolises are situated beside streams. The lapping waters seem to intone the eternal praises of the dead, as an epigram in *The Greek Anthology* puts it, and according to Aeschylus in the *Prometheus* [1] the flowing sources of the sacred streams murmur their grief. These again are no mere images but truths arising from the innermost content of the nature religions. For us, to be sure, such lines are only poetry, whose richest source would seem to lie in its disclosure of the intimate relation between the phenomena of lifeless nature and our own feelings.

All these impressions are made still more poignant by the utter remoteness and forlornness of the ancient burial sites. All who approach them have a sense of discovery. But this stillness strikes us as a homage of the living to the dead. Nothing intervenes between them and us. The sun warms and illuminates these resting places of the dead so wonderfully, and infuses the abodes of horror

† The last two towns have now been renamed respectively Toscania and Tarquinia.

with the magic of joyous life. What beauty there must have been in an age whose very tombs can still arouse so much yearning for it! What a vast abundance of beautiful ethical ideas the ancients drew from their myths. The treasure house that encompasses their oldest memories of history serves also as a source of the oldest ethical truths, and provides consolation and hope for the dying. The wounded Penthesilea seems doubly beautiful to her conqueror Achilles in the moment of her death; it is only as she is dying that he discovers the fullness of her charms. It is Plato who discloses this meaning of the image.

Yes, there is something in the walls of Rome that arouses what is deepest in man. When you strike a bronze disk, it resounds until you set a finger on it to stop the vibrations. That is how Rome affects the spirit that lives with antiquity. One stroke follows another, until every corner of our soul is stirred and we finally become aware of all that was slumbering within us. I returned home from my stay in Rome with an enriched spirit, a new seriousness of soul with which to confront my future, and a more living, positive background for my studies. There the wheel of life hollowed out a deeper track. Among the favorite images that I carried away with me is that of the Campagna. Often I draw aside the curtain and follow with delight the long shadows cast by the evening sun over this broad green plain that is so incomparably important for the history of the world. Here, to speak with Plato, the feet of the immortals have left more than one trace. But instead of following these traces, human scholarship has intentionally effaced more than one of them. Everything was dissolved in mist and fog by the Hyperboreans, who believed in their self-conceit that the great epochs of the ancient world could permanently be reduced to the petty proportions of their own minds.**

I went to Rome as a republican who wished to hear no more of the seven kings, as an unbeliever who respected no tradition, as an adventurer bent on entrusting his ship to the high seas instead of steering cautiously along the shore and keeping the solid ground in sight. All this I left behind in Italy. I should gladly have sacrificed this part of me to one of the old gods of the land as a parting gift.

** This is aimed at Barthold Georg Niebuhr (1776–1831) and Theodor Mommsen (1817–1903) the founders of the critical historical method.

But wrathful over my past sacrilege, they all veiled their faces. Little by little everything took on an entirely different form in my mind. Italy stepped down from the remote pedestal to which the scholars had so long relegated it. Its Eastern lineage became clear to me, and I saw that no culture can properly be understood in isolation. The force of tradition came to seem more and more firmly grounded. History stretched further and further back, and assumed more and more grandiose proportions. The founder of Rome had been represented to me as a kind of Italic Adam, but now I saw him as an extremely modern figure; Rome became the fulfillment and end of a cultural era spanning a millennium.

There are moments when the public life of states and nations succumbs to fatalism. We now stand at such a moment. When we consider particulars, much that is good can still be saved, much that is new and worth while still remains be done. My studies and past had prepared me for a bench in the provinces. In this position I followed the dictates of a truly historical sense, and I brought myself to subordinate the pardonable vanity of the scholar to the greater considerations of the public welfare. I learned to adjust myself with humility to given historical conditions.

The period whose endeavors and teachings I have been discussing extends up to 1848. Then I decided on a second stay in Rome. First my studies had inspired me with a yearning for Italy, and then Italy had awakened a desire for a new and more thorough association with the classics. This interchange began again, but now I had incomparably richer resources than before. I wished to round out my knowledge of various fields and I believed that Rome would give me new inspiration. But the peace of mind I should have required was soon shattered by the wild passions that had chosen Rome as their arena at this time. Rossi fell on the second day after my arrival. The storming of the Quirinal, the flight of the Pope, the Constituent Assembly, the proclamation of the Republic, followed in swift succession.

But for all the gruesome events, the atmosphere would have suggested a riotous but harmless carnival. And with the arrival of Garibaldi's band and the various patriotic legions from all over Italy, things became even more fantastic. Wherever Garibaldi appeared with his flaming red shirt and coal-black stallion, escorted by a Negro on a white horse, every hat in the quarter was tossed into the air. There was disorder of all sorts. Heaven had elected me to witness the first heroic deeds of the Italians against the advancing French; a little later in Tivoli I received a good deal of undesired attention from the populace, which suspected me of being a French spy; and finally, on my journey homeward, I beheld the breakdown of all order. Since then the storm has subsided. Once again Italy has become for me the land of antiquity and of tranquil studies. After such experiences I felt a redoubled need to rest among times and objects bathed in the stillness of the ages, in fields whence the floods of passion long ago subsided.

Despite the name he bears, a man is a highly anonymous being; the name remains identical however often its possessor may have changed his innermost being. I had known a period when the medieval processualists delighted me, and their long-forgotten names, that I had come across by chance, filled me with rejoicing. Later I was capable of forgetting the whole world for the sake of a fine passage in the Pandects, and regarded a successful interpretation as ample reward for protracted labors. But little by little all these pleasures forsook me. All my reading and studies, considered in the light of day, struck me as insignificant, as meager food for the soul, as irrelevant to the fulfillment of what is immortal in us. I found myself in a period of transition such as occurs in the life of every striving man. As to what brings it about—who can see so deeply into the human soul?

The transition was a painful one, but now I am thankful for it. A time inevitably comes when the scholar seriously examines his studies for their relation to the supreme truths. He becomes aware of a desire, an urgent need, to come a little closer to the eternal meaning of things. The husk no longer suffices. The thought of having struggled so long with mere worthless forms becomes a torment. And then one is saved by the realization that even in these things one may discover "the eternal footprint." I know full well what dangers beset me at this time. I might have strayed into metaphysical bypaths and lost sight of my right road forever. And the long circling about might have led to phantasms of the

Huschke †† variety. I thank the Lord that my soul is too sound for that sort of thing. I found a different solution. Ever since then my guiding thought has been the religious foundation of all ancient thinking and life. Here, I am confident, is a key that opens many locks. Sometimes it even seems to me that something of the divine, eternal meaning of human ideas will be revealed to me at the end of this road. If it is true, as Aristotle says, that like can be grasped only by like,[2] then the divine can only be apprehended by a divine mind, and not by the rationalistic self-conceit that sets itself above history. Abundance of information is not everything, it is not even the essential. It is one of my profoundest convictions that without a thorough transformation of our whole being, without a return to ancient simplicity and health of soul, one cannot gain the merest intimation of the greatness of those ancient times and their thinking, of those days when the human race had not yet, as it has today, departed from its harmony with creation and the transcendent creator. And the same idea, in which the political law of the ancients is grounded, dominates all other aspects of their thought and action. I see more and more that *one* law governs all things, and that primordial man planned and regulated his earthly life with the regularity, as it were, of animal instinct.

To explore this characteristic of the oldest thinking, particularly in matters of law and politics, is the aim of all my study and literary activity. What I am engaged upon now is true study of nature. The material alone is my preceptor. It must first be assembled, then observed and analyzed. Only in this way can one hope to disclose a law that is inherent in the matter itself and not in our subjective spirit. For how few scholars has the material been the supreme judge! My collection of excerpts has so increased in the course of my labors, so much material has accumulated, that, in order not to be overwhelmed by it, I must now think in all seriousness of setting chisel to the stone and advance in my work to the point where the image that still lies dormant within me will at length emerge, in crude form perhaps, but recognizable. In the course of these studies I have encountered so many books that brilliantly elucidate everything and yet fail to disclose any under-

†† Philipp Eduard Huschke (1801–86), professor of Roman law at Breslau, intermixed his legal studies with the mystical ideas of Schelling.

standing for the merest fragment of the ancient material that I doff my hat with true respect to anyone who can do so even in regard to the most trifling point. To perform my task quickly is not possible, nor is it my desire. I should like to give many years to the enjoyment of this occupation and for a long while experience the satisfaction of studying more for myself than for the public. But insofar as I, like every scholar, am concerned with my name, I hope to acquire glory rather than celebrity. At my present age it becomes necessary, of course, to keep my object well in view, and to limit my intellectual activity more than I should like to—all the more so as my judicial tasks and the legal studies connected with them demand a considerable share of my time.

A distraction of still another kind remains to be mentioned before I conclude this communication. Sometimes I am kept from home for months at a time by my travels. Since my first visit to England I have spent two periods of study at the British Museum, partly to consult literature that is elsewhere inaccessible, and partly for the sake of the Lycian and Assyrian sculpture. But still more important was a journey to Greece undertaken in the spring of 1851, which included all parts of the present kingdom and went off most successfully. Just as I had set out to cover the entire scope of ancient literature by continued reading, I planned in this journey to gain a personal knowledge of the most important scenes of classical antiquity and through this direct contact enhance my understanding of the literature. Now I have gained a living and colorful background for my study of the Greek authors. Whatever I read, a rich setting is present in my mind.

I have come to the end of my confessions. There is no doubt that I have spoken too much of myself and too little of my subject matter. I expect this criticism and find it justified. And I must also own that this communication has been too detailed and long-winded. But I beg your Excellency to pardon this latter fault as proof of a trusting devotion encouraged by your affable reception at Ragaz.*

Written between September 24th and 27th, 1854.
* The Swiss resort of Bad Ragaz.

From An Essay on

Ancient Mortuary Symbolism

1859

Foreword

THE VILLA PAMPHILI, so celebrated because of its magnificent situation near the Porta San Pancrazio on the ancient Via Aurelia near Rome, has at various times attracted the attention of students of antiquity by the columbaria * discovered in its grounds. These discoveries had almost been forgotten when a new one was made in the year 1838. The columbarium unearthed in that year was distinguished by the great number and unusual diversity of its mural paintings. Yet it attracted little notice. A brief description by the late Emil Braun [1] called it to my attention, and I visited the tomb late in 1842. It made a profound impression on me, particularly in view of the fact that I had never seen an edifice of the kind, except for the two columbaria Campana [2] discovered a few years before. The villa's proximity to the Vatican, in whose library I then spent a good many mornings, gave me an opportunity to visit the place repeatedly. The beauty of the gardens, the magnificent view, the ancient works of art which banish, for some moments at least, the centuries that separate us from antiquity, and in addition the novelty and freshness of a young man's first visit to Rome—all these combined to arouse an interest that has been with me ever since. It is to these visits that I owe my first impulse to study the world of the ancient tombs—a preoccupation which since then has brought me twice to Italy and has found new nourishment in Greece. In my constant reading of the ancient authors I have paid close attention to everything they say about tombs and tomb

* Columbarium (pl., columbaria), a tomb with niches to hold urns of ashes.

cults. Thus over a period of years I accumulated an abundance of material which seemed to call more and more urgently for scientific treatment. A series of lectures on the subject which I delivered at the Basel Antiquarian Society † met with considerable approval. Thus encouraged, I returned to the columbarium at the Villa Pamphili, the starting point for so enjoyable a study. I was continuously reminded of it by a number of tracings I had made of the wall itself. Two of the numerous murals interested me particularly. The one fascinated me by its new variant of the motif of Ocnus the rope plaiter, which occurs also in Campana's columbarium, and the other by its emphasis on three black and white eggs lying on a tripod.

The three mystery eggs and the rope plaiter provide the foundation and starting point for two essays on ancient tomb symbolism in which I attempt to disclose a meaning far beyond the sphere of art and archaeology. I discuss the more obscure aspects of this little-explored field in detail, and strive to relate the particular motifs to general ancient conceptions. The passing centuries and all the innovations they bring have little power over tombs and tomb cults. Their symbolism, rooted in the oldest intuitions of our race, passed unchanged, though ultimately no longer understood, into the era of waning paganism, and even into the new era opened by the Incarnation of Christ. It forms a bond between early and late generations, annulling distinctions in time, space, and nationality. The symbol of the egg provides a remarkable example for the transcending of time, while the motif of Ocnus the rope plaiter passes beyond national barriers and is encountered in Egypt, Asia, Greece, and Italy.

It is this character of permanence that makes the ancient tombs so very meaningful. And this wealth of meaning is further enhanced by the insight the tombs give us into the most beautiful aspect of the ancient spirit. Other spheres of archaeology may captivate our understanding, the contemplation of the tombs wins our hearts; it not only enriches our knowledge but provides food for our spiritual needs. Wherever possible I have taken this aspect into account and attempted to intimate those sublime ideas which the ancients conceived in the presence of death and which cannot

† On February 10, 24, and March 10, 1853.

be expressed in language but only in symbols. Herein I have primarily acceded to a need inherent in my own nature, but perhaps I have also come closer to realizing the supreme aim of archaeology than is possible through an approach limited to the form and surface of things. And this aim, I believe, consists in communicating the sublimely beautiful ideas of the past to an age that is very much in need of regeneration.

The Three Mystery Eggs

THE TOMB painting reproduced in plate I is perfectly definite and clear in all its details. A group of five young men are seated around a small three-legged table with three eggs on it. The figures present an almost complete uniformity, which, however, is saved from monotony by the variety in the arrangement of their dress, in their gestures and attitudes, and by the skillful composition of the whole. The bareheaded ephebes are sitting on benches; their attention is fixed on the table in the middle of the circle, and they seem to be earnestly discussing the eggs. The two in the right and left foreground seem to take the lead in the conversation, while those in the background appear to be relegated more to the role of listeners. The figure on the right side seems to be the most inactive: he is situated somewhat outside the group, and his inclusion would seem to have been imposed on the artist by the dictates of the number five. One of the youths is crowned with a myrtle wreath, another holds a burning oil lamp in the palm of his outstretched left hand. These two attributes would disclose the religious content of the work even if the absence of shoes and headdress did not make it sufficiently clear. The sacral significance of the lamp is made obvious by the daylight, which discloses the outlines of a temple and a house in the distance.

In our description of this picture we have thus far neglected a circumstance that will serve as the starting point of our whole discussion. The three eggs on the table present a feature which is

I. The Three Mystery Eggs

Tomb painting from a columbarium in the Villa Pamphili, Rome

brought out in our plate exactly as in the Munich copy.** They are not solid in color, but divided lengthwise, white above and dark below. And the division is equally sharp in all three. If this were an isolated phenomenon it would still be significant and call for explanation. But earlier tombs show the same feature, so that the hypothesis of optical illusion or of mere artistic fancy must be excluded.††

Its meaning is not open to doubt. The alternation of light and dark color expresses the continuous passage from darkness to light, from death to life. It shows us tellurian creation as the result of eternal becoming and eternal passing away, as a never-ending movement between two opposite poles. This idea deserves our fullest attention because of its inner truth, but we must also admire the simple expression of the symbol. The mere opposition of light and dark color concretizes a profound thought which the greatest of ancient philosophers seemed unable to express fully in words. Are we not justified in supposing that the earnest and animated conversation of the ephebes was concerned with this aspect of the symbolic eggs? Certainly no subject is so appropriate to the solemnity of the tomb. And assuredly the presence of death raises no more urgent question than that of the relation between the two poles between which all tellurian existence moves. And no symbol can be better calculated to raise the spirit above the limitations of corporeal existence to an intimation of one's own rebirth than the egg; it encompasses life and death, binding them into an inseparable unity and bringing forth anew everything that has sunk into invisibility. The sublime dignity and richness of the symbol reside precisely in the fact that it not only allows of but even encourages different levels of interpretation, and leads us from the truths of physical life to those of a higher spiritual order.

In religion the egg is a symbol of the material source of all things, of the ἀρχὴ γενέσεως (beginning of creation). The material source of things, which brings forth all life from out of itself,

** The Antiquarium in Munich exhibited a copy of the mural made by Carlo Ruspi, on which Bachofen's reproduction was based.
†† Here follow several pages of documentation from ancient art and literature, relating to the antithetical meanings of black and white. It should be pointed out, however, that in the present instance the black bottoms of the eggs probably are shaded for the sake of perspective.

comprises both becoming and passing away. It encompasses both the bright and the dark side of nature. The Orphic primordial egg is half white and half black or red—and it may be remembered that Typhon,[1] the destructive power, is represented as red. And these colors flow into one another as unremittingly as life and death, day and night, becoming and passing away. They do not exist merely in proximity but also within one another. Death is the precondition of life, and only in the same measure as destruction proceeds can the creative power be effective. In every moment becoming and passing away operate side by side. The life of every earthly organism is the product of a twofold force, creative and destructive. Only insofar as the former takes away can the latter restore. No other idea holds so large a place in the symbolism and mythology of the ancients. We recognize it in the rope of Ocnus * which the she-ass keeps devouring, or in the weaving of Penelope and the daughter of Tarchetius,† unraveled each night; [2] in the supremely guileful thieves of the Egyptian legend of Rhampsinitus,[3] and in the dice game with Demeter, in which the king alternately wins and loses: ** all images of the eternally vain labors of nature, which through eternal destruction brings about the eternal rejuvenation of the race. We find it in the ring of Gyges: alternately turned inward and outward, it strikingly symbolizes the unity of the two contrary potencies of nature.[4] The same idea recurs in the alternating life of the antithetical Dioscuri,[5] who issued from the same egg and embody the significance of the alternating colors. And similarly the Elean brothers, the Moliones, born from a single egg, drive their chariot together, inseparable as

---

* See pp. 51ff.

† The daughter of Tarchetius refused to cohabit with a phallus that had emerged from the hearth. Thrown into prison, she was advised by Hestia to weave a garment; upon its completion she would find a husband. But Tarchetius ordered his servants to undo every night the portion woven during the day.

** Rhampsinitus (Ramesses III of Egypt) had a treasury built to house his vast wealth. But the mason he employed so constructed it that one of the stones of the wall could be removed and replaced without trace. At his death the mason passed the secret on to his sons, who from time to time removed the stone and, employing various ruses, stole part of the treasure. Rhampsinitus is also said to have descended alive into Hades and played dice with Demeter, who presented him with a golden napkin to take back to earth.

life and death, flying headlong through the cosmos, like eternal becoming and eternal passing away.

Now these sons of Actor were twins; one held the reins at his leisure, Held the reins at his leisure, while the other lashed on the horses.[6]

Pictorially this idea is expressed by two horses of different colors, one light and one dark, racing side by side. Romulus and Remus also represent the bright and dark side of nature. And Hermes' hat, half black and half white, corresponds to his twofold nature, by virtue of which he dwells alternately in the luminous heights and in the empty chambers of the underworld. Like Castor and Pollux, the sons of Oedipus rule by turns. The flame on the altar separates into two pillars, eternally blowing in opposite directions. Silenus, captured in the rose garden, tells Midas the secret of the well of grief and the well of joy.[7] "The ever flowing stream of birth will never stand still, nor will the contrary stream of destruction, Acheron or Cocytus, or whatever the poets may call it," writes Plutarch to Apollonius,[8] and in numerous passages the ancients stress the same idea as the fundamental law of tellurian creation. "Everywhere in the mysteries and sacrifices, among the Greeks as well as the barbarians," writes Plutarch in *Isis and Osiris*,[9] "there are two fundamental beings and opposing powers, one of which leads with the right hand and straight ahead, while the other turns about and leads backward." The two are equally essential for the progress of creation. That is why Isis sets the imprisoned Typhon free. She knows that the eternal mixture of the two potencies is indispensable. Typhon may be defeated but not destroyed. Eternally the struggle continues, and as often as Typhon is captured, he breaks loose again and battles with Horus. "But Horus is the world surrounding the earth, the world in which genesis and destruction alternate." [10]

This accounts for the frequency of pairs of brothers, sometimes represented as forever struggling with one another, sometimes as friendly, and usually as twins. For they are at once hostile and friendly, two opposites joined into a unity. They battle with one another eternally, like life and death, coming into being and passing away, and so preserve the everlasting youth and freshness of creation. The twinship of the two forces is particularly characteristic. Sleep and death are twins in the same sense; they are similar, but sleep represents a reawakening of life. "Sleep, says the poet, is the lesser mysteries of death." [11] And the twins death and sleep on such mortuary steles as that of the Villa Albani †† express the same meaning as the Theban brothers murdering each other, so often represented on Etruscan cinerary urns. They are the two powers that dominate creation; they devour one another, but continuously lead life back from darkness to the light.

The alternation of the two colors is represented in countless ancient images as the fundamental law of tellurian life. In his beautiful letter to Apollonius consoling him for the death of his son, Plutarch quotes the following lines from ancient poets:

> The turning of the wheel brings up first one spoke
> And then alternately the other.[12]

And:

> The race of mortals moves like the realm of plants
> Forever in a circle. One flowers into life,
> While the other dies and is mown down.[13]

And what makes these formulations all the more meaningful is that the images of the wheel and of the circle forever returning to its starting point are not based on arbitrary poetic invention, but are taken from the oldest symbolism, that of the tombs.

This conception, underlying so many symbols and myths, belongs to the very foundations of all ancient religion; it tells us not so much about the nature of the gods as about the physical conditions of creation.[14] And it should not surprise us to find it playing so prominent a role in the Bacchic mysteries if we bear in mind that this cult is based entirely on matter and on the feminine-material principle of nature in its aspect of fecundation. The two-colored egg at the center of the Dionysian religion shows us the supreme law governing the transient world as a *fatum* inherent in feminine matter. Often the form of the egg is likened to that of the cosmos. Heaven and earth are the product of the two halves of the egg. In

†† In reality, two reliefs. See Helbig. *Führer* [3], No. 1840.

this unfolding the black half becomes the earth, the white half becomes heaven; the black half is the female-material principle, and the white half is the male-incorporeal potency. But once separated, these parts which were formerly one never cease yearning to be reunited. "So ancient is the desire of one another which is implanted in us, reuniting our original nature, making one of two, and healing the state of man." [15] This longing of the two halves of the egg for reunion gives rise to the genesis of all things, to the eternal stream of becoming and to the equally powerful contrary stream of passing away.

Thus the egg is in every respect the ἀρχὴ γενέσεως. It comprises all parts of the material world: heaven and earth, light and darkness, the male and the female potency of nature, the stream of becoming and that of passing away, the germ of all tellurian organisms, of the higher and lower creation, and the whole world of the gods who, of material origin like the entire tellurian world, have one and the same mother as men, animals, and plants—namely, the dark egg. In the Orphic-Bacchic mystery egg the initiate sees not only his own genesis but also that of his god, and from this insight he derives the hope that he will share in the lot of the god born of the same egg, the certainty that tellurian birth can rise to the immortality of the higher luminous world.

In our mural the initiate is crowned with a wreath. To be sure, it is not a wreath of ivy or laurel such as would seem to be required by the Bacchic rites and the close ties between Dionysus and Apollo. Various sources name the myrtle wreath as the mark of initiation.[16] But there is a still profounder connection, for the myrtle, like the egg, is associated with the feminine conception of the great nature principle. The myrtle is consecrated to Aphrodite-Venus, the primal mother of all tellurian creation.

Thus the two conspicuous objects in the Pamphilian grave painting, the eggs and the myrtle wreath, carry the initiation back to the primal material-maternal principle, which also gave rise to Dionysus Dimetor (the two-mothered). The phallic god striving toward the fertilization of matter is not the original datum: rather, he himself springs from the darkness of the maternal womb. He stands as a son to feminine matter; bursting the shell of the egg, he discloses the mystery of phallic masculinity that had hitherto been hidden within it, and the mother herself rejoices in him as in her own demon. The phallic god cannot be thought of separately from feminine materiality. Matter, the mother who bore him to the light, now becomes his wife. Bacchus is both the son and husband of Aphrodite. Mother, wife, sister merge into one. Matter takes all these attributes by turns.

Sexual union is always the fundamental Dionysian law; *gamos* (marriage) is its realization. Conceived sensuously on the tellurian level, it achieves on the uranian level the higher purity of exclusive marriage. In this sublimation the egg becomes the symbol of matrimonial consecration and of the *telos* (higher aim) which every *gamos* bears within itself. This explains why we have five ephebes in our mural. I have already pointed out * that the number cannot be based on artistic fancy, that from a purely artistic standpoint the figure on the extreme right would have been omitted. Its presence shows that we are dealing with a sacred number. For the ancients the number five represented marriage. It results from the male *trias* and the female *dyas*, and so signifies the conjugal union of the two sexes. Hence it is neither puzzling nor meaningless that there should be five youths in all. Their fiveness points to the female egg in its higher meaning as a symbol of the sexual union consecrated by marriage, in contrast to the three other representations in the same tomb, which emphasize the lower, Aphroditean, lawless fecundation condemned by the mysteries.

* See p. 24.

The Eggs at the Circus

SO FAR we have omitted to mention an entire class of monuments † in which the egg plays a significant role. I am referring to the representations of circus games in a number of sarcophagus reliefs. Here ovoid bodies—seven, five, or ten in number—are seen on a high platform, supported sometimes by four and sometimes by two columns. Another similar structure bears an equal number of dolphins. There can be no doubt as to the nature of these objects, because eggs as well as dolphins are stressed in literary records as attributes of the circus. In his *Roman History*, Cassius Dio mentions the eggs and the dolphins together: "When he (Agrippa) saw that the people in the circus could not tell the number of laps, he had the dolphins and ovoid forms set up, in order that they might indicate the number of laps." [1] Agrippa would seem to have made some new and practical innovation in regard to the arrangement of the dolphins and eggs in the circus, for the use of eggs in the circus games did not originate with him. In his *Roman History* Livy tells us that the practice existed as early as the year 578 of the founding of the city (175 B.C.). "The censors Quintus Fulvius Flaccus and Aulus Postumius Albinus let out contracts for the stalls in the circus and eggs to indicate the number of laps." [2] Even here he does not speak of a new custom. The censors merely provide for the construction of various parts of

† Bachofen finds the same or a related symbolism in a number of other ancient monuments, the discussion of which may be omitted from this section without detriment to the author's general picture.

31

the circus, including the eggs. The "ovoid structures" seem to have been built of wood or baked earth and to have been of considerable size. Varro's mention of them deserves special attention. In a conversation which he reports to have had in the temple of Tellus at the festival of the seed goddess, with C. Fundanius and other friends, he quotes C. Licinius Stolo as saying: "Not only has *the* egg which marked the last lap for the quadrigae in the circus games been removed; but neither did we see the one that is customarily carried in advance of the procession of Ceres." ** [3] These words show clearly that at each revolution of the chariots one of the eggs was removed from the frame, so that the last egg vanished at the end of the seventh circuit. Finally, the following passage from Juvenal's *Satires* assuredly relates to the eggs: "Plebeian destinies are determined in the Circus or on the ramparts: the woman who displays a long gold chain on her bare neck inquires before the pillars and the columns of dolphins whether she shall throw over the tavern-keeper and marry the old-clothes-man.[4]

For the poor plebeians eggs and dolphins are the *fatum* which they question concerning marriage, whereas rich women pay a foreign juggler large sums for a favorable oracle. In view of what has been said above, we no longer need ask why eggs and dolphins, the animals of the generative Neptune, should have been used for such prophecy. As ἀρχὴ γενέσεως the egg stands in the most intimate relation to marriage and generation. The egg of the circus is also regarded as the "beginning of creation," and that is why it can be mentioned in the same breath with the egg of the procession (*pompa*) of Ceres. In the circus, too, it represents the feminine principle of nature; it is older than the bird which bursts forth from it, winged and swift as the quadriga which bursts forth from the *carceres* (enclosure) with an irrepressible lust for life. The racing quadriga becomes an image of birth from the egg. As the bird shatters the shell of its egg and, freed from its confinement,

** Bachofen's reading *in cereali pompa* (in the procession of Ceres) in this passage from Varro is abandoned by modern editors in favor of *in cenali pompa* (in the procession at dinner), thus making Varro's remark irrelevant in the present context.

tries the strength of its wings, so the chariot storms forth from the restraining *carceres* in impatient winged flight. And here lies the connection between the eggs and the race.

From the records thus far considered, we may conclude that the eggs stand in an intimate relation to the circus games. True, they also served an outward purpose, namely to keep both racers and onlookers posted as to the number of laps completed. Natural eggs would have been too small for this; it was necessary to replace them with artificial ovoid bodies of considerable size. But this practical consideration hardly exhausts the relation of the egg to the circus and its games. The same purpose might have been served equally well by any other object. If eggs were chosen from time immemorial, the reason is to be sought in their religious significance. At every circuit one egg is removed. Even in a late period this inner relation of the egg to the chariot race was not wholly obscured. In certain superstitious practices of the people, particularly of the plebeian classes, the old consciousness survived, and as far as we can see from the writings of Cassiodorus, Juvenal, and Varro, it was always the idea of the maternal Ceres principle of creation, of marriage and birth, the feminine ἀρχή γενέσεως, which, sometimes clearly and sometimes obscurely, found its expression in such popular views.

We shall now attempt to elucidate the original idea underlying the connection between eggs and circus games. Here I should like to remind the reader of what has been said of the Dioscuri and the Elean Moliones.†† Both pairs of brothers sprang from the maternal egg. Both are distinguished by the unparalleled swiftness with which they fly along on their horse-drawn chariots. They spring from the primal maternal egg as mighty racers and chariot drivers. The creation that lay dormant in this germ of all things now issues visibly from the opened shell, and in this creation everything is restless, eternal motion. The life of tellurian generation suffers no halt. In it everything comes into being and vanishes. Material life moves between two poles. Its realm is not that of being but that of becoming and passing away, the eternal alternation of two colors, the white of life and the black of death. Only through the equal mixture of the two is the survival of the material world assured.

†† See pp. 26f.

from An Essay on Mortuary Symbolism

Without death no rejuvenation is possible, and in the eternal labor of nature the destructive power is no less indispensable for the preservation of eternally youthful life than is the creative, generative power. Indeed, the positive power cannot for one moment exist without the negative power. Death, then, is not the opposite but the helper of life, just as the negative pole of magnetism is not the adversary of the positive pole but its necessary complement, without which the positive pole would vanish immediately, and life give way to nothingness.

Thus two powers govern tellurian creation and, working together, assure the survival of all things. They were born together, twin brothers issuing from the same egg. They move side by side. They drive the same team, and their double striving toward the same goal accounts for their unequaled swiftness. It is to this joint exertion that the sons of Actor, the Moliones, owe the victory of their chariot. Swift as an arrow it flies along. And swift as an arrow is the flight of the tellurian world of appearance. The swiftness of the two forces which combine to move the created world is expressed by the chariot of the Moliones. The chariot returns forever to its starting point, like the circular line whose end is lost in its beginning. One of the powers drives straight ahead while the other steers around and leads back. The completion of every existence is a coming back to the beginning, and every departure contains a return. The two movements are connected with each other as inexplicably as the two forces to which they correspond. The product of their combined power is the cycle in which all tellurian life eternally moves. And this cycle is imaged in the circuits of the chariots which fly swiftly around the *metae,* only to start their circuit anew.

This clarifies two things: first, the connection between the egg and the chariot race in the circus; second, the analogy between the completion of the circuits and the removal of the egg. The ἀρχὴ γενέσεως is contained in the egg, and the chariot discloses the movement of the creation that comes forth from the womb of matter. With every return to the starting point the cycle of one existence is completed and another is about to begin. One offspring of the egg has come into being, grown, and vanished; a new one takes its place. Endlessly the generations follow one another, one

34

chick succeeds the last, and always with the lightning swiftness reflected in the myth of the Moliones, the twin charioteers. The team bursting forth from the enclosure is rightly represented as born of an egg. Winged, as the chick from the egg, the chariot bursts from the *carceres* which had hitherto prevented its movement. What was hidden becomes visible, what was motionless becomes restless haste. The first moment of existence brings with it the unrest that forms so striking a contrast to the stillness and immobility that prevailed in the egg.

Thus the eggs in the circus are not without meaning. No less than the egg carried in the procession of Ceres, they express the idea of generation from the original mother matter, the birth of a chick which no sooner comes to light than it succumbs to the law of matter. In the headlong flight of the chariots and in the corresponding disappearance of the eggs the onlookers recognize the drama of all tellurian life, the law governing their own existence, and in bestowing the palm of victory on the swiftest charioteer, they express their belief that the supreme glory of a nation and of each individual resides not in the longest possible life span but in the greatest possible unfolding—and hence consumption—of energy.

The same set of ideas governs the whole circus and all the gods, cults, and institutions connected with it. The power of nature, in its threefold tellurian, lunar, and solar gradation, its twofold feminine-passive, male-active potency, in its manifestation as a life-giving and destructive force, found so rich and varied a representation in the Roman circus that the Church Fathers looked upon the circus as a veritable pantheon, unclean, inhabited by pagan demons, a place strictly to be avoided by the faithful.[5] In Murcia, Cybele, the maternal triad Seia-Segetia-Tutilina, in Pollentia, Libera, and Ceres, the feminine principle of nature was given an expression comprehending the Aphroditean as well as the Demetrian aspect of material life; the male-generative, life-awakening, and fructifying principle is discernible in its tellurian-aquatic aspect as Consus-Neptune, while its celestial-luminous aspect is disclosed in the obelisks[6] and various other particulars. The connection between the tellurian and the solar level of the natural power deserves special attention. The male-generative power rests on more than one factor. It is physically grounded in the celestial light no less than in the moisture of the depths. And tellurian fertility results from their combined action on the feminine matter of the earth. But at the different stages of religious development the emphasis rests on one or the other, on the chthonian or the uranian principle, on the water or the light, on the Neptunian or the solar element. A more material and hence lower view will look upon the water as the seat and carrier of the generative power, while a more immaterial and hence purer view will find it in the imponderable sunlight.

In the shrines and cults of the Roman circus the Neptunian and solar stage of the power appear together. Some of the ancients [7] declare Neptune to be its master; others,[8] with equal conviction, call Sol, the sun, its overlord and regard the circus as an eminently solar institution. Neither of these two conceptions should be minimized. The tellurian-Neptunian element asserted itself to the end despite the steady growth of the solar element. Beside the primordial female egg stands a chthonian male god who works in the moist depths of matter. He represents the awakening principle and is hidden in the darkness of the earth, a true Zeus Arcanus (hidden Zeus), comparable to the Puer Jupiter Anxurus [9] (youthful Jupiter, tutelary deity of Anxur *), a god of hidden counsels, a demon of the phallic power from which Murcia awaits fecundation. Subterranean is his altar, Neptunian his nature; his physical foundation is the moisture that permeates the depths; the animal sacred to him is the horse, image of the generative waters; the games consecrated to him are real horse races, *hippocrateia* or Equiria. Murcia, an Aphroditean primordial mother, had her shrine in the damp valley between the Aventine and the Palatine. In the rich meadowland lay the divine stone, the *metae Murciae* (goal posts of Murcia), and the nearby Aventine itself bore the name of Murcus. Beside the mother stood Consus, a chthonian demon, just as Eros stood beside Aphrodite, who in Virgil addresses him as *mea magna potentia* (my great power).[10] He is the darling and fructifier, without whom Murcia can do nothing; he dwells by her in the depths, rests in her bosom, "by the goal posts under the earth she keeps him hidden." [11] Tarquin selected this

* Anxur is the Volscian for Terracina.

place in which to build his circus, and it seems certain that the indigenous cult of Murcia and of Consus, her *paredros*, or companion, was the chief reason for his choice.

There can be no doubt as to the religious phase to which this cult and the related circus games belonged. It is the tellurian-Neptunian phase, in which energy itself is conceived as chthonian-aquatic. In keeping with this conception of energy, the horse races and chariot races celebrated in its honor were held in rich, moist meadowlands on the shores of brooks and rivers. The proximity of the element regarded as the seat of energy, as the carrier of the earth's generative *lar* (godhead), meant the presence of the godhead itself. The horses raced headlong beside the bank, as Pindar describes in the first Olympian ode on the Elean games,[12] and in the spinning of the wheels and the swift strides of the foaming steeds one could behold an image of the water, the only element in static nature which possesses the distinction of mobility. The connection of the circus games with water, with rivers, swamps, damp grassy flats, is everywhere evident, particularly in Rome. The Equiria were celebrated in honor of the god of all earthly fertility, the Roman Mars Gradivus (striding Mars), whose footfalls conferred fruitfulness on the soil. The swampy, grassy plain which the Tiber fructifies with its yellowish waters, and frequently overflows, was eminently the possession of the god. Here the games were held in his honor. Running within sight of the river, the horses became images of the water, symbols of the god. The river bordered the race track, while swords, representations of the god, were implanted in the ground as *metae*. Mars himself looked on at the games. Horse, chariot, and wheel stood in a Neptunian relation to water. The victorious right-hand horse was sacrificed to the god. The bleeding trunk was fastened to the wall of the regia † and adorned with rings of bread, symbols of abundant harvest, which in turn were marked with the sign of the wheel.

In view of all this the Neptunian significance of the Roman circus and the games celebrated in it is not an isolated phenomenon, but rather an expression of the universal idea which situates the generative power in the tellurian waters. The watery element is

† Numa's royal hall in the Forum, later used for religious purposes.

indicated by the dolphins, whose connection with the eggs now becomes self-evident. "They dedicate the dolphins to Neptune," says Tertullian.[13] In the circus the god of the generative waters is not anthropomorphic, but takes the form of a fish, and in general the cult usages and representations of the circus have remained faithful to an earlier, archaic, more fundamental religious phase. Cassiodorus connects the Euripus with the dolphins. "The Euripus is a pictorial representation of a gleaming canal, from which the dolphins swim into the sea." [14] Here Euripus is not meant as a real canal, but rather as the *intermetium* (space), the *spina* (spinal cord), that stretched between the two *metae* in the center of the circus, dividing it lengthwise into two halves. We must think of it as an *agger* (dam), supported by two lateral walls. It supported the many sacred objects required by the games; the divine images, particularly of Cybele, presiding deity of the Euripus, and the three altars. If this earthen wall was interpreted as an image of the sea and related to the dolphins, those swift denizens of the deep characterized by their devotion to man, it is because of the original maritime nature of the circus. By extension of the same idea, the Euripus of the circus was compared with the Euripus which divides Euboea from the mainland of Boeotia. The sevenfold change of the tides which drives the water up and down the straits seemed to correspond to the sevenfold circuit of the chariots, the seven eggs, and seven dolphins, and to express the idea of the eternally rising and forever receding waves of existence.

As represented on sarcophagi, the circus games have no other meaning than the one they had in reality. The games were dedicated to material energy, at first conceived as wholly tellurian, the generative process which embraces all the factors contributing to the creation of the earth—life and death, matter and force—and which constitutes the idea of the godhead itself. Seen in this light, the games have a predominantly mortuary character, and in this they resemble the great national games of the Greeks, whose association with dead heroes lends them the aspect of funeral rites. We are reminded of the mythical games of the dead, particularly those represented on Etruscan cinerary urns. All games have a mortuary character. The *meta* is always a tombstone, and as such, the monument of a tellurian demon, a λίθος ἔμψυχος, animated stone, a ταράξιππος, frightener of horse, or a *meta sudans*, sweating stone, proclaiming its relation to the generative moisture of the depths. It is to this religious significance that the games owe their place in the world of the tomb, whether in murals (as at Corneto) or in sarcophagus reliefs. The funeral rite glorifies nature as a whole, with its twofold life- and death-giving principle. Death is represented as bound up with life, and even as its foundation. That is why the symbols of life are so frequent in the tombs; that is why in Campana's columbarium the phallic Priapus is called the "place of both life and death" (*mortis et vitae locus*). The circus games are a representation of life and death, and of the eternal cycle of tellurian creation called forth by their interaction. This is the basic idea underlying our sarcophagus figures, to which they owe their presence in the tombs. And from this idea arises a higher conception, that of deification, apotheosis. The games at Mincio beach were designed to proclaim that Augustus had been received among the immortals. The supreme idea of the circus relief was, then, that the deceased had passed into the company of the gods and donned the garment of immortality.

Sanctum and *Sacrum*

THE RELATION between egg and serpent is always the same: there the woman, here the man; there the material substrate, here developed life; there material abundance, here energy and domination; there immobility and conservation, here acquisition, increase, offensive and defensive struggle; there Fortuna by the hearth, here the serpent genius, devoted wholly to the life which it engenders, preserves, and dominates. Herein is grounded the duality of the kingdom as manifested at Rome in Romulus and Remus, in the consulate and duumvirate and in various magistracies—and in Sparta as well. If the feminine principle of nature were the prototype of government, it could rest only on one head. For primordial matter can only be one and undivided, but the life that issues from it is twofold, preserved and eternally rejuvenated by a twofold masculine power—which is at once becoming and passing away.

The opposition between egg and snake, between the primordial feminine-matter and the masculine kinetic principle, is expressed in two terms which play a prominent part in the religious law of the ancients: these are the terms *sanctum* (the untouchable) and *sacrum* (the consecrated). The *sanctum* has its root in an attribute of tellurian matter, while the *sacrum* derives from the luminous realm. The *sanctum* stands under the protection of the chthonian powers, the *sacrum* is dedicated to the higher gods: ** and the same

** "In a more general sense everything that has been dedicated to the gods as their property is called *sacrum*; the nature of the particular godhead is of no account. On the other hand, the idea of property is completely

40

distinction is expressed in the Greek terms ἱερόν and ὅσιον.[1] Among the *res sanctae* (divine things) a special significance must be accorded to walls. And ancient notions in regard to walls throw much light on the concept of *sanctitas*. In the *Laws* Plato writes that the legislator who forbade the construction of walls around the city of Sparta did well to "let them sleep in the earth."[2] Longinus finds this metaphor in bad taste and remarks that walls neither sleep nor wake.[3] But the Latin term *excitare muros*, to awaken walls, rests on the same fundamental intuition and shows that Plato's expression, even if borrowed from a poet, was close to a traditional conception. Evidently the traditional mind saw the walls rising from the depths of the earth as an offspring issuing from the maternal womb, a child which slept in the dark depths until the action of a male principle awakened it from slumber and raised it into the light. For the sexual act of the male is also called ἐγείρειν, to awaken, and corresponds exactly to *excitare*. Thus walls, like trees, are children of mother earth, and even after birth are everlastingly connected with the maternal womb by their foundations, as are the trees by their roots. In the wall as in the tree the male principle rises up to the light of day. The phallus, which unseen in the earth had fecundated matter, is now visibly represented in the manifest product. That is why the tree, as in the Bible, becomes the tree of life, and why according to Philostratus, the Lydians, starting from the same idea, believed the trees to be older than the earth which bears them.[4] For this reason the wall became the masculine *murus*, which the ancients often adorned with an image of the phallus, not only, as was later believed, in order to protect it by the *fascinus* (spell) of the phallus against enemy attack, but because the phallus lay at the very origin of the wall. We need only recall that the phallic Poseidon Genesios, in conjunction with Apollo, laid the foundations of Troy's walls deep in the earth.[5]

This intuition is to be found in still another ancient custom. The walls of conquered cities were destroyed to the sound of brazen trumpets. What is told of Jericho recurs among the

---

foreign to the *sanctum*. *Sanctitas* rests on the connection of an object with the maternal womb of earth. The quality of sacredness is constituted by legal action on man's part, that of sanctity is inherent in the object."
[From Bachofen's note.]

Romans. For the walls of Alba were torn down amid the blaring of trumpets and Mummius observed the same sacral rite when he demolished the walls of Corinth. Now this manner of destroying walls shows what conceptions must have governed the building of them. Numerous formulations of ancient law embody the notion that things must end as they began, and the principle is even stated in general terms.[6] A guilty man's chains are removed after he has undergone his punishment, those of a man whose innocence has been established are cut through with a file.[7] What has been fastened by violence must be loosed by counter violence. What the trumpet destroys was also built by the trumpet. The sense in which this is to be taken is shown by the myth about the walls of Thebes which, awakened by the tones of Amphion's lyre, build themselves of their own accord. But the brazen trumpet is closely related to phallic generation. It summons the bull of Dionysus from the generative waves of the sea, it brings forth Achilles from his hiding place among the women of Scyros, where his manhood lay hidden and unknown until the day when, like a son emerging from the womb, it rose up to the light. The Platonic and Roman terms take on their full meaning only when we conceive of the *excitatio*, the awakening, as induced by the sound of trumpets. The sleeper is awakened, the trumpet's mighty *taratantara* [8] raises the wall from its subterranean slumber.

Here again we have an act of male fecundation, to which the wall, like the tree, owes its origin. The wall is a creation of the tellurian phallus, which in it, as in a male child, attains to visible existence. It has its material foundation in the earth, which is why the mural crown (battlement) adorns the earth mother's head; but it owes its genesis to the masculine principle. It stands, therefore, in a hallowed relation to both these powers: as *sanctum* to the feminine-material principle, as *sacrum* to the male. It is solidly implanted in the womb of the earth, it is immovable; and this ἀκίνητον (immovable) is the basic meaning of *sanctum*. Rising above the earth, it is the phallic birth that has emerged into the light, and in this character is dedicated to the gods of light; in this relation it is *sacer*. *Sacrum* is everything that is dedicated to the gods above. It relates to the luminous nature of masculinity, just as *sanctum* relates to the earth. As *sancta res* (immovable thing) the wall is inseparable from the matter in which it is implanted; as *sacra res*, consecrated thing, it is confided to the protection of the higher luminous power, into whose realm it is born. In the *sanctum* resides the ἀκίνητον; thus it bears within it the guarantee of divine protection. The wall thereby has the character of the earth itself, immovable tranquillity and innate divinity, in which it is protected and defended by snakes, as well as by the phallus, from all hostile attack. On the gate of Mycenae stands the sun pillar held by the sun lions, symbols of supreme protection by the highest principle of divine power. The heavenly gods watch over the possession that man has made over to them. *Sanctitas* [earth-godliness] expresses only one attribute; though grounded in the religious intuitions of tellurism, it does not bear within it the concept of protection and defense. This lies in the *consecratio* [consecration, assignment to the light-godhead], and in the obligation to protect which thereby falls upon the godhead.

The Lamp in the Myth of
Amor and Psyche

IT IS more by her divine beauty than by any conscious decision that Psyche is drawn into the trammels of sensuality and the morass of matter. As Aphrodite's slave she must undergo a long list of penances and trials, and must even pass through the terrors of the underworld. Finally, overcome by Stygian sleep, a lifeless corpse, she is awakened by the touch of an arrow tip and given the chalice of immortality. In union with Eros she obtains all the blissful joys which she had vainly sought in the service of Aphrodite. Here two phases of feminine existence appear, comparable to the two series of women in so many vase paintings or to the two parts of Goethe's *Faust:* the feminine soul, first in the service of Aphrodite, a slave to matter, condemned at every step to new and unexpected sufferings, and finally led down into the deepest morass of sensuality—but then arising to a new and more powerful existence, passing from Aphroditean to Psychic life. The lower phase bears a tellurian, the higher a uranian character. From the chthonian earth Psyche is raised to the celestial earth (the moon). We recognize the Helen who, yielding to the natural law of Aphrodite, incurs sufferings and wanderings without end, until at last, on the glittering moon island, this most beautiful of women is united forever with the most glorious of heroes (Achilles) and finds the peace which not the tellurian Eros but only the heavenly Eros can confer. Below lie all unrest and suffering, all unexpected disappointments and inexplicable solutions; above, peace, eternal and secure enjoyment, the magic of the transfiguration which the

44

silent moonlight pours over the haunts of men so turbulent by day. Below, the impurity of tellurian matter, the serpent and the reed, which originate in the muck of the dark depths, witnesses and symbols of the unregulated marriage of water and earth; above, the butterfly, piercing the cocoon of matter to seek and find the light; below, the purely material Aphrodite; above, the uranian Aphrodite; below, the love of the hetaera; above, lawful marriage; below, soma (body); above, psyche; below, the lightless matter of earth; above, the purified celestial earth, the moon, the purest of the tellurian bodies. In Psyche Aphrodite herself achieves the lunar stage, the highest that woman's materiality can attain. Beside her stands Eros as Lunus.

Amor and Psyche are joined by the same bond as Lunus and Luna, Achilles and Helen. The kiss that unites them is the *basium* which the husband bestows on his wife, not the *suavium* which the lover gives the hetaera. The group of embracing and kissing figures (plate II) expresses the purity and chastity of love in its ultimate fulfillment with a perfection which no lyric poetry can achieve. And yet it would be wholly contrary to the conceptions of ancient art to call this a representation of purely spiritual love. It is not spiritual love, but earthly love exalted to the highest purity. The moon is the purest of earthly bodies and the impurest of heavenly bodies; and Psyche takes the same middle position between the two worlds. She combines the materiality of the one with the purity and tranquil clarity of the other; she compels the body to partake of the light, and the light to combine with the body; she remains equally removed from the immateriality of the one and the impurity of the other. Soma and nous are indissolubly combined in Psyche, so producing a creature who sublimates matter to its highest possible ennoblement. The idea of sexual love is not alien to this stage. But it has cast off its Aphroditean, hetaera-like character, and assumed that of a chaste conjugal union. Psyche's suffering and eventual redemption are only a consecration which raises the sexual life of the woman from the morass of impure matter, in which she meets destruction, to the luminous course which makes sexuality a starting point for a higher psychic existence. In this achievement of her ultimate vocation Psyche combines two concepts which seem to exclude one another and yet are intimately bound together in so many myths: supreme motherhood and perfect virginity. And herein again she is on a level with the moon. Eternally fecundated, it is eternally virginal, virgin as mother, mother as virgin. The concept of marriage and sexual union is necessarily bound up with the moon. By its nature the moon is a union of the two principles; it is hermaphroditic, Lunus and Luna, Eros and Psyche. It seeks the light, and the light never ceases to descend upon it. The fulfillment of this supreme yearning has found its expression in the σύμπλεγμα, embrace, in the kiss on the lips, in the eyes that meet. In this first kiss which seals the bond of marriage, the kiss "with which Cypria herself mixed a fifth part of her own nectar," [1] the cosmic law that governs the uranian bodies seems to be fulfilled among men, and the harmony of the higher and the lower world seems to be attained. The moon can do nothing by itself, but follows the sun and borrows its light to shine in silent splendor. And similarly it is only in conjugal union with man that woman can achieve the higher beauty which enables her materiality to captivate man's more spiritual nature.

We see now the relation of these mysteries of Eros to the Dionysian religion, and we know to what phase in this religion they correspond. Now the lamp, too, takes on a deeper meaning. By its light Psyche recognizes the divinely beautiful form of her nocturnal visitor, whom her sisters had described to her as a hideous dragon. The sword with which she intended to slay the monster falls from her hand. The flame flickers restlessly while Psyche gazes upon the forbidden sight: the beautiful face, the lovely golden curls, the bright-colored wings, faintly trembling at the tips. In her eagerness she scratches her thumb on an arrow tip. A drop of seething oil falls from her lamp to the god's right shoulder, as though driven by longing to join the lord of all fire. And Eros, awaking from deep sleep, punishes her disobedience by taking flight. Sinking exhausted to the ground, she sees the loved one snatched away just as she recognizes him in all his splendor. The episode forms a positive turning point in the trials to which Aphrodite had condemned her rival in beauty. Sexual enjoyment, shrouded in darkness, is replaced by a yearning to possess the god recognized in all his glory. To the physical wound is added the

II. Amor and Psyche

deeper suffering of psychic pain. For as Plutarch profoundly declared, wounding is the principle of love.[2] As the plowshare wounds the earth, as man's virility wounds woman and opens her womb, so, on the psychic plane, Eros' arrow wounds the maiden's heart, and her whole being is flooded by painful, ever-increasing yearning for union with the once-glimpsed heavenly bridegroom, now forever before her eyes.

The restlessly flickering flame, and the hot oil striving for union with Eros, typify Psyche herself; just as the moth whose wings she bears is drawn irresistibly to the flame, so Psyche seeks the light. Tellurian moisture is replaced by the higher phase of fire, darkness and chaos give way to light and order, and unregulated hetaerism to a yearning for conjugal union. The tellurian phase of pure materiality is followed by the lunar phase, in which matter itself attracts the luminous nature and so achieves a higher purification. This lunar-psychic stage of feminine being is symbolized in the burning lamp.

Symbol and Myth

MYTH IS the exegesis of the symbol. It unfolds in a series of out-wardly connected actions what the symbol embodies in a unity. It resembles a discursive philosophical treatise in so far as it splits the idea into a number of connected images and then leaves it to the reader to draw the ultimate inference. The combination of the symbol with the explanatory myth is a highly remarkable phenom-enon. In the Pamphilian grave painting the symbol in itself sufficed but not on the sarcophagus, †† where it seemed to require the support of the myth. In this combination the symbol finds the guarantee of its permanence. The myth restores the ancient dignity of the Orphic symbolism. To expound the mystery doctrine in words would be a sacrilege against the supreme law; it can only be represented in terms of myth. That is why mythology is the lan-guage of the tombs. As a rule the inscriptions are only statements of lesser importance; higher ideas inspired by death and tomb are expressed in the form of myth, aided by art. More and more the pure symbol is relegated to the background, while the myth becomes dominant. Gradually the entire mythology of the ancients enters into their tombs, so creating a drama that deserves our utmost attention. The treasury of myths, in which the ancients had set forth the earliest memories of their history, the entire sum of their physical knowledge, the recollection of earlier periods of creation and great tellurian transformations, is here employed to

†† The sarcophagus of Santa Chiara in Naples, which depicts the myth of Protesilaus and Laodamia; its discussion is omitted from this selection.

expound religious truths, to embody laws of nature, to express ethical and moral truths, and to awaken comforting intimations extending beyond the melancholy limits of the material *fatum*. Cloaked in mythical images, the content of the mysteries with their twofold physical and metaphysical significance is brought home to the beholder. Whereas heaven has descended to earth through the anthropomorphic vision of the divine, earth once more becomes heaven now that the myths have entered into the mystery and the human is traced back to the divine; in the lives of heroes valor and virtue are represented as the only means of transcending matter and achieving the ultimate reward: immortality. No longer an object of faith, the myth regains its highest dignity through its connection with mystery and tomb. The simple old symbolic faith, in part created and in part transmitted by Orpheus and the great religious teachers of the earliest times, is resurrected in new form in the mythology of the tombs. The later period created no new symbols and no new myths: it lacked the necessary freshness of youth. But with its more inward attitude it was able to give the traditional representations a new and transfigured meaning. Thus the myths, as Plutarch said,[1] became images and shadows of higher ideas, and by their mysterious character inculcated a profounder veneration. They resemble those mimetic καταδείξεις, representations in which the initiate beheld, as in a mirror, the more sublime truths of the mysteries. The whole composition suggests dramatized myth, and certain details are clearly modeled on performances of tragic works.

The static symbol and its mythical unfolding are the speech and writing, the language of the tombs. The higher meditations inspired by the riddle of death, the grief and consolation, the hope and fear, the foreboding and joyful anticipation, are expressed only in art. There is a profound reason for this. Human language is too feeble to convey all the thoughts aroused by the alternation of life and death and the sublime hopes of the initiate. Only the symbol and the related myth can meet this higher need. The symbol awakens intimations; speech can only explain. The symbol plucks all the strings of the human spirit at once; speech is compelled to take up a single thought at a time. The symbol strikes its roots in the most secret depths of the soul; language skims over the surface of the understanding like a soft breeze. The symbol aims inward; language outward. Only the symbol can combine the most disparate elements into a unitary impression. Language deals in successive particulars; it expresses bit by bit what must be brought home to the soul at a single glance if it is to affect us profoundly. Words make the infinite finite, symbols carry the spirit beyond the finite world of becoming into the realm of infinite being. Intimating the ineffable, they are mysterious as all religion by its very nature must be, a silent discourse appropriate to the quiet of the tomb, beyond the reach of mockery and doubt, those unripe fruits of wisdom. Therein lies the mysterious dignity of the symbol, which so eminently enhances the solemnity of the ancient tombs. Therein lies the spell of the mythical representations, which show us the great deeds of the primordial age in the muted light of distant melancholy recollection, and that is what lends them the aura of consecration characteristic of the ancient necropolises.

Ocnus the Rope Plaiter

THE SUBJECT of the following pages is provided by the picture, reproduced in our plate V, from the same tomb as that of the three mystery eggs. Composition and technique are extremely simple. A bearded man is shown sitting in the open country on a large stone block, his back to a farmstead formed of several buildings. His attitude suggests repose after the day's work, and a profound earnestness. His garment covers his head and falls in broad folds over his back; gathered in around the legs, it leaves chest, arms, and feet free. In his right hand the old man holds a long rope, upon which an ass lying nearby is nibbling. His left hand rests wearily on his knee. The whole scene, the old man, the animal, the farm, is bathed in the tranquillity of evening. Deep stillness prevails. The silence of the tomb seems infused into the picture.

What enhances the interest of this painting is its unusual interpretation of a familiar subject. The aged Ocnus is usually shown immersed in his eternally vain task; here he is resting from his labors. His hands, generally busy twisting the rope, lie idly in his lap. All thought of hardship, penance, and punishment is absent. And the setting also is very different from the usual one. The old man is resting in a peaceful countryside. The tree-shaded farm seems to have just been left by its owners. The old man, usually relegated to Hades and the sunless depths of the earth, is surrounded by all the joys of creation. The great penitents of the underworld would be quite out of place in this picture. The Danaïds, Ixion, Sisyphus, and Cerberus are related to the laboring

Ocnus, the penitent of Hades, but not to this old man resting from the day's work, this dweller in the luminous realm. The Pamphilian conception contrasts sharply with the others.

It is not artistic fancy but conscious purpose that has reversed the traditional myth. The suffering Ocnus has been set free. And the more one identifies the rope plaiter with punishment and penance, the more impressed one is by the message of peace and redemption in this picture. Ocnus was known as an aged plaiter of rope; here he is idle. The idea of eternally vain labor constituted his innermost being; here he has achieved peace and freedom from care. He has often been named as a dweller in Hades; here he is shown in the realm of the living. How strikingly the idea of liberation and redemption must have stood out against such a background; how powerful an impression our painting must have made when considered in the light of this contrast! And this is why we devote so much attention to it. The ethical idea embodied in it is the supreme spiritualization of a symbol whose original significance was purely physical and material. Here I shall attempt to investigate the original meaning of the symbol of Ocnus the rope plaiter, and to indicate the various transformations through which our hieroglyph developed from the purely physical and material to the immaterial and abstract.

To put ourselves on firm ground, we must undertake a brief survey of the monuments and written records that have come down to us. Most important of these is the grave painting which we show in plate III *b*. In 1832 Campana discovered one of those tombs, generally called columbaria, not far from the now walled-in Porta Latina at Rome. In the interior of the building the first of the small burial niches to catch the visitor's attention is that bearing the picture of Ocnus, for it is situated directly opposite the staircase leading down into the tomb. This columbarium has the shape of an aedicula surmounted by a frieze and pediment, both of which disclose remains of paintings (plate VI *a*). The entire center of the pediment is occupied by a painting of Chiron, the wise centaur, teaching the attentive young Achilles to play the lyre. Originally the entire frieze, over twenty Roman palms (*ca.* four feet) in length, was covered with paintings. Most of them have been effaced. Only the two outermost pieces have been preserved; to the right, the picture of Ocnus; to the left, the three-headed Cerberus. Surrounded by tall reeds, the bald-headed, bearded old man, clad in a sleeved garment, is plaiting his rope; as it falls to the ground, the finished end is being nibbled avidly by an ass. The old man's kneeling position and expression suggest painful exertion, and his whole aspect has an underworld character reminiscent of Charon, the melancholy ferryman. The nude figure of a young woman, holding her wind-blown garment with her fingertips, belongs to a second group, independent of Ocnus and his ass. This group, it seems almost certain, represented the myth of the Danaïds, although there is nothing about the fragment to suggest the labors of the youthful penitents. Still smaller is the fragment preserved at the left end. But the three-headed Cerberus makes it certain that the whole frieze was a running account of the underworld, and that Ocnus was shown among the great penitents of Hades.

The same theme is treated in other surviving monuments. On a round marble altar in the Museo Pio-Clementino [1] Ocnus appears in the company of the Danaïds (plate IV). Here there is so little division between the Danaïds and Ocnus that the first of the water carriers seems to stand directly behind the nibbling ass. The clothing is very similar to that in the Pamphilian tomb. Ocnus, like the Danaïds, is wholly immersed in his hopeless task. The treachery of the beast is stressed by its position behind the old man's back, which recalls the Apaturia,* in which the celebrants called to one another: "The man with the black goatskin is behind you." This altar was no doubt consecrated to chthonian deities; it was an *ara* and not an *altare*.

We also have a number of literary allusions, but it is noteworthy that most of them refer to artistic representations. Most famous of these was Polygnotus' painting in the lesche of Delphi. Pausanias

---

* Apaturia ('Απατούρια), annual Greek festival of "common relationship," held in all Ionian towns except Ephesus and Colophon. In Athens, held on the three days (at the end of October and beginning of November) when phratries of Attica met and registered children born within the year. Traditionally this festival was linked to ἀπάτη, "deceit," and commemorated the trick played by Melanthus (the Black One, representing the king of Attica), who won a fight with King Xanthus (the White One) of Boeotia by falsely warning that a man in a black goat's skin (Dionysus Melanaigis) was behind him. See Bachofen, *Gräbersymbolik*, in *Gesammelte Werke*, Vol. 4, pp. 58f.

gives us the following description: "After them comes a seated man, whom an inscription identifies as Ocnus; he is shown plaiting a rope; beside him stands a she-ass who secretly keeps eating the part he has just plaited. This Ocnus is said to have been a hard-working man, but to have had an extravagant wife who spent his substance as fast as he could earn it. The Delphians believe that Polygnotus was alluding to Ocnus' wife; but I know that when the Ionians see someone sweating under a futile occupation, they say he is plaiting Ocnus' rope. The fortunetellers who observe the flight of birds also call a certain bird ὄκνος, and this ὄκνος is the largest and most beautiful species of heron, but extremely rare." [2] And Ocnus was represented as an underworld penitent in a painting described by Plutarch.[3] An independent representation, unconnected with Hades, seems to have been a painting, mentioned by Pliny, which depicted "the lazy man called Ocnus (*piger qui appellatur Ocnus*), who plaits a rope which an ass is eating." [4]

And in classical comedy Ocnus also appears as a penitent in Hades. So he appears in Cratinus; [5] the latest reference occurs in Propertius, who declares that "the man [who] first plucked the soldier's stake from a tree" was deserving of Ocnus' punishment.[6] Here again we have the notion of penance and punishment.

Let us now seek to discover the original meaning of the rope-plaiting Ocnus.†

This meaning can only be basically physical. Ocnus the rope plaiter is a nature symbol. The history of words always begins with the sensuous, natural signification, and only in the course of development arrives at abstract, figurative meanings; and in religion, in the development of the human individual and of mankind, the same progress from the material to the psychic and spiritual can be noted. Likewise the symbols in which the earliest

---

† The grammarian Servius uses the form Aucnus beside Ocnus, thus deriving it from *augere, auctare* (to increase). This increasing "finds an exact expression in the pictorial representations of the old rope plaiter. He furthers his work without ceasing. . . . The proper name and the concept of ὄκνος form a whole. Their meanings stand in an inner relationship and yield a connected train of ideas. Transposed to the moral level of deliberating and testing, the idea of increase and continuous labor is transformed into that of cautiousness, of procrastination and tarrying." See Bachofen, *Gräbersymbolik*, in *Gesammelte Werke*, Vol. 4, pp. 412f.

mankind set forth its intuitions of nature and the environing world
began with purely physical and material meanings. Symbolism,
like language, is taught by nature. We shall soon see that this
comparison between language and symbolism is especially apt in
connection with Ocnus. There is an exact parallelism between the
aged rope plaiter and the various significations of the word ὄκνος.
Symbol and word develop side by side. And the meanings of the
word prove to be a late development of the symbol. Thus it
becomes clear that the explanations and implications we have
encountered in the course of the first section are relatively late
interpretations devised at a time when the original intuition
manifest in the symbol had been lost. Derived and wholly
secondary is the idea of *pigritia*, procrastination and laziness. No
less secondary is the interpretation of the Ionians, the diligent
husband, the extravagant wife, labor without benefit or profit; the
idea of punishment and penance is not fundamental either, nor the
opposite notion of redemption and liberation as it appears in the
Pamphilian painting. All these ideas deserve our consideration
because the ancients saw them in the picture of the aged rope
plaiter, but they themselves did not produce the symbol; they
merely became associated with it in a later day.

The original meaning can be discerned in an Egyptian ritual
described by Diodorus: "And many other elements of our mythology have been preserved in Egyptian customs down to the present
day, and not only as names but as actual practices. In the city of
Acanthus, beyond the Nile in the direction of Libya, a hundred
and twenty stadia from Memphis, there is a barrel full of holes into
which each day three hundred and sixty priests pour water from
the Nile. And not far from here one can see the fable of Ocnus
enacted in a society, one member of which plaits a long rope, while
others behind him undo what he had plaited." [7] What makes this
passage particularly important is that it is part of a long dissertation on the connection between Egyptian and Greek religion, which
argues the thesis that what the Greeks knew only as myth still
survived in Egypt as liturgical practice. The historical connection
may be minimized or rejected entirely as the private opinion of the
Greek historian; but the ritual practice of rope plaiting is presented as a fact and must be accepted as such.

Its meaning cannot be doubted for one moment. Rope plaiting

is frequently a symbolic action, based on the same conceptions as the spinning and weaving of the great nature mothers. The symbol of spinning and weaving represents the creative, formative power of nature. The labor of the great material primordial mothers is likened to the skillful plaiting and weaving which lends articulation, symmetrical form, and refinement to crude matter. The organisms all emerge in finished state from the womb of the earth. From their mother they have the subtle web of their body, which she fashioned with unparalleled mastery in the dark womb of matter. That is why Terra eminently deserves the name of artist (*daedala, artifex rerum*), that is why the primordial mother is known as the formative mother, μήτηρ πλαστήνη. This, too, is what gives the hand its high significance, especially its relation to natural generation and the maternity of matter. It is the hand, repository of all artistry, which gives crude matter its articulation and lends it beautiful form along with life. In the articulation of the hand lies its ability to fashion the most perfect work. It was for this reason that, according to Suetonius,[8] the cloven hoof of Caesar's horse was regarded as a token of the supreme power; and that conversely, according to Plutarch,[9] the lack of such articulation was held to confirm the demonic destructive nature of the ass. The Greek portrayals of Ocnus represent the creative principle in human form and the destructive principle in the form of an animal; and this antithesis also stressed the significance of the hand. Creation is an art; destruction is the work of brute force. Creation rests in the human hand; destruction is attributed to the demonic animal nature.

Thus the activity of nature, its skillful creation and formation, were symbolized in spinning, plaiting, and weaving; but these labors were related in still other ways to the work of tellurian creation. In the weaving of two threads could be seen the twofold power of nature, the interpenetration of the two sexual principles prerequisite to all generation. The sexual was still more manifest in the working of the loom. The crossing of the threads, their alternate appearance and disappearance, seemed to present a perfect image of the eternal process of natural life. Rhampsinitus, who alternately loses and wins in his subterranean dice game with Demeter, and to whom she gives a golden handkerchief in leave-taking,** represents the web of nature, in which light and shadow, appearance and disappearance, are seen as equally necessary factors. The myth of Arachne, who likes best to portray in her weaving the gods' amorous adventures with mortal women; [10] of Hephaestus, who catches Aphrodite and Ares in his net as they lie in passionate embrace; [11] of Eileithyia, [12] the good weaver who acts as a midwife, is persuaded by the offering of a ribbon nine ells long to assist Leto in her labor, and upon whom the Delian virgins bestow spindles entwined with locks of hair before they marry: [13] all these clearly show the erotic significance attributed to weaving and the warp and weft pattern of the threads.

This physico-erotic relation also comprises the idea of *fatum* and πεπρωμένη, destiny. The thread of death is woven into the web of which every tellurian organism consists. Death is the supreme natural law, the *fatum* of material life, to which the gods themselves bow, which they cannot claim to master. Thus the web of tellurian creation becomes the web of destiny, the thread becomes the carrier of human fate, Eileithyia, the midwife, the good spinstress, becomes the great Moira who is older even than Cronus himself.[14] The thread plays a salutary role in connection with the Dionysian Ariadne-Aphrodite. On the other hand, the thread which breaks in the shrine of the Erinyes is a bringer of doom; after Cylon's rebellion it delivers the fugitives who had placed their trust in it to the fury of the people.†† It followed from this same intuition that the veil of Helen, the necklace of Eriphyle, and the poison-soaked garment with which his wife slays Heracles, the hater of women, were seen as fabrics of fatality; that the taeniae, headbands, were chiefly consecrated to the tombs and subterranean powers; that the loom, carrier of the supreme law of creation written in the stars, was assigned to the uranian deities in their sidereal nature; and, finally, that human life and the entire cosmos were seen as a great web of destiny.[16]

All these conceptions go back to a single fundamental intuition, and purely physical intuition of spinning and weaving mothers. The rope is plaited of two cords. The two sexes, dual poles of life,

** See p. 26*n.*
†† Aided by his father-in-law, Theagenes of Megara, Cylon attempted to establish a tyranny at Athens, ca. 636 B.C.[15]

which as twin brothers drive the team of creation with head-long swiftness, become one, and give to visible creation the ὁρατὸς κόσμος,[17] its beginning, its continuous renewal, and its eternal rejuvenation. But the fabric is still a crude one. The plaiter produces no fine-spun thread or cunning texture. In all the monuments we have reproduced, what Ocnus turns out is a thick, coarsely twisted rope. And this is by no means irrelevant or meaningless. According to the oldest theology, and particularly that of the Orphics, matter develops from chaos to form, from imperfection to perfection, from crude disorder to increasingly more refined articulation and organization; the beautiful first originates in a formative progression from the lower to the higher. And similarly the outgrowths of tellurian matter disclose a gradual development from crude to artful, from disorder to refinement of form. The simple crude rope is followed by finer fabrics until the perfection of the divine hand is disclosed in transparent garments embroidered with ingenious images of the earth and the world of the gods. In his song about Aphrodite's contest with Athene in weaving, Leucus of Lesbos brings out this distinction between the crude, artless tissue and the fine, beautiful fabric. Aphrodite, the primordial mother of crude tellurian generation, cannot equal Athene's finished skill. Her hands are awkward at such work. The threads she produces are as thick as the rope of plaited willow withes with which the aged shipwright caulks the seams between the gaping planks of his craft. And Athene scoffs at the thick, clumsy cords turned out by the goddess unversed in fine work. Leaving her task unfinished, Aphrodite hastens back to Cyprus, and under her influence the work of tellurian generation begins anew.[18]

It is clear that here two stages of natural creation are distinguished. Aphrodite weaves the coarse fabric of tellurian forms from crude matter, Athene fashions fine garments of perfect beauty. Aphrodite's fabrics are compared to the willow withes of the swampy depths, earthy, the offspring of the earth. Athene's weaving achieves a higher, heavenly degree of perfection. Aphrodite's fabric remains unfinished and unravels; Athene's tissue is finished. Material fecundation and the pangs of childbirth attend Aphrodite's work. Athene brings purely Olympian existence, free from all material desire, free from labor pains, and she herself knows only her father, Zeus.

In view of all this there can be no doubt as to the true original meaning of the aged rope plaiter. Our hieroglyph is assuredly a symbol of the creative formative activity of the material principle. And this lends meaning to what might otherwise seem to be a trifling detail in the Campana mural. The old man is shown performing his endless task in a setting of great swamp plants. Here we may see an allusion to the swampy depths of Acheron. But there is more to it than this. The subterranean muck and its vegetation have a very special meaning in connection with Ocnus. By showing us the raw material from which the rope is plaited, the artists create a necessary connection between the crude rope and the lowest level of natural generation. Our symbol of nature's creative power is now specified more closely. The stage of tellurian generation symbolized by Ocnus is not that of the *laborata Ceres*, the active Ceres of agriculture, but the lower stage characterized by plants which grow without human aid, which thrive in the damp lowlands and marshes. The life of the swamps presented the whole drama of tellurian creation to the amazed eyes of earliest mankind. No seed fecundates the womb of the earth, no plow opens the furrow. Spontaneously matter sends forth into the light of day what it has fashioned in its dark depths. The stalks grow, mature, age, die away, and are replaced by new sprouts that embark on the same cycle of development. Here was the prototype of all earthly life. The swamp growth with its eternal cycle disclosed the law which also governs the world of animals and men. They too arise from the womb of matter, they too return to its darkness; and everywhere it is the eternal dying away of the individual which preserves the eternal youth of the species.

The ancients embodied all these ideas in the image of Ocnus, eternally plaiting his rope out of swamp plants. Clearly this symbolism was favored by the topography of the Nile valley. The phenomena to which Egypt owes its fertility and very existence gave rise to the intuition of the chthonian waters as bearer of phallic power; of the earth as the feminine-receptive matter; and of their union in the annual flood as the generative sexual act. The fecundating Nile appears as the physical substrate of Osiris.[19] Its waters are conceived as carrying the phallus of the male godhead. As Osiris is identified with the Nile, so Isis is identified with the land fructified by the overflowing waters. Their union constitutes the act of tellurian fecundation, which is completed when the waters vanish into the womb of matter. Imitating this natural event, the priests mix earth and water in a little golden chest; [20] and at Acanthus they pour the water of the Nile each day from 360 urns into a barrel full of holes, a ritual which symbolizes the impregnation of the earth womb by the generative moisture. The tellurian water is seen as the principle of creation, and by extension the swamp muck becomes the seat and vehicle of all earthly fertility.

The religious significance of swamp plants follows from this divine nature which the Egyptians imputed to the river mud. The mystery of generation proceeds in the dark damp depths, invisible to man, but the secret is revealed by the sprouting reed. The fruit of matter, conceiving in self-embrace, is manifested to mortal eyes in the swamp plants which spring upward to the light from the depths of the muck. The view of nature here expressed is easy to decipher. Swamp generation is identified with promiscuous sexual union. Hair and swamp plant are equated.

In opposition to the creative, increasing activity, there is an activity which dissolves and diminishes. Two forces are locked in eternal battle. Two equal currents oppose one another, and through their antagonism the eternal youth of creation is preserved. The short end of the rope which stands between the creative and the destructive principle is visible creation eternally in motion, never for one moment the same. Compared to all that through the ages has returned into the dark womb of the earth, the visible end pales to insignificance. What is the number of the living compared to the incalculable hordes of the dead? What is the span of time allotted to the living compared to the aeons, forever augmented by the fleeting present moment? Rightly the dead are called "the more," *plures*, πλείονες. To one who surveys all time and all being, human life cannot possibly seem great.[21] It becomes a mere mask worn for one brief moment. The veil of youth conceals the wrinkled forehead of the primordial mother. What seems real is not the real; becoming is the antithesis of being. All these ideas are suggested by the end of the rope, all that remains of centuries of work.

The choice of the ass to represent the evil principle is no free or arbitrary invention. It springs from the religious significance of the ass, whose sanctity is as old as the conceptions that crystallized in the figure of Ocnus himself. The role of the ass in the representations of Ocnus is in full accord with the Typhonian significance attributed to the beast in Egypt, thus supporting the hypothesis that the whole myth is of Libyan origin. The Egyptians identified the animal nature as such with Typhon's evil principle and, according to Plutarch,[22] represented only the female and never the male principle in animal form. This points to an inner relationship between the feminine and the principle of dissolution, and the connection is symbolized in the she-ass, θήλεια ὄνος.

Our discussion of the elements of the Campana mural (plate III b) is now complete. The meaning which we set forth at the outset has now been confirmed on all sides. The contrary activities of the aged rope plaiter and the nibbling she-ass constitute a nature symbol whose significance is no longer puzzling. What enhances this significance is that the symbol is not restricted to any particular aspect of tellurian life, but provides a simple and wholly comprehensible expression of the fundamental law governing all nature and all visible creation. Earthly life is manifested in its eternal flux, comparable to a stream with motion as its innermost principle, bursting incontinently from its source and at every moment being carried closer to the ocean in which it will vanish. Here we are brought face to face with the transience of all sublunary existence.

And yet this is not the ultimate reason why Ocnus was given a place in the ancient tombs. The myth implies another, far higher idea. It brings home to us an antithesis which pertains to an entirely new order of ideas and suggests entirely new meditations.

Thus far we have considered only the original meaning of the symbol of Ocnus. Now we shall have to account for its presence in the world of the tombs. Here the original religious idea has undergone an unexpected transformation. Ocnus is represented among the great penitents of Hades. Ixion, Tantalus, and the Danaïds are his companions. He is surrounded by the terrors of the underworld. Toil and hardship without end are his lot. The Campana mural (plate III *b*) suggests no other thought than suffering and penance by the shores of Acheron. But such an idea is far removed from the original meaning of the symbol. The original Ocnus has nothing to do with penance and pain, or with the terrors of the underworld, and we know of no crime to justify his punishment. The old man's unceasing toil suggests rather an attitude of benevolence to mortals; he appears in the role of an agathodaemon creating and preserving life. In contrast to the Typhonian she-ass, he is the embodiment of the good principle, forever at war with the demonic principle of destruction. The rope plaiter of Acanthus * would seem to be worlds apart from the penitent Ocnus of the Roman tombs.

Far from underestimating the difference, we must define it in all its sharpness. We have here a mythological phenomenon analogous to the development of the pierced barrel of the Danaïds, Ocnus has been consigned to the underworld. Like them, he has become a symbol of penitence. In both cases a blessing has become a curse; as in the case of the Danaïds any thought of a particular crime disappears, so with Ocnus his punishment and suffering are not connected with any particular crime. In the company of the water-gathering maidens [23] the old man becomes a symbol of the hopeless life and equally hopeless future of those who reject the blessings of the mysteries and so fall prey to pure material existence. This is the supreme idea that came to be associated with the aged rope plaiter; this is the idea that explains his presence in the tombs and speaks to us in the paintings. There is a possibility of salvation from the dark powers which threaten mortals with never-ending torments. Those who, through initiation into the mysteries, choose the god as their guide, will triumph over the dark powers, not only on the stormy sea but also in death, as Heracles triumphed over the dog of Hades, Oedipus over the sphinx, Orpheus over the sirens whose death-dealing song he countered with the saving melody of his higher wisdom. The Campana frieze shows not what the deceased must expect, but what he has

* See p. 55.

III. Pediment and frieze from an aedicula in the columbarium
at the Porta Latina, Rome

a   Pediment and frieze   *b*   Detail: Ocnus and a Danaïd

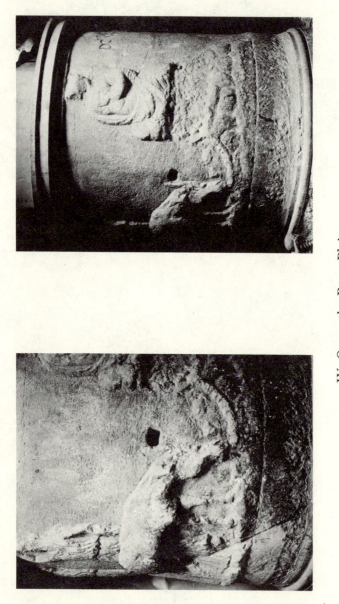

IV. Ocnus the Rope Plaiter

Relief on a round marble altar or well setting

Left: The ass, with two Danaïds (one barely visible); *right*: Ocnus and the ass

V. Ocnus Resting

Tomb painting from a columbarium in the Villa Pamphili, Rome

transcended: τῶν μὴ μεμυημένων (among the uninitiated), † this is the comforting explanation we should adopt for Ocnus as we read it over the heads of the Danaïds. What is uttered in words in the lesche of Delphi is here expressed in the painting of the pediment (plate III *a*). Achilles, instructed by the wise Chiron in the playing of the lyre, represents the positive aspect of the picture, which uses the shadow side of human destiny to open up an insight into the luminous realm. After viewing the terrors of Hades, the penitents of the dark depths, we gladly look up to the centaur and his attentive pupil, and find peace in contemplating the hero who has achieved the supreme bliss of eternal life.

The paintings on Campana's aedicula may then be taken as representations of two stages of life, a lower stage without the benefit of initiation and a higher stage in which the mystery rites confer hope of a better life to come. Or the distinction may be taken in a broader sense, as that between the material-tellurian and the immaterial-solar stage of religion, between a lower and a higher conception of the divine as revealed in nature, between a primordial and a more highly developed stage of culture. The religious development of the human race follows the same law that is disclosed in the education of the individual. It progresses from the lower to the higher, from the material to the psychic and spiritual, from the formless to the formed, from the impure to the pure, from darkness to light. According to the earliest Orphic view, there is an increasingly ample manifestation of divinity ever in progress, and in the ever-increasing perfection of created life, the creative principle itself comes to manifestation with increasing beauty as well. Like the graduated pyramid which finds a place in so many mortuary monuments, the religious development of our race starts from the broad base of a purely material conception and strives heavenward. Tellurism with its materiality gives way to the higher solar principle; the chthonian conception of energy to the recognition of its uranian nature. Over the Poseidonian-Plutonian principle rises the Apollonian principle of light. In comparison with the luminous principle the material principle not only appears as the impurer and lower stage of divinity, but is often seen as a power hostile to man, which can

† The words inscribed over Polygnotus' painting in the lesche at Delphi.[24]

63

only be transformed into a blessing through subordination to the higher law of the luminous realm. Thus the bloody justice of the Erinyes first gave way to and then became reconciled with Apollo's propitiating divinity. Tellurism with all its dark power bows to the higher, celestial, luminous justice of the Pythian and subordinates its old claims to those of the new god. And the same thought attaches to all those images which Polygnotus transplanted from the Greek Hades to the hall of Delphi. Over against them the beneficent purer nature of the Pythian god shines out all the more brightly.

Once we have recognized in the hall of Delphi the same idea that governs the contrast between the penitent Ocnus and the Apollonian Achilles on the aedicula of the Roman tomb, we shall have no difficulty in understanding the new transformation of the figure of Ocnus in the Pamphilian columbarium. The special interest of this painting lies in its deviation from all other literary and artistic interpretations of Ocnus. We are surprised by the attitude of repose in which the old man is shown. He has forsaken the labor of plaiting, hitherto his essential feature. His deep repose represents a striking—and intentional—contrast to the traditional conception of the rope plaiter. And the same is true of the ass, here shown recumbent. The underworld penitents, the terrors of Hades have vanished. Ocnus' inactivity dispels all thought of torment or punishment, and the surrounding landscape breathes only peace and calm. The old man seems to have come out into the courtyard to enjoy the stillness of the evening. As he rests here from the labors of the day, he lets the ass, his companion in toil, play with the rope. The Delphic prototype is entirely abandoned and everything consciously turned into its opposite. What thought could have moved the painter to this transformation?

If we take Ocnus in his original significance as a nature symbol, we shall find no explanation or justification. For the nature symbol the action of rope plaiting is indispensable, and cannot possibly be abandoned. We must seek our explanation elsewhere and consider the symbol in the meaning which it assumed for the mysteries. Now everything falls into place and the new idea stands out in all its beauty. With the simplest means, the Pamphilian painting sets forth a thought which no written words could have expressed so clearly and succinctly. The penitent Ocnus is redeemed. The bearded old man is the initiate, and like the whole work, he has a twofold implication. He is at once the mythological Ocnus and the nameless deceased who was the owner of the farm outside which he is seated. Thus he conveys two meanings: for Ocnus, the final liberation from his torment, for the owner of the farm, the beginning of eternal rest; for both, the victory of the higher mystery powers over the terrors of death.

This is the ultimate form taken by the nature symbol of the aged rope plaiter. The representation of tellurian life and its law has been transformed into a symbol of the highest stage of human existence. Confined at first to the material cycle, the symbol now passes beyond it to the realm of the life that begins with the death of the body. First an expression of becoming, now it is an image of being. At first bound up with the idea of transience, it now confers the hope of an unchanging future. Calmly and indifferently the initiate can now abandon the crude fabric of his body to the nibbling she-ass. Along with religion, Ocnus has risen from the dark marshy depths to the luminous heights. He symbolizes the lowest and highest that the earth offers, the entire weakness and greatness of the transient creature, man's subjugation to the law of death and his sublimation of it. The higher existence prevails. Two worlds stand side by side, one sensuous, the other transcendent. It would be absurd, as Aristotle puts it in his *Metaphysics,* to sacrifice the latter to the former.

> The life of man entire is misery:
> he finds no resting place, no haven from calamity
> But something other dearer still than life
> the darkness hides and mist encompasses;
> we are proved luckless lovers of this thing
> that glitters in the underworld: no man
> can tell us of the stuff of it, expounding
> what is, and what is not: we know nothing of it.[25]

From Mother Right

An Investigation of the Religious and Juridical

Character of Matriarchy

in the Ancient World

Introduction

T HE PRESENT work deals with a historical phenomenon which few have observed and no one has investigated in its full scope. Up until now archaeologists have had nothing to say of mother right. The term is new and the family situation it designates unknown. The subject is extremely attractive, but it also raises great difficulties. The most elementary spadework remains to be done, for the culture period to which mother right pertains has never been seriously studied. Thus we are entering upon virgin territory.

We find ourselves carried back to times antedating classical antiquity, to an older world of ideas totally different from those with which we are familiar. Leaving the nations we commonly associate with the glory of the ancient world, we find ourselves among peoples who never achieved the level of classical culture. An unknown world opens before our eyes, and the more we learn of it, the stranger it seems. Everything contrasts with the idea of a highly developed culture; everywhere we find older conceptions, an independent way of life that can only be judged according to its own fundamental law. The matriarchal organization of the family seems strange in the light not only of modern but also of classical ideas. And the more primitive way of life to which it pertains, from which it arose, and through which alone it can be explained, seems very strange beside the Hellenic. The main purpose of the following pages is to set forth the moving principle of the matriarchal age, and to give its proper place in relationship both to the lower stages of development and to the higher levels of culture. Thus the scope of this work is far broader than its title indicates. I propose to investigate all aspects of matriarchal culture, to disclose its diverse traits and the fundamental idea which unites them. In this way I hope to restore the picture of a cultural stage which was overlaid or totally destroyed by the later development of the ancient world. This is an ambitious undertaking. But it is only by broadening our horizon that we can achieve true understanding and carry scientific thinking to that clarity and completeness which are the very essence of knowledge.

And now I shall attempt a general survey of my ideas, which, I believe, will facilitate the study of the work itself.

Of all records relating and pertaining to mother right, those concerning the Lycian people are the clearest and most valuable. The Lycians, Herodotus [1] reports, did not name their children after their fathers like the Hellenes, but exclusively after their mothers; in their genealogical records they dealt entirely with the maternal line, and the status of children was defined solely in accordance with that of the mother. Nicolaus of Damascus [2] completes this testimony by telling us that only the daughters possessed the right of inheritance, and traces this institution back to the Lycian common law, the unwritten law which, as defined by Socrates, was handed down by the godhead itself. All these customs are manifestations of one and the same basic conception. Although Herodotus regards them merely as an odd deviation from Hellenic customs, closer observation must lead to a deeper view. We find not disorder but system, not fancy but necessity. And since it is expressly denied that these customs were influenced by any positive body of legislation, the hypothesis of a meaningless anomaly loses its last shred of justification. We find, then, side by side with the Hellenic-Roman father principle, a family organization which differs diametrically both in its foundation and in its development, as a comparison of the two clearly shows. This opinion is confirmed by the discovery of related conceptions among other peoples. The limitation of the right of inheritance to the daughters among the Lycians finds a parallel in the obligation (recorded by Diodorus for Egypt) of the daughters alone to provide for aged parents. And in line with the same basic conception Strabo [3] reports that among the Cantabri the sisters provided their brothers with dowries.

All these traits join to form a single picture and lead to the conclusion that mother right is not confined to any particular people but marks a cultural stage. In view of the universal qualities of human nature, this cultural stage cannot be restricted to any particular ethnic family. And consequently what must concern us is not so much the similarities between isolated phenomena as the unity of the basic conception. Polybius' [4] passage about the matriarchal genealogy of the hundred noble families among the Epizephyrian Locrians suggests two further observations which have been confirmed in the course of our investigation: (1) mother right belongs to a cultural period preceding that of the patriarchal system; (2) it began to decline only with the victorious development of the paternal system. The matriarchal forms are observed chiefly among the pre-Hellenic peoples and are an essential component of this archaic culture, upon which they set their imprint as much as do patriarchal forms upon Greek culture.

The principles which we have here deduced from a few observations are confirmed in the course of our investigation by an abundance of data. The Locrians lead us to the Leleges, Carians, Aetolians, Pelasgians, Caucones, Arcadians, Epeians, Minyae, and Teleboeans, who furnish a diversified picture of mother right and the culture based on it. The prestige of womanhood among these peoples was a source of astonishment to the ancients, and gives them all, regardless of individual coloration, a character of archaic sublimity that stands in striking contrast to Hellenic culture. Here we discern the basic idea from which sprang the genealogical system set forth in the Hesiodic *Eoiai* and "Catalogues," * the unions of immortal mothers wedded to mortal fathers, the emphasis on maternal property and the name of the maternal line, the closeness of maternal kinship, which gave rise to the term "mother country," the appellation "motherland," the greater sanctity of female sacrifices, and the inexpiability of matricide.

---

* Poems of Hesiod, now lost except for some fragments, which dealt with the mythical and legendary genealogy of the Greek peoples.

In these prefatory remarks, concerned not with individual data but with general perspectives, we must stress the importance of the mythical tradition for our investigation. In view of the central position of mother right among the earliest Greek peoples, we may expect this system to be reflected in myth. And accordingly this oldest form of tradition becomes an important source for our knowledge of matriarchal institutions. The question therefore arises: What importance may we impute to this primordial form of human tradition, and what use are we justified in making of its testimony? The answer to this question is provided by a single example drawn from Lycian mythology.

The maternal transmission of inheritance is attested for this sphere not only by the purely historical account of Herodotus but also by the mythical history of the Lycian kings. Not the sons of Sarpedon, but Laodamia, his daughter, is entitled to his heritage, and she passes the kingdom on to her son, to the exclusion of his uncles. A story recorded by Eustathius [5] gives this system of inheritance a symbolic expression, disclosing the basic idea of mother right in all its sensuous sexuality. If the reports of Herodotus and of Nicolaus had been lost, those who hold the prevailing view would have attempted to discredit Eustathius' story on the ground that its authenticity could not be supported by any older, not to mention contemporaneous sources; they would have argued that its cryptic character indicated invention by some foolish mythographer. They would have said, not that the myth had formed around the fact like a shell, but on the contrary, that the fact had been abstracted from the myth. They would have set it down as worthless rubbish and relegated it to the discard pile whose steady growth marks the destructive progress of the so-called "critical" approach to mythology. But comparison of the myth and the historical account shows the fallacy of this entire method. Tested by historically established truths, the mythical tradition is seen to be an authentic, independent record of the primordial age, a record in which invention plays no part. The preference of Laodamia over her brothers must then be taken as adequate proof that mother right prevailed in Lycia.

There is scarcely a feature of the matriarchal system that cannot be documented in this way, although the parallels cannot always be taken from one and the same people. In fact, we have such parallels even for the general picture of matriarchal culture; and the reason is that mother right was preserved at least partially down to relatively recent times. Both the mythical and the strictly historical traditions present very similar pictures of the system. Products of archaic and of much later periods show such an astonishing accord that we almost forget the long interval between the times when they originated. This parallelism proves the value of the mythical tradition and shows that the attitude of present-day scholarship toward it is untenable. Precisely in regard to the most important aspect of history, namely, the knowledge of ancient ideas and institutions, the already shaky distinction between historic and prehistoric times loses its last shred of justification.

Our question has been answered: the mythical tradition may be taken as a faithful reflection of the life of those times in which historical antiquity is rooted. It is a manifestation of primordial thinking, an immediate historical revelation, and consequently a highly reliable historical source.

Eustathius declares that the favoring of Laodamia over her brothers is entirely contrary to Hellenic attitudes. His remark is all the more noteworthy in view of its recent date. Unlike modern critics, the learned Byzantine does not question, much less modify the tradition because of the anomaly he seems to find in it. Such uncritical, candid acceptance of tradition, often attacked as thoughtless copying, provides the best pledge of the reliability of our sources even when they are relatively late. Among all the ancients who wrote about the earliest times we find the same meticulous fidelity in preserving and handing down tradition, the same reluctance to tamper with the vestiges of the primordial world. It is to this attitude that we owe the possibility of discerning with any degree of certainty the essential character of the most ancient periods and of tracing the history of human ideas back to their beginnings. The less inclined he is toward critique and subjective combination, the more reliable an author will be, and the less prone to falsification.

There is still another reason why myth demonstrates the authenticity of mother right. The contrast between mythical conceptions and those of subsequent days is so marked that where more recent ideas prevailed, it would not have been possible to invent the phenomena of matriarchy. The older system represented an utter puzzle to the patriarchal mind, which consequently could not have conceived any part of it. Hellenic thought could not possibly have fabricated Laodamia's priority, for it is in diametric opposition to such a conception. The same is true of the innumerable vestiges of matriarchal form woven into the prehistory of all ancient peoples—not excluding Athens and Rome, two most resolute advocates of paternity. The thinking and literature of any period unconsciously follow the laws of its life form. So great is the power of such laws that the natural tendency is always to set the new imprint on the divergent features of former times.

The matriarchal traditions did not escape this fate. We shall encounter some very surprising phenomena produced by the impact of late conceptions on the vestiges of older views and by the weakness which led some writers to replace the incomprehensible by what was comprehensible from the standpoint of their own culture. Old features are overlaid by new ones, the venerable figures of the matriarchal past are introduced to contemporaries in forms consonant with the spirit of the new period, harsh features are presented in a softened light; institutions, attitudes, motives, passions are reappraised from a contemporary point of view. Not infrequently new and old occur together; or the same fact, the same person, may appear in two versions, one prescribed by the earlier, one by the later world; one innocent, one criminal; one full of nobility and dignity, one an object of horror and the subject of a palinode. In other cases the mother gives way to the father, the sister to the brother, who now takes her place in the legend or alternates with her, while the feminine name is replaced by a masculine one. In a word, maternal conceptions cede to the requirements of patriarchal theory.

Thus, far from writing in the spirit of a surpassed, vanished culture, the later age will endeavor to extend the rule of its own ideas to ideas and facts that are alien to it. And this circumstance frequently guarantees the authenticity of the mythical vestiges of the matriarchal age, lending them the force of reliable proof. But where it has succumbed to later influence, myth becomes still more instructive. Since the changes usually result from the unconscious action of the new ideas, and only in exceptional cases from conscious hostility to the old, the legend becomes in its transformations a living expression of the stages in a people's development, and for the skillful observer, a faithful reflection of all the periods in the life of that people.

These considerations, I hope, will serve to justify the use that is made of the mythical tradition in the following. But the richness of the results it brings can only be appreciated in the course of detailed study. Preoccupied as they are with the facts, personalities, and institutions of particular epochs, our modern historians have drawn a sharp distinction between historical and mythical times and prolonged the so-called mythical era out of all proportion. Along these lines any penetrating and coherent understanding of antiquity is impossible. All historical institutions presuppose earlier stages of formation: nowhere in history do we find a beginning, but always a continuation, never a cause which is not at the same time an effect. True scientific knowledge cannot consist merely in an answer to the question, What? It must also discover the *whence* and tie it up with the *whither*. Knowledge becomes understanding only if it can encompass origin, progression, and end.

Since the beginning of all development lies in myth, myth must form the starting point for any serious investigation of ancient history. Myth contains the origins, and myth alone can reveal them. It is the origins which determine the subsequent development, which define its character and direction. Without knowledge of the origins, the science of history can come to no conclusion. A distinction between myth and history may be justified where it refers merely to a difference in mode of expression, but it has neither meaning nor justification when it creates a hiatus in the continuity of human development. The success of our undertaking depends essentially on the abandonment of any such distinction. The forms of family organization prevailing in the times known to us are not original forms, but the consequences of earlier stages. Considered alone, they disclose only themselves, not their causality; they are isolated data, elements of knowledge at most, but not of understanding. The strictness of the Roman patriarchal system points to an earlier system that had to be combatted and suppressed. And the same applies to the paternal system of Athens, the city of Athene, motherless daughter of Zeus.

With all its Apollonian purity, it too represents the peak of a development, the first stages of which must have belonged to a world characterized by entirely different ideas and institutions. How then shall we understand the end if the beginnings remain a riddle to us? But where are these beginnings to be found? The answer is not in doubt. In myth, the faithful picture of the oldest era, and nowhere else.

The thirst for systematic knowledge has inspired many attempts to arrive at a picture of the origins by philosophical speculation, to fill in the great gaps in our historical records with the shadowy figures of abstract reasoning. A strange inconsistency: to reject myth as invention and to accept one's own utopias so confidently. In the following investigations we shall painstakingly avoid temptations of this sort. Cautiously, perhaps overcautiously, we shall steer our course along the solid land, following the bends and bays of the shoreline, avoiding the dangers and accidents of the high seas. Where no earlier experience is available, one must pay the closest attention to detail. Only an abundance of particulars can supply the comparisons which will enble us to distinguish the essential from the accidental, the lawful and universal from the local, and to arrive at increasingly universal principles.

It has been said that myth, like quicksand, can never provide a firm foothold. This reproach applies, not to myth itself, but only to the way it has been handled. Multiform and shifting in its outward manifestation, myth nevertheless follows fixed laws, and can provide as definite and secure results as any other source of historical knowledge. Product of a cultural period in which life had not yet broken away from the harmony of nature, it shares with nature that unconscious lawfulness which is always lacking in the works of free reflection. Everywhere there is system, everywhere cohesion; in every detail the expression of a great fundamental law whose abundant manifestations demonstrate its inner truth and natural necessity.

In the matriarchal culture the homogeneity of a dominant idea is particularly apparent. All its manifestations are of one mold, disclosing a self-contained stage in the development of the human spirit. The primacy of motherhood in the family cannot be regarded as an isolated phenomenon. It is utterly incompatible with a culture such as that of the Greek classical period. The opposition between the paternal and maternal systems is bound to permeate the entire life form surrounding them.

This homogeneity of matriarchal ideas is confirmed by the favoring of the left over the right side. The left side belongs to the passive feminine principle, the right to the active masculine principle. The role played by the left hand of Isis in matriarchal Egypt suffices to make the connection clear. But a multitude of additional data prove its importance, universality, primordiality, and freedom from the influence of philosophical speculation. Customs and practices of civil and religious life, peculiarities of clothing and headdress, and certain linguistic usages reveal the same idea, the *major honos laevarum partium* (greater honor of the left side) and its close connection with mother right. Another no less significant manifestation of the same basic law is the primacy of the night over the day which issued from its womb. The opposite relation would be in direct contradiction to matriarchal ideas. Already the ancients identified the primacy of the night with that of the left, and both of these with the primacy of the mother. And here, too, age-old customs, the reckoning of time according to nights, the choice of the night as a time for battle, for taking counsel, for meting out justice, and for practicing the cult rites, show that we are not dealing with abstract philosophical ideas of later origin, but with the reality of an original mode of life. Extension of the same idea permits us to recognize the religious preference given to the moon over the sun, of the conceiving earth over the fecundating sea, of the dark aspect of death over the luminous aspect of growth, of the dead over the living, of mourning over rejoicing, as necessary characteristics of the predominantly matriarchal age. In the course of our investigation all these traits will appear many times over and take on an increasingly profound meaning.

Already we have before us a world in which mother right no longer appears as a strange, incomprehensible form, but rather as a homogeneous phenomenon. The picture, however, still presents

77

numerous gaps and obscurities. But it is characteristic of all profound perceptions that they quickly gather related objects into their sphere and find their way from the patent to the hidden. A gentle hint from the ancients often suffices to open up new insights. An example may be found in the favored position of the sister and of the youngest child. Both notions are aspects of the matriarchal principle and both demonstrate new ramifications of the basic idea. The significance of sisterhood among the Germanic people is disclosed by an observation of Tacitus,[6] and a corresponding statement from Plutarch [7] about Roman customs proves that this is no accidental local notion, but a consistent and fundamental idea. The favoring of the youngest child is attested by many passages in Philostratus' *Heroicus*, a work which, though late, is extremely important for the elucidation of the oldest ideas. And vast numbers of examples, some taken from mythical tradition and others from the history of ancient or still living peoples, prove the universality and primordiality of both phenomena. It is not difficult to ascertain the aspect of the matriarchal idea they are related to. The favoring of the sister over the brother merely lends new expression to the favoring of the daughter over the son, and the preference given to the youngest child identifies the survival of the clan with the youngest scion of the maternal line, who, because he is last born, will also be last to die.

There is scarcely any need to point out what new perspectives are disclosed by these two observations. The judgment of man according to the laws of natural life, which leads to preference for the shoots of the springtime, is in perfect accord with the Lycian metaphor of the leaves of the trees; † it characterizes mother right as the law of material-corporeal, not of higher spiritual life, and shows the matriarchal world as a whole to be a product of the maternal-tellurian, not of the paternal-uranian attitude toward human existence.

And it hardly seems necessary to point out how many passages in ancient writings, how many phenomena of matriarchal cultures, were illuminated and made available for this work by Tacitus' remarks about the far-reaching implications of sisterhood as the basis of the Germanic family. The greater love for the sister leads us

† See p. 127.

into one of the noblest aspects of matriarchal culture. Hitherto we have stressed the juridical aspect of mother right, but now we perceive its ethical significance. Its juridical forms surprised us by their contrast with what we have become accustomed to regarding as the natural organization of the family; at first sight they seemed incomprehensible. The ethical aspect strikes a resonance in a natural sentiment which is alien to no age: we understand it almost spontaneously. At the lowest, darkest stages of human existence the love between the mother and her offspring is the bright spot in life, the only light in the moral darkness, the only joy amid profound misery. By recalling this fact to our attention, the observation of still living peoples of other continents has clarified the mythical tradition which represents the appearance of the φιλοπάτορες (father lovers) as an important turning point in the development of human culture. The close relation between child and father, the son's self-sacrifice for his begetter, require a far higher degree of moral development than mother love, that mysterious power which equally permeates all earthly creatures. Paternal love appears later. The relationship which stands at the origin of all culture, of every virtue, of every nobler aspect of existence, is that between mother and child; it operates in a world of violence as the divine principle of love, of union, of peace. Raising her young, the woman learns earlier than the man to extend her loving care beyond the limits of the ego to another creature, and to direct whatever gift of invention she possesses to the preservation and improvement of this other's existence. Woman at this stage is the repository of all culture, of all benevolence, of all devotion, of all concern for the living and grief for the dead.

Myth and history express this idea in any number of ways. The Cretan expressed his love for the land of his birth by the term "mother country"; origin in a common womb is regarded as the closest bond, as the true and originally the only relation of kinship; to help, to protect, and to avenge the mother is seen as the highest duty, while to threaten her life is looked upon as a crime beyond all expiation, even if it is done in the service of offended fatherhood.

There is no need of further details. These suffice to arouse our

79

interest in the ethical character of matriarchal culture. How significant become all those examples of loyalty to mothers and sisters; of men inspired by the peril or death of a sister to undertake the gravest hardships; and, finally, of pairs of sisters who stand out as universal prototypes. Yet the love that arises from motherhood is not only more intense, but also more universal. Tacitus, who hints at this idea in his account of the Germani but speaks explicitly only of the sister relationship, can scarcely have realized its full significance and its full historical scope. Whereas the paternal principle is inherently restrictive, the maternal principle is universal; the paternal principle implies limitation to definite groups, but the maternal principle, like the life of nature, knows no barriers. The idea of motherhood produces a sense of universal fraternity among all men, which dies with the development of paternity. The family based on father right is a closed individual organism, whereas the matriarchal family bears the typically universal character that stands at the beginning of all development and distinguishes material life from higher spiritual life. Every woman's womb, the mortal image of the earth mother Demeter, will give brothers and sisters to the children of every other woman; the homeland will know only brothers and sisters until the day when the development of the paternal system dissolves the undifferentiated unity of the mass and introduces a principle of articulation.

The matriarchal cultures present many expressions and even juridical formulations of this aspect of the maternal principle. It is the basis of the universal freedom and equality so frequent among matriarchal peoples, of their hospitality, and of their aversion to restrictions of all sorts. It accounts for the broad significance of such concepts as the Roman *paricidium* (parricide, or murder of a relative), which only later exchanged its natural, universal meaning for an individual, restricted one. And in it is rooted the admirable sense of kinship and συμπάθεια (fellow feeling) which knows no barriers or dividing lines and embraces all members of a nation alike. Matriarchal states were particularly famed for their freedom from intestine strife and conflict. The great festivals where all sections of a nation delighted in a sense of brotherhood and common nationality were first introduced among these peoples, and here achieved their finest expression. The matriarchal peoples—and this is no less characteristic—assigned special culpability to the physical injury of one's fellow men or even of animals. The Roman women entreated the Great Mother to provide a husband not for their own but for their sisters' children; the Persians never prayed to the godhead except for the whole nation; the Carians saw the supreme virtue in συμπάθεια for one's kin: in all these traits we find the maternal principle translated into the reality of life. An air of tender humanity, discernible even in the facial expression of Egyptian statuary, permeates the culture of the matriarchal world. And now an aura of Saturnian innocence seems to surround that older race of men who, subordinating their whole existence to the law of motherhood, provided later generations with the main features of their picture of the silver age. How natural we now find Hesiod's world, with its dominant mother lavishing eternal loving care on an ever dependent son who, growing more physically than spiritually, lives beside his mother to a ripe old age, enjoying the peace and abundance of an agricultural life; how close it is to the pictures of a lost happiness which always center round the dominance of motherhood, and to those ἀρχαῖα φῦλα γυναικῶν (primordial race of women) with whom all peace vanished from the earth. Here the historicity of myth finds a surprising confirmation. All the free fancy and poetic ornament in which memory always shrouds itself has been powerless to eradicate the historic core of the tradition, to efface the salient feature and meaning of this earlier life.

At this point I may be permitted to rest for one moment and interrupt the development of my ideas with a few general remarks. Study of the basic matriarchal idea has opened up our understanding for a great number of particular facts and phenomena. Puzzling in isolation, they assume in context a character of inner necessity. But such results can be achieved only on one condition. The scholar must be able to renounce entirely the ideas of his own time, the beliefs with which these have filled his spirit, and transfer himself to the midpoint of a completely different world of thought. Without such self-abnegation no real success in the study of antiquity is thinkable. The scholar who takes the attitudes of later generations as his starting point will inevitably be turned away from an understanding of the earliest time. The contradictions multiply; when it seems impossible to explain a phenomenon, the only way out seems to be to doubt and ultimately deny its existence. And that is why the scholarship and criticism of our time produces so few great and lasting results. True criticism resides in the material itself, and knows no other standard than its own objective law; no other aim than to understand the alien system; no other test than the number of phenomena which its basic principle explains. Where scholarship requires distortions, the falsification rests with the scholar and not with the sources to which, in his ignorance, arrogance, and carelessness, he likes to impute his own failings. The serious scholar must bear in mind that the world he is exploring is infinitely different from the one he is familiar with, and that his knowledge of it, however considerable, must always be limited; that his experience of life is usually immature, based as it is on the observation of a brief interval of time, while the material at his disposal is a heap of isolated ruins and fragments which often, seen from a single angle, seem inauthentic, but later, when transposed into their true context, belie such premature judgment.

From the standpoint of the Roman patriarchate the appearance of the Sabine women in the midst of the battle line was as inexplicable as the genuinely matriarchal form of the Sabine treaty, which Plutarch [8] unquestionably took from Varro. But if we consider them in conjunction with similar phenomena as recorded both in the ancient world and among still living peoples of a lower cultural stage, and in relation to the basic idea of mother right, they cease to puzzle us. They emerge from the realm of poetic invention to which modern opinion has relegated them and take their place as historical reality, as a perfectly natural consequence of the nobility, inviolability, and religious consecration of motherhood. Hannibal's pact with the Gauls stipulated that all disputes were to be settled by the Gallic matrons; and there are innumerable mythical traditions concerning women who either singly or in groups, alone or in collaboration with the men, mete out justice, participate in popular assemblies, and arbitrate peace treaties; who sacrifice their children and lay down their own lives to save their country. Who can speak of improbability, or incompatibility with all our experience and with the laws of human nature as they appear to us now, not to speak of invoking the poetic aura that surrounds these memories of the primordial era as an argument against their historical recognition? Shall we sacrifice the past to the present, or, to speak with Simonides, shall we make the world over according to wick and lamp? ** Shall we expunge whole millennia and turn history into a plaything of passing opinion? [9]

The critics speak of improbability, but probabilities change with the times; what is out of tune with the spirit of one cultural stage is in harmony with that of the next; what seems improbable in one becomes probable in the other. They mention incompatibility with all our experience: but subjective experience and the law of subjective thought have no bearing on history, unless everything is to be reduced to the level of private opinion.

Need we reply separately to those who invoke the poetic aura of the primordial age? Any attempt to deny the existence of such an aura is silenced by ancient poetry, and even by modern poetry, which has borrowed its most beautiful and moving motifs from that primeval world. As though poetry and sculpture had vied with one another in inventiveness, there is something in ancient, and even more in primordial times, that lends wings to the soul and raises our thoughts above everyday life. But this quality lies in the very nature of the era and is inherent to it; accordingly, it is itself a subject of inquiry rather than a means of discrediting the age to which it belongs.

The matriarchal period is indeed the poetry of history by virtue of the sublimity, the heroic grandeur, even the beauty to which woman rose by inspiring bravery and chivalry in men, by virtue of the meaning she imparted to feminine love and the chastity and restraint that she exacted of young men. To the ancients all this appeared in very much the same light as the chivalric nobility of the Germanic world to our own eyes. Like us, the ancients asked: What has become of those women whose unblemished beauty, whose chastity and high-mindedness could

** Bachofen's memory failed him here: he is referring to Alcaeus, *frg.* 66 (*Lyra Graeca*, Vol. 1, p. 360) ; see also p. 154.

awaken love even in the immortals? What has become of the heroines whose praises were sung by Hesiod, poet of the matriarchy? What has become of the feminine assemblies with which Dike herself liked to engage in familiar discussions? But where, too, are those heroes without fear and without reproach, who, like the Lycian Bellerophon, great for his chivalry and blameless life, combined bravery with voluntary recognition of the feminine power? All warlike peoples, Aristotle [10] remarks, serve the woman, and the study of later epochs teaches the same lesson: to defy danger, to seek out adventure, and to serve beauty—these virtues betoken the fullness of a nation's youth. Present conditions make all this look like fiction. But the highest poetry, more vibrant and moving than any fantasy, is the reality of history. The human race has experienced greater adventures than our imagination can conceive. The matriarchal age, with its figures, deeds, upheavals, is beyond the poetry of cultivated but enfeebled times. Let us never forget that when the power to perform high deeds flags, the flight of the spirit falters also, and incipient rot permeates all spheres of life at once.

I hope that the foregoing remarks have thrown new light on the methods by which I am seeking to investigate an era hitherto relegated to the shadows of poetic fancy. In resuming my interrupted exposition of the matriarchal world, I shall endeavor not to lose myself in the mass of variegated and always surprising details, but to concentrate on its most important manifestation, which may be regarded as the culmination and substrate of all others.

The religious foundation of matriarchy discloses this system in its noblest form, links it with the highest aspects of life, and gives a profound insight into the dignity of that primordial era which Hellenism excelled only in outward radiance, not in depth and loftiness of conception. Here more than ever I am aware of the broad gulf dividing my view of antiquity from current theories and the modern view of history based upon them. The idea of treating religion as a profound influence on the life of nations, of ranking it first among the creative forces which mold man's whole existence, of consulting it for illumination of the obscurest aspects of ancient thought, strikes present-day historians as indicative of an unnatural penchant toward theocracy, as narrow-minded incompetence, as a deplorable relapse into the Dark Ages.

I have heard all these accusations, and yet I remain faithful to the old conservative spirit. I should still rather be ancient than modern when investigating antiquity; I should still rather seek the truth than cater to the opinions of my time. There is only one mighty lever of all civilization, and that is religion. Every rise and every decline of human existence springs from a movement that originates in this supreme sphere. Without it no aspect of ancient life is intelligible, and earliest times in particular remain an impenetrable riddle. Wholly dominated by its faith, mankind in this stage links every form of existence, every historical tradition, to the basic religious idea, sees every event in a religious light, and identifies itself completely with its gods. If especially matriarchate must bear this hieratic imprint, it is because of the essential feminine nature, that profound sense of the divine presence which, merging with the feeling of love, lends woman, and particularly the mother, a religious devotion that is most active in the most barbarous times. The elevation of woman over man arouses our amazement most especially by its contradiction to the relation of physical strength. The law of nature confers the scepter of power on the stronger. If it is torn away from him by feebler hands, other aspects of human nature must have been at work, deeper powers must have made their influence felt.

We scarcely need the help of ancient witnesses to realize what power had most to do with this victory. At all times woman has exerted a great influence on men and on the education and culture of nations through her inclination toward the supernatural and divine, the irrational and miraculous. Pythagoras [11] builds his address to the women of Croton round woman's special aptitude for εὐσέβεια (piety), her vocation for religion; and Strabo,[12] following Plato, pointed out that from time immemorial women had disseminated all δεισιδαιμονία (fear of the gods), all faith and all superstition as well. This observation is confirmed by the historical facts of all times and peoples. In innumerable cases woman was the repository of the first revelation, and women played the most active part in the propagation of most religions, sometimes engaging in active warfare and often employing their physical charms. Prophecy began with women; woman is more steadfast than man as a keeper of religion, she is "stiffer in the faith"; though physically weaker, woman is capable at times of rising far above man; she is more conservative, most especially in religious matters and in the preservation of ceremonial. Everywhere woman strives to extend her religious influence, her proselytizing fervor is spurred by a feeling of weakness which makes her take pride in subjugating the stronger. Endowed with such powers, the weaker sex can take up the struggle with the stronger and emerge triumphant. To man's superior physical strength woman opposes the mighty influence of her religious consecration; she counters violence with peace, enmity with conciliation, hate with love; and thus she guides the wild, lawless existence of the earliest period toward a milder, friendlier culture, in whose center she sits enthroned as the embodiment of the higher principle, as the manifestation of the divine commandment. Herein lies the magic power of the feminine figure, which disarms the wildest passions and parts battle lines, which makes woman the sacrosanct prophetess and judge, and in all things gives her will the prestige of supreme law. The almost divine veneration of Arete, queen of the Phaeacians, the sanctity in which her word was held, are regarded by so early a writer as Eustathius [13] as poetic touches in a wholly invented fairy tale; and yet they are no isolated manifestation, but rather the perfect expression of a matriarchy resting wholly on a religious foundation, with all the blessings and beauty it could confer upon a nation's existence.

We have numerous indications of the intimate connection between matriarchy and woman's religious character. Among the Locrians only a maiden could enact the rite of the φιαληφορία (bearing of the sacrificial bowl). In citing this custom as the proof that mother right prevailed among the Epizephyrians, Polybius [14] recognized its conection with the basic matriarchal idea. Moreover, the Locrians sacrificed a maiden in expiation of Ajax's sacrilege. This confirms the same relation and indicates the basis of the widespread belief that female sacrifices are more pleasing to the godhead. And this line of thought carries us to the deepest foundation and meaning of the matriarchal idea. Traced back to the prototype of Demeter, the earthly mother becomes the mortal representative of the primordial tellurian mother, her priestess and hierophant, entrusted with the administration of her mystery. All these phenomena are of a piece, manifestations of one and the same cultural stage. This religious primacy of motherhood leads to a primacy of the mortal woman; Demeter's exclusive bond with Kore leads to the no less exclusive relation of succession between mother and daughter; and finally, the inner link between the mystery and the chthonian-feminine cults leads to the priesthood of the mother, who here achieves the highest degree of religious consecration.

These considerations bring new insight into the cultural stage characterized by matriarchy. We are faced with the essential greatness of the pre-Hellenic culture: in the Demetrian mystery and the religious and civil primacy of womanhood it possessed the seed of noble achievement which was suppressed and often destroyed by later developments. The barbarity of the Pelasgian world, the incompatibility of matriarchy with a noble way of life, the late origin of the mysterious element in religion—such traditional opinions are dethroned once and for all. It has long been a hobby with students of antiquity to impute the noblest historical manifestations to the basest motives. Could they be expected to spare religion, to acknowledge that what was noblest in it—its concern with the supernatural, the transcendent, the mystical—was rooted in the profoundest needs of the human soul? In the opinion of these scholars only self-seeking false prophets could have darkened the limpid sky of the Hellenic world with such ugly clouds, only an era of decadence could have gone so far astray. But mystery is the true essence of every religion, and wherever woman dominates religion or life, she will cultivate the mysterious. Mystery is rooted in her very nature, with its close alliance between the material and the supersensory; mystery springs from her kinship with material nature, whose eternal death creates a need for comforting thoughts and awakens hope through pain; and mystery is inherent in the law of Demetrian motherhood, manifested to woman in the transformations of the seed grain and in the reciprocal relation between perishing and coming into being, disclosing death as the indispensable forerunner of higher rebirth, as prerequisite to the ἐπίκτησις τῆς τελετῆς (higher good of consecration).††

All these implications of the maternal are fully confirmed by history. Wherever we encounter matriarchy, it is bound up with the mystery of the chthonian religion, whether it invokes Demeter or is embodied by an equivalent goddess. The relation between the two phenomena is clearly exemplified in the lives of the Lycians and Epizephyrians, whose high development of the mystery—revealed by a number of remarkable phenomena that have hitherto been misunderstood—accounts for the unusual survival of mother right among them. This historical fact leads us to an inescapable conclusion. If we acknowledge the primordial character of mother right and its connection with an older cultural stage, we must say the same of the mystery, for the two phenomena are merely different aspects of the same cultural form; they are inseparable twins. And this is all the more certain when we consider that the religious aspect of matriarchy is at the root of its social manifestations. The cultic conceptions are the source, the social forms are their consequence and expression. Kore's bond with Demeter was the source of the primacy of mother over father, of daughter over son, and was not abstracted from the social relationship. Or, in ancient terms: the cultic-religious meaning of the maternal κτείς (weaver's shuttle, comb, weaving woman) is primary and dominant; while the social, juridical sense *pudenda* (shame) is derivative. The feminine *sporium* (womb) is seen primarily as a representation of the Demetrian mystery, both in its lower physical sense and in its higher transcendent implication, and only by derivation becomes an expression of the social matriarchy, as in the Lycian myth of Sarpedon. This refutes the assertion of modern historians that mystery is appropriate only to times of decadence and is a late degeneration of Hellenism. History reveals exactly the opposite relationship: the maternal mystery is the old

†† Bachofen says in *Gräbersymbolik* (*Gesammelte Werke*, Vol. 4, p. 44):
"The two blessings bestowed on mortal men by the Demetrian initiation are material well-being on earth and a higher hope in death. This latter is predominant in τελετή. Εὐθηνία,, the blessing of abundance and well-being, is the gain for the duration of this life; ἐπίκτησις is the higher gain, the *adventicium lucrum* (gratuitous gain) which grants a happy outlook for the time after death.

element, and the classic age represents a late stage of religious development; the later age, and not the mystery, may be regarded as a degeneration, as a religious leveling that sacrificed transcendence to immanence and the mysterious obscurity of higher hope to clarity of form.

Hellenism is hostile to such a world. The primacy of motherhood vanishes, and its consequences with it. The patriarchal development stresses a completely different aspect of human nature, which is reflected in entirely different social forms and ideas. In Egypt Herodotus finds the direct antithesis to Greek, and particularly Attic, civilization. Compared to his Hellenic surroundings, Egypt struck him as a world upside down. If the father of history had subjected the two great periods of Greek development to a similar comparison, he would have been equally amazed at the contrast between them. For Egypt is the land of stereotyped matriarchy, its whole culture is built essentially on the mother cult, on the primacy of Isis over Osiris; it offers striking parallels to countless matriarchal phenomena presented by the life of the pre-Hellenic peoples. And history has provided still another striking example of this same contrast between the two civilizations. In the midst of the Hellenic world Pythagoras restored religion and life to the old foundations, he attempted to give a new consecration to existence and to satisfy man's profounder religious needs by reviving the mystery of the chthonian-maternal cults. Essentially Pythagoreanism does not develop Hellenism but combats it. As one of our sources says, a breath of the hoariest antiquity blows through it. Its origins lie, not in the wisdom of the Greeks, but in the more ancient lore of the Orient, of the static African and Asian world. Pythagoras sought his followers chiefly among those peoples whose adherence to ancient tradition seemed to present the closest affinity to his doctrine, particularly among the tribes and cities of Hesperia (Italy), a land which would seem to have preserved down to our own day religious stages that have disappeared elsewhere.

This preference for an older view of life brought with it a decided recognition of the Demetrian mother principle, a distinct leaning toward the mysterious, transcendent, supersensory element in religion, and above all the appearance of sublime priestess figures: can we fail to recognize the inner unity of these phenomena and their bond with the pre-Hellenic culture? An earlier world rises from the grave; life strives back toward its beginnings. The long intervening years vanish, and late generations merge with those of the primordial era as thought here had been no change in times and ideas. Only the chthonian-maternal mystery of the Pelasgian religion can account for the Pythagorean women; their acts and spiritual attitude cannot be explained by the concepts of Greek classicism. Separated from that cultic foundation, the religious character of Theano, the "daughter of Pythagorean wisdom," is a mere anomaly, a puzzle which we shall not get rid of merely by referring to the mythical origin of Pythagoreanism. The ancients confirm this connection by grouping Theano, Diotima, and Sappho together. Wherein consists the similarity of these three figures belonging to different times and nations? Where else than in the mystery of the maternal-chthonian religion? It is in these three outstanding figures that the religious vocation of Pelasgian womanhood achieves its richest and loftiest unfolding. Sappho's home was one of the great centers of the Orphic mystery religion, Diotima dwelt in Arcadian Mantinea, famous for its archaic way of life and its cult of the Samothracian Demeter; one is Aeolian, the other Pelasgian; both belonged to nations whose religion and culture had remained faithful to the pre-Hellenic foundations. In a woman of unknown name living among an archaic people untouched by Hellenism, one of the greatest of philosophers discerned a religious illumination not to be found amid the brilliant culture of Attica.

The central idea that I have emphasized from the outset, the relationship between the primacy of women and the pre-Hellenic culture and religion, is eminently confirmed by the very phenomena which, when viewed superficially and out of context, seem to argue most against it. Wherever the older mystery religion is preserved or revived, woman emerges from the obscurity and servitude to which she was condemned amid the splendor of Ionian Greece and restored to all her pristine dignity. Is there any further room for doubt as to wherein lay the foundation of early matriarchy and the source of all the benefits it conferred on the peoples it encompassed? Socrates at the feet of Diotima, hardly able to follow the flight of her mysterious revelation, freely admitting his need for the woman's wisdom: can there be any nobler expression of matriarchy, any more moving evidence of the inner kinship between the Pelasgian-maternal mystery and the feminine nature? Where shall we find a more perfect lyrical expression of the ethical principle of matriarchal culture, of love, this sanctification of motherhood? All epochs have admired this image, but our admiration is further enhanced if we regard it not merely as the creation of a great mind but also as a picture of matriarchal religion, of the feminine priesthood. Here again history rises above poetic fancy.

I shall pursue the religious basis of matriarchy no further: it is most deeply rooted in woman's vocation for the religious life. Who will continue to ask why devotion, justice, and all the qualities that embellish man's life are known by feminine names, why τελετή (initiation) is personified by a woman? This choice is no free invention or accident, but is an expression of historical truth. We find the matriarchal peoples distinguished by εὐνομία, εὐσέβεια, παιδεία (rectitude, piety, and culture); we see women serving as conscientious guardians of the mystery, of justice and peace, and the accord between the historical facts and the linguistic phenomenon is evident. Seen in this light, matriarchy becomes a sign of cultural progress, a source and guarantee of its benefits, a necessary period in the education of mankind, and hence the fulfillment of a natural law which governs peoples as well as individuals.

Here we are carried back to our starting point. We began by showing matriarchy to be a universal phenomenon, independent of any special dogma or legislation. Now we can go further in our characterization and establish its quality of natural truth. Like childbearing motherhood, which is its physical image, matriarchy is entirely subservient to matter and to the phenomena of natural life, from which it derives the laws of its inner and outward existence; more strongly than later generations, the matriarchal peoples. feel the unity of all life, the harmony of the universe, which they have not yet outgrown; they are more keenly aware of the pain of death and the fragility of tellurian existence, lamented by woman and particularly the mother. They yearn more fervently for higher consolation, which they find in the phenomena of natural life, and they relate this consolation to the generative womb, to conceiving, sheltering, nurturing mother love. Obedient in all things to the laws of physical existence, they fasten their eyes upon the earth, setting the chthonian powers over the powers of uranian light. They identify the male principle chiefly with the tellurian waters and subordinate the generative moisture to the *gremium matris* (maternal womb), the ocean to the earth. In a wholly material sense they devote themselves to the embellishment of material existence, to the πρακτική ἀρετή (practical virtues). Both in agriculture, which was first fostered by women, and in the erection of walls, which the ancients identified with the chthonian cult, they achieved a perfection which astonished later generations. No era has attached so much importance to outward form, to the sanctity of the body, and so little to the inner spiritual factor; in juridical life no other era has so consistently advocated maternal dualism and the principle of actual possession; * and none has been so given to lyrical enthusiasm, this eminently feminine sentiment, rooted in the feeling of nature. In a word, matriarchal existence is regulated naturalism, its thinking is material, its development predominantly physical. Mother right is just as essential to this cultural stage as it is alien and unintelligible to the era of patriarchy.

Thus far we have concerned ourselves with the inner structure of the matriarchal system and of the whole related culture. Now our investigation takes a different turn. Having studied the essence of matriarchal culture, we shall now consider its history; we have laid bare its principle, now we shall seek to determine its relation to other cultural stages. We shall consider the earlier, lower stage as well as the higher conceptions of the later age, both in their struggle with Demetrian mother right. We shall come face to face with a new aspect of history. We shall encounter great transformations and upheavals which will throw a new light on the vicissi-

---

* Apparently Bachofen means the duality of birth and death which women experience in their own bodies, and the physical possession of the unborn child.

tudes of human destiny. Every change in the relation between the
sexes is attended by bloody events; peaceful and gradual change is
far less frequent than violent upheaval. Carried to the extreme,
every principle leads to the victory of its opposite; even abuse
becomes a lever of progress; supreme triumph is the beginning of
defeat. Nowhere is man's tendency to exceed the measure, his
inability to sustain an unnatural level, so evident; and nowhere is
the scholar's capacity for entering into the wild grandeur of crude
but gifted peoples, and for making himself at home among utterly
strange ideas and social forms, put to so rigorous a test.

Although the struggle of matriarchy against other forms is revealed by diverse phenomena, the underlying principle of development is clear. Matriarchy is followed by patriarchy and preceded
by unregulated hetaerism. The Demetrian ordered matriarchy
thus assumes a middle position, representing the transition of
mankind from the lowest stage of existence to the highest. With
the former it shares the material-maternal standpoint, with the
second, the exclusivity of marriage; it is distinguished from the
early stage by the Demetrian regulation of motherhood, through
which it rises above hetaerism, and from the later stage by the
primacy it accords to the generative womb, wherein it proves to be
a lower form than the fully developed patriarchal system. Our
exposition will follow this order of development. We shall investigate first the relation of matriarchy to hetaerism, then the progress
from matriarchy to the patriarchal system.

The exclusivity of the marriage bond seems so essential to the
nobility and higher calling of human nature that most writers
accept it as an original state of affairs, and regard the theory that it
was preceded by lower, unregulated sexual relations as an absurd
fallacy arising from useless speculation about the beginnings of
human existence. Who would not like to share in this opinion and
spare our race the memory of so unworthy a childhood? But the
testimony of history forbids us to heed the voices of pride and self-
love. It cannot be doubted that the institution of marriage was the
outgrowth of a very slow progress. A phalanx of strictly historical
data descends upon us, making all resistance impossible. The
observations of the ancients join with those of later generations,
and even in our own times contact with peoples of lower cultural

levels lends empirical confirmation to this tradition. Among all the peoples considered in the following investigation, and many others besides, we find distinct traces of original hetaeric forms, and their conflict with the higher Demetrian principle can often be followed on the basis of recorded phenomena pertaining to the innermost life of the peoples in question. There is no doubt that matriarchy everywhere grew out of woman's conscious, continued resistance to the debasing state of hetaerism. Defenseless against abuse by men, and according to an Arabian tradition preserved by Strabo, exhausted by their lusts, woman was first to feel the need for regulated conditions and a purer ethic, while men, conscious of their superior physical strength, accepted the new constraint only unwillingly. This context alone enables us to understand the full historical significance of the strict discipline which is one of the distinguishing features of matriarchal life, and to accord conjugal chastity, the highest principle of every mystery, its proper place in the history of human manners. Demetrian matriarchy is intelligible only if we assume the existence of earlier, cruder conditions; its fundamental principle presupposes a contrary principle, in opposition to which it came into being. Thus the historicity of matriarchy supports the historicity of hetaerism.

But the supreme proof for the soundness of this view is to be sought in the close contact between the diverse manifestations of the anti-Demetrian principle. On careful scrutiny, they always reveal system, and this system points back to a fundamental idea which is rooted in religion, and cannot be regarded as accidental, arbitrary, or merely local. A bitter surprise is in store for those who look on marriage as a necessary and primordial state. The ancients held exactly the reverse, they regarded the Demetrian principle as an infringement on an older principle and marriage as an offense against a religious commandment. Strange as this stage of affairs may seem to the modern mind, it is supported by the testimony of history. And it alone can account for many significant phenomena which have never been seen in their proper context. How else shall we explain the idea that marriage demanded propitiation of the godhead whose law it transgressed by its exclusivity? Woman is not endowed with all her charms in order to grow old in the arms of one man: the law of matter rejects all restrictions, abhors all fetters, and regards exclusivity as an offense against its divinity. This accounts for the hetaeric practices surrounding marriage. Diverse in form, they are perfectly homogeneous in idea. Marriage as a deviation from the natural law of matter must be expiated, the good will of the godhead regained through a period of hetaerism. Hetaerism and strict conjugal law— these two principles that would seem forever to exclude one another—now enter into the closest connection: prostitution itself becomes a pledge of marital chastity, which exacts a previous fulfillment of woman's natural vocation. In its struggle against such views supported by religion itself, the progress to a higher ethic was bound to be very slow, because it was threatened at every step.

The diversity of intermediary states between hetaerism and matriarchy indicate the ups and downs in this millenary struggle. The Demetrian principle triumphed gradually, and in the course of time the expiatory sacrifice was steadily restricted. The gradations are extremly interesting. The sacrifice which was first performed annually is later enacted but once; originally practiced by matrons, hetaerism is now restricted to young girls; it is practiced no longer during but only before marriage, and even then it is no longer promiscuous but narrowed down to certain selected persons. In keeping with this limitation special hierodules are appointed—an important step toward a higher morality, since it transferred the obligation of all womanhood to a restricted class and freed matrons from the duty of prostitution. The mildest form of personal expiation was the sacrifice of the hair, which, in some cases regarded as equivalent to the body, was generally identified with the chaos of hetaeric generation and with swamp vegetation, its natural prototype. All these phases of development have left numerous traces, not only in myth but also in the history of widely divergent nations. They find linguistic expression in the names of localities, gods, and peoples. Such vestiges show us the struggle between the Demetrian and the hetaeric principle as a religious and historical reality, and for the first time make many of the most famous myths intelligible. Finally, they show how the matriarchate carried on its cultural mission by strict observance of the Demetrian law and continued resistance to any return to the purely natural law.

Significant support for our theory is provided by the statements of the ancients regarding the dowries of brides. It is generally known that the Romans held the *indotata* (dowerless woman) in no higher esteem than a concubine. But this notion, so contrary to all our opinions, has not been understood. Its true historical explanation is to be found in the economic aspect of hetaerism. Observance of the natural principle enabled a woman to earn her own *dos* (dowry), and this was one of the chief obstacles to the triumph of the Demetrian principle. If hetaerism was to be eradicated, it was necessary that brides should be dowered by their families. This explains why the *indotata* was despised and why, even in a relatively late period, marriage without dowry was considered a punishable offense. The dowry was an important factor in the struggle between the Demetrian and the hetaeric form of life. Hence we should not be surprised to find it linked with the highest religious ideas of matriarchy, such as the εὐδαιμονία (beatitude) after death promised by the mysteries, nor to learn that a highly remarkable Lesbian-Egyptian myth attributes the compulsory dowry to the legislation of an illustrious princess. †

Thus new light is thrown on the profound relation between the Demetrian idea of matriarchy and the daughter's exclusive right of inheritance; we gain a new understanding of the moral idea expressed in this law of inheritance and of the part it played in the moral elevation of peoples, in producing the σωφροσύνη (thoughtful virtue) for which the Lycians were particularly famed. According to ancient testimony the son receives from his father spear and sword in order to secure his existence; he needs no more. But if the daughter does not inherit, she possesses only her body with which to acquire the fortune that will win her a husband. The same view is still held today in those Greek islands whose former inhabitants recognized the law of matriarchy, and even Attic writers observe that despite the highly developed patriarchy of their people the entire maternal fortune was set aside for the dowry of the daughter, who was thus preserved from profligacy. In no institution is the inner truth and dignity of the matriarchal ideas more

† Berenice II, wife of Ptolemy III of Egypt, promulgated a dotal law which enabled a daughter to sue for payment of dowry if the mother had died before she had found a husband.

beautifully expressed: nowhere did the social position, the intrinsic dignity and purity of woman, find a more effective support.

The phenomena we have so far discussed leave no possible doubt as to the fundamental view from which they arose. Beside the Demetrian elevation of motherhood, we find a lower, more primordial view, the full, unrestricted naturalness of pure tellurism. We recognize the contrast between agriculture and the *iniussa ultronea creatio,* the unbidden wild growth of mother earth,** manifested most abundantly and luxuriantly in the life of the swamps. Hetaerism follows the prototype of wild plant life; the strict Demetrian law of marriage as it prevailed in highly developed matriarchy follows that of the tilled field. Both stages of life rest on the same basic principle: the domination of the generative womb; the difference lies only in the degree of closeness to nature with which they interpret motherhood. Hetaerism is bound up with the lowest level of plant life, matriarchy with the higher stage of agriculture. Hetaerism finds its principle embodied in the vegetation and animals of the marshy lowlands, which become its chief gods; matriarchy reveres the ear of grain and the seed corn, which become the most sacred symbols of its maternal mystery. The difference between these two stages of maternity is meaningfully expressed in a vast number of myths and rites; and everywhere the conflict between them is manifested as a religious and historical fact, the progress from one to the other as a sublimation of all life, an ascent to a higher culture. Schoeneus, the man of the marshes, Atalanta's golden fruit, Carpus' victory over Calamus, all embody the same conflict and the same principle of development, which is exemplified historically by the victory of the sublime Eleusinian mystery over the matrilinear swamp cult of the Ioxids. Everywhere nature guided the development of man, taking him on her knee, as it were; everywhere his historical progress passes through the same stages as nature itself. The importance which myth imputes to the inauguration of monogamy, the aura with which it surrounds the name of Cecrops because of this cultural deed, its emphasis on legitimate birth, as in the stories of Theseus and the ring and of the testing of Horus by his father, or in the joining of the word ἐτεός (authentic) to the names of individuals, clans, gods, and nations;

** See p. 192.

the Roman concept of *patrem ciere* (to [be able to] name one's father): all these originate, not in idle or poetic fancy, but in the memory of a great and necessary turning point in the lives of peoples. The exclusive motherhood which knows no father, which designates children as ἀπάτορες (fatherless) or in the same sense as πολυπάτορες (descended from many fathers), as *spurii*, σπαρτοί (sown ones), or with like meaning as *unilaterales* (generated from one side), and the begetter himself as οὐδείς (no one), *Sertor*, *Semo* (sower), is just as historical as the Demetrian domination of this same motherhood over the principle of paternity. Indeed, the development of Demetrian matriarchy presupposes the early stage, just as it in turn was prerequisite to the development of the patriarchate.

Generally speaking, the development of the human race knows no leaps, no sudden progressions, but only gradual transitions; it passes through many stages, each of which may be said to bear within it the preceding and the following stage. All great nature goddesses, in whom the generative power of matter has assumed a name and a personal form, combine the two levels of maternity, the lower, purely natural stage, and the higher, conjugally regulated stage. It is only in the course of development and under the influence of conditions varying from people to people that one or the other becomes preponderant. And this is one of the most crucial proofs of the historicity of a premarital stage. The progressive purification of the idea of the godhead points to a corresponding sublimation of life, and can only have taken place in conjunction with it, just as, conversely, every relapse into lower, more material conditions has its corresponding expression in the sphere of religion. The principle that determines the character of the gods once governed life and gave form to a period of human culture; the religion based on the contemplation of nature is necessarily a living truth, and its content therefore belongs to the history of our race. None of my fundamental views finds such frequent confirmation in the course of this inquiry, none throws a brighter light on the conflict between hetaerism and conjugal matriarchy. Two stages of life confront one another, each nourished by a religious idea. The soundness of the theories I have thus far set forth is perhaps best confirmed by the history of the

Epizephyrian Locrians. Nowhere do we find more noteworthy manifestations of the gradual rise of Demetrian matriarchy over the original Aphroditean *ius naturale* (natural law); the history of no other people shows so clearly how all political development is contingent on the defeat of hetaerism, or illustrates so strikingly the ineradicable force of earlier religious ideas and their ability to reassert themselves.

Our ascribing so critical an influence on the vicissitudes of political life to circumstances and events pertaining to the hidden sphere of family life may seem strangely out of keeping with present-day conceptions. And indeed, our students of ancient history have paid no attention whatever to that aspect of human development. But it is precisely the connection of the sexual relationship and the lower or higher interpretation with the totality of life and the destinies of nations that relates our study directly to the cardinal questions of history. The first great encounter between the Asiatic and Greek worlds is represented as a struggle between the hetaerism of Aphrodite and the conjugal principle of Hera; we shall find the cause of the Trojan War in a violation of the marriage bed; and by an extension of the same idea, we shall date the ultimate defeat of Aphrodite, mother of the Aeneads, by the matronly Juno at the time of the Second Punic War, when the Roman nation was at the height of its inner greatness.

The connection between all these phenomena is unmistakable and is now perfectly intelligible. To the Occident, with its purer, chaster nature, history entrusted the task of bringing about the lasting victory of the higher Demetrian principle, so liberating mankind from the fetters of the lowest tellurism in which the magic of the Orientals held it fast. The political idea of the imperium with which Rome entered into world history enabled it to complete this development. Like the Epizephyrian Locrians the Romans were originally subservient to the Asiatic Aphrodite; at all times they preserved far closer bonds with the distant homeland, particularly in matters of religion, than did the Greeks, who were emancipated earlier and more completely; their Tarquinian kings brought them into close contact with the maternal Etruscan culture; and in times of stress the oracle announced that Rome was in need of the mother whom only Asia could provide. Without the support of its imperial idea this city destined to provide the connecting link between the old and new worlds could never have triumphed over the Asiatic nature-bound conceptions of material motherhood; it could never have completely cast off the *ius naturale* (natural law) of which it long preserved the empty framework; it could never have accomplished the triumph over the seductions of Egypt that was glorified and one might say imaged in the death of the last wholly Aphroditean-hetaeric Candace of the Orient (Cleopatra), and in Augustus' contemplation of her lifeless body.

The spread of the Dionysian religion brought about a new turn in the struggle between the hetaeric and the Demetrian principle, a regression that was disastrous to all ancient civilization. This event occupies an extremely important position in the history of the matriarchate. Dionysus is foremost among the great adversaries of matriarchy, particularly in its extreme Amazonian form. Irreconcilably opposed to this unnatural degeneration of feminine existence, he everywhere called for fulfillment of the marriage law, return to the maternal vocation of womanhood, recognition of the glorious superiority of his own male-phallic nature. Thus the Dionysian religion seems to imply support of the Demetrian principle of marriage and at the same time appears to be one of the chief causes for the victory of the paternal principle. None of this can be denied. Nevertheless the Bacchic cult must be regarded as the most powerful ally of the hetaeric trend, as shown by the history of its influence on the whole ancient world. This religion, with its central emphasis on marriage, did more than any other to reduce the life of womanhood to the natural level of Aphroditism; this religion, which developed the male principle at the expense of womanhood, did more than any other to degrade man below the level of woman.

One of the main causes for the rapid triumph of the new god was the extreme Amazonian form of the old matriarchy and the universal barbarism inseparable from it. The stricter the law of maternity, the less woman was able to sustain the unnatural grandeur of her Amazonian life. Joyfully she welcomed this god whose combination of sensuous beauty and transcendent radiance made him doubly seductive. The enthusiasm of women for his cult was irresistible. In a short time the Amazonian matriarchy's determined resistance to the new god shifted to an equally resolute devotion; the warlike women, formerly locked in struggle with Dionysus, became his crusading army of heroes. One extreme followed the other, showing how hard it is, at all times, for woman to observe moderation. The historical foundation is evident from the traditions which record the bloody events attending the first propagation of the Bacchic religion and the profound upheavals provoked by it. These upheavals recur independently among the most divergent peoples, but their character is always the same. They present so striking a contrast to the later Dionysian spirit, with its emphasis on peaceful enjoyment and the embellishment of existence, that it is impossible to regard them as the fabrication of a later period.

The magic power with which the phallic lord of exuberant natural life revolutionized the world of women is manifested in phenomena which surpass the limits of our experience and our imagination. Yet to relegate them to the realm of poetic invention would betoken little knowledge of the dark depths of human nature and failure to understand the power of a religion that satisfied sensual as well as transcendent needs. It would mean to ignore the emotional character of woman, which so indissolubly combines immanent and transcendent elements, as well as the overpowering magic of nature in the luxuriant south.

Throughout its development the Dionysian cult preserved the character it had when it first entered into history. With its sensuality and emphasis on sexual love, it presented a marked affinity to the feminine nature, and its appeal was primarily to women; it was among women that it found its most loyal supporters, its most assiduous servants, and their enthusiasm was the foundation of its power. Dionysus is a woman's god in the fullest sense of the word, the source of all woman's sensual and transcendent hopes, the center of her whole existence. It was to women that he was first revealed in his glory, and it was women who propagated his cult and brought about its triumph. A religion which based even its higher hopes on the fulfillment of the sexual commandment, which established the closest bond between the beatitude of supersensory existence and the satisfaction of the senses, could not fail, through the erotic tendency it introduced into the life of women, to undermine the Demetrian morality and ultimately to reduce matriarchal existence to an Aphroditean hetaerism patterned after the full spontaneity of natural life.

History fully supports this conclusion. Dionysus' tie with Demeter was soon submerged by his bond with Aphrodite and similar nature mothers; the symbols of Demetrian regulated maternity, the ear of grain and the loaf of bread, gave way to the Bacchic grape, the exuberant fruit of the virile god; milk, honey, and water, the chaste sacrifices of the old time, ceded to wine, the inducer of sensual frenzy; and the religion of the lowest tellurism, of swamp generation with all its products, its animals as well as plants, gained preponderance over agriculture and its gifts. All life was molded by this same trend, as is shown above all by the ancient tombs which, in a moving paradox, became the chief source of our knowledge of the erotic sensuality of Dionysian womanhood. Once again we recognize the profound influence of religion on the development of all culture. The Dionysian cult brought antiquity the highest development of a thoroughly Aphroditean civilization, and lent it that radiance which overshadows all the refinement and all the art of modern life. It loosed all fetters, removed all distinctions, and by orienting people's spirit toward matter and the embellishment of physical existence, carried life itself back to the laws of matter. This sensualization of existence coincides everywhere with the dissolution of political organization and the decline of political life. Intricate gradation gives way to democracy, the undifferentiated mass, the freedom and equality which distinguish natural life from ordered social life and pertain to the physical, material side of human nature.

The ancients were well aware of this connection; as they stated in no uncertain terms, they regarded carnal and political emancipation as inseparable twin brothers. The Dionysian religion represented the apotheosis both of Aphroditean pleasure and of universal brotherhood; hence it was readily accepted by the servile classes and encouraged by tyrants—by the Pisistratids, the Ptolemies, and Caesar—since it favored the democratic development on which their tyranny was based. All these manifestations spring from the same source and are only different aspects of what the ancients themselves called the Dionysian age. Offshoots of an essentially feminine culture, they restored to woman the scepter wielded by Basileia in Aristophanes' bird state, favored her strivings for emancipation, as represented by Lysistrata and the Ecclesiazusae—characters drawn from the real life of the Attic-Ionian states—and so established a new Dionysian matriarchy, which asserted itself less in legal forms than in the silent power of an Aphroditism dominating all existence.

A comparison between the new and the original matriarchy discloses the contrast between the chaste, Demetrian character of a life grounded in strict order and morality and the new form essentially rooted in the Aphroditean principle of carnal emancipation. The older matriarchy was a source of lofty virtues and of an existence which, though limited in its ideas, was nevertheless secure and well ordered; the new form, beneath the sheen of a rich material and intellectual life, concealed a diminished vitality, a moral decay, which contributed more than any other cause to the decline of the ancient world. Masculine bravery went hand in hand with the older matriarchy; the Dionysian matriarchy weakened and degraded men to such a degree that the women came to despise them. It is a mark of the inner strength of the Lycian and Elean peoples that they, longer than any other, preserved the Demetrian purity of their maternal principle from the disintegrating influence of the Dionysian religion. As the secret doctrine of Orphism—despite its high development of the male-phallic principle—moved closer to the old feminine mysteries, the danger of its defeat increased. The change and its consequences can be discerned most clearly among the Epizephyrian Locrians and the Aeolians of Lesbos. But it was in Africa and Asia that the original matriarchy underwent the most thorough Dionysian transformation.

History has repeatedly shown how the earliest phenomena in the lives of peoples tend to reappear at the end of their development. The cycle of life returns to its beginning. In the following investigation it will be our unpleasant duty to demonstrate this sad truth beyond any possible doubt. The manifestations of this law are found chiefly, but by no means exclusively in the Oriental countries. As the inner disintegration of the ancient world progresses, the maternal-material principle reasserts itself more and more and Aphroditean hetaerism submerges the Demetrian principle. The *ius naturale*, belonging to the lowest sphere of tellurian existence, is again in evidence. And we see this law, the historical reality of which has been doubted even for the lowest stage of human development, in full force at the latest stage, with its conscious deification of the bestial side of our nature. The *ius naturale* becomes the heart and core of secret doctrines and is praised as the ideal of all human perfection. And we find innumerable parallels to the most puzzling features of the oldest tradition. But the phenomena which we encounter in mythical garb at the beginning of our investigation now take on the historical character of a late day, so proving that despite all freedom of action human development follows strict laws.

In my exposition of the various stages of the maternal principle and the conflicts between them I have repeatedly mentioned the Amazonian extreme of matriarchy and hinted at the important role played by this phenomenon in the history of the relation between the sexes. Actually Amazonism is closely bound up with hetaerism. These two noteworthy manifestations of feminine life condition and explain each other. Here we shall seek to clarify the relation between them in accordance with the traditions that have come down to us.

In speaking of the Amazon Omphale, Clearchus [15] remarks that wherever such an intensification of feminine power occurs, it presupposes a previous degradation of woman and must be explained by the necessary succession of extremes. This idea is confirmed by several of the most celebrated myths, the deeds of the women of Lemnos,† of the Danaïds, even Clytaemnestra's murder. Everywhere it is an assault on woman's rights which provokes her resistance, which inspires self-defense followed by bloody vengeance. In accordance with this law grounded in human

†† See pp. 173ff.

and particularly in feminine nature, hetaerism must necessarily lead to Amazonism. Degraded by man's abuse, it is woman who first yearns for a more secure position and a purer life. The sense of degradation and fury of despair spur her on to armed resistance, exalting her to that warlike grandeur which, though it seems to exceed the bounds of womanhood, is rooted simply in her need for a higher life.

Two conclusions follow from this conception, and both are confirmed by history. First, Amazonism is a universal phenomenon. It is not based on the special physical or historical circumstances of any particular people, but on conditions that are characteristic of all human existence. And it shares this character of universality with hetaerism. The same cause everywhere calls forth the same result. Amazonian phenomena are interwoven with the origins of all peoples. They may be found from Central Asia to the Occident, from the Scythian north to West Africa; beyond the ocean they are no less numerous and no less certain; and even in times very close to our own Amazonism has been observed, accompanied by the same acts of bloody vengeance against the male sex. In accordance with the law of human nature, it is precisely the earliest phases of human development that disclose the most typical and universal character.

The second conclusion is that Amazonism, despite its savage degeneration, signifies an appreciable rise in human culture. A regression and perversion at later cultural stages, it is, in its first appearance, a step forward toward a purer form of life, and not only a necessary stage of human development, but one that is beneficial in its consequences. In it a feeling of the higher rights of motherhood first opposes the sensual demands of physical strength; in it lies the first germ of the matriarchy which founded the political civilization of peoples. And this is thoroughly confirmed by history. Though it cannot be denied that regulated matriarchy itself gradually degenerated into Amazonian severity and Amazonian customs, the converse relation was the rule: the Amazonian form of life is an earlier manifestation than conjugal matriarchy, and is in fact a preparation for it. This is made clear in the Lycian myth which represents Bellerophon both as the conqueror of the Amazons and as the founder of matriarchy, and by virtue of these two deeds as the founder of his country's whole civilization.

Thus the importance of the Amazonian struggle against hetaerism for the elevation of womanhood and of all human existence cannot be questioned. The same development appears in the cult. Although both Amazonism and conjugal matriarchy are closely bound up with the moon, although their preference of the moon over the sun is a prototype of all feminine domination, the Amazonian moon reveals a gloomier, sterner character than does that of the Demetrian matriarchy. For the Demetrian matriarchy the moon is the image of marital union, the highest cosmic expression of that exclusivity which characterizes the bond between sun and moon; for the Amazon, on the other hand, the lonely nocturnal moon fleeing from the sun is the stern virgin, the enemy of lasting union; with its grinning, eternally changing face it is the hideous, deathly Gorgon whose very name is associated with Amazonism. There is no doubt that of the two conceptions of the moon, the lower, Amazonian one is the older, and this supports the historical position we have assigned to Amazonism. In all these traditions the parallel between cult and social forms, between religion and life, is evident. A new light is thrown on the equestrian Amazons' campaigns of conquest; they may well be somewhat elaborated in the legends but this historical foundation remains firm. Their purpose must be sought above all in the propagation of a religious system. The warriors derived their enthusiasm from their religious idea combined with the hope of establishing their own rule along with that of the goddess.

The destinies of the states growing out of these conquests confirm our interpretation and lend coherence to the history of the matriarchal world. Mythical and historical traditions complement and support one another, permitting us to discern a succession of interrelated stages. After war and warlike undertakings the victorious warriors settle down, build cities, and engage in agriculture. From the banks of the Nile to the shores of the Black Sea, from Central Asia to Italy, Amazonian names and deeds are interwoven with the history of the founding of cities which later became famous. To be sure, this transition from nomadism to domestic settlement is a necessary part of human development, but it is particularly in keeping with the feminine nature and occurs most quickly where the influence of women is paramount. The observation of still living peoples has shown that human societies are impelled toward agriculture chiefly by the efforts of women, while the men tend to resist this change. Countless ancient traditions support this same historical fact: women put an end to the nomadic life by burning the ships; women gave most cities their names, and, as in Rome or in Elis, women inaugurated the first apportionment of the land. In bringing about fixed settlement, womanhood fulfills its natural vocation.

All civilization and culture are essentially grounded in the establishment and adornment of the hearth. By a perfectly consistent continuation of the same development, life takes more peaceful forms and warfare ceases to be the principal occupation of the group. The exercise of arms was never wholly relinquished by the women of matriarchal states, who could not but regard it as indispensable for the defense of their position at the head of warlike peoples, and their preoccupation with horses is reflected even in relatively late religious iconography. Soon, however, where warfare did not become the exclusive business of men, they came at least to share it. Sometimes the male armies marched along with the equestrian women; and sometimes, as in the case of the Mysian Hiera, * the order was reversed.

Yet despite this gradual change in forms, woman's domination of state and family long remained undiminished. But even here a progressive shift was inevitable. Step by step the matriarchy was restricted. This development took divergent forms. Sometimes it is woman's political power that was first lost, and sometimes her rule over the family. In Lycia we are informed only of her family position; no record of her political power has come down to us, although we know that it was also inherited according to mother right. Elsewhere, conversely, the political power remained either wholly or partly in the hands of the women, whereas the family

* Hiera, according to Philostratus, *Heroicus* (Kayser, 299.30f.) was wife of Telephus, king of Mysia, and fought at Troy as leader of the Mysian women troops; Homer, he says, does not mention her because she was the greatest and fairest of all women, and would have outshone his heroine Helen.

ceased to be governed by mother right. Those elements of the old system that were indissolubly bound up with religion were longest to resist the spirit of the times, protected by the higher sanction that attached to everything connected with the cult. But other factors played a part. The geographical isolation of the Lycians and Epizephyrians; the topography and climate of Egypt and of Africa in general, helped to preserve the matriarchy. Elsewhere the political matriarchy was protected by its very weakness, or bolstered by artificial forms, such as are indicated by imputing the origin of letter writing to Asiatic queens confined to the interior of their palaces. †

In conjunction with these fragments of what was once an all-embracing system, the reports of Chinese writers on the women's state in Central Asia, which preserved both political and social matriarchy down to the eighth century of our era, take on a very special interest. They accord in all characteristic features with the ancient reports on the Amazonian states, and their praise of the general εὐνομία and tranquillity supports my own findings. It was not violence such as early destroyed most of the Amazonian settlements, including the Italic settlement of the Cleitae, that put an end to this existence. It was the quiet workings of time and contact with the powerful neighbor states that here effaced a social condition which for European man represents one of the oldest and obscurest of memories, and even today must be regarded as a forgotten aspect of history.

In a realm of inquiry like this, which resembles a vast heap of ruins, the use of records originating at very divergent times and among many different peoples is often the only means of gaining any light. Only by considering all the hints at our disposal can we put order into our fragmentary material. The different forms and manifestations of matriarchy among the peoples of the ancient world now appear to us as so many stages in a great historical process which began in the primordial era and can be followed down to very late periods—a process that is still going on among the peoples of Africa. Starting from Demetrian ordered ma-

---

† Bachofen here refers to Atossa, the mother of Xerxes, who is credited by some late authors with the invention of letter writing. See *Mutterrecht* (in *Gesammelte Werke*, Vol. 3, p. 976).

triarchy, we have gained an understanding of ancient hetaerism and Amazonism. Having considered this lower stage of existence, we shall now be able to recognize the true significance of the higher stage, and give the victory of the patriarchate its proper position in the history of mankind.

The progress from the maternal to the paternal conception of man forms the most important turning point in the history of the relations between the sexes. The Demetrian and the Aphroditean-hetaeric stages both hold to the primacy of generative mother-hood, and it is only the greater or lesser purity of its interpreta-tion that distinguishes the two forms of existence. But with the transition to the paternal system occurs a change in fundamental principle; the older conception is wholly surpassed. An entirely new attitude makes itself felt. The mother's connection with the child is based on a material relationship, it is accessible to sense perception and remains always a natural truth. But the father as begetter presents an entirely different aspect. Standing in no visi-ble relation to the child, he can never, even in the marital relation, cast off a certain fictive character. Belonging to the offspring only through the mediation of the mother, he always appears as the remoter potency. As promoting cause, he discloses an immaterial-ity over against which the sheltering and nourishing mother ap-pears as ὕλη (matter), as χώρα καὶ δεξαμενὴ γενέσεως (place and house of generation), as τιθήνη (nurse).

All these attributes of fatherhood lead to one conclusion: the triumph of paternity brings with it the liberation of the spirit from the manifestations of nature, a sublimation of human existence over the laws of material life. While the principle of motherhood is common to all spheres of tellurian life, man, by the preponderant position he accords to the begetting potency, emerges from this relationship and becomes conscious of his higher calling. Spiritual life rises over corporeal existence, and the relation with the lower spheres of existence is restricted to the physical aspect. Maternity pertains to the physical side of man, the only thing he shares with the animals: the paternal-spiritual principle belongs to him alone. Here he breaks through the bonds of tellurism and lifts his eyes to the higher regions of the cosmos. Triumphant paternity partakes of the heavenly light, while childbearing motherhood is bound up with the earth that bears all things; the establishment of paternal right is universally represented as an act of the uranian solar hero, while the defense of mother right is the first duty of the chthonian mother goddesses.

Myth takes this view of the conflict between the old and the new principle in the matricide of Orestes and Alcmaeon, and links the great turning point of existence to the sublimation of religion. These traditions undoubtedly embody a memory of real experiences of the human race. If the historical character of matriarchy cannot be doubted, the events accompanying its downfall must also be more than a poetic fiction. In the adventures of Orestes we find a reflection of the upheavals and struggles leading to the triumph of paternity over the chthonian-maternal principle. Whatever influence we may impute to poetic fancy, there is historical truth in the struggle between the two principles as set forth by Aeschylus and Euripides. The old law is that of the Erinyes, according to which Orestes is guilty and his mother's blood inexpiable; but Apollo and Athene usher in the victory as a new law; that of the higher paternity and of the heavenly light. This is no dialectical opposition but a historical struggle, and the gods themselves decide its outcome. The old era dies, and another, the Apollonian age, rises on its ruins. A new ethos is in preparation, diametrically opposed to the old one. The divinity of the mother gives way to that of the father, the night cedes its primacy to the day, the left side to the right, and it is only in their contrast that the character of the two stages stands out sharply. The Pelasgian culture derives its stamp from its emphasis on maternity, Hellenism is inseparable from the patriarchal view. The Pelasgians present a picture of material confinement, the Hellenes of spiritual development; the life of the Pelasgians is marked by the operation of unconscious law, that of the Hellenes by individualism; on the one hand we find acceptance of nature, on the other, a transcending of nature; the old limits of existence are burst, the striving and suffering of Promethean life takes the place of perpetual rest, peaceful enjoyment, and eternal childhood in an aging body. The higher hope of the Demetrian mystery lies in the mother's free gift, which is seen in the sprouting of the seed corn; the Hellene wishes to achieve everything, even the supreme goal, by his own efforts. In struggle he becomes aware of his paternal nature, in battle he raises himself above the maternity to which he had wholly belonged, in battle he strives upward to his own divinity. For him the source of immortality is no longer the childbearing woman but the male-creative principle, which he endows with the divinity that the earlier world imputed only to the mother.

It is assuredly the Attic race that carried the Zeus character of paternity to its highest development. Though Athens itself has its roots in the Pelasgian culture, it wholly subordinated the Demetrian to the Apollonian principle in the course of its development. The Athenians revered Theseus as a second woman-hating Heracles; in the person of Athene they set motherless paternity in the place of fatherless maternity; and even in their legislation they endowed the universal principle of paternity with a character of inviolability which the old law of the Erinyes imputed only to motherhood. The virgin goddess is well disposed to the masculine, helpful to the heroes of the paternal solar law; in her, the warlike Amazonism of the old day reappears in spiritual form. Her city is hostile to the women who moor their ships on the coasts of Attica in search of help in defending the rights of their sex. Here the opposition between the Apollonian and the Demetrian principle stands out sharply. This city, whose earliest history discloses traces of matriarchal conditions, carried paternity to its highest development; and in one-sided exaggeration it condemned woman to a status of inferiority particularly surprising in its contrast to the foundations of the Eleusinian mysteries.

What makes the study of antiquity especially instructive is that in almost all spheres of life it carried its development to a conclusion and fully realized every principle. Though its traditions have come down to us only in fragments, in this important respect it represents a whole. And this gives the study of antiquity an advantage which no other period can offer. Our knowledge is assured of a conclusion. A comparison between beginning and end becomes a source of rich enlightenment as to the nature of both. It is only the contrast that makes the peculiarities of each stage wholly intelligible.

Thus it is no irrelevant extension but a necessary part of my task to devote myself closely to the growth of paternity and the attendant transformation of life. The change from a matriarchal to a patriarchal conception will be followed most particularly in two fields: in connection with the adoption of children and with mantic. The adoption of children, unthinkable where purely hetaeric conditions prevail, is bound to take entirely different forms under the Demetrian and under the Apollonian principle. In the Demetrian world it is governed by the principle of maternal birth and cannot be disengaged from natural truth; but an Apollonian world, with its fictive paternity, will rise to the idea of a purely spiritual generation, a motherless paternity divested of all materiality. This will lead to the idea, lacking in matriarchy, of succession in a direct line, and to the Apollonian notion of family immortality. The same development can be shown for mantic, especially in regard to Iamidian prophecy. Maternal-tellurian at its lowest, Melampodian stage, it becomes wholly paternal-Apollonian at its highest level. Here it too stresses the idea of unbroken lineage, so providing a parallel to the spiritualized form of adoption. But what makes this prophecy doubly instructive is that it takes us to Arcadia and Elis, two of the main centers of matriarchy, and enables us to observe the similarity in the development of family law on the one hand, and of mantic and religion in general on the other.

A comparison between these two spheres of life shows us the lawful development of the human spirit with a high degree of objective certainty. Everywhere the same ascent from earth to heaven, from matter to immateriality, from the mother to the father, everywhere the Orphic principle, which in the trend from below to above sees a successive purification of existence, and herein discloses its fundamental contrast with Christian doctrine and its dictum: "For the man is not of the woman, but the woman of the man." [16]

The second main line of my investigation, a historical inquiry into the matriarchy's struggle with the higher and lower stages of life, is grounded in a study of the inner relationship between the gradual spiritual progress of man and the hierarchy of cosmic manifestations. The absolute antithesis between our present-day thinking and that of antiquity is nowhere so startlingly disclosed as in the field upon which we are entering. The subordination of spiritual to physical laws, the dependence of human development on cosmic powers, seems so strange that one feels tempted to relegate it to the realm of philosophical dreams, or to put it down as "feverish fancy and higher nonsense." ** And yet it is no aberration of ancient or modern speculation, no unfounded parallel, no theory at all, but rather, if I may so express myself, objective truth, empiricism and speculation at once, a philosophy revealed in the historical development of the ancient world itself. All parts of ancient life are shot through with it, at all stages of religious development it stands out as a guiding principle, it is the foundation of all progress in the family law. It is this truth that sustains the whole edifice, and it is the only key to an understanding of numerous myths and symbols that have hitherto seemed inexplicable.

Our exposition up to this point already takes us one step closer to the ancient view of life. By showing how each stage in family organization depended on a religious idea, it implies that family relations must be subordinated to the same natural phenomena as religions. And at every step the study of antiquity provides new confirmation of this truth. The stages of sexual life, from Aphroditean hetaerism down to pure Apollonian paternity, all have their corresponding prototypes in the stages of natural life, from the wild vegetation of the swamps, the model of motherhood without marriage, down to the harmonious law of the uranian world and the heavenly light, the *flamma non urens* (flame without fire), which corresponds to the spiritual fatherhood that forever rejuvenates itself. So regular is the relationship that from the predominance of one or the other of the great heavenly bodies in the cult we can infer the form of the relation between the sexes. In one of the leading sites of the moon cult,†† for example, the masculine or

** The expression is from Conrad Bursian's devastating review of *Gräbersymbolik* in Zarncke's *Literarisches Centralblatt* (1860), pp. 228f.

†† Here Bachofen may have had in mind Carrhae, near Edessa in Syria, where the moon was worshiped as both Lunus (masc.) and Luna (fem.). See Aelius Spartianus, *Caracalla* 6.6 and 7.3–5, and cf. Tertullian, *Apology* 15.

feminine name given to the luminary can be taken as an expression of male or female dominance.

Of the three great cosmic bodies—earth, moon, sun—the first is the vehicle of maternity, while the last governs the development of the paternal principle; the lowest stage of religion, pure tellurism, insists on the primacy of the maternal womb. It situates the seat of virility in the tellurian waters and in the winds, which belong to the earth's atmosphere and hence to the chthonian system. It subordinates the male to the female principle, the ocean to the *gremium matris terrae* (womb of mother earth). The night is identified with the earth and interpreted as a maternal-chthonian power; here the night is the oldest of deities and stands in a special relation to woman. The sun, on the other hand, exalts men's eyes to contemplate the greater glory of the male power. The diurnal luminary ushers in the triumph of the patriarchate. The development takes place in three stages, two of which exactly follow the natural manifestation, while the third strives to transcend it. With the sunrise ancient religion associates the idea of triumph over the maternal darkness, and in the mysteries this idea often appears as the foundation of transcendent hopes. But in this early phase the radiant son is still wholly governed by his mother, the day is a ἡμέρη νυκτερινή (nocturnal day), and as fatherless scion of the great Eileithyia, the *mater matuta* (mother of dawn), it still belongs to the matriarchate. Total liberation from the maternal bond occurs only when the sun achieves the full unfolding of its luminous power. At the zenith, equidistant from the hour of birth and the hour of death, from the shepherd driving it into the fold and the shepherd who will drive it out again, it is triumphant paternity, subjugating the mother with its radiance, just as she dominated Poseidonian masculinity. This is the Dionysian stage of father right, the stage of the god who is celebrated both as the fully developed solar power and as the founder of paternity. The two manifestations of his nature correspond exactly. Like the sun in its fullest virility, Dionysian paternity is the phallic fecundator; like Sol, the Dionysian father forever seeks receptive matter in order to arouse it to life.

Wholly different and far purer is the third stage of solar development, the Apollonian stage. The phallic sun, forever fluctuating between rising and setting, coming into being and passing away, is transformed into the immutable source of light. It enters the realm of solar being, leaving behind it all idea of fecundation, all yearning for mixture with feminine matter. Dionysus merely raised paternity over the mother; Apollo frees himself entirely from any bond with woman. His paternity is motherless and spiritual, as in adoption, hence immortal, immune to the night of death which forever confronts Dionysus because he is phallic. It is thus that we perceive the relation between the two solar powers and the two paternities based on them in the *Ion* of Euripides, which exactly follows Delphic ideas and is even more significant than Heliodorus' novel for the following inquiry.

Between the two extremes, the earth and the sun, the moon takes the middle position which the ancients designate as the borderland between the two worlds. The purest of tellurian bodies, the impurest of uranian luminaries, it becomes the image of the maternity which attains its highest purification in the Demetrian principle; as a heavenly earth it contrasts with the chthonian earth, just as the Demetrian matron contrasts with the hetaeric woman. Accordingly, conjugal mother right is always bound up with the religious pre-eminence of the moon over the sun, and the higher religious idea of the Demetrian mystery, which provides the foundation of matriarchy, is seen as the gift of the moon. Luna, as also in the Dionysian mystery, is both mother and source of religion, and in both aspects she is the prototype of the matriarchal woman.

Here we have no need to go more deeply into the ideas of antiquity on this point: my investigation will show how indispensable they are for the understanding of a thousand details. But for now the basic principle suffices. The dependence of the different stages of sexual life on the cosmic phenomena is no freely constructed parallel, but a historical phenomenon, an idea conceived by history itself. Should man, the supreme manifestation of the cosmos, alone be free from its laws? Grounded in the hierarchy of the great cosmic bodies, which successively dominated the cult and ideas of the ancient peoples, the development of family organization takes on the highest degree of inner necessity and lawfulness; the passing manifestations of history become the expression of the divine creative ideas which are the foundation of religion.

The foregoing considerations also enable us to appreciate the final stage in the history of the sexual relation. Now that we have surveyed all the stages in the development, from unregulated tellurism down to the purest form of solar domination, and successively examined their historical, religious, and cosmic manifestations, one question still remains to be answered if our treatise is not to be incomplete. What is the ultimate form achieved by antiquity in this connection?

There would seem to have been two powers capable of fully realizing the paternal principle. These were the Delphic Apollo and the Roman political idea of the masculine imperium. History teaches that mankind owes less to Apollo than to the idea of the imperium. Though perhaps less spiritual than the Delphic idea, the imperial principle possessed in its juridical form an intimate bond with all public and private life, a support which was utterly lacking in the purely spiritual power of the god. Thus, while the idea of the imperium could triumph against all attacks and hold its own against barbarization and the steady relapse into material views, the Apollonian idea was unable to withstand the increasing assaults of baser doctrines. We see paternity falling back from Apollonian purity to Dionysian materiality, so preparing the way for a new victory of the feminine principle, for a new flowering of the mother cults. Although the intimate union which the two luminous powers concluded in Delphi seemed calculated to purify Dionysus' phallic exuberance through Apollo's immutable repose and clarity, and to lift it above itself, the consequence was the exact opposite: the greater sensuous appeal of the fecundating god outweighed his companion's more spiritual beauty, and increasingly usurped the power that should have been Apollo's. Instead of the Apollonian age, it was a Dionysian age that dawned; Zeus handed down the scepter of his power to none other than Dionysus, who assimilated all other cults, and finally became the focus of a universal religion which dominated the whole ancient world. In the *Dionysiaca* of Nonnus [17] the gods Apollo and Dionysus vie for the prize in the presence of the assembly. Apollo looks up, certain of victory, whereupon his adversary offers the fiery wine. Blushing, Apollo drops his eyes, for he has no comparable gift. This scene embodies both the sublimity and the weakness of Apollo and discloses the secret of Dionysus' victory. The encounter between the Greek and the Oriental world, brought about by Alexander, takes on a special importance in this connection. We see the two great antitheses locked in struggle, but finally reconciled in some measure by the Dionysian cult. Nowhere was Dionysus more worshiped, nowhere did he find a more exuberant cult, than in the house of the Ptolemies, who found in it a means of fusing the foreign with the indigenous elements.

The following treatise will give special attention to this historical conflict as it is manifested in sexual relations and observe the stubborn resistance of the indigenous Isis principle to the Greek theory of paternity. Two traditions, one mythical, the other historical, will concern us most particularly. In the story of the contest in wisdom between Alexander and the Indian-Meroitic Candace contemporary mankind set forth its view of the relation between the male-spiritual principle, eminently embodied in Alexander, and the maternal primacy of the Asiatic-Egyptian world. The story recognizes the higher divinity of the paternal principle, but at the same time suggests that the heroic youth who strode swiftly across the stage before the astonished eyes of two worlds could not lastingly subject the feminine principle, which he was condemned to acknowledge at every step. The second tradition is strictly historical and dates from the reign of Ptolemy I. This is the story of how Sarapis of Sinope [18] was introduced into Egypt while the Delphic god and the pure paternal principle were deliberately circumvented.

It is of the utmost interest that the Greek dynasty was compelled from the very start to take such measures in order to cement its rule. The records of political and of religious history are in full agreement. The spiritual principle of the Delphic Apollo could not set its imprint on the life of the older world, it was powerless to overcome the lower material views of the sexual relation. Mankind owes the enduring victory of paternity to the Roman political idea, which gave it a strict juridical form and consequently enabled it to develop in all spheres of existence; it made this principle the foundation of all life and safeguarded it against the decadence of religion, the corruption of manners, and a popular return to matriarchal views. Roman law maintained its traditional principle against all the assaults and threats of the Orient, against the spreading mother cult of Isis and Cybele, and even against the Dionysian mystery; it withstood the principle of feminine fertility, first introduced into legislation by Augustus; it withstood the influence of the imperial wives and mothers who, scorning the old Roman spirit, sought, not without success, to seize the *fasces* (rods, the judicial power) and the *signa* (insignia, military power); it held firm against Justinian's inclination toward the wholly natural view of the sexual relation, toward equal rights for women, and toward the veneration of childbearing motherhood. Even in the Orient it was able to combat with success the never fully extinguished resistance to the Roman deprecation of the feminine principle.

A comparison between this power of the Roman political idea and the weakness of a purely religious principle shows us all the frailty of human nature left to itself, unprotected by strict forms. The ancients looked on Augustus, the adoptive son who avenged the death of his spiritual father, as a second Orestes, and regarded his reign as the dawn of a new Apollonian era. Yet mankind does not owe the triumph of this highest stage to the inner strength of the religious idea, but essentially to the political formation of Rome, which could modify but never wholly relinquish its fundamental ideas. This belief is eminently confirmed by the relation between the propagation of the Roman juridical principle and the growth of the Egyptian mother cult. Precisely when the subjection of the Orient was complete and the last Candace had fallen, the maternal principle, defeated in the political arena, started with redoubled strength on a new triumphant march, winning back from the Occident in the religious field what seemed irrevocably lost in the political sphere. The struggle, concluded in one field, was transferred to another, higher sphere from which it would later shift back again. The new victories of the maternal principle over the revelation of purely spiritual paternity show how hard it has been for men, at all times and amid the most varied religious constellations, to overcome the inertia of material nature and to achieve the highest calling, the sublimation of earthly existence to the purity of the divine father principle.

These last considerations complete the circle of ideas within which the following dissertation will move. The limits at which our inquiry stops are not arbitrarily drawn, but set by the facts of history. And equally free from arbitrary choice are my methods of inquiry and presentation, concerning which I still owe the reader some explanation. A historical investigation which must be the first to gather, verify, and collate all its material, must everywhere stress the particular and only gradually progress to comprehensive ideas. Success depends on the most complete investigation and unprejudiced, purely objective appraisal of the material. From this circumstance follow the two criteria which will determine the organization of our forthcoming inquiry. The entire material is arranged according to nations; these supply our supreme principle of classification. Each section opens with a consideration of the most significant records. The very nature of this method precludes a logical progression in our exposition of the ideas relating to matriarchy; instead, we shall have to follow the documents regarding each people, stressing sometimes this and sometimes another aspect. Moreover, we shall have to deal repeatedly with one and the same question.

In a field of research offering so much that is new and wholly unknown, such differentiation and repetition should not be condemned or regretted. Both are inseparable from a system which otherwise possesses important advantages. The life of peoples is rich and varied. Influenced by circumstances and specific developments, the basic ideas of an individual nation at a given cultural stage take a great many different forms. Subsequently, similarities tend to recede and particular traits to come to the fore; and we shall see that under the influence of manifold circumstances a given aspect of life will decline at an early stage in one place and thrive in another. It is obvious that only a separate examination of each people can do justice to this wealth of historical formations and keep our investigation from dogmatic onesidedness. Research which aims at extending the field of history and the scope of our historical knowledge cannot content itself with merely erecting a system; rather it must strive to understand life in all its movements and manifestations. An all-embracing point of view may have great merit, but it can only be demonstrated by reference to detail: only when the general is combined with the specific and the total character of a cultural period is illustrated by the traits of individual peoples does the twofold need of the mind for unity and variety find satisfaction. Each nation that enters the sphere of our investigation provides the over-all picture and history of gynocracy with new facets and sheds new light on aspects formerly neglected. Thus our understanding will grow in the course of investigation; gaps will be filled in; initial observations will be confirmed, modified, or amplified by others; our knowledge will gradually be rounded out and gain inner cohesion; higher and higher perspectives will result; and finally they will all be joined in the unity of one supreme idea. Greater than our pleasure at the result is the satisfaction that comes from contemplation of its gradual development. If our book is not to lose this charm, we must concern ourselves less with noting results than with describing the gradual development by which they are achieved. We shall therefore require the co-operation of the reader at every step. The author will always be at pains not to inject his own presence between the reader's observation and the ancient material, not to distract the reader's attention from the object which alone warrants it. Only what one acquires by one's own effort is of value, and nothing is so repellent to human nature as a ready-packaged product. The present book makes no other claim than to provide the scholarly world with a new and well-nigh inexhaustible material for thought. If it has the power to stimulate, it will gladly content itself with the modest position of a preparatory work, and cheerfully accept the common fate of all first attempts, namely, to be disparaged by posterity and judged only on the basis of its shortcomings.

Lycia

ANY INVESTIGATION of matriarchy must start with the Lycians. It is in connection with this people that we possess the richest and most definite documentation. Hence our first task will be to gain a solid foundation by examining what the ancient writers say of them.

Herodotus reports that the Lycians originally came from Crete and that under Sarpedon they were known as Termilians, which name was still given them by their neighbors at a later date; but that when Lycus, son of Pandion, came from Athens to the land of the Termilians to visit Sarpedon, they were named Lycians after him.

The historian himself continues: "Their customs are partly Cretan and partly Carian. However, they have a strange custom which no other people has: they take their names from their mother, not from their father. For when one asks a Lycian who he is, he will indicate his descent on his mother's side, and list his mother's mothers, and when a woman citizen marries a slave, the children are regarded as nobly born; but if a male citizen, even the noblest, takes a foreign woman or a concubine, the children are dishonorable." [1] What makes this passage so remarkable is that it describes the custom of naming after the mother in connection with the legal position of the children, hence as part of a basic attitude whose consequences are fully realized.

Herodotus' observation is confirmed and completed by other writers. The following fragment has come down to us from

121

Nicolaus of Damascus' *Universal History:* "The Lycians show the women more honor than the men; they take their names from their mothers and leave their estates to their daughters, not to their sons." [2] Heraclides Ponticus has the brief notation: "They have no written laws but only unwritten usages. From time immemorial they have been ruled by their women." [3]

In addition we have the remarkable tale told by Plutarch, for which he cites the authority of Nymphis of Heraclea. Literally translated, it runs: "Nymphis relates in his fourth book on Heraclea that a wild boar once laid waste the region of Heraclea, destroying animals and fruits, until he was slain by Bellerophon. But when the hero received no thanks for his deed, he cursed the Xanthians and besought Poseidon to make the whole earth produce salt. And so everything went to ruin, because the earth had grown bitter, and this went on until Bellerophon, out of consideration for the pleas of the women, once again besought Poseidon to put an end to his devastation. Thence comes the custom among the Xanthians of taking their names not from their father but from their mother." [4] Nymphis' story represents matrilinear appellation as the outcome of a religious attitude; the fertility of the earth and the fertility of woman are seen as a single context.

This last notion is brought out even more strongly in another version of the same myth. In the same passage Plutarch relates: "The story that is said to have taken place in Lycia looks very much like a fable, but it is based on an old myth. According to this myth Amisodarus, or as the Lycians call him, Isaras, came from the Lycian settlement near Zeleia with several pirate ships, which were commanded by Cheimarrhus, a warlike but savage and cruel man. He sailed in a ship whose bow bore the sign of a lion and whose stern that of a serpent, and inflicted great harm on the Lycians, so that they could neither put out to sea nor inhabit the cities of the coast. Bellerophon killed him by pursuing him with Pegasus; he also drove out the Amazons, but could not obtain his merited reward, but was treated most unjustly by Iobates. Therefore he went into the sea and besought Poseidon to make this land barren and fruitless. When he went away after this prayer, a wave arose and flooded the land. It was terrible to see the sea rise and follow after him, covering the plain. The men could obtain nothing with their entreaty that Bellerophon halt the sea, but when the women, gathering up their garments, came toward him, he retreated out of modesty, and at the same time, as it is related, the waters went back with him." [5]

Here Bellerophon appears in a twofold relation to the race of women. On the one hand he combats and defeats the Amazons. On the other hand, he retreats at the sight of womanhood and cannot refuse to acknowledge the women, so that he becomes the virtual founder of Lycian matriarchy. This twofold relation, comprising both victory and defeat, is highly remarkable. It shows us mother right in conflict with father right, which carries off only a partial victory. Amazonism, this extreme offshoot of mother right, is destroyed by the Corinthian hero, the scion of Sisyphus. The warlike man-killing virgins are defeated. But the higher right of woman, restored to marriage and her sexual vocation, issues victorious from the struggle. Only the Amazonian perversion of matriarchy, not matriarchy itself, is destroyed.

Mother right is grounded in the material nature of woman. In the myths we have cited, woman is equated with the earth. Just as Bellerophon bows to the sign of feminine fertility, so Poseidon draws back his devastating waves from the menaced land. The male fecundating power cedes the higher right to receptive, generative matter. What the earth, mother of all things, is to Poseidon, the earthly mortal woman is to Bellerophon. Γῆ (earth) and γυνή (woman), or Gaia, are equated. Woman takes the place of the earth and continues the primordial motherhood of the earth among mortals. The fecundating male appears as representative of the all-begetting Oceanus. Water is the fecundating element. When it mixes with the feminine earth matter, which it permeates and fertilizes, the germ of all tellurian life is developed in the dark depths of the maternal womb. Thus Oceanus is set in opposition to the earth and man to woman. Who has first place in this union? Which member will be dominant, Poseidon or the earth, man or woman? This conflict is described in the myth we have cited. Bellerophon and Poseidon seek the victory of father right. But they both withdraw in defeat before the sign of receptive motherhood. Salt, symbol and content of the male power, will serve not to devastate matter, but to fecundate it. The material principle of motherhood triumphs over the immaterial awakening power of the man.

The same is suggested in other aspects of the myth. Bellerophon must content himself in the end with a half conquest. His victory is followed by defeat. Aided by Pegasus, whom he had tamed with Athene's help, he had fought and destroyed the Amazons. He had descended from the cool upper air above to attack them.[6] But when he undertook to mount still higher with his winged steed and gain the luminous heights of heaven, the anger of Zeus was aroused. Hurled down, Bellerophon fell into the Aleian meadow. His defeat distinguishes him from the other combaters of mother right, from Heracles, Dionysus, Perseus, and the Apollonian heroes, Achilles and Theseus. They destroy all matriarchy along with Amazonism; as pure powers of light, they exalt the incorporeal solar principle of paternity over material and tellurian mother right. But Bellerophon cannot attain the pure heights of celestial light. Fearfully he looks down at the earth, which takes him back as he falls headlong from the heights into which he has ventured. Pegasus, the winged steed born from the bleeding trunk of the Gorgon, the stallion whom Athene had taught her favorite to curb, attains the goal of his heavenward flight, but the earthly rider sinks back to earth, to which as Poseidon's son he belongs. In him the masculine is still the Poseidonian aquatic principle that plays so prominent a part in the Lycian cults. The physical foundation of his being is the tellurian water and the ether surrounding the earth, which takes its moisture and gives it back again in an endless cycle. He is not destined to rise beyond this tellurian sphere to the solar heights, to transfer the paternal principle from matter to the sun. He cannot follow the flight of the divine stallion.

The winged steed also belongs primarily to the tellurian water, the realm of Poseidon. From his hoof flows the fertilizing spring. But Pegasus has transcended that lower principle. Wings bear him up to heaven where dutifully he announces each morning to Aurora the approach of the radiant sun god. But he is not the sun itself, only its messenger. On earth and in heaven he obeys woman: on earth Athene, in heaven Mater Matuta, the Eos of the Greeks. He himself, like Bellerophon, still stands in mother right, but as

Aurora points to the approaching sun, so he points to the higher solar principle, in which father right reposes. Though he has surpassed the lowest stage, he has not yet achieved the highest.

Thus far we have only touched on that aspect of the Lycian myth that is closely connected with matriarchy. But the myth also contains another side, a discussion of which will contribute considerably to the understanding of our subject. Three children were born to the hero by Philonoë-Cassandra, daughter of Iobates: Isander, Laodamia, and Hippolochus. The first two were snatched away from him by the will of the gods. Hated by the gods, the lonely father wanders through the Aleian meadow, consumed with sorrow and avoiding the paths of mortals, until he too is struck down by bitter death. Thus the hero, who expects to achieve immortality, sees himself and his race succumb to the law of earthly matter. Like the Delian Anius,[7] man of sorrow (ἀνία), he must survive the death of his children and himself meet death in the end. Here is the root of his pain, of his feeling that he is detested by the gods. What Ovid says of Cinyras is true also of him: *si sine prole fuisset, inter felices Cinyras potuisset haberi* (if he were without progeny, Cinyras might be numbered among the happy).[8] Here again we see Bellerophon in the same light as above. The son of Poseidon belongs to the matter that is governed by death, not to the luminous heights were immortality reigns. It is not his lot to attain immortality. He falls to earth, where he meets his doom. He belongs to the world of endless becoming, not to the world of being. Everything that material energy brings forth is doomed to death. Though the energy itself may be immortal, everything that it produces is fated to be mortal. Poseidon represents the energy, Bellerophon the product.

Only in the sequence of the generations is the race immortal. "So one generation of men will grow while another dies."[9] "The race of mortals, like the realm of plants, always moves in a circle," says Plutarch. "The one blooms into life, while the other dies and is mown down."[10] And beautifully Virgil sings of the bees, in whose state nature has provided the purest prototype of mother right:

Though short their course of life, and death may catch them early,
  (Seven summers they have at most),
The race remains immortal, for many years survive

The family fortunes, their fathers are known to the fourth generation.

Death itself is the precondition of life, and life dissolves into death in order that the race may remain imperishable in the eternal alternation of the two poles. This identity of life and death, theme of an endless number of myths, has found sharp expression in Bellerophon. He bears within him the Poseidonian principle of fecundation, but at the same time, and we may say for this very reason, he is the servant of death, representative of the destructive principle of nature. He is so designated by his name, Bellerophontes or Laophontes: the fecund son of Poseidon, he is named "murderer of the people." His career opens with the involuntary slaying of his brother, with the "murder of his own blood." The generative power is at the same time the power of destruction. He who awakens life works for death. In tellurian creation coming into being and passing away run side by side. In no moment of earthly existence do they depart from one another. At no time, in no tellurian organism, is life conceivable without death. What one takes away the other replaces, and only as the old vanishes can the new arise.

The outward manifestation of the principle is prey to never-ending destruction; only the principle itself endures forever. Like the Chimaera, Bellerophon's threefold race is engendered for death. It is subject to the same law. The father may have failed to realize this in his youth, but in his old age he perceives it in his own progeny. Like Thetis, he vainly deludes himself that what mortal man has bred can be endowed with immortality. In vain he has escaped from the ambush laid him by Iobates, while the Moliones fall into Heracles' trap at Nemea. Now he becomes aware that one lot, one *fatum*, Diomedean * necessity, strikes lower and higher creation, that the gods surround all things earthly with the same wrath. The Lycian Daedalus, the masculine architect of life, is also stung by the swamp serpent, so meeting the death which he had thought to evade. That is why Bellerophon accuses the immortals of ingratitude. That is why he invokes Poseidon's vengeance on the Lycian earth. He wishes to punish with barren-

---

* See *Iliad* VIII, 133ff., and Graves, *Greek Myths*, 166, 1, end.

ness the maternal matter that has borne him children in vain, bringing forth only the mortal and providing nourishment only for death; hence, like Pygmalion,[12] he withdraws into solitude. Rather no progeny than such as succumb forever to destruction. What is the purpose of eternally fruitless labor? Why should Ocnus grow old plaiting his rope when the she-ass keeps eating it up? Why should the Danaïd keep pouring water into a barrel riddled with holes? Hereafter let the salt not engender but destroy, making the maternal matter not fertile but barren. So the disillusioned Sisyphid implores in his despair. The fool! He is blind to the innermost law of all tellurian life, the law to which he himself belongs, the law that governs the womb. Only in the halls of the sun, which he vainly seeks to reach, do immortality and imperishable existence reign; under the moon the law of matter prevails, with death assigned as twin brother to all life.

> Yet if one, keeping wealth, surpass in beauty likewise
> and show his strength by excellence in the games,
> let him yet remember the limbs he appoints are mortal
> and that he must put upon him earth, the end of all things.[13]

Wiser than his father is Hippolochus' noble son Glaucus, who bears the name of Poseidon himself.† When Diomedes meets him in battle and questions him about his lineage, he replies with the simile of the leaves with which Homer precedes his narration of the myth of Bellerophon:

> As is the generation of leaves, so is that of humanity.
> The wind scatters the leaves on the ground, but the live timber
> burgeons with leaves again in the season of spring returning.
> So one generation of men will grow while another dies.[14]

What Bellerophon did not know is here movingly stated by the son of Hippolochus. One law governs the highest and the lowest creation; as the leaves of the tree, so the generations of men. Sisyphus forever pushes the stone, and forever it rolls insidiously down toward the house of Aides. Leaves, animals, men are renewed by the eternal labors of nature, but always in vain. This is the law and destiny of matter, which Bellerophon too, at the sight

† Γλαυκός, "bluish-green," an epithet of the sea.

of the maternal furrow, recognizes finally as the lot of all children born of woman.

In the mouth of the Lycian the simile has a twofold meaning, for it unmistakably discloses the foundation of Lycian mother right. The leaves of the tree do not spring from one another, but all alike from the stem. Leaf does not generate leaf; rather, the tree is the common mother of all leaves. So are the generations of man according to the matriarchal view. For here the father signifies no more than the sower who vanishes once he has strewn the seed in the furrow. That which is begotten belongs to the maternal matter which has enclosed it, borne it to the light, and which now nurtures it. But this mother is always the same: ultimately she is the earth, represented by earthly woman throughout the succession of mothers and daughters. Just as the leaves spring not from one another but from the stem, so men spring not from one another but from the primordial principle of matter, from Poseidon Phytalmios (producer) or Genesios (originator), the stem of life. Consequently, it seems to Glaucus that Diomedes shows a lack of understanding in inquiring into his lineage. But the Greek who disregards the material standpoint, who derives the son from the father and reckons only with the awakening male principle, has a frame of mind which explains and justifies his question. The Lycian, on the other hand, answers him from the context of mother right, which does not distinguish man from the rest of tellurian creation and judges him, like animals and plants, only according to the matter from which he issued. The father's son has a line of ancestors who are joined by no bond perceptible to the senses; but the mother's son has but one ancestor throughout the generations, the primordial mother earth. Why then should one name the successive leaves?

The contrast between the two attitudes may be made still clearer. In the system of father right, *mulier familiae suae caput et finis est*,[15] (woman is the beginning and end of her family). Regardless of how many children a woman may bear, she founds no family, she has no continuation, but only a purely personal existence. Under mother right the same is true of man. Here the father, there the mother is the fallen leaf which, once dead, leaves no memory and is no longer named. The Lycian expected to name his fathers is like a man who might seek to list the fallen and forgotten leaves of a tree. Faithful to the material law of nature, he replies to Tydides with its eternal truth: the simile of the tree and its leaves. He justifies the Lycian attitude by showing its consonance with the material laws of nature, which the Greek patriarchate has forsaken.

The transience of material life goes hand in hand with mother right. Father right is bound up with the immortality of a supramaterial life belonging to the regions of light. As long as religion recognizes the seat of the generative principle in tellurian matter, the law of matter prevails: man is equated with unlamented lower creation and mother right governs the reproduction of man and beast. But once the creative principle is dissociated from earthly matter and joined with the sun, a higher state sets in. Mother right is left to the animals and the human family goes over to father right. At the same time mortality is restricted to matter, which returns to the womb whence it came, while the spirit, purified by fire from the slag of matter, rises up to the luminous heights of immortality and immateriality. Thus Bellerophon is a mortal representative of mother right, while Heracles, founder of father right, dwells in the luminous heights with the Olympian gods. Everything supports the inference that mother right pertains to matter and to a stage of religion which knows only the life of the body; consequently, like Bellerophon, it mourns the eternal death of all creatures. Father right, on the other hand, pertains to the supramaterial principle of life. It identifies itself with the incorporeal power of the sun, with a spirit which rises above all change and attains to the luminous heights of the divine. Mother right is the Bellerophontic, father right the Heraclean principle; the former is the Lycian, the latter the Hellenic stage of culture; matriarchal is the Lycian Apollo, whose mother is Latona, queen of the swamp bottoms, and who dwells in the land of his birth only during the six dead winter months; patriarchal is the Hellenic god exalted to metaphysical purity, who rules over Delos during the six life-giving summer months.

And now, in order to leave no possible room for doubt in this so little understood and yet so rich and meaningful Lycian-Corinthian myth, let us consider certain further details.

In Plutarch's narrative Bellerophon drives the Amazons from Lycia, which, like the rest of Asia Minor, they had invaded from the north. Other documents go into greater detail. According to the *Iliad* [16] and Pindar,[17] according to Apollodorus [18] and the scholia to Pindar [19] and Lycophron,[20] the army of female archers was wholly exterminated by the hero, and this deed was not inferior to his victories over the triform monster Chimaera, the devastating wild boar, or the devastating hordes of the Solymi. But the monuments of art seem to contradict this view; for here Bellerophon is supported by the Amazons in his battle against the Chimaera. His enemies have become his allies.[21]

This shift from hostility to alliance recurs in the myths of the great Amazon fighters, particularly Dionysus and Achilles. Both in literature and art the Amazons frequently appear in the train of the heroes whom they first confronted in battle. In some extremely well-known versions warfare turns into love. As Penthesilea dies in his arms, Achilles perceives her beauty and is smitten with passion for his defeated foe. Here and in many variants of the same motif the idea is always the same. The woman recognizes the higher strength and beauty of the man and gladly inclines to the victorious hero. Weary of her heroic Amazonian grandeur, which she can sustain only for a short time, she willingly bows down to the man who gives her back her natural vocation. She realizes that not warfare against man but love and fertility are her calling. Thus she willingly follows him who has redeemed her by his victory. She protects the fallen foe against the renewed assault of her furious sisters, as in a relief of the temple of Apollo at Bassae.[22] Like the Danaïd who alone of all the sisters spares the bridegroom, the maiden would now rather be soft than cruel and brave. Sensing that the enemy's victory restores her true nature, she renounces the hostility that had spurred her on to battle with him. Given back to the limitations of womanhood, she awakens the man's love; for the first time he recognizes her full beauty and is stricken with grief at the fatal wound which he himself had been compelled to deal. Not battle and murder should prevail between them, but love and marriage, in accordance with woman's natural vocation. Thus Bellerophon's alliance with the Amazons presents no contradiction to the literary versions that show them locked in battle. Like the last act of a tragedy, it restores the natural relationship that had been so violently upset by the Amazons.

Pindar represents Bellerophon as radiant with strength and youthful beauty. But because he is chaste, he is slandered and persecuted by Stheneboea-Anteia.[23] The names of Proetus' wife allude clearly enough to the nature of the maternal earthly matter, waiting and yearning for fecundation.** In the Corinthian woman we recognize the Platonic Penia (want), who is forever pursuing men, in order to obtain forever fresh fecundation, forever new children. Penia, as Plutarch explains, meant to Plato "matter which intrinsically requires the good, and is being filled with it, which forever yearns for it and forever partakes of it," [24] hence the earth in its hetaerism. In this episode Bellerophon represents the sanctity of conjugal union. He rejects hetaerism as well as Amazonism, resolutely opposing these two perversions of womanhood, alienation from its natural calling and unregulated indulgence in it. And in both these respects he became the benefactor of Lycia and earned the gratitude of women. The conquered army of Amazons followed him willingly. In the chastity of marriage, the handmaidens of Artemis found the fulfillment of their higher calling, from which they were diverted no less by the unregulated love of men than by hostility to men. Bellerophon is the adversary of all unregulated, wild, destructive strength. The slaying of the Chimaera made possible regulated argiculture; the destruction of Amazonism and hetaerism opened the paths to strictly exclusive marriage. The two deeds go hand in hand, wherefore the hero is rewarded by the hand of Philonoë and the gift of fertile fields.

The principle of agriculture is the principle of ordered sexual union. Mother right pertains to them both. Just as the grain of the field emerges from the furrow opened by the plow, so the child issues from the maternal *sporium* (womb), from the κῆπος (garden, vagina); for the Sabines called the feminine field

** *Stheneboea:* strength of cattle; *Anteia:* flowering (both according to Graves, *Greek Myths*, index).

sporium, whence *spurii,* "the sowed ones," from σπείρω (I sow). So Plutarch relates.[25] His, too, was the idea that the principle of love lies in wounding, which is why Amor bears arrows. The earth is wounded by the plowshare, the woman's womb is wounded by the man's *aratrum* (plow). Both these relations justify the connection between the plow and Poseidon, the fecundating water god.[26] What is born from the *sporium* has only a mother, whether it be earth or woman. The father is of no more importance than the plow, than the sower who passes over the tilled field, casting the grain in the opened furrow, and then disappears into oblivion. The Romans formulated this principle in juridical terms. "All produce is gathered not according to the right of the seed, but the right of the soil," says Julian; or again: "In gathering fruit, more heed is given to the right of the body from which they are taken, than to that of the seed from which they grow." [27] Cujacius recognizes the same principle in connection with illegitimate children. It is also stated in *Codex Iustianianus:* "It is the law that the slave girl takes her status from the mother and is unaffected by the position of the father." [28] For the slave girl is subject to the *ius naturale* of material creation, which equates the woman with the *solum* (soil) and the father with the sower; she has no rights, under the *ius civile,* which always modifies and curtails the *ius naturale.* "It is not the earth that imitates the mother," Cujacius remarks, "but the mother who imitates the earth." [29] The seed takes on the nature of the soil, not the soil that of the seed. "A seed sown in a foreign country," says Plato, "cannot maintain itself, but tends to be overpowered and to degenerate into the native seed." [30] Thus *one* law, the material law of matriarchy, governs both agriculture and marriage.

Special attention must be given to the connection between mother right and conjugal chastity. Although the consequences of mother right, the maternal derivation of name and status, presuppose and characterize extramarital relations where the paternal system is in force, under mother right they accompany marriage and imply strict marital chastity. Matriarchy subsists within and not outside of matrimony. It does not stand in opposition to marriage but is its necessary concomitant.

Indeed, the very word matrimony (literally mother-marriage)

is based on the fundamental idea of mother right. One said *matrimonium*, not *patrimonium* (father-marriage, paternal inheritance), just as one originally spoke of a *materfamilias. Paterfamilias* is unquestionably a later term. Plautus uses the word *materfamilias* several times, *paterfamilias* not once. According to mother right there is, to be sure, a *pater*, but no *paterfamilias. Familia* is a purely physical concept, and hence relates at first only to the mother. The transfer to the father is an *improprie dictum* (a derived term), adopted as a legal term but only later prevalent in common nonjuridical usage. The father is always a juridical fiction, the mother a physical fact. Paulus states: "The mother is always certain, even though she has conceived by all and sundry; the father, on the other hand, is only he who is mentioned in the marriage certificate." [31] As Paulus puts it, mother right is *natura verum* (true by nature), the father exists only *iure civili* (in civil law). But *natura* is the physical law of matter, hence the maternal aspect of nature. From this it follows that the right of adoption cannot be imputed to the mother. "Mother is a term of nature, not of civil law. Adoption, however, is a juridical term." [32] Because of this natural basis of motherhood, the child's love is directed first and foremost toward its mother. "A mother loves her child more than a father does," says Menander, "for she knows it's her own while he but thinks it's his." [33] In the *Odyssey* Telemachus says: "My mother says I am his son, I myself do not know; for no one of himself knows his father." [34] Consequently the *uterini* (those born of the mother) are closer to one another than the *consanguinei, eodem patre nati* [35] (those engendered by one father). Thus in the *Iliad* Helen explains her love for the Dioscuri on the ground that they were born of one mother.[36] But Lycaon, son of Priam, seeks to mollify the angry Achilles by calling out: "I am not from the same womb as Hector, he who killed your powerful and kindly companion." [37] For it was upon Laothoë, daughter of Altes, king of the Leleges, that Priam begot Lycaon.[38] Thus the *uterini* were held to be more closely related, bound by closer ties of friendship than the *consanguinei*, and this is fully in accord with mother right, grounded as it is in natural truth. *Matrimonium* is held to be an expression of higher love, and this corresponds to the Cretan term "beloved mother country," which, according to Plato, expresses a very special bond that is not embodied in the term "father-land." [39]

It would be a mistake to identify the peoples showing matriar-chal forms with that bottommost stage of life in which there is no marriage but only natural sexual relations, as among animals. Matriarchy does not precede culture but is itself a cultural phase. It corresponds to agriculture, to a regulated tilling of the soil, not to the natural generation of the earth, not to the swamp vegetation with which the ancients identified hetaeric sexuality. [40] The swamp growth was equated with the *nothus* (illegitimate child), the cultivated plant with the *legitimus*. Even though mother right is *iuris naturalis*, because it springs from the laws of matter, this *ius naturale* is already restricted by the positive institution of mar-riage; it is no longer in full force as in the animal world. It is circumscribed by *matrimonium*, and free sexual ralations are precluded.

For the sake of contrast let us now consider some ancient accounts of peoples who recognized no *matrimonium* but observed mother right in conjunction with wholly natural sex relations, among whom the *ius naturale* preserved unrestricted sway. We know of several transitional states between the completely natural life and the recognition of exclusive marriage—and even this last is sometimes darkened by vestiges of the old bestial condition. In my treatment of these matters I shall lay special stress on the stages by which the human race rose from wholly bestial conditions to the marriage bond, and so seek to show the gradual transformation from *ius naturale* to a positive *ius civile*.

At the lowest stage of existence man's sexual life is promis-cuous and public. Like the animals, he satisfies the urge of nature before the eyes of all, and forms no lasting bond with any particular woman. The common enjoyment of women and public intercourse are attested with the greatest certainty for the Massage-tae. Herodotus writes: "Each man marries a woman, but all are permitted to make use of her. For what the Greeks attribute to the Scythians is not true of the Scythians, but of the Massagetae. Whenever a man lusts after a woman, he hangs up his quiver in front of her wagon and calmly lies with her." [41] On this occasion he thrusts his staff in the earth,[42] an image of his own act. Concerning the same Massagetae Strabo writes: "Each man marries one woman, but they also use those of the others, and not covertly. The man who thus lies with a strange woman hangs his quiver in front of her wagon and cohabits with her quite openly." [43] Herodotus frequently groups the Nasamones with the Massagetae. For example: "In accordance with their custom each one has many women and they copulate with them in common. In so doing they observe the same custom as the Massagetae: they thrust their staffs into the ground." [44] In both cases sexual intercourse is public and promiscuous.

We find public cohabitation combined with marriage among the Mosynoeces, concerning whom we have reports both by Dionysius [45] and Diodorus: [46] "The soldiers [of Cyrus II] said that this was the most barbarous people they had encountered on their march; that the men had copulated with their women before the eyes of all." Xenophon says the same.[47] To this category, according to Herodotus, also belong the Ethiopian Ausians, who lived by the Tritonian lake: "They use their women in common and copulate with them after the manner of cattle, without living with them domestically." [48] Concerning the Garamantes, another large Ethiopian tribe, only their communal ownership of women is recorded.[49] Although the public character of their mating is not mentioned, it seems highly probable in view of the fact that the Ethiopians regarded the dog as the supreme symbol of the godhead. This we find attested by Pliny,[50] Aelian,[51] and Plutarch.[52] The dog is an image of the hetaeric earth which delights in all fecundation. Given to unregulated and always visible copulation, he represents the principle of animal reproduction in its crudest form. There is no doubt that κύων (dog) and κύειν (fecundate), associated by Plutarch,[53] originate in the same basic stem, although there is no justification for deriving the one from the other. In Egypt, Plutarch tells us, the dog had been held in the highest veneration from time immemorial.

In this connection I should like to cite a report from Nicolaus of Damascus' collection of strange customs, preserved by Stobaeus in his *Florilegium*: "The Ethiopians hold their sisters in particular honor. The kings leave their scepter not to their own children but to those of their sisters. If no heir is available, they choose the most beautiful and belligerent as their leader." [54] This last observation is confirmed by Herodotus [55] and Strabo. [56] The favoring of the sister's children is a necessary consequence of mother right and is also to be found elsewhere.

Other Ethiopian tribes restrict the hetaerism of their women to the marriage night. Concerning the Augiles, who knew no other god than the dead, Mela writes: "It is a solemn custom among their women that on their wedding night they are prepared to cohabit with all who bring presents, and the woman who has lain with the most men is held to be the most beautiful; aside from this, they are characterized by reserve." [57] This may be compared with the following report on the inhabitants of the Balearic Islands: "They have a strange marriage custom. At the wedding banquet the oldest of the friends and acquaintances lies first with the bride, and after him the others in their turn, according as one is younger than the other, and the bridegroom is the last to whom this honor falls." [58] Concerning the African Gindanes Herodotus relates: "Their women wear bands around their ankles, each one a great number. They are made of hides and have the following significance: Every time she lies with a man the woman puts on such a band. The one who has the most bands is regarded as the most excellent, since she has been loved by the most men." [59]

Sextus' observation on the origin of the *dos* (dowry), [60] which is supported by Plautus' well-known line, addressed to the Etruscan woman, "You earn your dowry with your body," [61] explains the presents which the Augiles bring the bride. They are the hetaera's fee, comprising her marriage portion, just as in the mysteries the initiate lays an *aes meretricium* (prostitute's fee), a *stipes* (tax) in Aphrodite's lap, and in return receives the phallus from her. [62] The married life of the Augiles is characterized by *pudicitia insignis* (distinctive modesty). But this does not preclude an initial hetaerism, which is regarded as a pledge of future chastity. All these features recur among the Babylonians, Locrians, Etruscans. And the Thracians, too, combine strict marriage with hetaerism among the young girls: "They do not guard the girls but leave them full freedom to lie with whomever they please. But they guard the women strictly; they buy them from their parents for much money." [63]

Similar to the Ethiopians are the nomads of Cyrenaica: "Although they are scattered in families without order and law, and never take counsel for a common end, they nevertheless are quite numerous, because the women belong in common to the individual clans and thus there are many children and relations. [64] Here we see the communal possession of women restricted to a particular clan. Only relatives remain together; but there are always many of them because the women are in the majority. Here the freedom of sexual relations provides the primary bond among members of a sizable human community.

Strabo reports a similar state of affairs among the Arabs: "The brothers are held in higher esteem than the children. Rule over the clan and other dignities are ordered according to primogeniture. All blood kin hold their property in common. But the oldest is the ruler. All have *one* woman. He who comes first goes in and lies with her. He leaves his staff standing before the door, for all carry staffs. She spends the night with the eldest. Thus they are all brothers to one another. They also cohabit with their mothers. Adultery is punished by death. An adulterer is a man belonging to another clan. One of their kings had a daughter who was very beautiful; she had fifteen brothers who all loved their sister and visited her one after another without stopping. Fatigued by this uninterrupted cohabitation, she devised a stratagem. She fashioned staffs like those of her brothers. Then when one of them left her, she set the staff corresponding to his before the door and soon thereafter another and still another, always taking care that the one whose turn it was should not find his own. Once when all were together at the market, one of them wanted to visit her, but found his staff before the door. From this he concluded that an adulterer must be with the girl. He ran to their father, and brought him to the house, but soon discovered how he had been deceived by his sister." [65] This tale is of special interest because it deals not with a unique episode but with a general state of affairs. In it we see the pure natural law of the animals restricted to the clan, but accorded full recognition within these limits.

Marriage is alien and positively repellent to the natural law of matter. Its exclusivity is an infringement on the rights of Mother Earth. Helen is not endowed with all the charms of Pandora in order to become the exclusive possession of one man. When she offends against the marriage bond and follows the fair Alexander (Paris) to Ilium, it is less in response to her own wishes than to the commandment of Aphrodite and to the femininity that made her proverbial as the "eternal woman," an epithet, we might mention in passing, which Plutarch applies to Alcibiades.[66] Accordingly, the woman who marries must propitiate Mother Nature by a period of free hetaerism, and purchase the chastity of matrimony by previous unchastity. The hetaerism of the marriage night, as we find it among the Augile, Balearic, and Thracian women, springs from this idea. It is a sacrifice to the material Nature Mother, by which to reconcile her with the ensuing chastity of marriage. That is why the bridegroom is last to receive the honor. In order to gain lasting possession of the woman, her husband must first leave her to others. According to the *ius naturale* the woman is a harlot, an Acca Larentia, who gives herself "to the chance comer" [67] like earthly matter, like Penia who yearns for ever-renewed fecundation. Like the Arabian princess, the woman should give herself to men to the point of exhaustion, just as the Roman temple of Horta always stood open.[68] It is a sin for her to obtain peace by trickery and by fashioning false staffs. She should be an *obsequens* (willing one), a Lubentina, always encouraging, never reluctant, a true Horta, a goader of men. The Arabian people have remained true to this natural law, which the Augile woman infringes but seeks to appease by her hetaerism of the first night. The adulterer is always the alien, never the blood kinsman.

Such a family perpetuates itself by self-embrace. It is this that makes it a perfect image of earthly matter, which also generates by perpetual self-fecundation. In the darkness of Rhea's womb Isis and Osiris already embrace one another.[69] In this brother and sister nature separates into its two principles. Their reunion by cohabitation is the law of matter. Consequently the brother and sister are dependent above all on each other. In this material view marriage between brother and sister is not only permissible but necessary. It is the natural law which, according to Plato, was confirmed also by the Delphic Pythia.[70] Such is the marriage between Isis and Osiris,

Zeus and Hera, Janus and Camisa, and how profoundly this material law was rooted in the ancient mind is shown by numerous vestiges in the law and custom of the Hebrews as well as the Greeks.

The self-reproduction of the Arabian clan implies the highest degree of internal kinship and the greatest seclusion from the outside world. The members of one clan stand to one another in the closest relationship, as blood kindred of the first degree; they are all brothers, all sisters, sons, and fathers; but there is no bond whatever between the different clans. The extremes of love and hatred face one another. Union comes from the women's side, disjunction from the side of the man. Seen in this light, free sexual relations within the clan become the necessary instrumentality by which alone the mankind of this cultural phase could arrive at any higher and more enduring bond.

All these traits of matriarchal life may be found in the life of the bees. This was remarked by many ancient writers, and the prototype of the hive played an important role in the development of the human race. The life of the bees shows us matriarchy in its clearest and purest form. Aristotle places the bees higher than the men of that early period because they embody the law of nature far more completely and rigorously; and the same idea recurs in Virgil. Thus the bee is rightly held to represent the feminine principle of nature. The queen bee is related to Demeter, Artemis, and Persephone; with its motherliness, its restless creativeness, it is a model of earthly matter and hence an image of the Demetrian earth soul in its supreme purity. The purest product of organic nature, in which animal and vegetable production are so intimately combined, is also the purest food for mothers. It was used by the most ancient mankind; and priestly men, the Pythagoreans, Melchizedek, St. John returned to it. Honey and milk pertain to motherhood, wine to the male Dionysian principle of nature.

Aristotle has given us an interesting note concerning the Libyan peoples, whose very name has been traced back to a γυνὴ αὐτόχθων (a woman sprouted from the earth).[71] In arguing against

Plato's contention that the communal holding of women and children would promote love and brotherhood, the Stagirite remarks that this institution would not even achieve its purpose of destroying all individual ties. "For," he continues, "it is certainly impossible to prevent some from guessing who are their brothers and children and fathers and mothers; for they are sure to derive proofs from the likeness that prevails between the children and their parents. How this is confirmed by experience is shown by the books dealing with geography and ethnology. For among certain tribes of upper Libya the women are held in common; but the children produced are selected according to likeness." [72] This selection of children according to resemblances is observed by Herodotus among the Tritonian Ausians. "When a child has grown up with its mother, the men meet together, which occurs every third month, and the child is held to be the offspring of whatever man it resembles." [73]

This custom discloses a transition from the mother right of the pure *ius naturale* to the principle of marriage. Here a mother does not suffice; the child must also have a father. The mother is always a physical certainty, *mater natura vera*; the father, on the other hand, is a mere presumption, in marriage as amid promiscuous sex relations. The father is always a fiction. Where conjugal relations prevail, this fiction is supported by marriage itself with its supposed exclusivity. *Pater est quem nuptiae demonstrant* (the father is he whom the marriage designates as such).†† Where there is no marriage, the legal fiction is replaced by a different sort of probability: the child's physical resemblance to his father. In one case the fiction is legal, in the other it is of a purely physical character. The one case corresponds to the positive *ius civile*, the other to the *ius naturale* of mother right and the communal holding of women. Here again motherhood is the unifying principle, paternity the separating principle. Those who are distributed among many fathers are joined into a unit by the mother. Over against wholly natural mother right, selection according to likeness appears as a curtailment of *ius naturale*, as the beginning of a movement away from it.

†† See p. 133, n. 31.

The holding of women in common necessarily implies the tyranny of an individual. This we have found among the Arabians, Troglodytes, Ethiopians, and the Iberians of the Caspian Sea.[74] Each tribe has its tyrant. This tyranny is based on the right of fecundation. Since no selection occurs in sexual relations and there is consequently no such thing as individual paternity, the whole tribe has only one father, the tyrant; all are his sons and daughters, and all property belongs to him.[75] The dominance of one man implies no deviation from the *ius naturale* which governs this stage. For the tyrant derives all his rights from woman. The *tyrannis* is transmitted by way of the womb. The Ethiopian leaves his kingdom not to his own children but to his sister's children. Thus, as in Lycia, the head of the tribe derives his right not from his father's but from his mother's side; in legitimizing his power he lists his mother's mothers or, what amounts to the same thing, the sisters of former kings. He takes a wife not in order to beget successors, for his sons will not succeed him but will lose themselves in the mass of the people; he takes a woman only because the male principle of nature must have a female principle beside it in order to embody fully the material power (as represented in the androgynous form of certain Libyans); in order to realize the idea of the double ax, as borne by the Amazons, by the people of Tenedos, by the Lydian Heraclids, and by the Romans, following the Etruscan custom, as a sign of their imperium. It is through this union that the *tyrannos* gains his physical relation with the tribe, and the Cephallenian *tyrannos* achieves it most fully by cohabiting with every bride. Marriage is without importance for the transmission of the royal power, and accordingly an offense against the marriage bond can be atoned by the contribution of one or a few sheep.

The *tyrannis* taken in conjunction with the communal possession of women throws important light on our story of the Arabian princess. Wearied by continuous cohabitation, the girl resorts to ruse. The swindled brother appeals to the king for vindication of his rights. The abuse of male rights, symbolized by the bearing of the staff, is a necessary consequence of this twofold power. And it in turn provokes resistance on the part of women, leading to matriarchy. In considering the Lydian matriarchy, Clearchus writes: "The rule of women is always the consequence of a violent revolt of the female sex against the humiliation of an earlier day; among the Lydians it was Omphale who first practiced such vengeance and subjected the men to matriarchy." [76]

Unquestionably this explanation is historically sound. To be sure, the mother right which embodies only the child's matrilinear descent is *iuris naturalis;* it is as old as the human race and not incompatible with sexual promiscuity; but the matriarchy which gives the mother *domination* over family and state is of later origin and wholly positive in nature. It grows from the woman's reaction to unregulated sexuality, from which she is first to seek liberation. The initial determined resistance to the bestial state of universal promiscuity is woman's. It is woman who artfully or forcefully puts an end to this degrading state. The staff is wrenched from the male, the woman becomes the master. This transition is inconceivable without individual marriage. The rule of woman over the males and children is impossible in the natural state of sexual promiscuity, and the matrilinear transmission of property and names is meaningful only where there is marriage. If women and children are held in common, property must also be held in common. In this phase proper names are also lacking, as Nicolaus of Damascus attests for the Libyan Atarantes. [77]

Civil law and a definite order of inheritance presuppose the elimination of the natural state. But this development from communal sexuality to exclusive marriage takes place in definite stages. Among the Massagetae and Troglodytes we find marriage combined with the communal possession of women. Each man has a wife, but all are permitted to cohabit with other men's wives. The Augiles, Balearics, and Thracians occupy a higher stage, for they observe the chastity of marriage and restrict hetaerism to the marriage night. Marriage combined with the communal possession of women is purer than the same stage without marriage, but less pure than exclusive marriage. Yet this mixed form prevailed among the Lacedaemonians even in a late period. According to Nicolaus of Damascus [78] they allowed their wives to be fecundated by the handsomest men both among citizens and foreigners.*

---

* Plutarch, *Lycurgus* 14–16, confirms and develops in detail the story of Nicolaus, and Lycurgus' principle that the children belong not to their fathers but to the state is also discussed.

The intermediary stage combining marriage and the communal possession of women discloses private property and an individual family, both of which are lacking in the lowest stage of promiscuity. Here mother right, which at the lowest, promiscuous stage was meaningless except for the transmission of the kingship, becomes significant for the inheritance of property. But this mother right does not yet imply matriarchy. As at the lowest stage, the male is still dominant; every tribe is headed by its *tyrannos*, whose power is transmitted according to mother right. Among the Abylles of Libya a man ruled over the men, a woman over the women.[79] Here we see mother right without matriarchy. And actually it may be found in conjunction with the extreme degradation of woman, who is defenseless against the lusts of men and must incline to the staff, which only the man carries. It is interesting to note that among the Arabs and Massagetae the whole male population carried staffs.[80] The man bore the σκίπων, and this gave him admittance to all the women of his tribe. It is the expression of the male, purely physical tyranny. At the next stage this male power is broken; in exclusive marriage woman finds the protection which the Arabian princess vainly sought by guile. Here mother right broadens into matriarchy. The matrilinear transmission of name and property is amplified by the exclusion of all male claims; women now rule over the family and the state. This total matriarchy did not occur amid the early promiscuity, but developed in resolute struggle against it. It was absent from the intermediary phase of marriage combined with the communal possession of women, and came into full force only after this phase was surpassed. Thus as a rule matriarchy presupposes exclusive marriage. It is a conjugal state and, like marriage itself, a positive institution; like marriage, it represents a curtailment of the bestial *ius naturale*, to which any domination and any law of inheritance based on recognition of private property are alien.

In this respect the establishment of matriarchy represents a step forward toward civilization. It represents an emancipation from the bonds of crudely sensual animal life. Woman counters man's abuse of his superior strength by the dignity of her enthroned motherhood—as in the myth of Bellerophon's encounter with the Lycian women. The more savage the men of this first period, the more necessary becomes the restraining force of women. As long as mankind is immersed in purely material life, woman must rule. Matriarchy is necessary to the education of mankind and particularly of men. Just as the child is first disciplined by his mother, so the races of men are first disciplined by woman. The male must serve before he can govern. It is the woman's vocation to tame man's primordial strength, to guide it into benign channels. Athene alone possesses the secret of attaching bridle and bit to the wild Scythius.† The greater the strength, the more it requires to be checked. According to the Bithynian legend recorded by Lucian,[81] Hera makes use of the dance to check the excessive manhood of her wild son Ares. This principle of harmonious movement is contained in marriage, whose rigorous law is upheld by woman. Without hesitation Bellerophon submitted to the will of the matrons and thus became his country's first culture-hero.

In a noteworthy passage Strabo imputes this culture-bringing, benign power of woman to δεισιδαιμονία (fear of God), which first dwelled in woman and which she implanted in the men.[82] It was believed that woman was closer than man to the godhead and endowed with a superior understanding of the divine will. She embodied the law of matter. She manifests justice unconsciously but with full certainty, she is the human conscience; she is naturally autonoë (in herself wise), dikaia (just), Fauna or Fatua; she is the prophetess who proclaims the *fatum;* she is Sibyl, Martha,[83] Phaënnis,[84] Themis. That is why women were held sacred, regarded as the repositories of justice, the source of prophecy. That is why the battle lines parted at their bidding, why the priestess was an arbiter who could compose quarrels among nations. And this was the religious foundation of matriarchy. Woman was the source of the first civilization, just as she has played a prominent part in every decline and every regeneration—an idea which Count Leopardi imparts to his sister Paolina in a magnificent epithalamion.[85]

The Liburnians and Scythians disclose a parallel to the above-cited examples of choosing a child's father in a marriageless society.

† The first horse, sprung from the earth at Poseidon's behest.

"The Liburnians," writes Nicolaus of Damascus, "hold their women in common and raise all their children in common up to their fifth year. In the sixth year they gather them together, seek out the likenesses between them and the men, and accordingly assign a father to each child. The man who thus receives a boy from his mother regards him as his son." [86] And regarding the Agathyrsi Herodotus writes: "They cohabit in common with the women, in order that they should all be blood kin and that their family relationship should prevent them from harboring envy and hostility toward one another." [87] Nicolaus tells us that the Galacto-phagi "are distinguished for righteousness and hold their women and property in common. Consequently they call all older men fathers, the younger men sons, and their contemporaries broth-ers." [88] Strabo reports that they held their property in common, excepting only sword and drinking bowl,[89] as was also the case among the Sardolibyans.[90] Women and children belonged to all. In this community of goods, women, and children Strabo finds the foundation of the love of justice which was so universally regarded as the distinctive feature of the Scythians and Getae, and which caused Aeschylus to call them εὔνομοι (observing good laws).[91] In striking contrast to Hellenic decadence, the primordial customs of the Scythians seemed to be a fulfillment of everything which philosophical theorists, including Plato [92] himself, sought vainly to achieve. Deploring the supposed benefits of culture, the best of the ancients looked with yearning at these nomads with their igno-rance of all cultural refinement. In his picture of Germanic customs Tacitus sought consolation for the degeneracy of the Roman world.

But it is just as absurd to look back nostalgically from the end of human development to its beginnings as it is to condemn early institutions from the standpoint of a later culture, or out of a sense of higher human dignity to deny that such institutions could ever have existed. True, one may apply to all advanced civilization Plato's saying about gold, namely, that it is the most beautiful and radiant of all metals but has more dross clinging to it than the lesser metals.[93] Nevertheless, we are not justified in condemning civilization, much less in seeking to exchange it for a precultural state. Higher human culture is like the soul. "Its condition," says

Plato, "resembles that of the sea-god Glaucus whose first nature can hardly be made out by those who catch glimpses of him, because the original members of his body are broken off and mutilated and crushed and in every way marred by the waves, and other parts have attached themselves to him, accretions of shells and sea-weed and rocks, so that he is more like any wild creature than what he was by nature." [94]

The strength and weakness of human institutions reside in the same point. Plato seeks to eradicate egotism and the resulting political disintegration by restoring common ownership of property and women, thus reviving the εὐνομία and δικαιοσύνη (righteousness) which Strabo praised so highly among the Scythians with their Platonic forms of life. Yet Aristotle, in a section of his *Politics* [95] specially devoted to this one subject, soundly argues that the perfect unity here represented as the supreme political good actually negates the state since it turns the state into a family and the family into an individual; and he argues further that what belongs to the greatest number of owners is always used most carelessly. The progress of human civilization lies not in the reduction of the many to the one, but conversely, in development from the original one to the many. We have found the Arabian, Libyan, and Scythian tribes to be a unity or even, in the person of the *tyrannos* at their head, an individual. The development of marriage brings fixed articulation into this chaotically unitary mass of men and property. It leads from unity to multiplicity and so brings the supreme principle of order into the world. That is why Cecrops, who first juxtaposed a father to the mother and gave to the child a twofold lineage, an androgynous double nature (as symbolized in the Ethiopian legend of the men with one male and one female breast) was looked upon as the founder of a truly human life; [96] and he was the first to worship the phallic Hermes.

The progress from material existence to a higher spiritual life coincides with the progress from the one to the many, from chaotic conditions to articulation. The human race begins with unity and material existence; multiplicity and higher spiritual existence are its goal, toward which it progresses unremittingly through all vicissitudes. "That was not first which is spiritual, but that which is natural; and afterward that which is spiritual," says St. Paul. [97] In this process of development marriage combined with matriarchy occupies the middle position. It is preceded by the pure *ius naturale* of undifferentiated sexual union, as we have found it in a great diversity of modifications and gradations among numerous peoples. And it is followed by the pure *ius civile*, that is, marriage combined with father right and patriarchy. In the intermediate stage of conjugal matriarchy the material and the spiritual principle are mingled. The material principle is no longer exclusively dominant, but the spiritual principle has not yet achieved full purity. Essential factors of the material *ius naturale* have been retained: the predominance of material, maternal birth with all its consequences, the matrilinear transmission of property, and the daughters' exclusive right of inheritance; but the principles of marriage and of a family authority that sustains it partake of the spiritual *ius civile*.

Upon the foundation of this intermediate stage there ultimately rises the supreme stage of purely spiritual father right, which subordinates the woman to the man and transfers all the mother's former significance to the father. This supreme law found its purest expression among the Romans. No other people so fully developed the idea of *potestas* (authority) over women and children; and consequently no other people so consciously pursued the corresponding idea of the unitary political imperium. From these heights Cicero looks down on that first condition which for Plato was the ideal of human society and sees it as a negation of every political principle, and of every spiritual principle as well, as a pure expression of the material side of our human nature: "For there was a time when men wandered about the country like beasts, living on wild fruits, acting not in accordance with reason and the spirit, but for the most part in accordance with their physical powers; the order of religion or human morality was not yet observed, no one had seen legal marriage or heirs who were of a certainty someone's children; no one had understood the benefits of just laws." [98]

Transferred to the cosmos—I take the word in the sense in which the Pythagoreans first used it—the three stages of human development appear as earth, moon, and sun. The purely extramarital natural law is the tellurian principle, pure father right is the solar principle. Halfway between the two stands the moon, the border zone between the tellurian and the solar region, the purest of the material and transient bodies, the impurest part of the immaterial, immutable world. Of ancient writers it was above all Plutarch who developed this view in *Isis and Osiris* and *The Face Which Appears in the Orb of the Moon*. The moon, this "other, celestial earth," is androgynous, Luna and Lunus in one, feminine in relation to the sun, but masculine in relation to the earth; [99] but its masculine nature is secondary, it is first woman, afterward man. It is fecundated by the sun and passes this fecundation on to the earth. Thus it maintains the unity of the cosmos, it is the interpreter between mortals and immortals.[100] With its twofold nature it corresponds to marriage in conjunction with matriarchy: to marriage because here man and woman are joined; to matriarchy because it is first woman, then man, thus exalting the feminine principle over the masculine principle. This intuition (as we shall demonstrate below **) underlies the whole religious system of the ancient world and has left echoes in Christianity.[101]

The moon governs the night as the sun governs the day. Mother right may be identified with the moon and the night, father right with the sun and the day. Or to put it differently: in matriarchy the night has primacy, bearing the day from within itself, as the mother bears the son; in father right, the day is dominant, standing to the night as affirmation to negation. The matriarchal system is reflected in the time reckoning that begins from midnight,[102] the patriarchal system in the time reckoning that starts with the day. The lunar month corresponds to matriarchy, the solar year to patriarchy.

The relation between the sexes has always found its cosmic expression in the relation between moon and sun. The battle between the sexes is a battle between sun and moon for preeminence in relation to the earth. All the great heroes who triumphed over matriarchy take their place in the heavens as solar powers. Earthly events become an expression of cosmic events. It was a universal belief of the ancients that heaven and earth must

** See p. 178.

obey the same laws, with one great harmony pervading the transient and the eternal. The earth's development is a striving to copy faithfully the cosmic prototype of the celestial bodies. And this process is completed only with the domination of man over woman, of the sun over the moon.

It is this intuition that makes intelligible the Indian-Egyptian myth of the phoenix with its egg of myrrh and gives it profound meaning. Previous interpretations [103] have brought out the bird's relation—already stressed by ancient writers [104]—to the sun and the great Year of the Phoenix or of Sothis, at the end of which begins a new age of the world, a *novus saeclorum ordo*—and explained the many attributes of the miraculous bird on the basis of this relation. But there is one point that has been overlooked: the relation of the sun to father right. In this solar myth there is no mother but only a father. The father is followed by a son who everlastingly regenerates himself. The miraculous bird lays down his burden at the temple of Heliopolis, on the altar of the supreme sun god. He had shaped an egg of myrrh and hollowed it out. Within it he had concealed his father. When he had sealed up the opening, the egg was no heavier than before.

The egg represents the maternal principle of nature, from which everything arises, to which everything returns. But here the egg is no longer the ultimate foundation of things: it is fecundated by a higher power, the sun. The sun implants in the egg the *vis genitalis* that engenders the fetus. So says Tacitus.[105] The egg does not become heavier because the fecundating power of the sun is immaterial and incorporeal. It is this immaterial power that distinguishes the highest stage of the male principle of nature from the lower stage built on the material water. To be sure, the phoenix is no stranger to the watery principle. In the *Physiologus* Epiphanius relates that he lives in the Orient by a bay in the river Oceanus,†† [106] and Philostratus represents him as a swan dwelling in marshy waters, singing his own song of leave-taking and death.[107] But he rises from the waters and accompanies the sun; his

†† Bachofen's memory failed him here. The *Physiologus* (of which Epiphanius' authorship is not now generally accepted) says this not of the phoenix, but of the "hydrops"—an unidentified animal, perhaps a kind of antelope—and its references to the phoenix suggest no connection with the "watery principle."

plumage is purple and gold; his wings are inscribed with the word φωτοειδές (luminous); and his watery origin disappears entirely beneath his luminous nature. The material is wholly surpassed by the immaterial. The fire burns away the slag of mortality, and the son rises from the ashes. The sun confers its principle, which is the epitome of the consuming fire, upon the myrrh and frankincense.

In this form the phoenix is the exact image of the Heliopolitan Zeus, just as the griffon guarding the gold is that of the Apollonian sun principle. And for this very reason the arrival of the phoenix in Egypt can be linked with the close of the old great solar year and the beginning of a new one. In its purely metaphysical aspect the phoenix becomes the idea of abstract time, just as Apollo, who in his highest form is equally metaphysical, is associated with the beginning of the great cosmic year. In the phoenix, then, the luminous principle is developed in supreme incorporeality and identified with paternity. The maternal principle is surpassed. The young phoenix is born of fire alone, motherless, in the manner of Athene springing from the head of Zeus; he is πυριγενής (born of fire) in a far purer sense than Dionysus. The maternal egg is no longer the principle of life; it is ruled by the fecundating power of the sun, whose nature it has assumed. In no myth has the triumph of the paternal solar principle over the maternal lunar principle been embodied with such purity as in this Indo-Egyptian conception of the great year of the Phoenix.

The realm of the idea belongs to the man, the realm of material life to the woman. In the struggle between the two sexes that ultimately ends with the victory of the man, every great turning point is connected with an exaggeration of the preceding system. Man's abuse of woman leads to conjugal matriarchy; the Amazonian perversion of womanhood, with its unnatural intensification of woman's power, provokes a male uprising which sometimes ends with the restoration of natural marriage, as in Lycia, but sometimes with the downfall of the matriarchy and the introduction of father right, as associated with Heracles, Dionysus, Apollo. For in all things it is abuse and perversion that provide the greatest stimulus to development.

All the myths relating to our subject embody a memory of real events experienced by the human race. They represent not fictions but historical realities. The stories of the Amazons and Bellerophon are real and not poetic. Based on the experiences of mortal man, they are expressions of events. History has risen to even greater heights than the creative imagination.

As we have seen, the Lycian matriarchy does not antedate marriage, but is a conjugal institution. And it is illuminating in another respect as well. One might suppose the men of this society to have been cowardly, effeminate, degenerate, because they accepted feminine rule. The spectacle of the Lycian people shows how mistaken such an inference would be. Their bravery was proverbial, and the heroic death of the men of Xanthus [108] is among the noblest examples of courage and self-sacrifice bequeathed us by antiquity. And Bellerophon, whose name is bound up with mother right, appears as a blameless hero, worshiped by the Amazons for his beauty, a man both chaste and bold, who performed Heraclean deeds and whose people observed the watchword which Posidonius proclaimed to Pompey when they met in Rhodes: [109] "Strive always to be first and to excel all others." [110] This combination of matriarchy and warlike bravery on the part of the men is found not only in Lycia but elsewhere as well, particularly among the Carians, who had close ties with Crete and Lycia. For Aristotle the relationship is universal. In speaking of the Laconian matriarchy, which struck him as the great weakness of the Lycurgan legislation, he remarks that "most of the warlike and belligerent peoples are ruled by women." [111] Far from precluding warlike bravery, matriarchy vastly encourages it. At all times chivalry has gone hand in hand with the cult of the woman. Courage in battle and the veneration of women have always been qualities of virile, youthful peoples.

Thus the customs and institutions attending Lycian matriarchy characterize it as a source of lofty qualities. Chastity in marriage, bravery and chivalry among the men, authority and matronly gravity among the women, whose religious consecration even the immortals dared not assail: these are elements of the strength whereby a nation secures its future. And this may explain, if such historical facts are susceptible of explanation, why the Lycians preserved their mother right for so long. It is surely no accident that the Locrians and the Lycians, two peoples who were especially famed in the ancient world for their εὐνομία (lawfulness) and σωφροσύνη (wisdom), should have preserved their matriarchy for so long. Undoubtedly the exalted position of women among them discloses a strong conservative element. Among other peoples mother right early gave way to father right, and Herodotus was not a little surprised to find it preserved among the Lycians. True, it had lost its political importance. According to Strabo, the Lycian league at least was ruled by a male λυκιάρχης.[112]

The connection between matriarchy and warlike courage among the men may be explained in another way. In those early times when the men were engaged exclusively in warfare which carried them far away from home, only the woman could attend to the children and property, which as a rule were wholly entrusted to her supervision. The clearest picture of such conditions is provided by the ancient records of the remote expeditions of conquest carried on by the Scythian tribes.[113] Devastation marked their path. Like the Cimmerians, they were unable to capture fortified cities.[114] They were interested only in plunder. Undertakings of this sort are in keeping only with the customs of nomadic shepherd tribes. Sometimes raiding parties were fostered by intestine strife, sometimes by the advance of neighboring tribes. However, the women remained at home, taking care of the children and the cattle. The belief in their inviolability protected them from the enemy, and the slaves were blinded.

Matriarchy is fully consonant with such conditions. Hunting, warring, and pillaging filled the life of the men, keeping them far from the women and children. The family, the cart, the hearth, the slaves were entrusted to the women. And here lay the root of their dominant social position and exclusive claim to inheritance. The son was expected to maintain himself by hunting and warfare. The daughter, excluded from these opportunities, was dependent on the family wealth. She alone inherited; the man had his weapons, his bow and his spear were his livelihood. He acquired wealth for his wife and daughter, not for himself or his male descendants. Thus matriarchy and warlike life are concomitant. Effect becomes cause and cause effect. The man's exclusion from all inheritance spurred him on to warlike undertakings; his release from all domestic cares enabled him to maintain himself by distant expeditions of rapine and conquest. The men of Lemnos sailed to the coasts of Thrace, and on their return, settled down with the captive maidens. Instead of warfare, handicraft now became the occupation of the males. We find this state of affairs among the Minyae and the Ozolian Locrians. Excluded from warfare and pillage, the men fell into ways which struck even the women as contemptible. The Egyptian tended the loom and, the Minyan worked in the smithy; the Locrian shepherd took his name from the smell of sheepskins.[115] And the women, exalted by their social position, favored by their exclusive right of inheritance, towered over the men. The woman's nature is ennobled in the same measure as that of the man is debased by his twofold humiliation. Thus as the mode of life changes, the very same custom appears in a different light.

The ancients attributed the origin of Amazonism to the conditions of an earlier warlike life. Amazonism was only an unnatural exaggerated matriarchy, however, brought about by a corresponding degeneration of the male sex. It was the union of the men with the Thracian girls they had captured on their expeditions that drove the women of Lemnos to commit the crime that has become proverbial: they murdered all the males and resorted to the Amazonian life.* The Argonauts were hospitably received on the island denuded of men. The Scythian women of Thermodon saw their men defeated in battle. Now they themselves were compelled to take up arms, and bands of warlike maidens poured triumphantly through Asia Minor, Greece, Italy, Gaul, repeating in these regions what, it would seem, had taken place independently in Africa. While others, such as the Scythians, the Lacedaemonians, and the Greeks during the Trojan War, wearied of their men's absence and united with slaves and foreigners, the Amazons renounced marriage and founded a society which not only played an outstanding part in the history of our race through the devastation which it brought on the world, but also contributed more than anything else to the downfall of the matriarchate.

* See p. 173.

The rise of father right begins with the war against the Amazons. The lunar principle is destroyed by the luminous powers, woman's natural vocation is restored to her, and spiritual father right becomes dominant for all time over material motherhood. The greatest exaggeration leads to total downfall. Only mother right and the consequent warfare makes the Amazonism of Asia and Africa intelligible; for despite all the embellishments of legend and art, the historical foundation of the ancient reports, which Strabo [116] contests on such absurd grounds, cannot be doubted. Modern scholarship has denied what it should have sought to understand. Herein lies its weakness: concerned less with ancient than with modern ideas, it supplies explanations that partake more of the modern than of the ancient world. The inevitable end is skepticism, confusion, and hopeless nihilism. It is impossible to prove the existence of Amazonian states. But this is implicit in the very nature of history. No single historical tradition has ever been proved. We hearken only to rumor. To deny traditions of this kind is, to speak with Simonides, to battle with the millennia; [117] to judge them according to modern standards is, as Alcaeus put it, "not to paint the lion according to the claw, but to fashion the universe and the heavens according to lamp and wick." † [118]

We have still another bit of information relating to Lycian mother right. Plutarch writes in his *Letter of Consolation to Apollonius:* "The lawgiver of the Lycians, they relate, ordered his citizens to don women's clothing whenever they were in mourning." [119] Since the name of this lawgiver is not added and we have no other record of a Lycian nomothete, it may be stated with certainty that the wearing of women's clothing by men was one of those unwritten customs which Heraclides claims to have found among the Lycians in the place of written laws.[120] This gives the custom the higher significance of a tradition removed from any arbitrary human decision. Plutarch derives it from an ethical meaning. Mourning,

---

† Alcaeus said "painting a lion from the claw," whereas it was one Demetrius who made the whole statement in connection with the fact that the priests of Ammon used less oil every year for the perpetual lamp; the story is recorded by Plutarch in *On the Cessation of Oracles* 2, 3.

he contends, is something feminine, weak, ignoble; women are more inclined to it than men, barbarians than Hellenes, commoners than aristocrats. But the Lycian usage has a deeper root. It stems from the material religious view that we have described above. At the summit of all tellurian life stands the feminine principle, the Great Mother, whom the Lycians called Lada, synonymous with Latona, Lara, Lasa, Lala. Its physical foundation is the earth, its mortal representative is earthly woman. From this principle all things are born, to it all things return.[121] The womb from which the child springs takes it back again in death. That is why the harpies are represented in maternal ovoid form on a well-known Lycian tomb.[122] And it is why only the mother originally mourned the dead. Only woman, who by conception and childbearing fulfills the destiny of matter, laments the end of matter. From the lofty crags of Sipylus Niobe pours down inexhaustible tears for the death of her children. An image of the earth exhausted by generation, she weeps because not one of her offspring remains to comfort her.

Thus mourning is itself a religious cult dedicated to Mother Earth, practiced by barbarian peoples in subterranean, sunless chambers, as Plutarch, citing the tragic poet Ion, tells us in his discussion of the Lycian custom.[123] If a man wishes to engage in mourning for the dead, he himself must assume the character of Mother Earth. The dead become Demetrians, and the grief of the earth can only be expressed by the mother and in the maternal form. The connection between the women's garments of the Lycian men and Lycian matriarchy is apparent. If the father is without meaning for the living child, he has no right to mourn for the dead one. The son of the Lycian earth is not the father's but the mother's child. If fatherhood has no meaning beyond that of physical fecundation, it loses all claim to consideration once the child has died. Only the maternal matter which takes the dead back again has a bond with them; once life vanishes, the virile power that awakened it sinks into oblivion. That is why Virgil, in describing the underworld, uses the term *matres atque viri* (mothers and men), not *matres atque patres*.[124] After death only *viri* remain, and no *patres*. Certain of the heroes bring back their mothers, but never their fathers, from the realm of the dead. On the Lycian tomb only the mother and the mother's mother are named, not the father,[125] just as even Strabo the Amasean always stresses his maternal lineage,[126] and only the mother, not the father, can grieve at the tomb. There is a necessary connection between the two motifs. And for this reason the father's maternal clothing is the supreme expression of matriarchy. We encounter such a change of clothing in many cults. But in connection with the funeral service and the rituals of mourning it is recorded only for the Lycians, among whom the custom survived as long as matriarchy itself.

If we sum up the records of the ancients concerning Lycian mother right, the following conclusions stand out.

Its outward expression is to be found in the naming of the child after its mother. But its significance is manifested in several other points. First, in the status of the children, which is taken from the mother, not the father; secondly, in the inheritance of property, which is handed down not to the sons but to the daughters; thirdly, in the government of the family, which falls not to the father but to the mother, and by a consequent extension of this last principle, government of the state was also entrusted to the women.

Thus we have not an outward peculiarity of nomenclature but a thoroughgoing system; it is bound up with a religious intuition and belongs to an older period of human development than father right.

Athens

LYCIA HAS close bonds not only with Crete * but with Athens as well. For in the passage quoted above † Herodotus tells us (and the tale was later recorded by Strabo [1]) that Lycus, son of Pandion, when driven out of Athens by his brother Aegeus, took refuge with Sarpedon in the land of the Termilians. Does this mean that mother right prevailed at one time in Athens? There are numerous indications that such was the case.

In his *City of God* St. Augustine quotes [2] a passage from Varro telling of a twofold miracle that occurred during the reign of Cecrops. An olive tree sprang from the earth, and in another spot water gushed forth. Frightened, the king sent to Delphi and inquired what this meant and what was to be done. The god replied that the olive tree meant Minerva and the water Neptune, and it was for the citizens to decide after which of the two deities they wished to name their city. Thereupon Cecrops called an assembly of the citizens, both men and women, for in those days the women also took part in public deliberations. The men voted for Neptune, the women for Minerva, and since there was one more woman, Minerva won out. Neptune was angry at this, and the sea flooded the entire Athenian territory. To appease the god's wrath, the citizens imposed a threefold punishment on their women: they should lose their right of suffrage, their children should no longer

* The chapter on Crete is omitted here.   † See p. 121.

take the names of their mothers, and they themselves should no longer bear the title of Athenians (after the goddess).

In this myth Neptune represents father right and Athene mother right. While mother right prevailed, the children were named after their mothers and all the women bore the name of the goddess. As long as they were called Athenaeae, they were true citizens of Athens. Afterward they were merely citizens' wives. The law of the pre-Cecropian period was replaced by father right. Aristophanes was mistaken when he wrote in the *Ecclesiazusae* (455–7) that rule by women was the one thing that had never existed in Athens. It not only existed, it was the oldest form of law. The Lycian usage prevailed also in Attica. Here as in Asia it was the primordial law, closely bound up with local religion, the cult of the goddess Athene, and with the feminine name of the city.

And we have still another highly remarkable allusion to the existence of mother right in archaic Attica. I am referring to the *Eumenides* of Aeschylus. The two principles, mother right and father right, represented by Minerva and Neptune in the passage from Varro, are here championed by the Erinyes on the one hand, by Apollo and Athene on the other. Orestes kills his mother in order to avenge his father. Which of the two weighs heavier in the balance, father or mother? Which of the two stands closer to the child? Athene ordains a court of justice. The most respected of her citizens shall decide. The Erinyes testify against the matricide; Apollo, who commanded Orestes to act and purged him of blood guilt, is his defender. The Erinyes argue the cause of Clytaemnestra while Apollo takes the part of Agamemnon. The Erinyes are the champions of mother right, Apollo the advocate of father right. The position of the Erinyes is made clear in their dialogue with Orestes:

CHORUS: The Prophet guided you into this matricide?
ORESTES: Yes. I have never complained of this. I do not now.
CHORUS: When sentence seizes you, you will talk a different way.
ORESTES: I have no fear. My father will aid me from the grave.
CHORUS: Kill your mother, then put trust in a corpse! Trust on.
ORESTES: Yes. She was dirtied twice over with disgrace.
CHORUS: Tell me how, and explain it to the judges here.
ORESTES: She murdered her husband, and thereby my father too.

CHORUS: Of this stain, death has set her free. But you still live.
ORESTES: When she lived, why did you not descend and drive her out?
CHORUS: The man she killed was not of blood congenital.
ORESTES: But am I then involved with my mother by blood-bond?
CHORUS: Murderer, yes. How else could she have nursed you beneath
Her heart? Do you forswear your mother's intimate blood? [3]

It is plain that the Erinyes do not recognize the law of the father and husband, for they leave Clytaemnestra's deed unpunished. They know only the law of the mother, the rights of the mother's blood; they demand the punishment of the matricide in accordance with old law and custom. Not so Apollo. He ordered the deed to avenge the father, having received his own orders from Zeus, the god of heaven. And now he defends Orestes against the Erinyes, championing father right against mother right. He reveals himself as Patroos (paternal god), and indeed this was his epithet as tutelary god of Athens. He speaks to the judges as follows:

I will tell you, and I will answer correctly. Watch.
The mother is no parent of that which is called
her child, but only nurse of the new-planted seed
that grows. The parent is he who mounts. A stranger she
preserves a stranger's seed, if no god interfere.
I will show you proof of what I have explained. There can
be a father without any mother. There she stands,
the living witness, daughter of Olympian Zeus,
she who was never fostered in the dark of the womb,
yet such a child as no goddess could bring to birth.[4]

Thus Apollo champions the right of the begetter, while the Erinyes defend the rights of the blood, of the maternal matter. Apollo's is the new law, theirs is the old. To Apollo's arguments the Erinyes reply:

You won the ancient goddesses over with wine
and so destroyed the orders of an elder time.[5]

and further on:

Since you, a young god, would ride down my elder age . . .[6]

Now the judges, enlightened by the arguments on both sides, step up to the voting urn. Athene also takes up a stone from the altar, holds it in her hand, and speaks:

It is my task to render final judgment here.
This is a ballot for Orestes I shall cast.
There is no mother anywhere who gave me birth,
and, but for marriage, I am always for the male
with all my heart, and strongly on my father's side.
So, in a case where the wife has killed her husband, lord
of the house, her death shall not mean most to me. And if
the other votes are even, then Orestes wins.[7]

Thus it is the father, protector of the house, and not the mother, who has the superior right. According to this right, which comes from Zeus, father of both Apollo and Athene, Orestes is acquitted. In this first trial for murder ever to have been held among mortals, an equal number of votes is cast on each side and the decision is carried by the *calculus Minervae* [Minerva's stone]. But this is the new law of the new gods. Of Apollo it is said that he "blighted age-old distributions of power," [8] and "destroyed the orders of an elder time." The semichorus of the Erinyes sings:

Gods of the younger generation, you have ridden down
the laws of the elder time, torn them out of my hands.[9]

The old juridical state of mankind is now deprived of every support, the foundation of all well-being is shattered. No longer shall anyone cry out: "O Justice! Throned powers of the Erinyes." [10] Fuming with rage, the goddesses, childless daughters of the night, resolve to hide in the subterranean depths to destroy the fertility of the earth and the growth of the infant in the womb. But Athene wins them over and reconciles them with the new law. Henceforth they shall serve piously by her side. They are not banished, they are not fallen. No:

And you, in your place
of eminence beside Erechtheus in his house

shall win from female and from male processionals
more than all lands of men beside could ever give.[11]

And gladly they agree to dwell and serve beside Pallas;
henceforth, beloved of maidens, they will prepare nuptial joys—
they, the primordial goddesses, now spirits of peace and concord.
The throng of pious maidens and aged mothers then conducts the
reconciled corulers of the land back to their realm, down to Hades,
the dark abode of the dead. For the people of Athens, Moira and
Zeus the all-seeing are joyfully united.

The child's predominant connection with its mother is relinquished. Man is raised above woman. The material principle is
subordinated to the spiritual principle. Thus marriage for the first
time attains its true height. For the Erinyes, as Apollo held up to
them,[12] failed to honor Hera's decree, the sacred marriage bond.
Clytaemnestra's infringement of it was nothing to them: in their
eyes it could not excuse Orestes' just, though bloody, deed. In this
sense father right is tantamount to marriage right, hence the starting point of a new era, an era of fixed order in family and state,
which bore within it the germs of a great unfolding and flowering.

In order to illuminate from all sides the antithesis between
father right and mother right, let us consider a few details of
Aeschylus' version. First, this point: the Hill of Ares, which
Athene designated for all time as the site of the penal court, and
where the old law of the earth was defeated in the person of
Clytaemnestra, is the very same spot where the Amazons had set up
their camp.

Here is the Hill of Ares, here the Amazons
encamped and built their shelters when they came in arms
for spite of Theseus, here they piled their rival towers
to rise, new city, and dare his city long ago,
and slew their beasts for Ares. So this rock is named
from then the Hill of Ares.[13]

Here we see a new antithesis between father right and mother
right. As Theseus represents the patriarchal state, so the Amazons
represent the matriarchal state. Enraged with envy they erect their
towering fortress to rival Theseus' newly founded city. Enraged

161

with envy: for Theseus has defeated Antiope [the queen of the Amazons] and captured her girdle; in Theseus there arises a new principle, directly opposed and inwardly hostile to theirs. The Amazonian state—if one may apply the word state to a nation of women—comprises the most complete realization of matriarchy. And Theseus builds his new state on the opposite principle. The history of Athens begins with the struggle between the two, and that is why Theseus' victory over the Amazons assumes such outstanding importance. Later generations look back with pride at this event, calling it the greatest of Athens' benefits to all Hellas.[14] It is the first act in the struggle between Europe and Asia that is the very essence of Greek history.

Theseus was to Attica what Bellerophon had been to Lycia. He defeated the Amazons, who joyfully and willingly entered into marriage. But he rose still higher than the Corinthian-Lycian hero. The decline not only of Amazonism but also of conjugal matriarchy is bound up with his name. He fully attained to the luminous nature of the male. He appears in Apollonian purity.

But Aeschylus casts further light on our subject. In his work the antithesis between father right and mother right takes still another form. The new law is the celestial law of the Olympian Zeus; the old law is the chthonian right of the subterranean powers. Orestes himself, in a speech immediately after his acquittal by Athene, proclaims that the Olympians are the source of the new law:

Pallas Athene, you have kept my house alive.
When I had lost the land of my fathers you gave me
a place to live. Among the Hellenes they shall say:
"A man of Argos lives again in the estates
of his father, all by grace of Pallas Athene, and
Apollo, and with them the all-ordaining god
the Savior"—who remembers my father's death, who looked
upon my mother's advocates, and rescues me.[15]

And Athene herself proclaims:

        . . . but the luminous evidence of Zeus
was there, and he who spoke the oracle was he
who ordered Orestes so to act and not be hurt.[16]

Contrary to this the Erinys cries out:

Is there a man who does not fear
this, does not shrink to hear
how my place has been ordained,
granted and given by destiny
and god, absolute? Privilege
primeval yet is mine, nor am I without place,
though it be underneath the ground
and in no sunlight and in gloom that I must stand.[17]

And then, after Orestes has been acquitted:

Gods of the younger generation, you have ridden down
the laws of the elder time, torn them out of my hands.
I, disinherited, suffering, heavy with anger
shall let loose on the land
the vindictive poison
dripping deadly out of my heart upon the ground.[18]

And again:

That they could treat me so!
I, the mind of the past, to be driven under the ground,
outcast like dirt!
The wind I breathe is fury and utter hate.[19]

The antithesis is clear: celestial and Olympian is the right of the father, proclaimed by Zeus, although he himself, as the Erinyes hold up to him, did not act in accordance with it when he chained his aged father Cronus; and chthonian, subterranean, is the right of the mother; like its advocates, the Erinyes, it springs from the depths of the earth. And the Erinyes are the powers at work in the depths; in the dark ground of matter they, children of the night, generate all life; everything that grows from the earth is their gift, their creation. To men and beasts they give nourishment, they cause the fruit of the womb to thrive. When they are angry, everything goes to ruin—the fruit of the soil, the offspring of men and beasts. Men sacrifice the first fruits of the land to them to assure the fertility of marriage and the well-being of the children. What further proof do we need when they themselves tell us this in Aeschylus:

Let there blow no wind that wrecks the trees.
I pronounce words of grace.
Nor blaze of heat blind the blossoms of grown plants, nor
cross the circles of its right
place. Let no barren deadly sickness creep and kill.
Flocks fatten. Earth be kind
to them, with double fold of fruit
in time appointed for its yielding. Secret child
of earth, her hidden wealth, bestow
blessing and surprise of gods.[20]

Deep under the earth, in Ogygian depths, they receive honor
and sacrifice and ritual fire, offered them in order that they may
withhold all catastrophe from the land, in order that they may send
up all blessings to the city. They are the friendly gods, who secure
the prosperity and well-being of men, they are true Eumenides
(kindly ones), related in their whole chthonian nature to the
agathodaemon, to the Roman Bona Dea.

In the Ogygian dark depths of the earth they weave all life and
send it upward into the sunlight; and in death everything returns to
them. All life repays its debt to nature, that is, to matter. Thus the
Erinyes, like the earth to which they belong, are rulers over death
as well as life, for both are encompassed by material, tellurian
being. All personifications of the chthonian power of earth combine these two aspects, coming into being and passing away, the
two poles between which, as Plato said, the cycle of all things
moves.[21] Thus Venus, goddess of material generation, is also
Libitina, the goddess of death. At Delphi there is a pillar named
Epitymbia (on the tomb), and hither the departed are summoned
to partake of the sacrifices offered up to them.[22] In the Roman
mortuary inscription found near Campana's columbarium,
Priapus is called *mortis et vitai locus*. And no motif is more
frequent in the tombs than Priapus, symbol of material generation.

In their other aspect the friendly Eumenides are the terrible
cruel goddesses, hostile to all earthly life. In this aspect they
delight in catastrophe, blood, and death, in this aspect they are
detested, accursed monsters, bloodthirsty and hideous, whom Zeus

"has ruled outcast." [23] In this aspect they mete out to each man his merited reward.

> Hades is great . . . Hades calls men to reckoning . . .[24]

As goddesses of doom they are also goddesses of fate and just retribution; they received their office from Moira:

> When we were born such lots were assigned for our keeping.
> So the immortals must hold hands off, nor is there
> one who shall sit at our feasting.
> For sheer white robes I have no right and no portion.

> I have chosen overthrow
> of houses, where the Battlegod
> grown within strikes near and dear
> down. So we swoop upon this man
> here. He is strong, but we wear him down
> for the blood that is still wet on him.[25]

All these aspects of their nature unite in a single fundamental idea; all follow from their material tellurian nature. The Erinyes, like *era* (earth), are an expression of earthly corporeal life, of tellurian existence.

A story of Herodotus' shows how the friendship between the Aeginetans and the Athenians played an important role in the history of Athenian marriage law. Once when the land of Epidaurus would bear no fruit, Pythia prophesied that the famine would cease if the Epidaurians were to carve statues of Damia and Auxesia from the wood of a cultivated olive tree. Thereupon the Epidaurians appealed to the Athenians for permission to fell one of their sacred olive trees. The request was granted on condition that the Epidaurians would offer up sacrifices each year to the Athenian Pallas and to Erechtheus. The condition was fulfilled as long as the Epidaurians were in possession of the two statues. But when the Aeginetans rebelled against the Epidaurians, their former masters, and stole the statues, the Epidaurians ceased to keep their promise. Thereupon the Athenians demanded the return of the two statues, and invaded Aegina when this was not done.

But the undertaking ended badly. For although force was used, the statues would not budge from their sockets, and the Athenians fell beneath the blows of the Aeginetans and the Epidaurians who had hastened to the spot—or else, as the Athenians said, they were smitten by the angry goddesses theselves. A single soldier returned to Athens, but once there, he too lost his life.

For when he came to Athens, he announced the defeat, and when the wives of the men who had gone off to war in Aegina learned this, they grew angry that he alone had escaped, and surrounded him and pricked him with the clasps of their cloaks, each one asking him where her husband was, and in this way the man had been killed; and to the Athenians this act of their women seemed still more terrible than the defeat, and they did not know how to punish the women; but they changed their dress into the Ionian style. For previously the Athenian women had worn Dorian dress, like the Corinthian; this they changed to long tunics, in order that they should require no clasps. Strictly speaking, this dress is not originally Ionian, but Carian; for in the old time Greek women's dress was everywhere one and the same, namely, the dress that we now call Dorian. But the Argives and the Aeginetans thereupon introduced a law making their clasps half again as long as they had been and requiring the women to consecrate clasps in the temples of those goddesses; thenceforth they were to bring nothing Attic into the temple, not even earthenware pottery, but in future it should be the custom to make drink offerings from little household pots. And from that time onward the women of Argos and Aegina have preserved, out of hatred for the Athenians, the custom which still endured in my time, of wearing larger clasps than before.[26]

In Herodotus' narrative the divergence between the Carian-Ionian and the Dorian-Hellenic dress takes on a religious significance. A symbolic meaning attaches particularly to the clasp pins. These are taken away from the Athenian women, while the Argives and Aeginetans make them longer by half again, and consecrate them to the maternal goddesses Auxesia and Damia. What then is this symbolic meaning? The Aphroditean-erotic significance of the episode cannot be doubted. The consecration of the clasp pin (περόνη , πόρπη, the latter signifying the ring in the clasp, the former the pin that passes through it) that held the cloak together has the same meaning as the dedication of the woman's girdle. Both signify the sacrifice of virginity. The consecration of the clasp signifies the transition to motherhood, the entrance into marriage, the fulfillment of the feminine vocation through "marriage in the flower of youth." [27] The closed garment is now opened. The clasp, formerly symbol of chaste virginity, becomes an image of marriage. The ring traversed by the pin is itself an image of the sexes united for generation.

Every detail of Herodotus' narrative fits in with this erotic interpretation. First there is the maternal nature of the two goddesses Damia and Auxesia, whose Demetrian significance is unmistakable. Both goddesses are representations of tellurian motherhood, true θάλειαι (goddesses of abundance),[28] as their very names indicate. For Auxesia is derived from αὐξάνω (increase), and in Damia we have a stem [dā, gē] which recurs in a great number of terms and always has as its foundation the material stuff of earth. Accordingly, the divine statues are made from the trunk of a tree which eminently represents the earth's fertility. Just as the earth finds its pleasure in unremitting fecundation, so Damia and Auxesia awaken the germ of life in women's wombs. They foster the marriage bond and incline toward everything masculine.

The fact that there are two mothers implies the same dual power of nature as such twins as the Dioscuri or the Moliones illustrate. Death and life, passing away and coming into being, are the two aspects of the principle which moves eternally between two poles. As twin brothers or sisters they stand inseparably side by side, issue of one mother. Auxesia sends forth life and Damia takes it back again into her womb. Auxesia expresses the bright side of natural life, Damia the nocturnal aspect. Herein Damia reveals herself to be Lamia, the great cruel harlot. The two designations are synonymous.

This duality has still another meaning. It refers to the two potencies that are united in the natural principle—the masculine added to the feminine. More perfect than the two is the three, because here offspring is added to the father and the mother, so that unity of the natural principle is restored. The one is the little unity, the three the great unity; the one is self-contained, the latter is developed unity, unity in threeness. The child combines the potencies that were separate in father and mother. In every childbirth an insoluble bond is forged between the two sexual potencies; their original unity is refashioned. Through the child the two parents are chained together. When the Argives and Aeginetans enlarge their clasp pins by half again, it signifies such an advance from the two to the three, from the feminine to the masculine, conceived in the symbolic spirit of the ancient religion. In the tenness of the chorus leaders who lead the round of women at the festival of the goddesses,[29] each member of the duality is multiplied by five. To the ancients five meant marriage. It arises through the combination of the female two with the male three. In their fiveness the two mothers truly reveal themselves to be, like the Argive Hera, goddesses of marriage and union.

All this accounts for the erotic-Aphroditic significance of the clasp pin: περόνη and πόρπη were a true expression of the motherhood which gives itself to the masculine and delights in childbearing. The Athenian women's use of their clasp pins to commit murder was bound to appear as a signal sacrilege. In the hands of the Athenian matrons the symbol of generation had become an instrument of death. For woman should find her joy not in death but in the enjoyment of virility. It was for failing to heed this commandment that the Cyprian Leucomantis and the Cretan Gorgo ** had been turned into statues.[30] And because the Athenian women had defied this principle by slaying the single soldier whom the goddesses had spared, they lost the privilege of wearing the clasp that symbolized the conjugal motherhood they had desecrated.

The bearing of this narrative on the social position of the Athenian matron is clear. The change of dress is accompanied by a change of status. The high honor which the Athenian woman had enjoyed was taken from her. In the cult of the great nature mothers earthly woman was also sanctified, and thus she was shielded from the dominion of man. To male authority the matron opposed the religious character of her matronhood, based on the prototype of

---

** Two women, otherwise unknown, who had to die, "because each refused her lover, and rejoiced more at his death than his love." See Bachofen, *Gräbersymbolik,* in *Gesammelte Werke,* Vol. 4, p. 91.

the great tellurian primal mother who rises up to protect her mortal representatives. This safeguard was now withdrawn from the Athenian women. Damia and Auxesia had refused to return to Athens; by their abuse of the clasp the matrons had forfeited all claim to protection. Defenseless, they were delivered over to the law of the men. The symbol of the mother goddess, which they had hitherto worn, was taken away from them. And the power of the men rose accordingly. As the cult of the nature mother gave way to that of the fecundating god, mother right declined.

The exchange of Doric for Ionian dress marks a decisive step in this development; it is not a cause but an outward indication. The dominant position of the Doric women was reflected in their dress, which concealed little and favored freedom of movement. It was sleeveless, held together at the shoulders by clasps; it left the thighs bare and altogether disclosed a nudity which struck many of the Ionians as indecent. The exchange of the Doric dress for the radically different Ionian costume, with its pleated linen robes that well concealed the body and clasps that held together the slitted sleeves, implied a return of womanhood from virile public life to the obscurity and subservience which characterize Oriental customs, and quickly result in Oriental degeneration.

In contrast to this Ionian development in Athens, the Aeginetans and Argives retained the Dorian customs and dress. They remained true to the old material-feminine principle of nature. Hence the conflict between the two systems. The Dorian women preserved their ancient garb and the old hieratic significance of the clasp pin. In order to mark the distinction even more sharply, they lengthened the clasp by half again. No Attic vessels might be brought into the temple of the mother goddesses. The Attic earth had lost its sanctity, its law had been broken. Drinking vessels now had to be fashioned of native clay. The earth which constituted the physical foundation, the womb of Damia, could alone be pleasing to the goddess. The baked clay stands in the same close relation to her as to Demeter and all the earth mothers and tomb goddesses of the dead; for this reason Pyrrhus, who was killed by a tile, was regarded as Demeter's darling.[31] If water must be drunk from native vessels, it is because the native maternal soil is held to be the repository and bestower of the water which awakens life in its womb. Thus the cult of Damia and Auxesia is surrounded by ordinances and usages based on the material motherhood of the all-generating earth and placing this motherhood at the summit of nature and religion. While Athens increasingly relinquished the material standpoint and forsook the feminine principle in religion and family for the masculine principle, the Dorians clung to the old law of the earth. In this regard they preserved an attachment to tradition and a character of permanence, while the Ionians were caught up in a restless striving for progress.

The old matriarchal tradition is most strikingly reflected in the Dorian dress. Even among men the Spartan maiden wears a simple garment which conceals little. Wearing only a chiton, Melissa the fair Epidaurian pours out wine for the workmen. It was thus that the Corinthian Periander saw her and fell in love with her.[32] And the Dorian maidens were clad the same way in their dances. Nude, says Plutarch,[33] they sing and lead the round. This offended the Athenians; their attitude was like that of the Romans toward the Germanic women. And yet it is certain that as a rule strict modesty in dress appears only when all is hopelessly lost and debauchery holds full sway. What Tacitus says of the Germanic women [34] is equally true of the Dorian women; they wore their arms bare up to the shoulder; even one side of the bosom was bare; and yet for them the marriage bond was inviolable, and no aspect of their mores was more praiseworthy. What a lovely arm, said someone of Theano the Pythagorean, and she replied: Yes, but not for everyone.[35] We also know the reply which Geradas, a Spartan of the earliest period, is said to have made to a stranger who asked him how adulterers were punished in Sparta. "Stranger," replied the Spartan, "in our country there are no adulterers." The stranger persisted: "But if there were an adulterer?" "Then," said Geradas, "he would have to offer up an ox so large that his head would stretch across the Taygetus and drink from the Eurotas." To which the amazed stranger remarked: "How is it possible that an ox can be so large?" And Geradas laughed: "How is it possible that there should be an adulterer in Sparta?" [36]

In this same passage Plutarch quotes Aristotle's criticism of the Lycurgan code for the freedom it accorded to women.[37] Plutarch himself shows a profound understanding of the old Dorian spirit when he writes: "There was nothing shameful about the nakedness of the virgins, for they were always accompanied by modesty and lechery was banned. Rather, it gave them a taste for simplicity and a care for outward dignity. The female sex accustomed themselves to male bravery, for they could make an equal claim to honor. Hence the Spartan women could boast, as Gorgo, the wife of Leonidas is said to have done when a foreign woman said to her, 'You Lacedaemonian women are the only women who rule over your men': 'We are also the only ones who bring men into the world.' " [38] Numerous replies of this sort have been recorded. And the experience of later days shows how fruitful this freedom of Spartan womanhood could be for public as well as private life, thus brilliantly controverting Aristotle's assertion that women have never been of any use to their country. The honorific titles μεσσόδομα (lady of the house) and δέσποινα (woman who commands) were frequently conferred on Spartan women.

By and large the decline in women's virtue sets in when the men begin to look down on them, when with advancing civilization the males develop a foppishness for which our own cultivated times have coined so many euphemistic terms. The progress of civilization is not favorable to woman. She is at her best in the so-called barbaric periods; later epochs destroy her hegemony, curtail her physical beauty, reduce her from the lofty position she enjoyed among the Dorian tribes to the bejeweled servitude that was her lot in Ionia and Attica, and ultimately compel her to regain through hetaerism the influence of which she has been deprived in marital relations.

All these phenomena disclose the same law: the more primordial the people, the more the feminine nature principle will dominate religious life and the higher woman's social position will be. Matriarchy is the heritage of those peoples whom Strabo calls barbarians—the first pre-Hellenic inhabitants of Greece and Asia Minor whose continuous migrations represent the beginning of ancient history, just as the migrations of the Nordic tribes ushered in the history of our own era. Carians, Leleges, Caucones, Pelasgians, are foremost among these πλανητικοί (migratory peoples). They disappear or take on other names, and the ideas and customs of the primordial age die with them. Only here and there do we find recognizable vestiges of a once universal system based on the pre-eminence of the feminine nature principle, a system which was partially preserved largely because of this religious foundation, but which we can reconstitute as a whole only by noting and comparing the elements that survived in a number of different places.

Lemnos

THE CRIME of the women of Lemnos has been mentioned above *
and compared to Clytaemnestra's murder of her husband. In the
Choephoroi of Aeschylus the chorus sings:

> Of all foul things legends tell the Lemnian
> outranks, a vile wizard's charm, detestable
> so that man names a hideous
> crime "Lemnian" in memory of their wickedness.[1]

Apollodorus narrates the event as follows: "Led by Jason the
Argonauts first sailed to Lemnos. At that time the island was
wholly bereft of men and ruled by Hypsipyle, daughter of Thoas.
This state of affairs came about as follows: The women of Lemnos
had neglected the cult of Aphrodite. As a punishment the goddess
afflicted them with δυσοσμία (foul smell). From disgust the men
allied themselves with captive maidens from nearby Thrace.
Enraged at this humiliation, the Lemnian women murdered their
fathers and husbands. Only Hypsipyle hid her father, Thoas, and
spared him. Thus Lemnos was governed by the women at that time.
The Argonauts lay with them. Hypsipyle shared Jason's bed and
bore Euneus and Nebrophonus."[2]

What gives Apollodorus' account a particular significance is
his use of the term γυναικοκρατουμένη (governed by women) in
connection with Lemnos. Here matriarchy takes its extreme form
of man-murdering Amazonism. The narrative we have cited not

* See pp. 104, 153.

only confirms the existence of Amazonism on Lemnos, but also throws light on the events that brought about the change from conjugal matriarchy to anticonjugal Amazonism. And herein lies the chief meaning of the Lemnian massacre. Aphrodite was hostile to the women of Lemnos because they had neglected her cult. The meaning is evident. The women of Lemnos found greater pleasure in the warlike life of the Amazon than in the fulfillment of their feminine calling. The law of Aphrodite, according to which marriage and childbearing are women's highest duty, was not fulfilled. Warlike valor was set above motherhood. Aphrodite avenged the women's neglect of her cult by destroying their charms. The δυσοσμία that she inflicted on the Lemnian women signifies the forfeiture, through Amazonism and its mannish practices, of true feminine beauty, of all those lures by which Pandora captivates men. The same idea is implicit in the myths of Achilles and Perseus, who recognize the full beauty of Penthesilea and the Gorgon only when they are wounded, breathing out their life in the arms of their conqueror. Warlike valor destroys all woman's charms. But death puts an end to this depravity. Only now does the queen awaken her adversary's love, never to be fulfilled.

Repelled by the δυσοσμία of their women, the men of Lemnos cohabit with the Thracian girls. These are prisoners whom they have captured in the course of pillaging expeditions on the nearby mainland. Here we see the Lemnian matriarchy amid the customs and social conditions that we have recognized above as the original background of matriarchal life.† Warfare removes the men for long periods from home and family, so that the domination of the women becomes a necessity. The mother cares for the children, tills the field, rules over the house and servants, and when necessary takes up arms to defend her hearth and home. The exercise of this domination, combined with her skill in handling weapons, increases the woman's sense of dignity and power. She towers high above the man, and the physical beauty which distinguishes the women of matriarchal states, and particularly of Lemnos, reflects the prestige of her position.

† See pp. 151ff.

Conversely, the name Sintian (σίντης, spoiler, thief) reflects the contempt inspired by the marauding life of the men. This most ancient name of the Lemnian people recalls the Ozolae (ὄζη, bad smell) and the Psoloeis (ψόλος, soot, smoke). The ignominy implied in all these names marks the contrast between the dominant woman and the servile man among matriarchal peoples. The Psoloeis of Minya are represented as grimy blacksmiths. The Locrian shepherds are said to have been named Ozolae from the smell of goatskins. Two explanations have been offered for the name Sintian: some interpreted it as an allusion to a wild marauding life; Hellanicus, on the other hand, regarded it as a reference to the blacksmith's trade and the forging of weapons, first practiced by the Sintians of Hephaestian Lemnos.[3] According to both explanations the men occupy a position which could not but enhance the women's sense of spiritual and physical superiority. If we bear this in mind, it becomes evident that conjugal matriarchy was bound to degenerate into Amazonism and that ultimately the thirst for vengeance against more fortunate rivals, and the lust for power, would goad the Lemnian women to their bloody crime.

Those who relegate the massacre of the men to the realm of invention fail to appreciate woman's insatiable bloodthirst [4] and to realize how the habit of domination was bound to exacerbate her natural passions. They divest the history of the human race of a memory which may strike milder and more cultivated generations as an absurdity, but which nevertheless must be counted undeniably among the real experiences of mankind.

The bloody crime of the Lemnian women is the supreme expression of matriarchy at its peak. The offense against the marriage bond is avenged, the rival is slain, her race wiped out. The women of Lemnos take on a heroic stature, they are grandiose Amazonian figures who have cast off all the weakness of their sex. But this supreme triumph is also a degeneration. Such heroic grandeur is not proper to women. And the myth shows that this extreme embodiment of matriarchy contained the seeds of its own downfall. For amidst these blood-drenched Amazons appears their queen, innocent and obedient to love, a model of womanly affection and tenderness. Hypsipyle cannot subordinate her natural feeling to the interests of the Amazonian state. She spares her father, Thoas. And this saving of her father becomes all the more meaningful when we consider that she bears Jason two sons, one of whom, Euneus, is called Jasonides in Homer.[5] Thus Hypsipyle marks the transition from mother right to father right. She is an Amazon, exponent of mother right, yet she becomes the mother of a race which traces its lineage back to the father; and, alone among the women of Lemnos, she professes the paternal principle by abstaining from patricide. In Apollonius [6] the queen promises the departing hero Jason that if he should ever return, he will inherit her father's scepter, not her own. Her own, as we learn from Strabo,[7] later passed to Euneus the Jasonid. And Hyginus, surely drawing an old tradition, tells us that all the women of Lemnos named the children begotten by the Argonauts after their fathers.[8] This is significant because the patronymic was contrary to the basic idea of Amazonism. If the Lemnian women gave their children their fathers' names, if Hypsipyle's sons came to be known as Jasonids, it meant that Amazonism and all mother right had been transcended and the principle of paternity established.

The union of Hypsipyle with Jason makes it seem likely that father right was introduced to Lemnos by a band of Minyae driven from home by similar Amazonian conditions. The literature contains a number of passages indicating that the island was populated by Jasonids or Minyae.[9] And this may be why the island of Lemnos found its place in the saga of the Argonauts.

It is characteristic that Heracles alone of all the heroes remained on board the *Argo* and reproached his friends for lying with the Amazons. Since the accounts of this brief visit stress the nature of Amazonian life, Heracles appears fully in character. In all his myths he is the irreconcilable foe of matriarchy, the indefatigable battler of Amazons, the misogynist, in whose sacrifice no woman takes part, by whose name no woman swears, and who finally meets his death from a woman's poisoned garment. He preserves this same character among the Argonauts. He has his fit place among the Minyae, establishers of father right, but this destroyer of Amazons cannot set foot on the manless island ruled by women.

Hypsipyle's father, Thoas, finds an illuminating parallel in Achilles, who is also truly θόας (swift). In fact, swiftness of foot is one of his distinguishing attributes, and recurs in the Ἀχιλλέως δρόμοι (races of Achilles). His fleetness belongs to him as a water god, and also as Deus Lunus—in which form he dwells, wedded to Helen, on Leuce, the island of the moon, and runs around it daily as Talos ran around Crete; and, finally, swiftness is his attribute as an Apollonian sun hero, in which quality he is represented as persecuting Hemithea on Tenedos. What gives this parallel a special interest is that, no less than Dionysus and the other solar heroes, the fleet Achilles is associated with the conquest of Amazonism. He, in whose lineage the mother overshadows the father, battles triumphantly for solar father right, and on the island of Leuce he completes the struggle against the Amazonian principle that he had begun on earth. As an Apollonian sun hero he excels all in swiftness, and this characteristic becomes an expression of the dominance of the male over the female principle.

Herein lies the root of the often recurring mythological fiction of the Amazonian virgin who races with the hero and is carried off as the prize of his victory. Hippodamia is the prize won by Pelops. The Amazonian virgin is defeated, and gladly she follows the male hero whose higher nature she recognizes. Marriage takes the place of hostility, and in the newly established race it is the father who rules. The Pelopids bear the paternal sign of Neptune on their right arm, the maternal symbol on their left arm.** This fully confirms the significance of Thoas, Hypsipyle's father, in the Lemnian myth. His name and his genealogical connection with Dionysus-Ariadne (he was regarded as their son), are proofs of his relation to Amazonian mother right, which in him and his line gave way to the higher Dionysian principle.

** A passage from *Gräbersymbolik* (in *Gesammelte Werke*, Vol. 4, p. 208) may serve to elucidate this: "The Pelopids are said to have shown on their right shoulder the Neptunian trident, and on their left upper arm the Gorgon's head. The former indicates their descent on the father's side from Poseidon Genesios who had helped Pelops to win Hippodamia, the latter that on the female side." [10]

Egypt

THE EGYPTIAN STAGE of marriage law may be designated as the lunar stage. We have no longer the purely tellurian, nor yet the exclusively solar principle.

This lunar stage is grounded in the marriage bond. Sun and moon represent a model of the exclusive relation between husband and wife. At this stage the woman towers above the man, the material principle overshadows the awakening cause. The children are no longer *unilaterales,* no longer like swamp plants exclusively children of the mother; they are διφυεῖς, *bilaterales, tam patris quam matris* (dual-natured, bilateral, as much the father's as the mother's).* Here we first encounter the concept of authentic birth, in the light of which the offspring of purely tellurian motherhood are regarded as inauthentic. This feature is definitely emphasized in the myth of Isis. After the death of Osiris Typhon contests the authentic birth of Horus, while the heavenly gods, supported by Hermes, set it forth as a certainty. From Typhon's tellurian standpoint there is no such thing as authenticity. But from the higher standpoint of the cosmic-celestial order Horus is seen as an authentic scion. For it was not as Terra, not as swamp mother, but as Luna that Isis bore him to her heavenly husband, Osiris. Through the lunar nature of his mother the son became διφυής, hence the authentic, legitimate scion. His mother's *matrimonium* gives the son a definite father. But this father is his only through

* See p. 146.

the mediation of the mother. Horus is first the son of Isis, and only as such is he the son of Osiris. The father is second to the mother, the higher but also the more remote causality. Thus the lunar stage is superior to the tellurian stage, since it involves matrimony and authentic birth, but inferior to the solar stage in that it sets mother above father. Osiris enters into the moon and becomes Lunus through Luna, not the other way round. Apollo and Athene manifest a motherless paternity; with Isis and Osiris the paternal principle is contained in motherhood. We have, then, three stages: the tellurian, corresponding to motherhood without marriage; the lunar, corresponding to conjugal motherhood and authentic birth; the solar, corresponding to conjugal father right.

For the lunar stage of nature religion there is only transience. It has not yet risen from the mortality of the creature to the immortality of the principle. Osiris himself, like the Cretan Zeus, is still mortal. The center of gravity is still on the maternal side and the solar principle is secondary. But just as the moon is bound to the sun in chaste wedlock and is fecundated by no one else, so the mortal woman is faithful to her wedded husband; her offspring is an authentic, legitimate child. Here mother right is bound up with the certainty of the father. Horus, the authentic scion of Osiris, is still first and foremost his mother's son. Marriage and mother right are concomitant; an expression of the lunar religious stage which interprets life only in its transient appearance, not in the immutability of the male solar principle. This is the intermediary stage of human development; the supreme Apollonian stage is still to come. And now we shall show how the inclusion of the Oedipus myth in the corpus of the Pythian (Apollonian) religion reflects the transition to this ultimate stage.

My introductory remarks on the Oedipus myth are drawn from the passage in which Sophocles likens the daughters of Oedipus, who faithfully follow their father in his wanderings, to the women of Egypt:

Ah! They behave as if they were Egyptians,
Bred the Egyptian way! Down there, the men

Sit indoors all day long, weaving;
The women go out and attend to business.
Just so your brothers, who should have done this work,
Sit by the fire like home-loving girls,
And you two, in their place, must bear my hardships.[1]

Such a comparison in the work of a Greek tragic poet would have
seemed very strange if it had not been grounded in tradition. The
Sphinx, such an important part of the Oedipus myth, originated in
Egypt. And furthermore Cadmus, from whom Oedipus and the
Labdacids are descended, was associated with Egypt, as we are
told in both Diodorus [2] and Pausanias.[3] It is this association that
led Sophocles to speak of the Egyptian women, and through it the
myth of Oedipus takes on a relevance for Egypt. Here we shall not
consider the myth in detail. A few general remarks will suffice to
show its bearing on our investigation.

The religious ideas underlying the mythical figure of Oedipus
(Swollen Foot) are self-evident. The swollen foot from which he
takes his name shows him to be an embodiment of the male
fecundating principle, which in its tellurian-Poseidonian aspect is
not infrequently associated with the foot or the shoe. The Neptunian significance of the chariot that caused the swelling is well
known. Hyginus calls Oedipus *impudens* [4] (shameless), quite aside
from his relation to his mother. This is an allusion to the
exuberantly sensual fecundating principle prevailing in the unregulated tellurian sexuality of the swamp, and it is this "shameless-
ness" that gives the swollen foot its meaning. In this stage of the
natural principle, as many myths show, the mother is seen also as
the wife, even as the daughter of the man who fecundates her: each
generation of men in turn fecundates the maternal matter of earth.
The son becomes husband and father, the same primordial woman
is today impregnated by the grandfather, tomorrow by the grandson. Hence the riddle regarding Iocasta: *avia filiorum est, quae
mater mariti* [5] (grandmother to her sons, mother to her husband).
According to this conception, Oedipus belongs to the race of the
Spartoi, the *genus draconteum* (the dragon people), called to life
by the virile dragon, the Ladon of the moist depths; the Spartoi
have no recognizable father but only a mother, like the *spurii*,

whose name is identical in meaning. The child does not know his own begetter, and this is what makes the patricide possible. Iocasta (who, very characteristically, is also called Epicasta), daughter of Menoeceus, is the mother of Oedipus. But Menoeceus is definitely descended from the *draconteum genus*, the Spartoi.† The Spartoi, as we might expect, observed the maternal, matrilinear system. Creon, represented in the myth as a usurper, seeks to attain legitimacy through union with his sister Iocasta, widow of Laius, and in line with the same juridical system he marries his youngest daughter Glauce to Jason. We have already become familiar with this significance of sisterhood.**

The Sphinx is an embodiment of tellurian motherhood; she represents the feminine right of the earth in its dark aspect as the inexorable law of death.†† [6] She comes from the remotest ends of the earth, from Ethiopia, the land of Queen Aso, the ally of Typhon, the land whose queens, down to the latest times, have borne the name of Candace. In the riddle whose solution will put an end to the Sphinx's power, man is considered only in his transient aspect, mortality; the downward path to the tomb is the sole and ultimate idea of his existence. This is the religious stage at which tellurian matter alone is dominant; this is the stage of mankind which knows only a mother and no father. The life-law of the *draconteum genus* is embodied in the riddle of the Sphinx; once it is understood, once its utter hopelessness is recognized, this law will be at an end. The race of the Spartoi, who have only a mother and are engendered by the dragon of the dark depths, recognize the Typhonian Sphinx as their ruler. She sends forth matter from darkness to light, and she will again consume it. This people's lot is no different from that of the swamp plants which come into being and pass away unwept. Man has not yet risen above the lowest stage of tellurian generation.

Oedipus marks the advance to a higher stage of existence. He is one of those great figures whose suffering and torment lead to higher human civilization, who, themselves still rooted in the older

† They might also be called *parthenopaei*, children of a virgin; Diodorus 4. 65.4 tells us that Atalanta's son, grandson of Schoeneus the rush man, was called Parthenopaeus. [B.]
** See p. 138f.
†† As emblem of Parthenopaeus the Sphinx takes on added significance. [B.]

state of things, represent the last great victim of this condition and by this same token the founder of a new era. With the Sphinx Iocasta's father, Menoeceus, the last of the *draconteum genus,* meets his end. The leap from the wall, which recurs in so many myths, always discloses the same connection with maternal tellurism, to whose realm the wall belongs because it is a product of the earth and hence partakes of chthonian *sanctitas* (inviolability).* The simultaneous downfall of the Spartoi and the Sphinx shows that they are based on the same principle. It is against the background of this principle that Oedipus makes his appearance.

In the son of Laius the male principle takes on independent significance side by side with the female. In the name Oedipus virility is dominant. Moreover, his male lineage is stressed in the myth. The son mourns the death of Polybus, his supposed father, and the condition of his feet reveals the paternity of Laius. The authentic birth of children begins with Oedipus. The men of this new race are no longer Spartoi or *spurii,* but sons of Oedipus, or traced back to the first tribal chiefs, Cadmaeans and Labdacids, authentic sons and διφυεῖς: a transition which also throws light on the history of the Spartans and Laconians or Lacedaemonians. The old condition of exclusive motherhood corresponding to tellurian swamp generation, in which only the feminine matter is considered, now gives way to the Demetrian stage grounded in marriage. Oedipus breaks with hetaerism to find peace in bond with Demeter. He lies buried in her temple, named Oedipodeum after him. And the oracle commanded that his body never be removed from this temple.

Iocasta's clasp conveys the same meaning. It carries the same Aphroditean significance as in the Aeginetan-Athenian tradition discussed above.† It is with this clasp, symbol of Aphroditean union, that Oedipus puts out his eyes, because by lying with his mother he has offended against the purer law of the gods of light. His act is a condemnation of the impure hetaeric-tellurian motherhood to which he owed all his sufferings, and which he transcends in favor of the pure Demetrian law. That is why the people came to regard him as a beneficent demon with power to ward off evil. In Colonus and in the Attic-Boeotian border town of Eteonus his tomb

* See pp. 40ff.   † See p. 166.

182

was held to be a protection against marauders. And woman in particular venerated Oedipus as the institutor of her higher condition. By initiating Demetrian life he became her benefactor, her redeemer. Breaking the curse of Aphroditean hetaerism that attached to Harmonia's necklace and Iocasta's clasp, Demeter's law brought woman peace and all the happiness of a love life regulated by exclusive marriage; hetaerism gave way to motherhood. This is the profounder meaning of the self-sacrifice of Ismene and Antigone. Woman, who in her earlier state had been the source of all evil, now becomes a blessing to man. Hetaeric lust was subservient only to Aphrodite's sensual law; it was in obeying this law and desecrating Pelops' son Chrysippus that Laius had brought a curse on his race. Now hetaerism was replaced by the self-sacrificing love which sought to reconcile all strife among men. The blood-drenched Erinyes became Eumenides (Gracious Ones). Reconciled, they received Oedipus into their sacred grove. And Oedipus, who had borne all the sufferings of the former age, found peace with them.

In his Oedipus trilogy Aeschylus contrasted the bloody primordial law of the earth—which creates murder from murder, the law of talion, which requites crime with crime and knows no atonement, but only the disastrous riddle of the Sphinx, and destroys entire peoples, root and branch—with the new, milder law of Apollo. It is the same contrast as we have seen in the *Oresteia*. As in the *Eumenides* the Erinyes yearn to cast off their bloody office, to change from avenging earth goddesses to mothers of all blessing, here too they take under their protection him whom they have so long persecuted [7] and make him one of their own. He comes to be worshiped in union with the Erinyes as well as Demeter. When the wrath of the tellurian earth mothers threatens the fruitfulness of their people, the oracle advises the Theban Aegids to erect a common shrine to Oedipus and the Erinyes. [8] Here the mothers are clearly subordinated to the purer Apollonian law. For the god of the Aegids is Apollo, whose Carnean festival extends from Thebes to Sparta, from Thera to the Battiads of Cyrene. Salvation comes from Apollo, and the Erinyes bow willingly to his higher law; to him they gladly sacrifice their bloody office. The god of the Aegids had ordered the propitiation of

Oedipus and the Erinyes of Laius. Here the earth mothers become the avenging spirits of the father, just as in the *Oresteia,* matricide summons them from the depths. This does not contradict their exclusive maternal nature but merely amplifies it, grounding it even in the Apollonian law. Only their subordination to Apollo has made possible a bond between them and the father, a bond resulting from the fusion of the cult of the Erinyes with the higher Apollonian cult; the introduction of the Pythian oracle into all parts of the *Oedipodeia* [9] is a reflection of this development.

According to the primordial manner of thinking, the earth mothers could no more have risen up in behalf of Laius than of the slain Agamemnon. It was their subordination to Apollo that first made them champions of the father and his injured right. In this new connection they are no longer the irreconcilable, bloody mothers who know only the law of the earth; they have become conciliatory, well-disposed powers who gladly acknowledge the higher atonement. When the oracle decrees the building of a temple to Oedipus and the Erinyes of Laius, it speaks not to the bloody primordial powers, but to the friendly mothers now allied with Apollo, who have exchanged hatred and vengeance for love and solicitude.

Thus the *Oedipodeia* takes its place beside the *Oresteia.* In both, the tellurian law of the Erinyes is transcended and subordinated to the higher Apollonian law. The *Oedipodeia* is thus a completion and continuation of the *Oresteia.* Through Orestes Apollo battled with the maternal Erinyes and defeated them in their own exclusive realm, while the ultimate pardon of Oedipus shows that a crime even against the paternal principle of Apollo can be atoned. Now the milder law of the Pythian god becomes universal. The paternal Erinyes of Laius, reconciled with Oedipus, show the beneficent power of Apollo in its supreme perfection. In the *Oresteia* the Σεμναί (Venerable Ones) are conciliated, but they still remain representatives of maternity, hence fundamentally alien to Apollo; now they enter into the closest union with the paternal god. It is in the temple of the venerable mothers that Apollo announces to Oedipus the final solution of his destiny, and the Apollonian Aegids themselves propagate the cult of the mothers. Oedipus and the paternal Erinyes of Laius are drawn into the Pythian religion; they become, as it were, a part of the

Apollonian nature, hence far closer to luminous father right than were the maternal Erinyes of Clytaemnestra, whose bond with the feminine principle excluded them forever from any such union with the Pythian.

What makes this gradual development particularly meaningful is that it corresponds to a historical advance of human institutions. The memory of the transition from older religious stages to purer ideas, and of all the sufferings and catastrophes which induced and accompanied this transformation, underlie the myths of both Oedipus and Orestes. Deposits of the earliest national memories, such myths are at the same time a source of knowledge concerning the oldest religious ideas. Historical events provide the content, religion the form and expression. In the human memory all events take on religious form. In that primordial era faith governed man's whole manner of thinking. Events and their heroes appear in the cloak of religion. One and the same myth encompasses religious and historical facts, and the two are not separate but identical. Oedipus and Orestes belong both to religion and to history, and the one by virtue of the other. Every great step in the development of the human race is situated in the realm of religion, which is always the greatest vehicle of civilization, and in the primordial era the only one. But although I have gone to some pains in developing the religious idea in accordance with which legend took form, I do not mean to deny the historical foundation of the destinies of the Labdacids. I do not mean to reduce the positive elements to a phantasm, but only to provide a key to the hieroglyph. If we can decipher this hieroglyph, we shall acquire an otherwise unobtainable insight into the earliest times of our race. Even though the picture that unrolls before us may offer little comfort, even though it may not encourage much pride in our beginnings, still, the spectacle of man gradually transcending the bestial in his nature may offer firm ground for a confident belief that through all vicissitudes the human race will find the power to complete its triumphant journey upward from the depths, from the night of matter to the light of a celestial-spiritual principle.

The feminine principle of nature as expression and source of law is not a conception limited to Egypt. Beside Isis, other nature mothers appear in the same significance. The principle that stands at the summit of material creation must also be the source and foundation of a justice concerned solely with the material life of man. This conception stands out in the Pythagorean number mysticism. The basic number of *iustitia* (justice) is the feminine two. Two opens the numerical series, just as the woman stands at the summit of the material world, of the ὁρατὸς κόσμος (visible cosmos). The number one admits of no differentiation between even and odd. It designates the unity of the natural principle. With two begins the differentiation of two numerical natures, of the even and odd; it designates the advance from the unity of the principle to the δυάς (duality) of the sexes, as manifested in material creation. Therefore the two is matter itself, and as matter it is woman, the ὑλικόν, παθητικόν [10] (the material, passive principle), the χώρα καὶ δεξαμενὴ γενέσεως [11] (the seat and matter of becoming), and at the same time it is justice, which has its seat and expression in matter and its equal division.

Thus the number two unites the same attributes as are combined in Isis and all the nature mothers. The idea of matter and the receptive principle on the one hand, and the idea of justice and equal division on the other, are merely different aspects of the same maternity, so that *iustitia* and *aequitas* are innate attributes of the feminine nature principle. Consequently the number two is synonymous with the left side. For the left, as we have seen,** is the feminine side and at the same time the side of justice. And indeed, the ancients identified the even numbers with the left side, the odd numbers with the right side. The former belong to the woman, the latter to the man. Correspondingly, Plato assigned the right side and the odd numbers to the Olympian gods, their counterparts to the demons, that is, to the earthly and mortal. To the gods of the earth should be sacrificed second-choice animals in even number and parts from the left side; while odd numbers, the first choice, and parts from the right side should be offered to the Olympian gods. [12] Here the even number is connected with the left side, and both are assigned to tellurism, to the female nature principle.

** See pp. 76f., 110.

Thus justice is linked to the feminine-material aspect of nature, to the even number and the left side. The character of this justice is self-evident. The *dyas* is the number of perfectly equal parts without the slightest residue. From this it follows that the justice based on duality must be the law of talion. The punishment must fit the crime, the two pans of the scale must be evenly balanced. Retaliation and retribution are the entire content of such dualist justice. It is a play of two contrary forces which cancel suffering by suffering, hence Pythagoras' "suffering as counterweight to suffering"; [13] hence Aristotle's "suffering of numbers"; [14] hence Plutarch's "to do injustice and suffer injustice"; [15] hence the suffering that follows action and makes two from one, the *secundus motus* that opposes a *primus motus*. The justice represented by the number two is bloody, always assuring the subterranean gods of two sacrifices, as we have seen above in connection with the tellurian justice of the Erinyes.†† The dual justice is strife and conflict, and according to Plutarch, it is in these terms that the Pythagoreans defined the *dyas*.[16] Justice and strife coincide. The two are identical.

An image of such retributive justice, which the ancients called Νεοπτολέμειος τίσις (Neoptolemean retribution), was the double murder of the Theban brothers. Their father Oedipus had ordained that each in turn should rule for a year. But at the end of the year Eteocles refused to hand over the government to Polynices. They fought and both were killed, "Polynices finding his end according to the law of nature, and Eteocles, too, in accordance with justice" [δίκαιον].[17] Here justice is a perfect *dyas:* first the alternation of the kingship, then the double murder, in which Eteocles atones for the death of Polynices by his own death, so fulfilling the law of talion. But such justice never brings a solution. Even after death the two flames part and blow eternally in opposite directions.[18] The *dyas* proves to be discord. The justice conceived as duality is an eternal, never-ending conflict. Murder begets murder and the demon of the race rages down through the generations until all are destroyed.

In its application to justice the *dyas* proves once again to be an

†† See p. 164.

"indefinite number," as it was often called by the ancients. Its attribute is indeterminacy and endlessness, for it never leads to a conclusion, its innermost law is eternal fission.[19] It is the number of death and destruction, the *mortalis numerus*. Conceived as *dyas*, justice is the law of death. Dual justice is a repetition of the conflict between the two eternally opposing forces which dominate the "visible cosmos"—between the force of creation and the force of destruction. Justice itself is only a copy of natural life, which moves eternally back and forth between two poles; a double movement, attack and counterattack, with never a conclusion. The law of material life becomes a juridical concept, death is seen as a *debitum naturae* [20] (our debt to nature). And this is more than a mere image; it is a statement that natural life is justice, that φύσις and δίκαιον are identical.

The same relationship recurs in the Dioscuri. Their ἐτερημερία (daily alternating life) is an image not only of the alternation between life and death, day and night, that governs the world, but also of the highest justice, in recognition of which the surviving brother voluntarily shares his immortality with the dead one.

Justice conceived as consisting of two contrary movements recurs in the doctrine which Plato attributes to the Mysteries: ". . . that story [shall be mentioned] which is believed by many when they hear it from the lips of those who seriously relate such things at their mystic rites,—that vengeance for such acts is exacted in Hades, and that those who return again to this earth are bound to pay the natural penalty,—each culprit the same, that is, which he inflicted on his victim,—and that their life on earth must end in their meeting a like fate at the hands of another" [21] (Neoptolemean retribution). Here again, natural life and justice are identical. A twofold movement constitutes both life and justice, and this interaction of two forces is as inconclusive as the interchange of life and death in visible creation; every "doing of injustice" results in a "suffering of injustice," which provokes another equal injustice. The action which is supposed to restore the balance, the ἴσον καὶ δίκαιον (equal and just), brings about a new disturbance in the *partium aequa libratio* (the equilibrium of the parts). The *summum ius* is at the same time a *summa iniuria*, Orestes the avenger of the murder is *facto pius et sceleratus eodem* (virtuous and criminal by the same act).

Justice bound up with the material feminine principle means natural freedom and equality. This is the *ius naturale* of which the Roman jurists speak. It is assuredly no accident that Ulpian, who was of Phoenician origin, should resolutely have upheld this physical-natural justice and defined it wholly in the spirit of the ancient mother religion. "Natural justice is the justice that nature has taught all living creatures; for this justice is not specific to the human race but common to all living creatures who are born on earth and in the sea and to the birds as well. It gives rise to the union of man and woman which we call marriage, to the bearing and rearing of children; for we also see the other living creatures, even the wild beasts, evaluated according to their knowledge of this justice." [22] Ulpian's *ius naturale* proves to be the Aphroditean law which permeates matter and causes it to be fertilized. It is Aphrodite who fills the two sexes with the urge for generation, who implants solicitude for the offspring, who forges the bond between mother and child and secures the freedom and equality of all the progeny. All special privilege is odious to this goddess. Hence the equal right of all to the sea, the seashore, the air; and the *communis omnium possessio* [23] (common property) may be traced back to the *ius naturale*. And in recognizing the principle of *vim vi repellere* [24] (repelling force by force) as natural law, the same Ulpian again manifests a preoccupation with physical existence and with the dualist justice of the female nature principle, which has a profounder kinship with the *natura iustum* (that which is just by nature) than does the male sex, with its greater susceptibility to the principle of domination and of positive legislation.

The frequent emphasis on a purely natural point of view in law deserves the highest consideration. It is a reaction against the positive political standpoint to which Rome subordinated all life and an endeavor to escape the domination of form. Such a movement toward the purely physical law of nature confirms the dictum that the end of human institutions is close to their beginning.

One great law governs the juridical development of man. It advances from the material to the immaterial, from the physical to the metaphysical, from tellurism to spirituality. The ultimate goal can be attained only through the united effort of all peoples and ages, but attained it assuredly will be despite all ups and downs. What begins materially must end immaterially. At the end of all juridical development there stands a new *ius naturale*, now not of matter but of spirit; an ultimate justice which will be universal, just as the primordial justice was universal; which, like the primordial law, will be free from all arbitrariness; dictated by the things themselves; not invented but discovered by man, just as the primordial physical law appeared as an immanent material order. The Persians believed that there would someday be one justice and one language. "When Ahriman is destroyed the earth will be flat and level, and happy mankind will have one mode of life, one form of government, and one language." [25] This last justice expresses the pure radiance of the good principle. It is not tellurian like the bloody dark justice of the first material era, but celestial and luminous, the perfect law of Zeus. But its ultimate sublimation must also imply its dissolution. Through liberation from all material admixture, law becomes love. Love is the highest justice. And this justice again appears in the dual, but not, like the old tellurian justice, in the duality of conflict and never-ending annihilation: now it discloses the duality that offers the other cheek and gladly gives away the second cloak. In this doctrine the highest justice is realized. Its perfection transcends even the concept of justice and so becomes the ultimate and complete negation of matter, the resolution of all dissonance.

Thus far * our discussion of the relation between justice and the material-feminine nature principle has been limited to the lowest, purely Aphroditean stage of tellurian life. This stage is characterized by unregulated sexual relation, the absence of all individual possessions or private rights of any kind, by the communal holding of women, children, and consequently of all property; it is a stage of formless, orderless freedom, and the only bond between creatures is that of Aphroditean desire. There is as yet no state or fixed abode, but a nomadic life which ends only with death and knows no stable resting place other than the tomb. Debased and humiliat-

* The following section up through the paragraph ending at the top of p. 193 is taken from sect. 16 of *Gräbersymbolik*.

ing as they may now seem, such conditions were no doubt indispensable for the early propagation and rapid growth of our race.

Religion and law achieved a higher form through the transition to agriculture. Pure Aphroditism gave way to the Demetrian principle. Communal property was superseded by individual ownership and hetaerism by matrimony as the Aphroditean self-generating swamp vegetation gave way to the *laborata Ceres* [26] (the tilled soil). The transition was marked by the contest between Carpus and Calamus (grain and rush). Nonnus assuredly cites the myth in its traditional form.[27] Attracted by the golden fruits, Atalanta turns aside from her race, sacrificing victory and freedom to the lure of possession. The *Schoeneia virgo*, the daughter of Schoeneus the rush man, renounces her proud freedom and resigns herself to her new fate.[28] The gods of the purely natural life are hostile to the new culture, for marriage and the Demetrian mystery that it introduces are hateful to the primordial gods of matter. Although these primordial powers include egg mothers such as Demeter and like gods of the grain give and destroy life, they now become dark destroyers in the presence of the new life. They are irrevocably hostile to the marriage rite. The human race breaks away from the bond that had hitherto encompassed all material creation, and at first this vast advance of mankind disturbs the harmony of earthly life. The *ius naturale* is abandoned, only to be reinstated in an ennobled form. With agriculture, motherhood takes on a new significance, a higher form. The wild swamp generation, which eternally rejuvenates matter in everlasting self-embrace, which brings forth only reeds and rushes or the "swampy offspring of the sources," [29] and which springs up uselessly without regard to man, is replaced by the act of the tiller of the soil, who opens the womb of the earth with his plow, who lays the seed in the furrow, and harvests nutritious fruit, Demeter's food, "when the joyous harvesters cut the limbs of Ceres." [30]

The earth becomes wife and mother, the man who guides the plow and scatters the seed becomes husband and father. The man is joined in wedlock with feminine matter, and this provides the model for an intimate, enduring, and exclusive relation between the sexes. The male plow opens up the womb of the earth and of woman as well; this twofold act is indeed but one, and in respect to the earth as to woman, it is no longer a passing hetaeric episode but a conjugal union. The man's act does not aim at the satisfaction of sensual lust, but at the production of golden fruit. The sexes meet *liberorum quaerendorum causa* [31] (to acquire children), not "for the sake of desire." It is by this sublimation that woman first gains peace. In her lasting union with Eros, Psyche achieves the happiness which she vainly sought to capture in unregulated hetaerism, in the base promiscuity of the swamp. Woman has risen from pure tellurism to the lunar stage of existence; she is given to the man for his enduring and exclusive possession, as Luna is given to Sol-Lunus. The children now have a father as well as a mother, they are legitimate offspring.

This stage of life has a new justice. The Aphroditean *ius naturale* gives way to a Demetrian *ius naturale*. But the new justice too is bound up with the feminine nature principle. It preserves the material-maternal character of the old stage. Demeter becomes θεσμοφόρος,[32] Ceres becomes *legifera* [33] (lawgiver), just as Aphrodite governed the old *ius naturale*. The Demetrian law is also a true *ius naturale*, but its foundation is a vegetation regulated by agriculture, not left to itself; *laborata Ceres*, not the *creatio ultronea* (wild plant life) † of Aphrodite. At this stage the exclusive conjugal principle predominates over hetaeric universality. Gaia, the earth, and mortal woman in her image, gives herself to man as his exclusive possession. Gaia is no longer a mother in an unrestricted universal sense; now she has this quality in respect to a definite man, whose seed she receives, for whose benefit she conceives, and to whom finally she gives her fruit. She is no longer Penia, who follows all men and rejoices in all fecundation, she is no longer the daughter who inclines without will of her own to the male scepter. Rather, she shuns all that is masculine, endures violence and rape, and preserves the mystery character of undesecrated matronhood. Thus she becomes the vehicle of a higher law which extends to all spheres of life and may be designated as conjugal mother right. It has been asserted that the θεσμοί (decrees) of Demeter referred only to the marriage bond among men. This is true to the extent that marriage actually forms

† See also p. 97. Elsewhere Bachofen cites Servius, *Georgics* 2. 11 as his source for *creatio ultronea*, but the expression does not occur there.

the center of all Demetrian law. But marriage itself cannot be restricted to human beings. It also comprised man's relation to the earth, to the field. It encompassed agriculture and sexual union in one concept and one mystery; it provided one justice for field and family.

Justice forms a part of religion. It is θεσμός in the strict sense, "given by the gods," as Aeschylus adds.[34] As priests of Ceres the aediles have charge of the law. Their various attributes may be explained through this connection with the great mother goddess. They stand in the same relation as the goddess herself to the community, to the market, to the buildings, to public life and justice. And the praetors stand in a similar relation to Bona Dea. Plutarch tells us that the festival of Bona Dea was always celebrated in the house of a praetor or consul.[35] This house became the temple of the goddess whom the Greeks simply called γυναικεία θεός (feminine godhead).[36] Bona Dea is the maternal nature principle that generates and nourishes all material life and promotes the material well-being of the people. Thus she was the maternal foundation of the state's welfare; it was through their bond with her that praetor and consul represented the material side of the nation's existence and administered justice. Justice resided in the same primordial mother who created material wealth. And the praetor gave expression to justice as the organ and *viva vox* of Bona Dea-Fauna-Fatua. Through this tie with the material primordial mother he was enabled to observe the practical justice of the *ius naturale*, the equity of the left hand, often in opposition to the strictly formal logic of the civil law. As "feminine godhead" Bona Dea became equivalent to Themis, in whose mysteries the worship of the feminine κτείς, the *sporium muliebre* (womb), plays so prominent a part. The name "feminine godhead" takes on its full meaning only when the same physical, sensuous implication is recognized. Thus the cult of the κτείς involved not only the idea of maternal fertility but the maternal mystery of justice, the ὄργια θεσμῶν (cult of the laws) as well. And the term *ius Quiritium*, which was limited to civil law, also recalls the feminine origins of justice. For the Romans were Quirites in their feminine-material aspect, in view of their maternal Sabine origin, hence in their physical, not their political existence.

Another manifestation of the feminine as vehicle of justice is

Juno Moneta, whom Suidas identifies with a *iustitia in bellis*.[37] She assists the injured party and favors his undertakings.[38] Her temple was situated in the Area M. Manlii Capitolini. By his assault on Roman freedom Manlius had offended against the material-feminine principle of justice, which the Romans propitiated by dedicating the site of the Manlian house to Juno Moneta.[39] The epithet Moneta implies a relationship both to the source of material wealth and to the justice which admonishes and metes out punishment. Everywhere the mother of wealth is also the mother of the justice that governs it.

A further aspect of this conception is the connection between the *ovatio* and the feminine nature principle. The *triumphus* belonged to the patrician state and its underlying paternal solar principle.[40] The *ovatio*, on the other hand, had a feminine-material character. It was associated with Murcia, celebrated by a tellurian sacrifice of sheep, and approved whenever any inexactitude was noted in the observance of the formalities of the positive law.[41] The decrees of the positive law were repellent to the feminine nature principle. Thus the *ovatio* may be termed the little triumph of the *ius naturale*, while the *triumphus* was a manifestation of the positive, patrician political law. Hence the nonpatrician classes, particularly the knights, also took part in the *ovatio*. The plebs (πλῆθος) was held to be descended from feminine-material motherhood, while the patriciate derived its title and higher religious position from father right and the *patrem ciere*.

Ceres is the great protectress of the plebs. The plebeian community is dedicated chiefly to her, just as in Athens the popular assembly was closely related to Demeter. The community confided its treasury, its laws, and the decisions of the Senate to the temple of Ceres, where they were secure against falsification.[42] The assembly met under the protection of Ceres. To the higher solar consecration of the patriciate the people opposed the sanctity of the material primal mother. The plebs entered into the state from the feminine-material side; it partook of the *ius Quiritium*, not of the political ordinances based on the higher paternal consecration, on the *patrem ciere posse*. That is why King Servius,** as son of his mother (a maidservant), dedicated the

** See pp. 213ff.

Latin League to the Aventine temple of Diana, who in Italy bore the name of Ops.[43] Only from the feminine-material side could Rome found a political league with the Latin peoples, not from the paternal side, on which the imperium rested. It is the natural, not the political family that is headed by the feminine element.

We have demonstrated the bond between justice and material motherhood in two stages of human development, the lower Aphroditean-hetaeric stage and the higher Demetrian-conjugal stage. The former corresponds to the unregulated swamp generation, the latter to ordered agriculture. At both cultural stages natural life is the model and measure of human institutions. It was nature that reared justice. Agriculture is the prototype of the marriage bond between man and woman. It is not the earth that imitates woman, but woman who imitates the earth. The ancients looked on marriage as an agrarian relationship, and borrowed the whole terminology of marriage law from agricultural conditions. We find such expressions as ἀροῦν (to plow), σπείρειν (to sow seed), φυτεύειν (to plant), γεωργεῖν (to till), for the act of the male; further the Sabinian usage of *sporium* [44] for the female field, the σάκανδρον[45] (vulva). This terminology is not merely figurative, but reflects the fundamental idea that agriculture was the model of human marriage. Thus even the decision in questions of marriage law was derived from the law of agriculture.

Now we can understand the full meaning of a custom recorded by Plutarch at the beginning of his *Praecepta coniugalia,* namely that the newly wedded bride and groom were shut up in their chamber with the priestess of Demeter, who taught them the θεσμός of the earth mother as the highest law of marriage.[46] Marriage was a Demetrian mystery, every γάμος was a τέλος (every marriage an initiation into the supreme goal of life), so that fidelity in marriage was sworn by the Eleusinian gods, maidens prayed to Demeter for a husband, and Dido at her marriage honored Ceres Legifera with a sacrifice.[47] The Demetrian θεσμοί make up the law of agriculture to which they subordinate marriage law. The mystery of the seed grain was the mystery of marriage. Agriculture and exclusive marriage were the twofold foundation of a cultural stage whose entire juridical form was derived from Demetrian motherhood. In this extended sense the goddess was called θεσμοφόρος and *legifera.* Not only the marital θεσμοί in the strict sense, but all justice and all law arising from the cultural stage of agriculture have their source in Demetrian motherhood, so that all *leges aere incisae* (laws inscribed in bronze), whatever their content, were rightly received into the temple of Ceres. And it was the women, again with good reason, who bore the temple's legal scrolls in the Eleusinian procession.

The origin not only of customs and laws, but also of cities, may be traced back to Demeter. Cities were founded amid Demetrian rites, the walls arose from the womb of the earth, and their inviolability was rooted precisely in this relation to maternal matter. There is no part of agricultural life that does not go back to Demeter, that does not have its foundation in her maternal nature. The religious consecration of motherhood is the foundation of this whole stage of life. The profanation of the maternal mystery was regarded as a relapse into hetaeric life. At the festival of Ceres neither father nor son might be named, lest the pure mystery of the mother be desecrated by any memory of masculinity, marriage, or father right. All Demetrian ordinances bear the character of *sanctitas*.†† This *sanctitas* lies in the inviolability of motherhood, in which the law has its foundation.

†† See pp. 40ff.

India

UNDER "ALEXANDER" the *Lexicon* of Suidas tells the story of Candace, the Indian queen who recognized the Macedonian despite his disguise. Impressed by her astuteness, Alexander promised to leave her and her kingdom in peace. The same event is mentioned by several other authors.[1]

Georgius Cedrenus in the eleventh century relates the story as follows: After defeating Porus, Alexander continued on to the remotest parts of India as far as the kingdom of the widowed Candace. Disguised according to his wont, he himself took part in the embassy to the princess. When Candace heard this, she ordered a portrait of him to be fashioned, and recognized him among the kings. She said to him: O King Alexander, thou hast conquered the world, yet a woman has bested thee. Taken aback, the king abstained from all hostility toward the queen and her land.[2]

Julius Valerius * proves this legend was in existence as early as the third or fourth century A.D. His account [3] opens with an exchange of letters. Recalling the ancient bond between India and Egypt, Alexander invites Candace to join him in a visit to the Ammonium to pay homage to the god, who is closely related to them both, and whose cult is carried on by matron priestesses. But the princess declines, invoking the prohibition of the Ammonian oracle, and contents herself with demonstrating her friendship by rich presents to both oracle and king. The king is now seized with

---

* His *Res gestae Alexandri Macedonis* is a Latin version of a Greek novel.

an irresistible desire to visit the queen herself. Informed of his forthcoming visit, she secretly has a portrait of him made, in order to be sure of recognizing him.

An unexpected event now helps Alexander to realize his desire. Accompanied by several horsemen, Candaules, one of Candace's sons, is found near the Macedonian camp. Seized and brought before Ptolemy Soter, whom he mistakes for Alexander, he reveals his identity and the reason for his journey. His wife had been stolen from him by Amazonian women in the service of the Bebrycians, and he is on his way to avenge the affront. Alexander is informed, and soon realizes that Candaules' mistake can be put to good use. Ptolemy is invested with the royal insignia. Alexander himself plays the role of Antigonus and takes a servile attitude before Ptolemy his overlord. When consulted, Alexander-Antigonus advises Ptolemy to help Candaules in his undertaking and so enhance the honor of his own mother Olympias. The expedition is arranged and, still on the advice of the false Antigonus, a night attack on the Bebrycians is planned. Candaules is amazed at so much craftiness, which to his mind offers the greatest promise of success and seems worthy of Alexander himself.

The plan is carried out, Candaules recovers his wife, and Alexander's own designs are on the way to fulfillment, for Candaules invites him to the royal city to receive his just recompense from Candace herself. But here Alexander is outdone in guile by the woman. Amazed at the splendor of the royal halls through which Candace leads him, he suddenly hears his true name from her lips. He recognizes his defeat at the hands of a woman, but is reassured by her promise of secrecy. Now a dangerous new complication arises. For Choragus, Candace's younger son, demands the emissary's life as vengeance for the Macedonians' murder of Porus, his father-in-law. The two sons quarrel and are on the point of coming to blows. Candaules thinks only of the favor that has been done him, Choragus only of his loss. Finding no solution to the conflict, Candace appeals to Alexander's superior wisdom. The king lives up to his fame. He promises to send Alexander himself to receive his presents, thus delivering him into the hands of Choragus. Reconciled, the two brothers bow down to the stranger, whom they still do not recognize. Candace sees herself outdone in craftiness. Full of admiration she recognizes Alexander as the supreme model not only of warlike bravery but also of guile. She desires him for a son; as Alexander's mother, she says, she will be sure of ruling the world. Secretly the woman invests him with the crown and all the insignia of kingship, and the hero, escorted by Candace's satraps, starts on his journey homeward.

But a still greater reward is in store for him. For in the temple he is welcomed by the celestial gods as one of them. Sesonchosis-Sesostris promises him future immortality. In the city of Alexandria to be founded by him he will receive the same veneration as Sarapis; with this twofold reward, the crown bestowed by Candace and the promise of the gods of heavenly light, Alexander rejoins his army and hastens to conquer the Amazons.

Now we are in a position to interpret the myth of Candace. It embodies the conflict between the higher masculine and the lower feminine principle. In the Orient the two principles meet. Candace is the representative of mother right, as recognized particularly in Egypt and Ethiopia; Alexander embodies the higher standpoint, to which mother right is subordinated.

It is no longer possible to discover whether this meeting is based on a definite event which was subsequently embroidered until it assumed the fabulous form in which we find it in pseudo-Callisthenes. Although this is by no means impossible, none of the historians of Alexander, neither Diodorus nor Plutarch, neither Curtius nor Arrian nor Justin mentions any such incident. Yet even if the whole story is taken as a fable, its significance is not diminished—but rather enhanced. For in this case the myth is no longer an elaboration on a single isolated incident but the expression of a great and universal manifestation of the times—thought, expressed, and handed down in the form of a single real event. We must distinguish between the form of the tale and its content or idea. The form lies in the fiction of a single definite event, which takes its course and moves toward its conclusion through a concatenation of circumstances and the intervention of a number of persons. This formal element must be discarded as a fabrication, a fable, a fairy tale, or whatever we may term such products of the free fancy, and excluded from the realm of historical truth. But in respect to the guiding thought, we must apply a different standard. This retains its significance even though the garment in which it is shrouded may merit little regard. In fact, when dissociated from this single incident, it takes on the greater dimension of a general historicity, not bound by specific localities or persons. In this sense the myth of Candace has a high historical significance.

Alexander's entrance into the lands of the African and Asiatic Orient brought about an encounter between different religions, outlooks, and civilizations. Two worlds came face to face, and only then became fully aware of the intrinsic differences between them. As the historical Alexander grew more and more remote from men's recollection, the popular mind found free play. It was this popular mind which reflected the conflict between Orient and Occident, between Greek and Asiatic institutions in so many miraculous tales. Accordingly, the story of Alexander more than any other is composed, at its very source, of truth and poetry, so that the dividing line between factual history and traditional fabrication is impossible to determine. The work that the hero began was completed and developed in the popular mind. The creation of the popular mind shows us best how his contemporaries and immediate successors judged Alexander's impact on the lands through which he passed, and how they appraised his relation to indigenous conditions, customs, and institutions. One of the most meaningful traditions of this sort is the story of Alexander's encounter with Candace. No doubt it originated in Egypt. It was here, most of all, that the question of the mighty conqueror's relation to the indigenous matriarchal views was bound to arise. The essential is the content of the story. The only true standard by which to judge it lies in the tale itself. And here it is highly noteworthy that the tale preserves throughout the standpoint of mother right, not only adopting the name of Candace (Mother Earth), but reflecting the entire system of matriarchy.

Lesbos

THERE IS much that is puzzling about Sappho's island, and thus far our scholars, despite all their efforts, have achieved little understanding of its special circumstances. They have simply been baffled by Sappho and her circle of poetesses who left the obscurity of domestic life to engage in an effort worthy of men. Praise has alternated with blame, and in the main they have been judged according to the ethical concepts of Christianity. But both the eulogies and the condemnations of modern writers seem very flat when compared with the brief but powerful statements of a Plutarch[1] or a Horace.[2] Such praise and blame are equally unfounded and fruitless for understanding.

Yet it is certain that no historical phenomenon can be fully explained, least of all one that is supreme in its kind, and ancient opinion was unanimous in attributing such supremacy to Sappho. The problem of Sappho makes us perceive more strongly than ever the futility of a science which deals principally with externals. An explanation for the phenomenon of the Lesbian women has been sought in the natural disposition of the Pelasgian and Aeolian people; in the matriarchal institutions of the Italic and Greek Locrians; and finally in the high degree of independence enjoyed by Dorian and particularly Spartan women. Assuredly all these perspectives have their justification. But they do not suggest the one explanation that really throws light on the matter. We have suggested it in our remarks on the Dionysian women.* It is to be

---

* Bachofen says earlier (*Mutterrecht*, in *Gesammelte Werke*, Vol. 3, p. 585): "Dionysus is primarily the god of women. All aspects of female

found in the Orphic religion, which strongly influenced the Lesbian women. Aeolian lyricism, the most distinguished exponents of which were women, is saturated with its spirit.

I need not discuss all the numerous proofs of the importance of the Bacchic cult on Lesbos. But it seems worth while to recall the tradition that attributes the poetic fame of the Lesbians to their friendly reception of Orpheus' head when it arrived singing on their island, having floated down the Thracian Hebrus and across the sea. In accordance with a deplorable present-day trend, this myth, like so many others, is regarded as a late fabrication suggested by conditions prevailing in another age. But we need not argue the point, for whatever the myth's age and source, it proves that Lesbos was regarded as one of the most celebrated sites of Dionysian Orphism. And the same conclusion must be drawn from the legend that Terpander possessed Orpheus' lyre, from the legend that Arion [3] came from Lesbos, and from Pythagoras' sojourn there.[4] Despite differences in detail, these legends all agree in the essential point, namely, the connection between the Orphic muse and Lesbian poetry. And the contrasting behavior of the Thracian and Lesbian women throws much light on this relationship. The Thracian women were hostile to the Orphic doctrine, whereas the women of Lesbos welcomed it and developed it to its highest expression. Orpheus was slain by the Thracian women, the Lesbians gladly buried his singing head in Aeolian soil.

The myth reveals its underlying idea by the connection it draws between the crime of the Ciconian [5] mothers and the brandmarks on their skin. Many writers have reported that the Thracian women wore tattoo marks down to a very late period. On women the tattoo mark was a sign of maternal nobility, a σύνθημα τῆς εὐγενείας (sign of noble birth), as Dio Chrysostom stresses.[6] Only the queen and the free-born women were entitled to such a marking. On boys it was a sign of nobility transferred to them from the maternal side.

---

nature find satisfaction in him. Youthful and fair, the master of life, he is kindly disposed toward women; he opposes to Amazonian misanthropy and the unruly hetaeric union the order of marriage and of the exclusive matrimonial bond. As τελεσσίγαμος (perfector of marriage), as the ally of Hymenaeus, as Liber next to Libera, as prototype of the ἱερὸς γάμος, he shows woman the great law in which alone her nature can find lasting peace."

Here again the prominent position of the mother characterized a lower, purely material stage of existence. This is manifested in the hetaeric sexuality of the Thracian women,[7] in the clasp pins used to scratch in the tattoo marks (their sexual significance has been discussed above †), and in the lambda form of the stigma, which is related to the cross and, in line with a symbolism widely distributed in the New World as well as the Old, to the sexual act.

Orpheus was the enemy of this lower religious stage. The purer, luminous doctrine proclaimed by the Apollonian priest stirred the women to bloody vengeance. All our sources agree that the women resisted the purified doctrine, and every version of the legend stresses the profound conflict between the new religion and mother right.[8] From the standpoint of the higher doctrine the tattooing of the women could only be regarded as punishment for their resistance. Originally a sign of noble birth, the tattoo became a mark of shame and crime. This accounts for the tradition that the stigmata were a punishment for the murder of Orpheus, and explains why among the Getae only the slaves were tattooed, and why Clearchus [9] and Eustathius [10] could finally consider the brands as mere ornaments.

These circumstances not only elucidate the Orphic legend (most amply recorded by Phanocles [11]), but also disclose the true significance of the ἄρρενες ἔρωτες (male homosexuality). These "masculine loves" stood in opposition to the purely sensual and sexual desire aroused by woman. Orpheus gave a new direction to this mightiest of emotions. For the Apollonian prophet, ἄρρενες ἔρωτες were a means of raising man from the morass of hetaeric sensuality to a higher stage of existence. The original idea was not sensuality, as Ovid, poet of a decadent age, supposes,[12] but precisely a sublimation, an ethical transcending of the lower Eros. It is an idea which holds an important place in the history of religion. We have seen it at work in Pelops, who is also connected with Mytilene. Chrysippus stands in the same relation to the Achaean hero (Laius) as Ganymede to Zeus and Pelops himself to Poseidon,** and no doubt the homosexuality of the Cretans, Eleans, Megarians, Thebans, and Chalcidians may originally have

† See pp. 166f.
** Bachofen apparently confuses Pelops and Laius (see p. 183).

had the same religious significance. The more puzzling this phenomenon may seem to us, the more imperative it becomes that we strictly follow historical evidence. The masculine Eros was welcomed as a promoter of virtue by the ancients,[13] particularly by the Aeolians and the Dorians. Like Orpheus, they made it the foundation of a higher Apollonian existence. Socrates attributes the first rising of man to ἄρρενες ἔρωτες; in them he perceives a liberation from the dominion of matter, an ascent from the body to the soul, a transfiguration in which love rises above sexuality; and he declares them to be the best road to perfection.[14] And in Xenophon's *Symposium* a large part of the conversation with which Callias' friends season his banquet in honor of his beloved Autolycus revolves around the same question and expresses the same point of view. Both authors clearly express the idea which provoked the resistance of the Thracian women.

Thus there is no doubt that the Orphic ἄρρενες ἔρωτες played a vital part in man's cultural development. And in this light the relation between the Thracian and the Lesbian worlds stands out clearly. The Thracian women were hostile to the Orphic doctrine and remained faithful to the sensual stage of existence; the Lesbian women, on the other hand, chose the Orphic life over their old Amazonian ways: to Orphism they owed the higher spiritual development which culminated in Sappho and her circle. Aphrodite and Eros play an essential role in Orphic poetry. In this it derives from the most ancient Samothracian Orphism, and the development of the two figures in Lesbian poetry follows the Orphic religious idea. Removed from this background, the women of Lesbos present a hopeless riddle; but bearing it in mind, even the strangest aspects of their life become comprehensible.

The love of women for their own sex was equivalent to the Orphic ἄρρενες ἔρωτες. Here again the sole purpose was to transcend the lower sensuality, to make physical beauty into a purified psychic beauty. Sappho's striving to elevate her sex was the source of all her joys and sorrows,[15] and it was Eros who inspired her in this attempt. Her ardent words flowed not from maternal solicitude but from amorous passion, and yet this enthusiasm, which seized upon the sensuous and the transcendent, the physical and the psychic, with equal vigor, had its ultimate and richest source in religion. Love and identity of sex, which had seemed mutually exclusive, were now united. Passionately Sappho sought the love of the Lesbian maidens; [16] she served those who were her inferiors in an effort to win them. And she was concerned not with one alone; Eros drove her to them all; her task was to elevate and educate her sex.[17] Wherever she found physical beauty, Eros impelled her to create spiritual beauty as well. Her songs were his doing, and so likewise was the madness of her heart, which accomplished greater things than human reason.

The religious nature of this madness is reflected in the aim expressed over and over again in Sappho's poetry. She hated disorder and gracelessness, even in dress and outward appearance; [18] for her, beauty was *one*, the center of her whole spiritual world, the beginning of all ennoblement. But above physical beauty stood spiritual beauty,[19] the ultimate goal of all striving.[20] She opposed and punished all hetaerism, every passion that disturbed the harmony of Orphic life; [21] for her the chaste brow betokened chastity of soul, which she regarded as woman's highest ornament. Thus rising from the lower to the higher aspect, transfiguring the body and making physical life itself into a foundation of psychic life, she led her maidens beyond the limits of physical existence, opened up to them a vision of the immortality that partakes of the higher Eros, showed them the golden, enduring value of that beauty which neither worms nor rust [22] can destroy, and so awakened in these women's hearts a yearning for the eternal glory which the Muses, leaving their father's golden house, had bestowed upon her through the gift of her works.[23] In the presence of this idea she came to look with indifference on everything she had valued as a young girl, wealth, jewels, the ornaments of outward sweet existence.[24] How she pities the rich woman whose soul, exalted by no higher striving, would slip away, silent and forgotten amid the dark shades, and enjoy no share in the Pierian roses.[25] But Eros' greatest gift to her was to exalt her winged soul above grief and death. She was expressing the highest thought of the Orphic religion when she called it a sin (οὐ θέμις) to intone dirges in the house of the Muses,[26] for had not the head of the Apollonian prophet, borne by the lyre, come singing to her island shores? "Ah, that I might die, listening to such song!" had been Solon's wish.[27]

In this attitude toward death many writers have seen a mere

insistence on the enjoyment of life, which they regard as a salient feature of Sapphism. They are blind to the true nature of Sapphic exaltation. To overlook the religious idea that pervades Lesbian poetry is to miss its chief beauty. A correct view of the higher mystery idea, underlying Sappho's song about Selene's love for Endymion,[28] provides a key to the most troubling aspect of the Aeolian muse: the fusion of sadness, grief at the eternal passing away of all creatures, with the serene confidence in immortality which banishes all grief. The contradiction is resolved in Orphism. The Orphic religion presents the same Janus head: the one face discloses pain and lamentation, the other confidence and joy, and the two are united in the idea that above the endless transience of all tellurian existence there dwells the consoling eternity of uranian life.

The Orphic quality of the Sapphic muse accounts for the sacred character the ancients ascribed to the poetess. Still more eloquent is Socrates' view of her. In the *Phaedrus* he names Sappho the fair at the head of those who have filled his heart "like a pitcher" and provided the substance of his enthusiastic speech in praise of Eros. To this wonderful woman he attributes all his knowledge of the higher Orphic god,[29] and this conception is supported no less by the mystical flight of the speech in which he communicates this knowledge than by the truly vestal dignity which clothes Sappho in artistic representations.[30] Here, then, Socrates follows the wisdom of Sappho, and in the *Symposium* he puts the loftiest, most mysterious part of his doctrine of love into the mouth of Mantinean Diotima. It is to her that he appeals to reveal what is beyond him. And he bows to her higher wisdom as to an inspired Pythia, freely admitting that he can follow her only with difficulty into the depths of the mystery.[31] Both women have the same character; to both Socrates imputes the same sublimity, the same immediate insight, the same prophetic, priestly character. Wholly religious is their being and all their knowledge; mysterious is the god whose supreme essence they disclose; mysterious is the flight of their discourse and the source of their enthusiasm. This sublimity of woman is a consequence of her relation to the hidden doctrine. The mystery is entrusted to the woman; it is she who safeguards and administers it, and she who communicates it to men.

Singing both nature and womanhood, Sappho encompasses all sides of the goddess she serves, and in the popular legends of Phaon and the Leucadian leap, she becomes one with her. The stage of spiritual development which is manifested in Sappho and constitutes the whole essence of the Aeolian world is the intermediate stage that in the cosmos marks the position of the psyche between *nous* and *soma*. And Diotima ascribes this same position to Eros; for she calls him not ugly and not beautiful, but something between the two; neither mortal nor immortal, but something intermediate; not man and not god but both; not wise and not foolish, but philosophically speaking, in between; not unitary and absolutely pure, but of twofold origin. Like the moon, combining the different laws of two worlds, the Aeolian stage of culture is not a negation but a purification and transfiguration of the feminine-material principle, hence even at its highest level characterized by finiteness and a certain uniformity of emotion; captive to the senses, distinguished less by sharpness and freedom of outline than by prophetic feeling; governed more by sentiment than by thought, subject always to division of mind (δύο νοήματα) and the strange, aimless striving peculiar to women and deplored by Sappho; [32] hovering between frenzy and reflection, between voluptuousness and virtue—thus in all things feminine-material, not paternal-Apollonian; governed wholly by Aphrodite, partaking both of her greatness and her limitation, dwelling with her on the dizzy heights where passion and reason are locked in eternal conflict.

From The Myth of Tanaquil

A Study of Orientalism in Rome and Italy

Introduction*

IS THE culture of Italy autochthonous or was it a foreign importation? Was Hellenism the only outside influence, or was there an older Oriental period? The present work is an attempt to answer this question. No one will deny the importance of the problem. For a sound approach to the subsequent history of the peninsula calls for a sound view of the beginnings. But, it may be asked, is a satisfying solution possible? In this era that has long since discarded the ancient traditions, what value can we impute to the ancient records of immigrations from Asia? It is useless to point out that the agreement between the Roman, the Etruscan, and various lesser traditions strongly supports the belief of the Romans and Etruscans in their Oriental origin. It is useless to point out that these peoples not only knew but never forgot their Oriental origin, that they faithfully preserved this tradition through all the vicissitudes of their history. The critical enlightenment of our time has long since graduated from such direct proofs, and today none of the many scholars who pride themselves on their discernment would dare to give them credence, not to speak of attaching any essential importance to them. What these scholars demand is incontrovertible proof of the proof.

Since no progress is possible along these lines, we are reduced

---

* This "Introduction" is an outline of the contents of the book itself; in the interest of reading continuity statements referring to this aspect (including a few repetitions) have been omitted or, if made in the future tense, changed to the present. [Ed.]

to the monuments as the only source of enlightenment. And who will deny that a people's literature, language, architecture, and art can provide a certain amount of information about its character and origins? For comparative method applied to all fields of human endeavor is assuredly one of the most fruitful implements of research. But here new difficulties arise, some inherent in the material that has come down to us, others rooted in the spirit of our times. What can comparative linguistics accomplish when it lacks material? What can it tell us of Etruria as long as the few remnants of its language remain more obscure than the language of Mesopotamia? To be sure, the architectural monuments and other remains through which extinct peoples speak to posterity are far more abundant; moreover, they need not be deciphered and are subject to no serious suspicion of forgery: but even they do not meet the requirements of our *Zeitgeist.* Neither the proof of incontestable Oriental influence in mythical motifs and artistic forms, in the attributes and representation of certain gods, in the systems of measures and weights, nor the authority of the most reliable, persevering, and independent observers, such as G. Conestabile, Noel des Vergers, J. de Witte, Micali in his late period, has thus far convinced our scholars that the Etruscans came from the Orient, or achieved any considerable influence on our courses of study. Where the advocates of Hellenism can find no other objections, the fact that our academic studies of ancient languages are usually limited to Greek is regarded as a valid argument against the permissibility of remoter parallels.

Thus we are denied lines of inquiry that might encourage the highest hopes. But just as there is no historical source, even though it may have been used for centuries, that has yielded everything it contains, so there is no fundamental fact whose truth or falsity has been tested by all the means available to us. Aside from language and the works of human hands, there is still another class of monument available for our comparative research, namely myth. Indeed, it is myth that provides our richest and most reliable insights regarding the cultural relations among the various peoples. For although migrant peoples not infrequently change their language along with their abode or, through their contacts with other peoples, quickly distort it to the point of unrecognizability, although the products of the arts and crafts are very much affected by climate and other local conditions, no nation, in changing its abode, changes its god, its basic religious view, and its traditional ritual observances. Myth is nothing other than a picture of the national experience in the light of religious faith. From this it may safely be concluded that agreement in idea and form between the mythologies of countries far removed from one another discloses a cultural connection which can be explained only by migration.

The incredible fury with which the Romans destroyed Etruria and eradicated every trace of its culture did not succeed in suppressing every monument of this sort. Even after the people, their entire literature, and even their language had disappeared, a fragment of Etruscan history was preserved in Roman history. For a whole century the Romans were vassals of this people which they ultimately subjugated. Three mighty figures of Etruscan origin [Tarquinius Priscus, Servius Tullius, and Tarquinius Superbus] were the last of the Roman kings. Their history reflects the history of the mighty neighboring people, their myths fully disclose the beliefs of the time.

The myth of Tanaquil occupies an outstanding position among the traditions of this period. It is interwoven not only with the history of the first Tarquin, but even more intimately with that of Servius Tullius. It is mentioned again in connection with Tarquin the Proud, so that it runs through the entire century of foreign domination. And the legend itself is exceedingly rich. Tanaquil not only confers the crown on her favorites, but also plays an important role in connection with the birth of King Servius, that is, in an entirely different function. She is portrayed in tombs and temples, and her figure is reflected in attributes, customs, religious and civic honors which long survived men's understanding of their origin. And the sources provide us with a material rarely available in connection with such early traditions.

So far our scholars have ignored this rich and well-documented tradition. They have concerned themselves solely with the eternally hopeless task of investigating "historical truth," taking no interest in a legend full of miraculous tales and impossibilities of all sorts which forever exclude it from the realm of history. Either they disparage it or they say nothing at all. But to deny the historicity of a legend does not divest it of value. What cannot have happened was nonetheless thought. External truth is replaced by inner truth. Instead of facts we find actions of the spirit. Banished from the realm of history, the Tanaquil tradition is a monument from the world of ideas. This ideal element suffices for our purposes. Not the historical events but the ideas embodied in a tradition form the object of our comparative study. Where the same complex of ideas produces analogous modes of expression, we are justified in assuming a close cultural connection. If we can also determine which of the similar myth cycles is closer to the basic idea and which one is further removed from it, we have determined which people received it from the other. In an age when we consult comparative linguistics regarding the kinship between peoples, we can scarcely place less trust in a comparison of myths and ideas.

We shall restrict our study to a single monument. Our hope of providing a secure demonstration lies not in the number of parallels adduced, but in the exhaustive treatment of a single motif. In the following survey we shall show the gradual development of our ideas and reveal the inner connections between the different parts of our demonstration.

Our attention was first called to the remarkable figure of Tanaquil by a single aspect of the legend, which also plays the most conspicuous role in the historical narrative. The older Tarquin owed his accession to the Roman throne to the assistance of a woman. The same motif is repeated, though in modified form, with the accession of Servius Tullius. In both cases the crown is the gift of a woman; in both cases the good fortune is unexpected. Finally, Tarquin the Proud, in line with the same idea, obtains the supreme power with the help of the criminal Tullia, and Tullia is represented as an imitator of Tanaquil.

Here, then, we have a fundamental idea: the feminine origin of the supreme power. Is this a Roman idea? No one will say that it is. On the contrary, it presents so striking a contrast to the political principles of Rome that analogies can be found only in the late imperial age, when Oriental conceptions had made a place for themselves in Rome. Nor does the Hellenic world offer any point of contact. But Asiatic mythology provides such a vast number of parallels that a connection between Roman and Oriental views imposes itself. The legends of the Asiatic dynasties disclose more than one Tanaquil. Throughout the Assyrian world it is a woman who confers the throne. The three Italic peoples to whom the tradition particularly attributes a bond with the Orient [Etruscans, Tyrrhenian Lydians, Sabines] all present memorable parallels. It is with these peoples that we shall first concern ourselves. Next we shall turn to the traditions of the Carians and Mysians, Aramaeans and Phoenicians, Persians and Assyrians. We find infinite variety in the mythical forms, but the idea remains the same. The presence of this common feature among so many peoples proves the belief in a feminine origin of the royal power to be among the distinguishing marks of a great cultural period.

Now we have a basis on which to follow the parallels in detail. Similarity of general outlines does not suffice. We shall go on to show that the characteristic attributes of the Asiatic king-woman are repeated in Tanaquil. Three such attributes stand out everywhere: The king-woman of the Asiatic dynasties is invariably conceived as a hetaera; she is invariably connected with Heracles; and she invariably dominates her male companion. Now if Tanaquil is one of these Asiatic king-women, her legend must disclose the same attributes.

Here our investigation runs into difficulty. The Roman tradition took over, unchanged, the idea of the feminine origin of the royal power, but divested the figure of Tanaquil of all those traits with which the Oriental world endowed its feminine bestowers of thrones. Indeed, the high regard which this exalted figure enjoyed even in the latest Roman times is largely based on attributes that are contrary to the base, sensuous conceptions of the Orient. If this final version of the legend is also its original form, if Tanaquil was never other than as the late Romans saw her, then our parallel is ruined, despite the concurrence of the broad outlines, and this line of proof must be abandoned. Here, then, we must take a different direction. We are compelled to strip our monument of all the alterations made in it over the centuries and sift out its original content from all later admixtures; for however thoroughly a monument may have been made over in accordance with later ideas, its original form is never fully concealed, the cracks and gaps can never be so completely filled in as to frustrate all insight into its original character.

In certain parts of the Tanaquil legend the hetaeric ideas and customs of the Orient are still clearly discernible. The Romans glossed them over as much as possible and reinterpreted them according to their own diametrically opposed ideas and taste. But the explanations are never wholly satisfactory, and this very inadequacy shows that an attempt has been made to interpret from a new standpoint what sprang from an older and entirely different law of formation. This knowledge enables us to go back from the later to the earlier ideas, from the Roman national Tanaquil to the original figure of the Asiatic king-woman, from divergence to agreement between East and West. This woman, who for the later period was the embodiment of all matronly virtues, was in her origin of the same class as the hetaeric king-women of Asia.

The connection between Tanaquil and Heracles is no less certain. In the historical legend, to be sure, it has found no expression, but the choice of the temple of Heracles on the Quirinal as the site on which to erect the wonder-working statue of Tanaquil and in which to keep her feminine paraphernalia is explained by the system of the Assyrian religion, which consistently represents the women who conferred the royal power as paramours of Heracles. And the original Tanaquil also provides an exact parallel to the Oriental conceptions of a hetaera exalted above her male consort. The feminine power and independence preserved in the late Roman tradition of Tanaquil were a mere vestige of older, more far-reaching matriarchal forms. Tanaquil was not only an *imperiosa coniux* [1] (dominating consort) within the limits of Roman marriage law, though as such her name remained proverbial down to the latest Roman times; her original relation to Heracles was that of the Lydian Omphale toward her husband, who was dominated and debased by her sensual charms. But the higher moral feeling of the Occident was resolutely opposed to this aspect of the Oriental attitude; the political thinking of Rome, based on the exclusive rights of the father and husband, could grant such a Tanaquil no place among the venerable figures of the past. This is evident from the care with which all the Omphale-like traits of the original picture were painted over or disguised by anachronistic explanations. But here again the eye trained by previous investigations can easily discover the dividing line between the old and the new and distribute the material correctly between the two strata.

In this study we have not taken the currency of the Omphale-Heracles myth in Etruria, the home of Tanaquil, as our guiding thread, although this consideration has led other scholars back to the tradition of a migration from Lydia. Instead we have started from the Sabine origin of the temple of Heracles, containing Tanaquil's statue and paraphernalia, and consulted the Sabine traditions for enlightenment as to the earliest meaning of Tanaquil's connection with Heracles. Our hopes have not been disappointed. The entire complex of Oriental conceptions regarding a hetaeric king-woman who confers power and reduces her husband to servitude is preserved more purely in the Sabine myths than in the legends of the Romanized Tanaquil. The tradition concerning the power-conferring Tarpeia, concerning Heracles' amours with Larentia and Flora's similar relationship with Mars-Heracles, the legend about the founding of the old hetaeric festivals, are all Sabine. And these Oriental vestiges are closely related to the hitherto neglected and at all times misunderstood traditions which irrefutably show that the Sabine family was governed by a matriarchal principle raised to its Amazonian extreme. If we bear in mind that in early cultural stages a cleavage between articles of faith and principles of social life was unheard of, it becomes clear that the relation of the Sabine Heracles to Tanaquil can only have been conceived in terms of the subordination of man to woman, thus constituting a parallel to the Lydian Omphale-Heracles relationship. And this conclusion becomes a certainty when we explain the feminine paraphernalia which were preserved along with the statue of Tanaquil in the temple of Heracles, and which were completely reinterpreted in a later period. At this point we may definitely identify Tanaquil with the Oriental king-woman. Not only does her myth embody the basic motif of the Asiatic king-legends, the bestowal of power by a woman, but moreover the earliest version of Tanaquil reveals all the characteristic features of the Oriental king-woman as most distinctly exemplified in the Lydian Omphale.

A third point still remains to be considered. If our parallel is to hold, there must be the same correspondence between the Heracles of the Heracles-Tanaquil conjunction and the Assyrian Bel-Heracles as between Tanaquil and the Assyrian-Lydian hetaera. The Sabine consort of Tanaquil bears the indigenous name of Semo Sancus Dius Fidius, which was preserved in the temple on the Quirinal. Our first question then must be: Is the god whom the Sabines and after them the Romans saw in Semo Sancus similar to the Assyrian Bel-Heracles? If so, the identity of the Roman Tanaquil-Heracles with the Lydian-Assyrian Omphale-Heracles and similar Oriental pairs is confirmed, and it becomes a certainty that not merely a single Asiatic tradition but the whole of the Oriental Heracles system was transplanted into Italy; if not, our whole demonstration must be discarded on the ground that it is based on a mere agreement in names, not on a factual identity. Consequently, we have taken the greatest pains over this bit of comparative religion. The reader will find that the usual method of handling mythological material has here been abandoned as utterly inadequate. We have aimed not only at the fullest possible documentation of the facts, but above all at the understanding and comparison of ideas. We must first of all determine the position of the Assyrian Heracles in the system of the religion of Bel, and show the various stages by which the pure Heracles idea degenerated into the conception of a hero succumbing to the sensuous charm of tellurism and enslaved by the hetaera. Then we must compare this complex of ideas with that surrounding the Sabine Semo Sancus Dius Fidius in such a way as to demonstrate that the Sabine-Roman Heracles is directly and immediately derived from the Assyrian-Phoenician god. Nowhere does the scholar's ability to move among unaccustomed ideas face a severer test.

But our pains are richly rewarded. Our comparison throws a light on the obscurest part of the Italic religion, one that cannot be gained, and thus far has not been gained, through the derived and utterly atrophied Hellenic idea of Heracles. Furthermore, the Sabine people take their place among the most important carriers of Italian Orientalism and enter into a relation with the Etruscan Heraclids, which to be sure was suggested quite some time ago by K. O. Müller,[2] but has never been taken up by our scholars.

Finally, the completion of the parallel between Tanaquil and the king-women of the Assyrian legends by a corresponding parallel between her male consorts in Rome and Asia definitely demonstrates the historicity of a period of Oriental culture in Italy.

A single mythical monument has led us to this conclusion. But such an abundance of Oriental ideas presupposes the presence of Oriental peoples in Italy, and the deep-rootedness of these ideas shows that the period of Assyrian culture was of long duration. The Apennine peninsula was an Asiatic colony long before it became a colony of expanding Hellenism. At all times Italy has presented the same phenomenon. It has been the last refuge of cultures elsewhere on the wane, of declining ideas and defeated parties. Here the religions of the Orient struck deep and vital roots which Hellenism could not eradicate, even at the time of its greatest influence.

The derivation of the Roman Tanaquil from the Oriental prototype of an Aphrodite-Mylitta (Ishtar) who conferred kingship, became clearer at every step in our investigation. It was confirmed by the identical relation of the two legendary women with Heracles, and by the parallel between the Assyrian-Lydian and the Sabine-Roman conceptions of Heracles. The demonstration which was the object of our comparative research is now complete. But it is desirable to subject its results to a test. The requisite material is at hand, provided by a second group of legends concerning Tanaquil, namely, those surrounding the birth of Servius Tullius. These we examine carefully in our second section. For if Tanaquil's position as a bestower of the throne ultimately reflects the Assyrian conception of Mylitta, her relation to the birth legend must be rooted in the principles and usages of the Mylitta cult. The two traditions are so closely interwoven that they can only have sprung from the same prototype. It follows that the conclusion at which we arrived in our first investigation will either be proved beyond all doubt or controverted by the results of the second inquiry.

When we embarked on this second inquiry it could not be foreseen to what extent it would corroborate the Oriental origin of the Roman tradition. After the results of our previous research it can no longer surprise us to find a relation between one of the most familiar Roman legends and the Assyrian cult of a nature-mother manifesting herself in the most unrestrained hetaerism. But what far exceeds all our expectation is to find that the very rite which presented the wildest, and to the Western mind, most repugnant expression of Aphroditism was unmistakably the immediate proto-type of the Roman Servius legend, which follows it in every particular. For our second group of Tanaquil myths is simply a historicization of the Sacaea, of those festive rites which are a perfect expression of the basely sensual law of Mylitta.† The characteristic features of the Roman legend are equally common to the hetaeric slave festivals of Babylonia and Assyria; the functions of Tanaquil duplicate those ascribed to the divine queen of the Sacaea. When the Roman legend is traced back to this prototype, its numerous contradictions are resolved. Seemingly incompatible elements enter into a coherent whole, seeming anomalies take their place as parts of a perfectly consistent development.

This inquiry points over and over again to a fact that has already come to our attention. Contexts which in Italy are discernible only in dispersed and much overlaid fragments occur in the Orient in their original complete and coherent form. And it is thanks to this fully preserved Asiatic context that our dispersed fragments now arrange themselves, each in its original place.

Thus securely guided, we need not be troubled by the futility of the Roman attempts to explain these myths. Such explanations are of interest to us, for they serve to point up the contrast between Roman national ideology and the earlier world of ideas. But far more important for our purposes is a class of religious traditions which, like everything connected with religious festivals, was relatively immune to the influence of new ideas. For the derivation of the Servian nativity legend from the ceremonies of the Sacaea will seem plausible only if we can prove that festivals of this type were held in Italy and in Rome itself. How could the popular mind of Italy have fashioned its conceptions of their beloved king's birth

---

† Bachofen characterizes this festival: "All civic and social regulations which interfere with the *ius naturale* are suspended. For five days, starting on July 9th, the law of Mylitta reigns supreme. The Sacaea is a festival of universal equality and liberty" (from *Die Sage von Tanaquil*, in *Gesammelte Werke*, Vol. 6, p. 100).

according to a religious prototype that was not known to it from actual practice?

Our mythologies offer us mere facts. They tell us nothing of sources or underlying creative ideas, and everything remains a riddle. Let us first consider the significant number of festivals of the Sacaea type in Rome and Latium. There are the Nonae Caprotinae, the Quinquatrus minores, the Tubilustria, the Floralia, the days of Anna Perenna, and the days of the Servian Fortuna, celebrated by the banks of the Tiber outside the city. Though the old idea and the old spirit had gone out of them, though their popularity down to very late times resulted mainly from the appeal of unrestrained merrymaking to the rabble of all classes—even so, we have no difficulty in recognizing the Sacaea in all these festivals. We must bear in mind that the cult itself had undergone a profound change. It differed from the Oriental model chiefly by the suppression of practices that offended the Western spirit of moderation.

A further source of information is to be found in the great number of myths relating to the origin of the cults and attempting to account for certain conspicuous festive usages. In all this we have a vastly rich, cohesive, and reliable material for our comparisons. Once more we can do without the late Roman explanations. Fabrications intended to reconcile ceremonies which had come to seem strange with the new *Zeitgeist,* they are a source of knowledge concerning their own era but cast no light on the original idea. Often ancient substance has been preserved not because its underlying idea was understood, but in spite and because of the loss of this idea. At the end of our study of the vestiges of the Sacaea in Rome and Latium, the parallel between East and West takes on far greater breadth than the Tanaquil legend itself had led us to hope. Yet no one will accuse us of going beyond the sphere of ideas to which the myth belongs. This we carefully avoid in the interest of a strict demonstration; yet it is essential on the other hand that we consider all phenomena having a common source with the Tanaquil legend. For the value of a sound idea lies in the light it casts on puzzling points, and the value of an investigation resides in the spiritual tie it creates between seemingly unrelated facts.

The final conclusion to which we are led by this investigation is as follows: In the view of his grateful contemporaries King Servius, founder of the Roman community, author of popular freedom, was a product of those hetaeric slave festivals in which the peoples of the Assyrian cultural sphere celebrated with the unrestrained enthusiasm the return of men to the commandments of the great mother of life, to the freedom and equality of all. Every phase of the legend concurs in this idea, which provides an explanation of its puzzling features. The hetaera who arbitrarily disposes of life and throne, whom we found in the king-woman of Tarquin the Elder, is none other than the lascivious goddess of the Sacaea, seen in her full natural freedom and exuberance, and it is she again who appears as foster mother and protectress of the boy Servius. The functions she fulfills in both legends spring from the same religious system and show the same basic idea, although they are developed to two different conclusions. Here as always the popular mind, which gave form to the legend, is thoroughly consistent. It observes a lawfulness which rivals that of natural creation, and once again discloses the primitive cultural stage above which it cannot rise.

Up to this point we have demonstrated the Oriental origin of the Tanaquil myths without the help of etymologies and word comparisons. Our aim has been to establish a parallel based solely on an agreement of ideas. But now that this aim can be regarded as attained, it will be of closely related interest to determine whether the demonstrated analogy is supported by the names of the gods.

After this linguistic digression, our second section concludes with a discussion of the myths regarding the birth of the Spartan King Demaratus, who presents a distinct analogy to the Roman Servius Tullius. His myth is related in great detail by Herodotus.[3] Here we attempt to trace it back in every particular to the religion of Heracles-Bel, thus showing that the Spartan nativity legend, like its Roman companion piece, is not a product of free invention, but that both grew out of the religious views of the people with the regularity characteristic of nature itself. In the course of this comparison the parallel between the Spartan and the Roman myths and their derivation from the Asiatic prototype become perfectly clear. All the features of the Servian nativity legend pass once more before our eyes. The conceptions of maternal and paternal lineage are the same. At every step we encounter the ideas of the Italic myth, though expressed in a different form.

Thus it is shown that an ethnic tie may have existed between Sparta, the Asiatic mainland, and the Italic West, so that the tradition to this effect must be regarded as indispensable. For to the ancients the conclusion at which we arrive by comparative mythology was a historical belief. The Sabine people, whom we have come to know as one of the chief repositories of Orientalism in Italy, and with whose tribal god, Semo Sancus, Tanaquil, the divine protectress of Servius, was closely related—this same Sabine people is now seen to be linked with the Asiatic homeland of the Sacaea, and at the same time with Sparta, home of the Demaratus myth. And an inquiry which seemed to have no connection with the Tanaquil myths comes back to them at last.

We next turn our undivided attention to the history of the Oriental tradition in Italy.

Thus far we have seen that the Italic peoples borrowed innumerable ideas and customs from the Orient; now we shall marvel at their ability to transform these imported elements and adapt them to their own modes of thought. For is it not remarkable that Anahita, the Asiatic king-woman, the companion of Omphale, the Amazonian hetaera of Anaïtis, the Sacaean mother worshiped in lewd sexual festivals, should have been transformed into the Tanaquil described by the Roman authors, the Tanaquil who has been impressed on our minds in Latin school, that model of all matronly virtue and dignity, divested of every trace of hetaeric leanings, of every sign of the overbearing Amazon, a perfect expression of the pure, ethical view of family life. And is the metamorphosis of an inner religious intuition into a historical personality, of religious ideas and customs into a tissue of human relations and destinies, any less surprising?

Here we cannot attempt to elucidate this historical process itself, to explain the secret of human development. The mystery of growth can be solved by the methods neither of historical nor of physical science. We know that the plant changes with the nature of the soil, that the fruit takes on a different taste in a new country, and that full development may require more than one change of climate. But all this does not give us an insight into the essence of growth itself. We can only establish the fact of metamorphosis and regard it as a part of our scientific experience. But in the present case it does not suffice to place the Oriental and Occidental versions of Tanaquil side by side; we must show that the later conception must have derived from the older one in a natural process of transformation. The metamorphosis has two aspects, each of which, for the sake of clarity, we take up separately.

First we consider the transformation of the hetaeric king-woman into the model of all matronly virtues. Here we show that despite the repression of the hetaeric idea, the distinguishing features of the Oriental harlots are still discernible in the Roman Tanaquil, and that consequently the late ideas can only be understood in the light of the early ones. A Tanaquil resembling the overbearing matriarchal Omphale, who enslaves her mate and makes him into a woman, could not have survived in the hearts of the Roman people. Casting off her hetaerism and Amazonism, Tanaquil became the advocate and protectress of maternal rights against men's stern insistence on the power conferred on them by the positive civil law, and her prestige grew as the law of the state left motherhood increasingly defenseless. Reinterpreted in the same way, her conjunction with Heracles retained its importance. No longer was the man enslaved by the woman's abuse of her sensuous charms: what remained was the respect owed by the men to a matron class founded on the strict fulfillment of domestic duty. The statue of Tanaquil with distaff, spinning wheel, and sandals in the temple of Dius Fidius became for the dutiful Roman woman a symbol of the protection provided by the avenger against male brutality and injustice. The traditional conjunction was preserved, but Rome imbued it with its own spirit and higher morality. And the new Tanaquil was still an expression of universal freedom and equality among humankind, among the children of *one* mother, as embodied in the Sacaea. True, the basely sensuous form which Asia gave this idea could not survive among the Roman people; but as advocate of the servile classes' natural right over against the rigors of official law, the foster mother of the slave child remained at all times dear to the popular memory. Casting off all hetaeric Aphroditism, this originally Asiatic figure came more and more to embody the idea of ennobled love and self-sacrifice. More and more she became the champion of humanity in a society weighed down by the severity of the positive state order.

We go on to show how other representatives of the old Sacaean system underwent the same transformation, how the common people looked upon Tutela Philotis, who led their procession in the Nonae Caprotinae, and the Phoenician Anna of Bovillae, kindly foster mother of the hungry plebeians thirsting for freedom, with the same feeling as upon Tanaquil and Ocrisia,** and how, finally, the consciousness of a sin committed against the mother goddesses through the severity of the state law was expressed in numerous religious rites, in myths, and even in entirely historical events. Such festivals of atonement had for the most part, though not entirely—one need only consider the Sabine Floralia—been purged of the hetaeric excesses which sullied the Asiatic Sacaea; but the idea of a periodic return to the happiness of an older, natural social order still found its expression in the traditional forms. The ideas and religious usages of the Orient were not simply relinquished, but reduced to a more moderate form. The more passionate Asia, which gave the whole world its religions, felt more deeply and expressed its natural emotions more violently. In the essentially uncreative West the atmosphere was cooler; everything was made over in the interests of a higher view of life and, thus transformed, the Asiatic heritage was enabled to survive under totally different spiritual conditions.

We cannot let so remarkable a development stand without a parallel. To be sure, our investigations have largely dispelled its puzzling character, but our scientific consciousness cannot fully accept it unless we can demonstrate its consistency by adducing an analogous phenomenon. Strange as it may seem, we find the desired parallel not in some obscure secondary field, but in one of the most important aspects of sacral law. No priesthood was so

---

** Ocrisia, the mother of Servius Tullius, came to the house of Tarquinius Priscus as a slave girl. One day when she was sacrificing at the hearth a phallus reached for her. Tanaquil realized that a superhuman race was to issue from the royal hearth and commanded Ocrisia to put on the bridal gown. And either Vulcan or a *lar* begat Servius Tullius on her.

national as the flamines, no sacral law was so fundamentally and purely Roman as that of the three great flamines which occupied first place in the *ordo sacerdotum*, ranking before even the pontifices. And yet this autochthony is an illusion. Like Tanaquil and her myths, the flamines show their Oriental origin in the divine triad to which they are dedicated and by a great number of ceremonial observances which defy all explanation on the basis of Roman or Greek ideas. Moreover, the Roman priesthood with its law springs from the same Bel-Heracles system as Tanaquil, from the system that we have studied at its highest and lowest levels in our previous investigation. And all the elements we have found in our first two sections now recur. The primacy and hetaeric conception of motherhood, the investiture of the man by a superior hetaeric woman, the conjunction of an Omphale-like queen with a male consort dedicated to Heracles: every one of these characteristic features of the Assyrian Heracles religion may be recognized in the original relation of the *flaminica* to the flamen, each one is the source of sacral regulations for which the later period, having grown away from its Oriental background, could no longer find an adequate explanation. But these traditional elements, like those underlying the Tanaquil myth, could not escape reformation. On Italic soil the old was imbued with new spirit and so underwent a complete change. The Omphale-like harlot became the *flaminica*, the prototype of the Roman matron, with her virtues and respected position. Effaced were all traces of hetaeric Amazonism: what remained was the lofty independence which the *flaminica* preserved in her relation to the flamen, and which, like Tanaquil's similar position, all matrons regarded with pride and joy as a pledge that the dutiful wife would be protected against the stern ordinances of the civil law. The parallel is complete.

It is a recognized and well-grounded truth that the severity of certain Roman laws can only be explained as a reaction against foreign ideas that had grown intolerable. We often speak of a "historical heritage" of the Roman people, forgetting that what we are supposedly explaining by this meaningless term was largely the fruit of a struggle, and that without such a struggle neither a people nor an individual can fully develop its strength and special character. If we think away the Orientalism from Rome's background, if we forget the deep roots which it had struck in Italian soil over the centuries, we cannot possibly understand Rome's ruthless striving to raise the state over religion and father right over the matriarchal system; we cannot see why so much importance should have been attached to substitution of the dowry for the harlot's marriage portion, or why the behavior and dress of the *flaminica* should have been regulated with such Mosaic severity.

An extreme can be explained only in terms of its opposite, which provokes resistance; an extreme hetaerism engenders a no less extreme puritanism. It is no paradox but a great truth borne out by all history that human culture advances only through the clash of opposites. Should the Roman people, with their meager theory but vast experience of life, have been alone in failing to perceive this truth? If I am not mistaken, the most widely read of all Roman authors fully supports my view of the flamines and of the history of Oriental culture in Italy. Let us for a moment consult this ancient authority. Throughout his great epic Virgil represents Aeneas as a flamen, Dido as a *flaminica*. He represents both figures in a religious light which submerges their political character, and moreover his whole narrative alludes to this first and highest of all priesthoods. And since both Aeneas and Dido have their roots in the Orient, since in Virgil's conception they are closely related through the kinship between the Tyrians and Trojans [4] — the poet must have ascribed a pre-Roman, Asiatic origin to the flamines.

The crucial meeting in Carthage shows the parting of the cultural ways. Dido is the Oriental king-woman, planning to enslave the man by her harlot's arts. She seeks to dominate Aeneas as Omphale dominated Heracles, Semiramis Ninus, Delilah Samson. She strives to embody the power which Asia gave the hetaeric queen over the life and throne of her husband. When Dido accuses her fugitive lover of faithlessness, her reproach is perfectly founded from the standpoint of the traditional Asiatic law, and Dido knows no other. But Aeneas represents the new view of life to which Rome was destined to elevate mankind.[5] Though his whole past is rooted in the culture of Asia, though his Heracles character is grounded in the very religious idea from which Dido derives her rights, his eyes are turned toward his new home and the new era which he, in accordance with a higher decision, is destined to inaugurate. No tender memory, no consideration of their common Asiatic origin, can shake him. Under the impact of the Roman national hero, the throne of the Oriental hetaera, which Cleopatra-Isis would like to erect anew, sinks into ruins. The pyre of the Assyrian Sacaea, kindled to unite Zoganes with his prototype Heracles, consumes the vanquished Dido, but Aeneas is burned only in lifeless effigy. This is the turning point. On the ruins of the old flaminate rises the new, Aeneas leads it to victory, and Dido strives in vain to perpetuate the old flaminate in the West. In Latium the *flaminica* ceases to be the commanding Omphale and becomes the pure companion of the pure priest of light; Asia's sensual maternity never reaches this land which the *Weltgeist* has chosen as the birthplace of a new era.

Virgil gives the broadest extension to this idea. He does not restrict it merely to the reformation of a single priesthood. As the Trojan hero arrives at the mouth of the Tiber, everything Asiatic is destroyed. Aeneas—here again in the image of Heracles—visits the Assyrian ancestors and Dido the hetaeric king-woman herself, in the Cumaean realm of the dead. These figures out of the Asiatic past have ceased to be anything more than lifeless shadows. Neither they nor their dead world will live again in Latium. Anchises, Creusa, the nurse Caieta, Palinurus, and all these representatives of Oriental ideas fail to reach the land of promise. Aeneas avoids the alluring isle of Circe the harlot. And finally it is Ascanius, who was taken from his home as a boy, and not Aeneas, who founds the first Latin kingdom. If we read the *Aeneid* for its ideas, we find a single conception throughout. Virgil gives equal emphasis to the two factors underlying all cultural development: the bond with tradition and the ulterior development that transcends it. The current view that Virgil had in mind only the ties between Italy and Asia is utterly one-sided. No less important is the emancipation of the Roman world from the fetters of Oriental tradition. Actually the central idea of the whole epic is that Oriental culture, defeated in the East, was to fulfill a higher destiny in the distant West. Built on Asiatic foundations, Rome becomes the ultimate conqueror of Asia. Herein lies the essence of the *Aeneid. Occidit occideritque sinas cum nomine Troia* (Troy has fallen, and let it be fallen forever, even to its name).[6]

Was the poet right in his interpretation of Roman history? Does his narrative accord with the actual development of the Roman West? Does it express the national idea? This question is not irrelevant to our inquiry. If the metamorphoses of Tanaquil and the flaminate indicate the destiny of the Oriental traditions on Italian soil, then all Roman history must follow the same movement. For must not the part observe the same law as the whole and must there not be a consonance between outward and inward development? Can we conceive of a spiritual conquest of the Orient without a national struggle in the same direction? And indeed, the relations between Italy and the Orient constitute the universal aspect of Roman history. The supreme purpose and consequence of this development was to transfer the cultural center of the world from the East to the West. All the crucial events group themselves around this central idea.

For centuries Italy seemed destined to remain forever a dependency of Asia. By land and sea, by way of the Hellespont, the Adriatic, the Iberian peninsula, Oriental peoples or peoples of Oriental culture poured into Italy. The harbors provided by its coasts and islands, its situation in the center of the Mediterranean basin, seemed designed to make the peninsula a meeting place of the nations. After the eventful period of the great migrations which ushered in the first as well as the middle period of Italian history, we see the peoples and religions of Asia in possession of the whole country, from the foothills of the Alps to the fertile fields of Campania: in the north and south Etruscan preponderance was rooted in an age-old cultural tradition; they exerted the greatest influence on the history of Italy, and particularly of Rome. In the mountains of central Italy the Sabines, more closely related than is commonly supposed to the Etruscans, were among the chief pillars of Oriental culture; in the western plain the kingdom of Alba was most prominent among a group of similar kingdoms. All were purely Asiatic in origin and tradition. Rome sprang from their womb, and derived its strength and ideas from them. Rome, too, traced its past to dying Asia rather than victorious Hellenism, and preserved this belief even in a day when Greek lineage and Greek culture constituted the supreme titles to glory. As son of Mylitta and priest-king, the Roman national figure, the Trojan

Aeneas, was a true expression of theocratic Asia, and this he always remained; the Oriental in him was never submerged by the Hellenized hero—and here it should be remembered that Greek colonization never gained a foothold north of the Tiber.†† The exodus from Alba to an inhospitable marshy region, although ill justifying any hope of future prosperity, represented a first attempt at emancipation from the traditional fetters; nevertheless the dynasty of Sabine priest-kings and, after their banishment, that of the Etruscan princes provided new and powerful support for Oriental ideas in the city as it grew. Although Cicero [7] tells us that even in the days of the Tarquins Greek culture had seriously taken up the struggle against Oriental conceptions in Rome, although Mastarna's ordinances show that the old era was already on the verge of collapse—still, the fact that the legend of Servius was wholly conceived and developed after an Asiatic prototype shows that Oriental beliefs were deep-rooted in Italy and preserved their force for many centuries. A long period of arduous apprenticeship was indispensable to this first of Western states if it was to be equal to its vocation of permanently raising mankind to a higher stage of existence.

The first great outbreak of long-growing reaction was evinced in the fall of the last Tarquin, a ruler of true Oriental stamp who shows us once more that history owes its greatest advances to extremes. Every step in the development of Rome is a victory of the purer outlook of the Occidental spirit. The Roman national idea, the Occidental idea, grew strong in struggle against the restoration of the Etruscan dynasty. The Romans became more and more clearly aware of the antagonism between them and the alien culture around them, and at the same time of their historical calling. The destruction of the Asiatic element was prerequisite first to the existence, then to the power of Rome, and usually to both at once.

Hence the unparalleled fury with which everything that could not be assimilated to the new idea was swept from the face of the earth; hence that equally amazing tenacity and single-mindedness which knew no half measures or compromises. Porsena's tempo-

†† No trace is left of an Aeginetan colony in Umbria mentioned by Strabo 8. 376. [B.]

rary success accomplished nothing. It neither restored the Tarquins nor reduced Rome to the insignificance of a peaceful trading
center. As Alba fell, so fell Veii and the other Etruscan cities, one
stronghold of Orientalism after another. The fall of Capua, doubly
dangerous by reason of its proximity, teaches us how contemp-
tuously history can crush the proudest abodes of wealth, art, and
refinement. A single year saw the destruction of Aphroditean
Corinth, crossroads between two worlds, and Phoenician Carthage
—all for the benefit of mankind, whose rise to a purer stage of life
required the annihilation of the older sensualistic civilizations and
of their commercial and industrial foundations. Like the ruins of
Mesopotamia, their forsaken cities, some of them hard by the gates
of Rome, proclaim the end of a condemned era.

The Punic Wars can be properly evaluated only as part of this
great historical process. Here in the West, Asia had mustered its
last forces for the decisive struggle. Was European mankind to
succumb once more to the Oriental life principle, this time
forever? Living closer to Asia, the Greeks had cast off Asiatic
domination more quickly and completely; but soon local interests
had deflected them from any great national idea. More given to the
glitter of genius than to greatness of character, they disintegrated
everything they touched, first and most completely themselves. In
their heroic undertakings against the powers of the Orient they
remind us of those Olympic champions who, after achieving fame
in their youth, soon sank into oblivion. The types of Greek genius
are Achilles, Alexander, Pyrrhus, who rise and fall like meteors on
the horizon of history. Greece began the work but lacked the
decisive moral strength to complete it. With its fresh vitality
Macedonia brought the same ruin on the Asiatic and Greek worlds
and finally on itself. Contrary to what Lycophron, living at the time
of the Pyrrhic war, supposed,[8] not Alexander but Rome completed
the millennial struggle against the East which was the leitmotiv of
Herodotus' history; hence it was Rome and not Greece which
transferred the universal monarchy from the East to the West, and
so put an end to the old world. What is Marathon, what are
Salamis and Plataea, compared to the war against Hannibal? As
infinitesimal as the brief decades of Athenian power compared to
Roman eternity. What were Agathocles' battles against Carthage

compared to the Roman campaigns? The Greek thought it a simple matter to subjugate the Phoenician city, and what did he accomplish? The destruction of Carthage, this greatest turning point in the destinies of mankind, was the work of the Italic nations united under the Republican leadership of Rome; more than any other accomplishment, it sprang from the innermost core of the Western spirit. In these years the city fulfilled its true historical mission. The West had conquered the inheritance of the East for all time, and the victorious nation had achieved its ethical summit.

Great knowledge and experience were lost through the destruction of Carthage. But we have no regrets. It was fifteen hundred years before its earth-spanning enterprises were revived. Yet the victory of the higher ethical principle of Western European mankind over the base sensuality of Asia makes us forget this impoverishment. In the midst of its decisive struggle the Roman nation became doubly conscious of its Asiatic origins. To save Italy from the scourge of Hannibal, the formless aerolite * was brought to Rome from the Phrygian homeland. Rome, the city of Aphrodite, took fright at its long neglect of the mother and its exclusive devotion to the political principle of the paternal imperium. Virgil was neither the first nor the only Roman to see a close connection between the Punic Wars and the myth of Aeneas, and to regard them as the culmination of a development begun thousands of years before.[9] So thought the contemporaries of the Scipios, and if we wish to judge correctly, we must take equally vast periods of time under consideration, because history always operates in long perspectives. We men of the nineteenth century, who are content for the most part if we know what we are going to eat and drink, how we are going to dress and amuse ourselves, have difficulty in appreciating the vigor that lofty aims can lend a whole people, not to mention the part that popular traditions such as the legend of Aeneas can play in the history of a nation. We regard them as literary fabrications, subjects of literary controversy, fairy tales of a later day, or mythical prototypes of historical events. But for the ancients they were elements of power, and like

* A meteor in Pessinus, Phrygia, which was believed to represent Cybele; in 204 B.C. it was taken to Rome and a temple was dedicated to Cybele as Magna Mater.

our legend of William Tell, a decisive influence on the morale of a nation and the course of its history. Virgil's poem was the Roman's favorite book only because in it he recognized himself, his destinies, his guiding national idea.

After the struggle with Hannibal Rome waged only foreign wars. What the armies of Alexander in the East and of Carthage in the West had occupied for a brief time became the lasting possession of the western Aeneads. Everywhere the West imposed its higher idea by virtue of its inner strength, despite the increasing corruption of Rome. Even in the immense confusion of the civil wars the world question—Orient or Occident?—was bound up with the question of parties. With Pompey, Brutus, Cassius, and above all Mark Antony, the East succumbed to the West, and their downfall completed the ruin of Asia. It was not the lover of the Egyptian Cleopatra, any more than his predecessor Alexander, to whom the legend imputes a similar encounter with the Meroitic Candace,† but the second conqueror of the Oriental king-woman (Octavian-Augustus), the new Orestes,** avenger of parricide, whom the spirit of history entrusted with the task of establishing the imperium: its Western idea lies at the root of modern civilization. The warriors of the Oriental world seem alien and incomprehensible to us. We feel the gulf that separates us from men like Hannibal, Mithridates, Jugurtha. But in the Scipios, Catos, Julians lives a European spirit that we can understand; their political and legal creations embody ideas whose adoption today is still a possibility, usually a necessity, and not infrequently a source of comfort.

Rome introduced something absolutely new into the world. The Roman nation could look back with pride to the plains near Mount Ida, for its Trojan origin was no mere delusion. But it was not the Trojans and not the Assyrian Heraclids who were reborn on the banks of the Tiber, as the Aeacid Pyrrhus tried to tell himself; [11] rather, a new Western political idea had sprung from the ruins of the Eastern world. Those who believed that Caesar intended a return to the origins lacked understanding.[12] True, the cradle of his

† See pp. 197ff.
** Pausanius [10] relates that a statue of Orestes stood in front of the temple of Hera at Mycenae, inscribed with the name of Augustus. [B.]

race had been in Asia, but the son of the Oriental Aphrodite had established the Western Empire. Caesar was eminently the Western hero; the imperial Rome that he built rested wholly on Western foundations, and has thus been identified with the West for two thousand years. The mission of Rome was not to give mankind back to a transcended life principle, but to secure and reinforce the new principle against the mighty reaction of the Eastern world, made doubly dangerous by the Hellenization of the Orient.

Through its religions the Orient attempted once again to impress its yoke on the Occident. The mother goddesses of Asia and Egypt advanced in triumph. Down to the remotest corners of the Western Empire the Occidental spirit was shaken by this eminently feminine, eminently hetaeric pantheon, which exerted a power never possessed by the externalized figures of the Greek national cult. Formerly the corrupting influence of the Asiatic mysteries of Dionysus-Sandon had been countered by the devastation of Italy; but now Elagabalus could seriously attempt to restore the Babylonian Mylitta principle with all its consequences at the very center of the Empire. The sisters of Nitocris †† surrounded the thrones of the Roman emperors, endangering the foundation of political life. But the menace was withstood, thanks to the inner strength which ultimately enables every higher principle to recover from all setbacks. Zenobia, the Palmyran Candace, was led through Rome in triumph by Aurelian, so fulfilling a desire of Octavian's which Cleopatra's suicide had frustrated three and a half centuries before.

Now that we understand the inner law governing this development, we can assign the greatest event since the downfall of Carthage, the destruction of Jerusalem, its proper place in Roman history. Through the fall of the temple of Jehovah Rome, and with it the West, inherited a new empire, the empire of religion—at a time when the Flavians were putting the finishing touches on the

†† Probably Queen Nit-aqerti (Nitocris), the last ruler of the VI Dynasty, mentioned by Herodotus (1 . 184ff.). In Strabo (17 . 808) and Aelian (*Varia historia* 13 . 33) she was a Memphite hetaera who married the king of Egypt and received as her tomb a pyramid, called the Hetaera's Tomb (see *Die Sage von Tanaquil*, in *Gesammelte Werke*, Vol. 6, pp. 107ff). By her "sisters" Bachofen means women such as Julia Maesa, grandmother of Elagabalus (emperor, A.D. 218–22), and Julia Mamaea, mother of Alexianus (Alexander Severus, emperor, A.D. 222–35).

Caesarism established by the Julians and by the defeat of Julius Civilis' attempt to set up the first independent northern state in opposition to the Roman Empire. The fall of Carthage and that of Jerusalem are not merely tragic episodes in the most amazing of all dramas—Roman history—they are also the two most important turning points in the history of the world. While Scipio's deed guaranteed for all time the political emancipation of the West from the East, the Flavian triumph, commemorated by the still extant Arch of Titus—the most significant of all ancient monuments—meant the liberation of the religion of the future from Mosaic Orientalism and secured Rome's claim to the spiritual heritage of the Orient. Not Byzantium, not Antioch, neither Alexandria nor the African Hippo, but Rome took the place of Jerusalem. Christianity became Occidental, and through this assimilation Rome became so identified with the Occident that for the whole ensuing era all struggles against the Orient were waged by them in common.

Italy proceeded to take up Christianity with the same fervor it had displayed in a former era toward the religious idea of the East; and again Rome so radically adapted the foreign material to its own character that the importation soon took on the appearance of a national product. Of all these imported ideas, the most long-lived has been the Oriental conception of the priesthood, which Rome has preserved down to our own day in the midst of totally different *Weltanschauungen*. On this idea Rome built a world hegemony which the Greeks, although earlier to adopt the gospel, could not achieve. But these considerations, however instructive, lie outside the limits of our inquiry. Suffice it to say that throughout its history Rome discloses the same twofold relation to the Orient as we have seen embodied in the history of the Tanaquil myth: while retaining its roots in the East, Rome continuously transcended the Asiatic view of man and the world, both in an inward and an outward sense. Its victorious armies reached the Tigris and Euphrates sooner than our Alps. The Nordic world, hard by the gates of Italy, remained for Rome the hidden seed of a new and higher era, dimly foreseen but never understood. If we dwell on this general historical reflection longer than our immediate subject seems to require, this is justified by the ultimate purpose of our book. For our intention is to arrive, through the analysis of a single monument, at an insight into a universal law of history, and to establish the standpoint which, though essential to an understanding of the Roman development in all spheres of life, has hitherto been wholly disregarded.

The transformation of Tanaquil on Italian soil goes beyond the development from the hetaeric principle to the ideal of the Roman matron. It expresses the new Western spirit in still another way. Not only is Tanaquil transformed from the hetaeric king-woman of Asiatic dynasties into the prototype of the virtuous, respected Roman wife: she is also transformed from a religious to a historical figure. And this process throws new light on the Roman mind and its relation to the older Asiatic culture. The West replaced the natural standpoint of the Orient by a historical view. Rome, in particular, saw everything in terms of its own political life. Our investigation reveals numerous examples illustrating the transition from a physical to a historic-political attitude. Like Tanaquil, all the figures of Sacaean origin enter into a relationship with the Roman state and the crucial events in its development. Tutela Philotis as well as Anna Perenna of Bovillae no longer owe their cult to the natural idea of Asia, from which they and their rituals sprang, but above all to the influence which, as the myth tells us, they exerted on the course of political events. The same development may be observed throughout the Roman religion. We find scarcely a temple, scarcely an important religious rite, which did not ultimately derive its prestige from a historical motivation. We might be tempted to regard this subordination of the divine to a human idea as the last stage in a process of degeneration from an earlier, more sublime standpoint. And indeed, who will deny that beside the cosmic world-spanning ideas of the Bel-Heracles religion, which gave rise to the notion of a woman commanding over life and throne, the humanized Tanaquil of the Roman tradition, adapted as she is to everyday life, seems an impoverished figure, scarcely comparable to the colossal Oriental conception. And yet this regression contains the germ of a very important advance. For every step that liberates our spirit from the paralyzing fetters of a cosmic-physical view of life must be so regarded.

The most comprehensive and sublime natural systems show no spiritual achievement to equal the recognition of man as the first and most important factor in history. What reduced the cultures of the Orient to the base sensualism manifested in the deification of the harlot? Beyond a doubt it was the attitude that places man at the mercy of natural forces. And what enabled Rome to transcend this stage and endowed it with the superiority that makes its colossal work of destruction seem justified? Surely it was the spiritual liberation following the ascendancy of historical consciousness over the natural idea. Here again Rome introduced something entirely new into the world. In the field of its supreme achievement the Greek genius never relinquished its bond with the outward manifestation of material life; the Greek ideal of beauty has at all times aroused sensualism and given rise to aesthetic judgment, the badge of ethically enfeebled peoples. Rome's central idea, on the other hand, the idea underlying its historical state and its law, is wholly independent of matter; it is an eminently ethical achievement, the most spiritual of antiquity's bequests to the ensuing age. And here again it is clear that our Western life truly begins with Rome.

Roman is the idea through which European mankind prepared to set its own imprint on the entire globe, namely, the idea that no material law but only the free activity of the spirit determines the destinies of peoples. While the Etruscan reflected sorrowfully on the transience of his race, the Roman delighted in the eternity of his state, a prospect he was utterly incapable of doubting. In the legend of the fall of Veii * the Oriental resigns himself in impotent fatalism, but the Roman stands up self-reliantly to the incomprehensible natural phenomenon, rejects the law of material necessity, and masters the flood that has terrified the Oriental. In accordance with the same principle, the Asiatic passively bows to the most trifling natural phenomenon and wastes his mental energies in timidly hearkening to the slightest message of nature, but the Roman feels free to reject the augury, and thus upholds the superiority of the human mind. Everywhere he regards himself as

---

* In the tenth year of the siege (396 B.C.) the lake in the woods of Alba swelled to an unusual height, although there had been no rain. A captive Etruscan soothsayer explained that Veii would not fall before the water receded; but Camillus drained the lake and conquered the city through an underground passage.[13]

the first factor in historical life. Casting off the chains imposed on him by the naturalism of the Orient, he makes religion with all its fictions subservient to the purposes of the state, quite aware that these fictions were becoming more and more indispensable to its headlong growth. The principle that not the first but the last word is decisive, the restless striving that is the hallmark of European mankind, came to the fore with Rome; that is why the world-wide victory of Rome prefaced the great struggle for freedom from natural necessity that marks the historical trend of Christianity.

It is in this light that we consider the historization of the Tanaquil myth. In the process a static traditional idea is transformed into a living picture of human deeds and destinies, religious intuitions are woven into the history of the development of a state, the natural idea gives way to a political idea that molds everything to its needs. The same phenomenon may be observed in a number of familiar historical myths. But the tradition of Tanaquil grants the deepest insight into the spiritual process. Nowhere else is the dividing line between the religious and the historical factors so evident. For we are aided by the extraordinary circumstance that the religious content of Tanaquil was transferred to another mother goddess of related origin, the Praenestine Fortuna, so facilitating the historization of the Etruscan king-woman. We first examine this substitution of an indigenous for a foreign figure. We show how the forward-looking Latin element turned from Tanaquil to Fortuna, how the Latins sought to eliminate not only the Etruscan but the related Sabine element from the legend, and were not content until they had freed their hero, King Servius Tullius, the author of their freedom, from his bond with Tanaquil, representing him as Fortuna's son and the grateful founder of her Roman cult. But the people did not succeed in casting off the conceptions of the primordial age. All the distinguishing features of Tanaquil, the Asiatic king-woman, recur in Fortuna. The myth of Servius' relation to Fortuna reproduces the basic hetaeric idea of the Mylitta principle, and hetaeric usages, which in the historized legend of Tanaquil became mere ornamental trappings, preserve their religious character in the legend of Fortuna. Even the Sacaea survive in the cult of the Latin goddess, while in the myth of Tanaquil they became mere fragmentary memories.

We show that the victorious struggle of Roman matronhood against the hetaeric principle of the Orient, and of the higher morality against sensualism, is also reflected in the history of the Fortuna cult. Here again the prestige of woman is not destroyed along with the hetaeric conception of motherhood, for like Tanaquil and the *flaminica,* Fortuna Muliebris protects faithful wives against male high-handedness. We have not sufficiently remembered that the high standing of motherhood in cult and myth was eminently traced back to the very same king who contributed more than any other to the political development of Rome. Banished from the law of the state, the prestige of maternity was preserved in religion and in the historical myths that sprang from religious ideas. Here it found a salutary barrier against the ruthless enforcement of the civil law, a defense that was doubly necessary in view of the unbending consistency of the Roman character. Our study of the substitution of Fortuna for Tanaquil in the cult concludes with an observation that throws much light on the special character of Rome. The nation wholly relinquished none of its experiences. It sought to repress everything that was contrary to its spirit; but once the victory was won, it knew how to bend to its purposes elements that had at first been fiercely combated. Subordinated to the idea of the state, the old elements retained their force and prestige in spheres where the political idea proved inadequate.

The complete transference of Tanaquil's religious significance to Fortuna (even Tanaquil's wonder-working statue in the temple of Semo Sancus ceased to be an object of religious worship), removed all obstacles to the historization of the traditional religious idea. Two stages in this development may be differentiated. In the first stage the religious idea alone is significant; in the second stage it is replaced by the petty pragmatism of a purely human historical probability. Let us examine each of these stages separately.

The original form of the historical tradition of Tanaquil is a faithful copy of the religious original. The exact transference is evident not only in the broad outlines of the narrative, but also in trifling details. The popular spirit still feels no need to give the legend a rational human motivation. Despite their entrance into human relations, persons and events reveal the supernatural home in which they originated. The human and divine move undifferentiated side by side. The temporal limits of human existence are unimportant. Chronology is not taken into account. There is still no need to round out the story and smooth off rough edges. As in the buildings of the oldest peoples, the masses stand side by side, bound by no mortar, finished by no artist's hand. The impression they arouse is one of archaic grandeur and permanence. As long as the creative religious idea retains its power and remains understood, no change is made, no deficiency is felt.

The second stage of development begins only when the religious idea is obscured and the key to its understanding is lost. Now the need arises for a human pragmatism. The vestiges of the supernatural and miraculous, of transcendent beliefs, arouse contradiction; they are replaced by rational causalities, or merely ridiculed as the absurd products of a childish past. Cracks and crevices in the ancient structure are filled in with small stones, dead surfaces are animated, chronological impossibilities removed, genealogies improved, names introduced where they were previously lacking, and by all these means narratives are created in which the modern spirit can take pleasure.

Compared to the first stage of history-making, this second one is small in its methods, artificial, full of hair-splitting cleverness. In place of divine truth, a human truth is sought, so that justice is done to neither. The final outcome is a petty empirical pragmatism, in which the religious figures of the older Asiatic mankind are reduced to mortal figures of the new era. The original historization is exclusively the work of the people, the later elaboration is the work of individual critics; the former is a product of an unconscious natural activity, the latter is a product of the reasoning intellect; the former, with all the crudity of its masses, is as natural as the primordial mountains; the latter is artificially ordered, like a formal garden at the bottom of a valley.

The outcome of the struggle between the two stages was highly characteristic of the Roman mind. Rationalism was not successful; it achieved only isolated results, and even these were not universally accepted. The popular spirit guarded its creation, whose religious character made it inviolable. No annalist living in those times would have dared to infringe on this national heritage. It is absurd to call their record of the past incomplete, falsified, unreliable: it is characteristic of a cultural stage, and in these terms it is an absolutely complete, thoroughly authentic tradition, but religious in nature. It is only a later epoch that created and favored a more exact, realistic approach—in Rome inaugurated by the Greek Polybius, whose own country had come to the end of its development; the older epoch perceived and judged everything in the light of faith and set religious truth over human truth.

Rome never wholly overcame this view. But in the early period it alone was dominant. Nothing in the legends we have considered was based on free invention, no single trait was picked out of the void, none sprang from the uncontrolled fancy of Greek myth makers. Everything was cast in the religious mold, just as the Roman annalists found it and recorded it for later times. The Italic people possessed but one kind of imagination, and it was religious; they had little poetic fancy, and it played no part in creating the historical tradition. Faith created the atmosphere of solemnity which distinguishes the older tradition as a whole, a quality the historical realism of a later day could never achieve. The Tanaquil tradition as a whole is full of divine grace and wrath, guilt and punishment, crime and catastrophe. Everything is judgment, an expression of the national conscience. In this tragedy all things earthly are measured by their relation to the divine. Who will say that such an approach to the national destiny lacks sublimity, and hence justification? We may call it one-sided, because without human truth divine truth cannot satisfy the Western mind. But the opposite extreme, so highly regarded today, is assuredly far worse, namely, the exclusive emphasis on human truth, which without divine truth remains sterile and unsanctified.

The reader who has followed this analysis of my book with some degree of attention will not fail to observe the contrast it presents to the prevailing view. This contrast, which indeed could scarcely be more radical, exerts a profound effect both on our methods and on our findings. The findings carry us back to historical facts which a dogmatic prejudice regards as no longer valid, and which

are nevertheless essential to any general understanding of history.†
The method is based on our view of the nature of history, namely,
that this supreme manifestation of the divine idea shares with the
lower manifestations of nature its absolute origin, its lawfulness, its
ultimate aim, and that consequently its investigation depends on
the same conditions. It is not my intention to present the
philosophical arguments for this similarity as opposed to the older
view, according to which the two realms are sharply differentiated,
and to the prevailing modern view, according to which history is a
natural process set in motion by material forces, so that any
distinction between the ideal and the physical manifestation of the
divine is annulled. Nor shall I go to any length to point out that the
ancients, over against the later mankind molded by Christianity
and its revelation of the infinite, were largely taken up with the
natural aspect of existence, and could not, even in their struggles
for redemption from material fetters, cast off this preoccupation. I
merely feel that it is my duty to state as clearly as possible the
logical implications of this parallel for our methods of inquiry.

What distinguishes our scientific method from the modern
method that likes to call itself critical is chiefly our conception of
the object of investigation and attitude toward it. As to the
object of inquiry, it seems to me incontestable that since all human
activity on earth is transient and ephemeral, empirical events in
themselves can never be objects of our observations. We can only
fixate the ephemeral through the intermediary of tradition. But the
tradition too shares the nature of the underlying event. Like the
outward action, the inner act by which beliefs and traditions are
formed springs from a principle that is not stable and immutable
but fluid and transient, and hence, like everything in which there is
life, itself subject to history. From this it follows that historical
inquiry always deals with a spiritual manifestation which develops
and progresses, that the factual and ideal elements of a tradition
are not juxtaposed, but are so interwoven as to defy any attempt to
sift them apart, and finally that the truth we can attain in regard to
the history of the past is not of a physical but of a purely spiritual
character. When pretentious scholars approach a tradition (for

† I have in mind the Roman and Etruscan migration legends; the latter is
mentioned by Herodotus, Strabo, and Tertullian.[14] [B.]

example, the tradition regarding the accession of the older Tarquin or of Servius Tullius) with the question of what "actually happened," and, by a so-called critical sifting of the material at hand, seek to determine the actual course of events, it would be basically unsound and ineffectual for us to counter their denial of factuality (this is the "critical approach" to the traditions) with an affirmation of factuality, or to examine the likelihood of any new hypothesis regarding the actual course of events—for such an argument would imply an acceptance of the false notion that the investigation of former times revolves around the discovery of factual rather than spiritual truth, around empirical events rather than the spirit of the times as disclosed in tradition.

No truth is more strongly supported by all our experience. None of the heated arguments between orthodox and heretical historians has ever convinced anyone of the factual reality or unreality of a set of events; all their proofs and counterproofs are powerless to inspire belief. The subjective constructions spun by pretentious skeptical historians have resulted in the most blatant absurdities. Or consider the empty narratives of those modern historians who, hovering between heaven and hell, have lost the courage either of simple faith or of resolute negation, and who, by accepting certain selected traits and discarding everything else, try to combine two irreconcilable tendencies of thought. All this shows that where we are dealing with knowledge that is communicated by the medium of tradition, hence through the creative human spirit, what matters is the reality not of the fact but of the idea, not the greater or lesser probability of an event or an attendant circumstance but a sound understanding of the way in which the knowledge of it has been handed down.

What is the attitude of our scientific method toward this tradition? The question might be answered in a phrase—objective observation—were it not necessary, particularly in the present case, to specify what such observation requires and what it precludes. The first concern of objective historical research is to represent the object of inquiry in its unfalsified purity. Since the tradition in all its stages of development can be gleaned only from written works, we shall begin by investigating what each single author has said and by safeguarding our findings against all arguments that may be raised against the authenticity of the text or the soundness of the exegesis. Philological criticism is valid only within these strict limits. The very nature of the scientific method forbids philology to ask whether or not the content of our sources is probable, reasonable, or logical. For the existence of a record is not disproved by the incredibility, impossibility, or faulty logic of its content. Likewise excluded are all those operations springing from a purely mechanical formalism, those operations which are impressively termed criticism or verification of sources and currently classified among the higher functions of scientific research. Here I am referring to the rejection of an author because he wrote at a relatively late date, because he used older sources carelessly or not at all; the selection of a single authority at the expense of all others; the mutilation of source material by the arbitrary selection of elements to be emphasized or by the piecing together of approved fragments into an entirely new narrative; the discarding of a document because of its author's real or supposed pseudonymity. For such questions find their solution not in the realm of philology but in the higher sphere of the explanation of ideas, which calls for recognition of the entire tradition, regardless of the competence of the authors who transmitted it. I find one of the chief causes for the increasing flatness of our study of antiquity in the attitude that makes it a mere appendage of philology, a discipline which regards the manipulation of syllables and letters as an ultimate aim rather than a mere beginning, and seriously imagines that the forms of a hypothetical Indo-European language provide a guarantee of sound historical insight. Over against these unwarranted claims of a linguistic science inflated with the arrogance of youth, we must take the greatest pains to develop the true instruments of historical research.

Here I come to the crux of the matter, namely our approach to the material of tradition. Here again it would be difficult to elucidate the scientific method without reference to its antithesis. Accordingly I shall not content myself with saying that we must regard every phenomenon presented by tradition as an independent spiritual organism justified by its mere existence, that we must interpret each such phenomenon according to the law of its genesis and all ideas only in terms of themselves, but add that the capital offense against this principle consists in injecting ourselves into the objects of observation, of carrying our own ideas into a foreign subject matter instead of apprehending the ideas inherent in the things themselves, in approaching nature in a carping, argumentative frame of mind instead of subordinating ourselves to the phenomenon and seeking to discern its special character. Proceeding from these general considerations to their specific application, we must recall what has been said above regarding the nature of tradition. Events, which are always ephemeral, can only be fixated through the intermediary of tradition, but since the molding of a tradition is a spiritual fact, dependent on the cultural level and habits of thought prevailing in a particular period, and hence on a definite law, true objectivity can consist only in arriving, through exact empirical observation of the phenomenon, at a knowledge of the formative law from which it sprang. Because of its spiritual nature a tradition cannot possibly be free from change and development, but must be affected by transformations in habits of thought. Thus in the course of the centuries different types of tradition arise, each according to a definite formative law. Consequently the work of truly objective explanation must be done not once, but as often as the phenomena change. The links in this succession must be kept carefully apart; the formative law of each one must be explained only through the phenomenon itself, and in the language appropriate to it. Since the development of tradition as of human culture in general can only be gradual and therefore partial, since every stage will contain a mixture of old and new ideas, it follows that a truly objective inquiry can never limit itself to a single phenomenon or a particular period, but must relate every period to those before and those after it. In short, every investigation of the past must be undertaken in the spirit of the whole.

There is no doubt that all this requires far greater depth of mind and presents far graver difficulties than does the modernizing historiography, so popular today, that is turning more and more into a handmaiden of current interests. But in no other way can we achieve solid results comparable to those upon which modern natural science, after long groping in the dark, has built its achievement and prestige. The main advantage of our method is that it enables us to arrive at an inherent structure of history. The scientific approach to history recognizes the stratification of the spiritual modes that have gradually made their appearance, assigns to each stratum the phenomena that pertain to it, and shows the genesis of ideas. Proceeding thus through all the stages of reality, it leads us to realize what this spirit of ours once was, through the passage of the ages, but is today no more. The resulting scientific edifice will not be shaken or made uncertain by hypotheses, probabilities, surmises; it is independent of all subjective judgments and opinions, consisting from top to bottom of sheer affirmations. The realm of ideal revelations takes on a lawful structure, as solid and unshakable as the material realm of physical development. The truth is seen in the necessary combination of all the parts, in the whole context, not in fragments. It is no longer the purely empirical truth of outward factuality, but the higher truth, essentially the only real spiritual truth, which rises above all ephemeral things to the idea that is manifested in them. Thus our results are in keeping with the idea underlying our method. Our scholarship acquires a scientific principle, and with it a definite goal, such as is unknown to the so-called critical school.

Our investigation of the Tanaquil myth aims to show, by a study of one fragment, how we should evaluate the Roman tradition for the historical structure of the future. Assuredly it falls short of its guiding idea. For even with courage and determination we can achieve absolute objectivity only gradually and progressively. But a book can foster what it cannot fully accomplish, and what book has set itself a higher aim? We must all strive to exceed our powers if we would not fall short of them.

Written at Basel, in the summer of 1869.

NOTES

Abbreviations

For full references, see list of works cited.

FHG	Müller. *Fragmenta Historicorum Graecorum*
FPhilG	Mullach. *Fragmenta Philosophorum Graecorum*
LCL	Loeb Classical Library, London and Cambridge, Mass. (or New York)
PG	Migne. *Patrologiae cursus completus: Series Graeca*
PL	Migne. *Patrologiae cursus completus: Series Latina*
Plutarch	

De Is. et Os.	*De Iside et Osiride*
Consol. ad Apoll.	*Consolatio ad Apollonium*
Quaest. Graec.	*Quaestiones Graecae*
Quaest. Rom.	*Quaestiones Romanae*

My Life in Retrospect

1 Aeschylus, *Prometheus Bound*, 434f.

2 Aristotle, *Metaphysics* 3 . 4 . 17.

From An Essay on Mortuary Symbolism

FOREWORD

1 Emil Braun, "Scavi romani: Villa Pamfili."

2 Giovanni Pietro Campana, *Illustrazione.*

THE THREE MYSTERY EGGS

1 Plutarch, *De Is. et Os.* 22 . 359 E; 31 . 363 A.

2 Plutarch, *Romulus* 2 . 4ff.

3 Herodotus 2 . 121–3.

4 Plato, *Republic* 2 . 359 D.

5 Homer, *Odyssey* XI . 298.

6 Homer, *Iliad* XXIII . 641f. (tr. Lattimore).

7 Aelian, *Varia Historia* 3 . 18.

8 Plutarch, *Consol. ad Apoll.* 10 . 106 F.

9 Plutarch, *De Is. et Os.* 45 . 369.

10 Ibid., 19; 40; 43.

11 Plutarch, *Consol. ad Apoll.* 12 . 107.

12 Ibid., 5 . 103 F.

13 Ibid., 6 . 104 B (= Euripides, *frg.* 418 N [1]).

14 Cicero, *De natura deorum* 1 . 119.

15 Plato, *Symposium* 191 D (tr. Jowett, Vol. 1, p. 317f.).

16 Chiefly Aristophanes, *Frogs* 330.

THE EGGS AT THE CIRCUS

1 Cassius Dio 49 . 43 . 2.

2 Livy 41 . 27 . 6.

3 Varro, *De re rustica* 1 . 2 . 11.

4 Juvenal, *Satires* 6. 588–92 (tr. Ramsay, p. 131).

5 Tertullian, *De spectaculis* 8.

6 Ibid.

7 Lactantius 6 . 20 . 35; Tertullian, op. cit., 9; and others.

8 Cassiodorus, *Variae* 3.51.6:
Tertullian, op. cit., 8: and
others.

9 Virgil, *Aeneid* 7.799.

10 Ibid. 1.664.

11 Tertullian, op. cit., 8: *apud
metas sub terra delitescit.*

12 Pindar, *Olympian Odes* 1.31ff.

13 Tertullian, op cit., 8: *delphinos
Neptuno vovent* (this is the
older reading, the reading now
accepted being: *delphines Neptuno vomunt*).

14 Cassiodorus, *Variae* 3.51.8:
*Euripus maris vitrei reddit
imaginem, unde illuc delphini
aequorei aquas influunt.*

SANCTUM AND SACRUM

1 Plutarch, *De Is. et Os.* 61 is
very certain about this.

2 Plato, *Laws* 6.778 D

3 "Longinus," *On the Sublime*
4.6.

4 Philostratus, *Vita Apollonii* 6.
37.

5 Homer, *Iliad* XXI.441ff.

6 Ulpian, *Digestae* 50.17.35.

7 Josephus, *Bellum Judaicum* 4.
10.7.

8 Ennius: *"At tuba terribili soni-
tu taratantara dixit"* (and the
trumpet said with terrible
sound *taratantara*), in Servius,
Aeneid 9.501.

THE LAMP IN THE MYTH OF AMOR AND PSYCHE

1 Horace, *Carmina* 1.13.15.

2 Plutarch, *Amatorius* 24.769 E.

SYMBOL AND MYTH

1 Plutarch, *De genio Socratis* 20.
589 B.

OCNUS THE ROPE PLAITER

1 Now in the Vatican Museum;
see Helbig, *Führer*[3], Vol. 1,
No. 359/= Salomon Reinach,
Répertoire de reliefs 3.358.

2 Pausanias 10.29.1–2.

3 Plutarch, *De tranquillitate
animi* 14.

4 Pliny, *Natural History* 35.40.
137.

5 Cratinus, *frg.* 348 (Kock);
Photius, *Lexicon*, col. 246.

6 Propertius 4.3.21ff. (tr. Butler, p. 283).

7 Diodorus Siculus 1.97.1ff.

8 Suetonius, *Julius Caesar* 61.

9 Plutarch, *De Is. et Os.* 30.
362ff.

10 Ovid, *Metamorphoses* 6.5ff.

11 Homer, *Odyssey* VIII.266ff.

12 *Homeric Hymn III to Apollo*
103ff.

13 Creuzer, *Symbolik*[3], Vol. 4,
p. 132.

14 Pausanias 8.21.4.

15 Plutarch, *Solon* 12.

16 Euripides, *Orestes* 12.

17 Plato, *Timaeus* 28 B.

18 Nonnus, *Dionysiaca* 24.242ff.

19 Plutarch, *De Is. et Os.* 33.
364 A.

20 Ibid., 39.366f.

21 Plato, *Republic* 6.486 A.

22 Plutarch, *De Is. et Os.*, cited by
Bachofen, does not contain this
remark.

23 Pausanias 10.31.9.

24 Aristotle, *Metaphysics* 4.5.
1010a.31f.

25 Euripides, *Hippolytus* 189–96
(tr. Grene, p. 171).

From Mother Right

INTRODUCTION

1 Herodotus 1 . 173.
2 *Frg.* 129 (*FHG*, Vol. 3, p. 461).
3 Strabo 34 . 18.
4 Polybius 12 . 5 . 4.
5 *Commentarii* (*Iliad*) 12 . 1 . 101, 894 (Vol. 3, p. 100).
6 Tacitus, *Germania* 20.
7 Plutarch, *Quaest. Rom.* 17 . 267.
8 Ibid., 85 . 284.
9 Simonides, *frg.* 99 (*Lyra Graeca*, Vol. 2, p. 341).
10 *Politics* 2 . 9.
11 Iamblichus, *De Vita Pythagorica* 11 . 56 (ed. Deubner, p. 31).
12 Strabo 7 . 3 . 4.
13 *Commentarii* (*Odyssey*) 7 . 11 . 50, 148ff., 1567, 1575 (Vol. 5, pp. 259, 270).
14 Polybius 12 . 5 . 9–11.
15 *FHG*, Vol. 2, p. 305; Athenaeus 12 . 515e–516.
16 I Cor. 11 : 9.
17 Nonnus, *Dionysiaca* 19 . 253ff.
18 Tacitus, *Historiae* 4 . 83.

LYCIA

1 Herodotus 1 . 173.
2 *FHG*, Vol. 3, p. 461, *frg.* 129.
3 Aristotle, *frg.* 611 . 43 (ed. Rose, p. 379, 21).
4 Plutarch, *De mulierum virtutes* 248 D.
5 Ibid., 248 A B.
6 Pindar, *Olympian Odes* 13 . 88.
7 Ovid, *Metamorphoses* 13 . 632ff.
8 Ibid., 10 . 298.
9 *Iliad* VI . 149 (tr. Lattimore).
10 Plutarch, *Consol. ad Apoll.* 7 . 322.

11 Virgil, *Georgics* 4 . 206ff. (tr. C. Day Lewis).
12 Ovid, *Metamorphoses* 10 . 245.
13 Pindar, *Nemean Odes* 11 . 13–16 (tr. Lattimore).
14 *Iliad* VI . 146–50 (tr. Lattimore).
15 Ulpian, *Digestae* 50 . 16 . 195 . 5.
16 *Iliad* VI . 186.
17 Pindar, *Olympian Odes* 13 . 87ff.
18 Apollodorus 2 . 3 . 2.
19 Scholia to *Olympian Odes* 13 . 118 (84).
20 Scholia to Lycophron, *Cassandra* 17.
21 Fellows, *Account of Discoveries*, pl. for pp. 136, 118, 209.
22 Stackelberg, *Apollotempel*, pl. 9.
23 Pindar, *Olympian Odes* 13 . 85. [ED.] Homer, *Iliad* VI . 160ff.
24 Plutarch, *De Is. et Os.* 57 . 374 C D.
25 Plutarch, *Quaest. Rom.* 103 . 288 F. Cf. Plato, *Symposium* 203 C.
26 Philostratus, *Imagines* 2 . 17.
27 Julian, *Digestae* 22 . 1 . 25: *omnis fructus non iure seminis, sed iure soli percipitur; . . . in percipiendis fructibus magis corporis ius, ex quo percipiuntur, quam seminis, ex quo oriuntur, aspicitur.*
28 *Codex Iustinianus* 3 . 32 . 7: *partum ancillae matris sequi condicionem nec statum in hac specie patris considerari explorati iuris est.*
29 Cujacius, *Opera* 6, col. 219 (E) :

mater enim est similis solo, non solum simile matri.

30 Plato, *Republic* 6 . 497 B.
31 Paulus, *Digesta* 2 . 4 . 5: [*mater*] *semper certa est, etiamsi vulgo conceperit, pater vero is tantum, quem nuptiae demonstrant.*
32 Cujacius, *op. cit.*, 5, col. 85 (E): *mater naturae vocabulum est, non civile, adoptio autem civilis.*
33 Menander, *frg.* 657 . 1 K (LCL, p. 516).
34 *Odyssey* I . 215.
35 Gaius, *Institutiones* 3 . 10.
36 *Iliad* III . 238.
37 *Iliad* XXI . 95f. (tr. Lattimore).
38 *Ibid.*, 85
39 Plato, *Republic* 9 . 575 D.
40 Plutarch, *De Is. et Os.* 38.
41 Herodotus 1 . 216.
42 *Ibid.*, 4 . 172.
43 Strabo 11 . 513.
44 Herodotus 4 . 172.
45 Dionysius Periegetes 766.
46 Diodorus 14 . 30 . 7.
47 Xenophon, *Anabasis* 5 . 4 . 34.
48 Herodotus 4 . 180.
49 Solinus 30 . 2, 3: Mela 1 . 45; Pliny, *Historia naturalis* 5 . 8 . 45; Martianus Capella 6 . 674.
50 Pliny, *Historia naturalis* 6 . 35 . 192.
51 Aelian, *De natura animalium* 7 . 40.
52 Plutarch, *De communibus notitiis adv. Stoicos* 11 . 1064b.
53 Plutarch, *De Is. et Os.* 44 . 369 E, F.
54 Stobaeus, *Florilegium*, ed. Meineke, Vol. 2, p. 186 = *FHG* Vol. 3, p. 463, *frg.* 142.
55 Herodotus 3 . 20.
56 Strabo 17 . 822.
57 Mela 1 . 46.
58 Diodorus 5 . 18 . 1.
59 Herodotus 4 . 176.
60 Sextus Empiricus, *Pyrrhoneioi hypotyposeis* 3 . 201.
61 Plautus, *Cistellaria* 563.
62 Arnobius 5 . 19.
63 Herodotus 5 . 6.
64 Mela 1 . 42.
65 Strabo 16 . 783.
66 Plutarch, *Alcibiades* 23 . 6.
67 Plutarch, *Quaest. Rom.* 35 . 273.
68 *Ibid.*, 46 . 275.
69 Plutarch, *De Is. et Os.* 12 . 356 A.
70 Plato, *Republic* 5 . 461 D.
71 Herodotus 4 . 45.
72 Aristotle, *Politics* 2 . 1 . 13 (1262 a 14).
73 Herodotus 4 . 180.
74 Strabo 11 . 501.
75 Ephorus, in Strabo 10 . 480.
76 Athenaeus 12 . 11 . 516a.
77 *FHG*, Vol. 3, p. 463, *frg.* 140.
78 *FHG*, Vol. 3, p. 458, *frg.* 114.
79 *FHG*, Vol. 3, p. 462, *frg.* 133.
80 Strabo 14 . 663; 16 . 783; Herodotus 4 . 172; 1 . 195 (Assyrians).
81 Lucian, *De Saltatio* 21.
82 Strabo 7 . 297.
83 Plutarch, *Marius* 17 . 2.
84 Pausanias 10 . 12 . 10.
85 Giacomo Leopardi, *Poems* (tr. Bickersteth, pp. 166ff.).
86 *FHG*, Vol. 3, p. 458, *frg.* 111.
87 Herodotus 4 . 104.
88 *FHG*, Vol. 3, p. 460, *frg.* 123.
89 Strabo 7 . 300.
90 *FHG*, Vol. 3, p. 463, *frg.* 137.
91 Aeschylus. *frg.* 198 N^2 (ed. Smyth, Vol. 2, *frg.* 111, p. 452).
92 Plato, *Republic* 5, 457 A–461 E.
93 *Ibid.*, 3 . 416 E.
94 *Ibid.*, 10 . 611 D (tr. Shorey).

95 Aristotle, *Politics* 2.1.4 (1261 a 10ff.).

96 Athenaeus 13.2.555e.

97 I Cor. 15 : 46.

98 Cicero, *De inventione rhetorica* 1.2.

99 See also Plato, *Symposium* 190 B.

100 Plutarch, *De defectu oraculorum* 13.416 D E.

101 I Cor. 15 : 40, 41.

102 Plutarch, *Quaest. Rom.* 84. 284; Gellius, *Noctes Atticae* 3.2.2.

103 Creuzer, *Symbolik* [3], 2.163–70; Martini, *Lactanti Carmen de Ave Phoenix.*

104 Herodotus 2.73; Tacitus, *Annals* 6.28.1; Pliny, *Natural History* 10.2.3; Horapollo 1.34.

105 Tacitus, *op. cit.*, 6.28.5.

106 *Physiologus* (ed. Sbordone, p. 154, 4).

107 Philostratus, *Vita Apollonii* 3.49.

108 Herodotus 1.176.

109 Strabo 11.492.

110 *Iliad* VI, 208.

111 Aristotle, *Politics* 2.6.4 (1269 b 24).

112 Strabo 14.665.

113 Justin 2.3–5; Herodotus 4.1.11; 1.15.103.105; Strabo 1.61; 11.511; 15.687.

114 Herodotus 1.6.

115 Plutarch, *Quaest. Graec.* 15. 294 E.

116 Strabo 11, 504–5.

117 Simonides, *frg.* 99 (*Lyra Graeca*, Vol. 2, p. 340).

118 Alcaeus, *frg.* 66 (*Lyra Graeca*, Vol. 1, p. 360).

119 Plutarch, *Consol. ad Apoll.* 22.113 A.

120 *FHG*, Vol. 2, *frg.* 15, p. 217.

121 Cicero, *De natura deorum* 2. 66: *Et recidunt omnia in terras et oriuntur e terris.*

122 F. Winter, *Kunstgeschichte in Bildern* 208.4.

123 Plutarch, *Consol. ad Apoll.* 22.113 B.

124 Virgil, *Georgics* 4.475.

125 F. N. Pryce, *Catalogue of Sculpture*, Vol. 1, Pt. 1, p. 128.

126 Strabo 10.478; 11.499; 12. 557.

ATHENS

1 Strabo 12.573.

2 *City of God* 18.9.

3 Aeschylus, *The Eumenides* 595–608 (tr. Lattimore).

4 Ibid., 657–66.

5 Ibid., 727f.

6 Ibid., 731.

7 Ibid., 734–41.

8 Ibid., 171.

9 Ibid., 808f.

10 Ibid., 511f.

11 Ibid., 854–57.

12 Ibid., 213ff.

13 Ibid., 685–90.

14 Herodotus 9.27; Pausanias 5. 11.7.

15 Aeschylus, *op. cit.*, 754–61 (tr. Lattimore).

16 Ibid., 797ff.

17 Ibid., 389–96.

18 Ibid., 778–83.

19 Ibid., 837–40.

20 Ibid., 938–48.

21 Plato, *Timaeus* 34 A B.

22 Plutarch, *Quaest. Rom.* 23. 269 B.

23 Aeschylus, *op. cit.*, 365f. (tr. Lattimore).

24 Ibid., 273.

25 Ibid., 347–59.

26 Herodotus 5 . 82–8.
27 Odyssey XX . 74.
28 Plutarch, *Quaestionem convivia-lium* 9 . 14 . 4.
29 Herodotus 5 . 83.
30 Plutarch, *Amatorius* 20 . 766 c.
31 Pausanias 1 . 13 . 8.
32 Pythainetos in *FHG*, Vol. 4, p. 487, *frg.* 6.
33 Plutarch, *Lycurgus* 14 . 4.
34 Tacitus, *Germania* 17 . 2; 18 . 1.
35 *FPhilG*, Vol. 2, p. 115, *frg.* 3.
36 Plutarch, *Lycurgus* 15 . 10.
37 Aristotle, *Politics* 2 . 6 . 7; 1269 b 39.
38 Plutarch, *Lycurgus* 14 . 4.

LEMNOS

1 Aeschylus, *Choephoroi* 631–34 (tr. Lattimore).
2 Apollodorus 1 . 9 . 17.
3 *FHG*, Vol. 1, p. 59, *frg.* 112.
4 Cf. Euripides, *Ion* 628; *Medea* 264.
5 *Iliad* VII . 468.
6 Apollonius Rhodius 1 . 828–9.
7 Strabo 1 . 45.
8 Hyginus, *fab.* 15.
9 Strabo 1 . 45; Herodotus 4 . 145; Pindar, *Pythian Odes* 4 . 252.
10 Scholia to *Olympian Odes* 1 . 37.

EGYPT

1 Sophocles, *Oedipus at Colonus* 337 (tr. Fitzgerald, p. 27).
2 Diodorus 1 . 23 . 4.
3 Pausanias 9 . 12 . 2.
4 Hyginus, *fab.* 67.
5 Diomedes, in Keil, *Grammatici Latini* 1 . 450 . 26.
6 Cf. Pausanias 5 . 11 . 2.
7 *Iliad* XXIII . 679.

8 Herodotus 4 . 149.
9 Pindar, *Olympian Odes* 2 . 39.
10 Plutarch, *De placitis philoso-phorum* 1 . 3 . 876.
11 Plato, *Timaeus* 52 D, 53 A.
12 Plato, *Laws* 4 . 717 A B.
13 Aristotle, *Ethica Nicomachea* 5 . 5 . 1; 1132 b 21.
14 Aristotle, *Metaphysica* 1 . 5 . 2; 985 b 29.
15 Plutarch, *De Is. et Os.* 75 . 381 F.
16 Ibid.
17 Pausanias 5 . 19 . 6; Hyginus, *fab.* 67, 68.
18 Ibid., *fab.* 68.
19 Plutarch, *De defectu oraculorum* 35 . 428.
20 Plutarch, *Consol. ad Apoll.* 23 . 113 c.
21 Plato, *Laws* 9 . 870 D E (tr. Bury).
22 Ulpian, *Digestae* 1 . 1 . 3.
23 Ibid., 47 . 10 . 13 . 7; 8 . 4 . 13 pr.
24 Ibid., 4 . 2 . 12 . 1, citing Pomponius.
25 Plutarch, *De Is. et Os.* 47 . 370 B.
26 Virgil, *Aeneid* 8 . 181.
27 Nonnus, *Dionysiaca* 11 . 370ff.
28 Ovid, *Metamorphoses* 10 . 660.
29 Aristophanes, *Frogs* 211.
30 Plutarch, *De Is. et Os.* 66 . 377 E.
31 Plautus, *Captivi* 889.
32 Herodotus 6 . 91, 134.
33 Virgil, *Aeneid* 4 . 58.
34 Aeschylus, *Eumenides* 392.
35 Plutarch, *Julius Caesar* 9 . 4.
36 Plutarch, *Quaest. Rom.* 20 . 268 D.
37 Suidas *s.v.* Μονῆτα.
38 Lucan 1 . 380.

39 Livy 7.28.4ff; Ovid, *Fasti* 6.
    183.
40 Livy 5.23.5f., emphasizes this
    in connection with Camillus.
41 Gellius 5.6.21.
42 Livy 3.55.13.
43 Livy 1.45.2. Plutarch, *Quaest.
    Rom.* 4.264 C D.
44 Plutarch, *Quaest. Rom.* 103,
    288 F.
45 Suidas *s.v.* σάκανδρον·
46 Plutarch, *Coniugalia praecepta*
    138 B.
47 Virgil, *Aeneid* 4.58.

INDIA

1 Tzetzes, *Historiarum variarum
   Chiliades* 3.885f.; Malalas,
   Chronographia 8.194 (*PG*,
   Vol. 97, col. 306).
2 Georgius Cedrenus, *Compend-
   ium Historiarum* 1.267 (*PG*,
   Vol. 121, col. 302).
3 Julius Valerius, *Res Gestae Al-
   exandri Macedonis* 3.28
   (XVIIIff.).

LESBOS

1 Plutarch, *Amatorius* 18.762.
2 Horace, *Odes* 4.9.10.
3 Herodotus 1.23.
4 Diogenes Laertius 8.1.2.
5 Virgil, *Georgics* 4.520.
6 Dio Chrysostom, *Orationes* 14.
   19.

7 Herodotus 5.3–6.
8 Pausanias 9.30.5; Ovid, *Metamorphoses* 10.80.
9 Clearchus, in *FHG*, Vol. 2, p.
   306.
10 Eustathius, *Commentarii* (*Odys-
    sey*) 24.1.230.
11 Phanocles, in Powell, *Collec-
    tanea Alexandrina*, p. 106.
12 Ovid, *Metamorphoses* 10.83ff.
13 Plutarch, *Lycurgus* 18.2.
14 Plato, *Symposium* 211 B.
15 Sappho, *frg.* 13 (ed. Edmonds).
16 Idem, *frg.* 1.22.23.48.
17 Idem, *frg.* 12.14.
18 Idem, *frg.* 98, 115.
19 Idem, *frg.* 58.72.
20 Idem, *frg.* 100.
21 Idem, *frg.* 119.
22 Idem, *frg.* 109.110.
23 Idem, *frg.* 10.76.
24 Idem, *frg.* 51.
25 Idem, *frg.* 71.
26 Idem, *frg.* 108.
27 Stobaeus, *Florilegium* 29.58;
    cited in *Lyra Graeca*, Vol. 1,
    p. 141.
28 Sappho, *frg.* 167 (ed. Ed-
    monds).
29 Plato, *Phaedrus* 235 C.
30 See Karl Schefold, *Die Bild-
    nisse der antiken Dichter, Red-
    ner und Denker*, 54f., 203.
31 Plato, *Symposium* 210.
32 Sappho, *frg.* 52 (ed. Edmonds).

From The Myth of Tanaquil

1 Ovid, *Ibis* 536.
2 K. O. Müller, *Die Etrusker*[2],
   Vol. 1, p. 103; Vol. 2, pp. 44,
   66ff.
3 Herodotus 6.61–75.

4 Virgil, *Aeneid* 1.574.
5 Ibid., 4.338; 4.373.
6 Ibid., 12.828.
7 Cicero, *De republica* 2.34.
8 Lycophron, *Cassandra* [*Alexan-*

dra] 1439ff.

9 Virgil, *Aeneid* 10.11–15; 4.
622ff.

10 Pausanias 2.17.3.

11 Pausanias 1.12.1.

12 Suetonius, *Julius Caesar* 79

13 Livy 5.15–22.

14 Herodotus 1.94; Strabo 5.
221; Tertullian, *De spectaculis*
5.

BIBLIOGRAPHY

Sources

My Life in Retrospect

First published in 1916 under the title "Lebens-Rückschau" (see below, J. J. Bachofen: Selected Bibliography). Here slightly condensed from the version published in *Zeitschrift für vergleichende Rechtswissenschaft*, pp. 337–45, 348–64, 368–80.

The volume and page numbers of the following selections are cited according to the *Gesammelte Werke* (Basel, 1943–   ):

From An Essay on Ancient Mortuary Symbolism (Vol. 4)

Foreword, pp. 7–9
The Three Mystery Eggs, pp. 11, 12, 18f., 22, 23, 24, 25f., 27, 30, 32, 33, 35ff., 39f., 41, 42
The Eggs at the Circus, pp. 263, 264f., 267, 268–76, 277, 282f., 288f.
Sanctum and Sacrum, pp. 190f., 192–7
The Lamp in the Myth of Amor and Psyche, pp. 115–19
Symbol and Myth, pp. 61–3
Ocnus the Rope Plaiter, pp. 352–4, 355, 356, 357, 358ff. 362ff., 365ff., 369f., 372ff., 375, 376, 380f., 434f., 458f., 462f., 465, 472, 473f., 479f., 481, 482ff.

From Mother Right (Vols. 2 and 3)

Introduction, pp. 9–66
Lycia, pp. 85–8, 89–110, 111f., 113, 114, 115, 117–25, 126–33, 134–42

From The Myth of Tanaquil (Vol. 6)

J. J. Bachofen:
Selected Bibliography

Original Editions

Versuch über die Gräbersymbolik der Alten. Basel, 1859. Reprinted, with a Foreword by C. A. Bernoulli and an Appreciation by Ludwig Klages. Basel, 1925.

Das Mutterrecht: Eine Untersuchung über die Gynaikokratie der alten Welt nach ihrer religiösen und rechtlichen Natur. Stuttgart, 1861. Reprinted, Basel, 1897.

Die Sage von Tanaquil. Heidelberg, 1870.

"Lebens-Rückschau," in *Zeitschrift für vergleichende Rechtswissenschaft*, Vol. 34 (1916), pp. 337–80. Also published under the title "Selbstbiographie," in *Basler Jahrbuch 1917* (pp. 298–343).

Collected Works

Johann Jakob Bachofens Gesammelte Werke. Edited by Karl Meuli. Basel, 1943– . (8 vols. by 1966.)

Related Literature

BAEUMLER, ALFRED. "Bachofen, der Mythologe der Romantik," in *Der Mythus von Orient und Okzident.* Ed. Manfred Schröter (Munich, 1926).

BERNOULLI, C. A., *J. J. Bachofen und das Natursymbol.* Basel, 1924.

——. *J. J. Bachofen als Religionsforscher.* Leigzig, 1924.

BIBLIOGRAPHY

KERÉNYI, KARL. *Bachofen und die Zukunft des Humanismus.* Zürich, 1945.

MORGAN, LEWIS HENRY. *Systems of Consanguinity and Affinity of the Human Family.* Washington, 1871.

——. *Ancient Society.* London, 1877.

SCHMIDT, GEORG. *J. J. Bachofens Geschichtsphilosophie.* Munich, 1929.

List of Works Cited

AELIAN (CLAUDIUS AELIANUS). *De natura animalium* (*On Animals*). Ed. and tr. A. F. Scholfield. LCL, 1958–59. 3 vols.

——. *Varia Historia, Epistolae, Fragmenta*. Ed. Rudolf Hercher. Leipzig, 1866.

AESCHYLUS. [*Plays.*] Ed. and tr. H. Weir Smyth. LCL, 1922–26. 2 vols. (Vol. 1: *Prometheus Bound*.)

——. [*Plays.*] Tr. Richmond Lattimore. (Complete Greek Tragedies.) Chicago, 1953–56. 2 vols. (Vol. 1: *Oresteia: Agamemnon, The Libation Bearers* [*Choiphoroi*], *The Eumenides*.)

ALCAEUS. In: *Lyra Graeca* (q.v.), Vol. 1.

APOLLODORUS. *Bibliotheca*. Ed. and tr. Sir James George Frazer. LCL, 1921. 2 vols.

APOLLONIUS RHODIUS. *Argonautica*. Ed. and tr. R. C. Seaton. LCL, 1912.

ARISTOPHANES. [*Comedies.*] Ed. and tr. Benjamin Bickley Rogers. LCL, 1924. 2 vols. (Vol. 2: *The Birds, The Frogs;* Vol. 3: *Ecclesiazusae, Lysistrata*.)

ARISTOTLE. [*Aristotelis qui ferebantur*] *Fragmenta*. Ed. Valentine Rose. Leipzig, 1886.

——. *Metaphysics*. Ed. and tr. H. Tredennick. LCL, 1933–35. 2 vols.

——. *Nicomachaean Ethics*. Ed. and tr. H. Rackham. LCL, 1926.

——. *Politics*. Ed. and tr. H. Rackham. LCL, 1932.

ARNOBIUS. *Adversus nationes*. Ed. August Reifferscheid. (Corpus Scriptorum Ecclesiasticorum Latinorum.) Vienna, 1875. / = *The Seven Books of Arnobius adversus Gentes*. Tr. Archibald Hamilton Bryce and Hugh Campbell. (Ante-Nicene Christian Library, 19.) Edinburgh, 1871.

ATHENAEUS. *The Deipnosophists.* Ed. and tr. Charles Burton Gulick. LCL, 1927–41. 7 vols.

AUGUSTINE, ST. *The City of God.* Ed. and tr. G. E. McCracken and others. LCL, 1957– . 7 vols.

AULUS GELLIUS. See GELLIUS, AULUS.

BLUME, FRIEDRICH. *Iter Italicum.* Vol. 1, Berlin and Stettin; Vols. 2–4, Halle: 1824–36. 4 vols.

BRAUN, EMIL. "Scavi romani: Villa Pamfili," in *Bullettino dell' Instituto di Corrispondenza Archeologica.* Rome, 1838.

BULFINCH, THOMAS. *The Age of Fable.* Boston, 1855.

BURCKHARDT, JAKOB. *The Civilization of the Renaissance in Italy.* Tr. S. G. C. Middlemore. New York and London, 1944. (Originally published in German, Basel, 1860.)

CAMPANA, GIOVANNI PIETRO. *Illustrazione di due sepolcri romani del secolo di Augusto scoperti . . . presso la tomba degli Scipioni.* Rome, 1840.

CASSIODORUS, FLAVIUS MAGNUS AURELIUS. *Variae.* Ed. Theodor Mommsen. (Monumenta Germaniae Historica, Auctores Antiquissimi, XII.) Berlin, 1894.

CASSIUS DIO. See DIO CASSIUS.

CEDRENUS, GEORGIUS. *Compendium historiarum.* In: *PG,* Vol. 121 and Vol. 122, cols. 1–367.

CICERO, MARCUS TULLIUS. *De inventione rhetorica.* . . . Ed. and tr. H. M. Hubbell. LCL, 1949.

——. *De natura deorum.* . . . Ed. and tr. H. Rackham. LCL, 1933.

——. *De oratore.* Ed. and tr. E. W. Sutton and H. Rackham. LCL, 1942. 2 vols.

——. *De republica.* In: *Laws, Republic.* Ed. and tr. Clinton Walker. LCL, 1928.

——. *Letters to Atticus.* Tr. E. O. Winstedt. LCL, 1912–18. 3 vols.

CLEARCHUS OF SOLI. *Fragmenta.* In: *FHG* (q.v.), Vol. 2.

Codex Iustinianus. In: *Corpus Juris Civilis* (q.v.), Vol. 2.

Corpus Juris Civilis. Ed. P. Krueger and T. Mommsen, 9th edn., Berlin, 1902. 2 vols.

CRATINUS. See THEODOR KOCK, *Comicorum Atticorum Fragmenta.*

CREUZER, FRIEDRICH. *Symbolik und Mythologie der alten Völker.* Darmstadt, 1810–23. 6 vols. 3rd edn., Darmstadt, 1836–42. 4 vols.

CUJACIUS, JACOBUS (JACQUES CUJAS). *Opera.* Venice and Modena, 1758–83. 11 vols.

DIO CASSIUS. *Roman History.* Ed. and tr. E. Cary. LCL, 1914–27. 9 vols.

DIO CHRYSOSTOM. [*Discourses.*] Ed. and tr. J. W. Cohoon and H. Lamar Crosby. LCL, 1932–35. 5 vols.

DIODORUS SICULUS. *Historical Library.* Ed. and tr. C. H. Oldfather and others. LCL, 1933–57. 12 vols.

DIOGENES LAERTIUS. *Lives of Eminent Philosophers.* Ed. and tr. R. D. Hicks. LCL, 1925. 2 vols.

DIOMEDES. *Ars Grammatica.* In: Heinrich Keil, *Grammatici Latini.*

DIONYSIUS PERIEGETES. In: *Geographi Graeci Minores*, ed. Karl Müller. Paris, 1855–61. 2 vols. (Vol. 2, pp. 104–76.)

ENNIUS, QUINTUS. See SERVIUS.

EPHORUS. See STRABO.

EPIPHANIUS. See *Physiologus.*

EURIPIDES. [*Plays.*] Ed. and tr. Arthur S. Way. LCL, 1912. 4 vols. (Vol. 2: *Orestes;* Vol. 4: *Hippolytus, Ion, Medea.*)

——. *Fragments.* In: *Euripidis Periditarum Tragoediarum Fragmenta.* Ed. August Nauck. Leipzig. 1885.

——. *Hippolytus.* In: *Euripides*, Vol. 1. Tr. David Grene. (Complete Greek Tragedies.) Chicago, 1955.

EUSTATHIUS. *Commentarii ad Homeri Iliadem et Odysseam.* Leipzig, 1825–28. 7 vols. (Repr., Hildesheim, 1960, identical pagination, 7 vols. in 4.)

FELLOWS, CHARLES. *An Account of Discoveries in Lycia.* London, 1841.

Fragmenta Historicorum Graecorum. See MÜLLER, CARL and THEODOR.

Fragmenta Philosophorum Graecorum. See MULLACH, F. W. A.

FREEMAN, KATHLEEN. *Ancilla to the Pre-Socratic Philosophers.* Oxford, 1948.

GAIUS. *Institutiones.* Ed. Paul Krüger and Wilhelm Studemund. (Collectio Librorum Juris Anteiustiniani, 1.) 6th edn., Berlin, 1912.

GELLIUS, AULUS. *Attic Nights.* Ed. and tr. John C. Rolfe. LCL, 1927. 3 vols.

GRAVES, ROBERT. *The Greek Myths.* 3rd rev. edn., Baltimore and Harmondsworth, 1960.

Greek Anthology, The. Ed. and tr. W. R. Paton. LCL, 1916–18. 5 vols.

HELBIG, WOLFGANG. *Führer durch die öffentlichen Sammlungen klassischer Altertümer in Rom.* 3rd edn., Leipzig, 1912–13. 2 vols.

HERODOTUS. [*The Histories.*] Ed. and tr. A. D. Godley. LCL, 1921–24. 4 vols.

[HESIOD.] *Hesiod and the Homeric Hymns*. Ed. and tr. H. G. Evelyn-White. LCL, 1914.

HOMER. *The Iliad*. Ed. and tr. A. C. Murray. LCL, 1924–25. 2 vols.

——. *The Iliad*. Tr. Richmond Lattimore. Chicago, 1951.

——. *The Odyssey*. Ed. and tr. A. C. Murray. LCL, 1919. 2 vols.

Homeric Hymn to Apollo. See HESIOD.

HORACE. *Odes and Epodes*. Ed. and tr. C. E. Bennett. LCL, 1914.

HORAPOLLO NILIACUS. *Hieroglyphica*. Ed. C. Leemans. Amsterdam, 1835./ = *The Hieroglyphics of Horapollo*. Tr. George Boas. New York (Bollingen Series XXIII), 1950.

HYGINUS, GAIUS JULIUS. *Fabulae*. Ed. M. Schmidt. Jena, 1872.

IAMBLICHUS. *De Vita Pythagorica*. Ed. Ludwig Deubner. Leipzig, 1937./=*Iamblichus' Life of Pythagoras*. Tr. Thomas Taylor. London, 1926.

JOSEPHUS, FLAVIUS. *The Jewish War*. Ed. and tr. H. Thackeray. LCL, 1927–28. 2 vols.

JULIAN (ANTECESSOR). *Digestae*. In: *Corpus Juris Civilis* (q.v.), Vol. 1.

JULIUS VALERIUS. *Res Gestae Alexandri Macedonis*. Ed. Bernhard Kübler. Leipzig, 1888.

JUSTIN (MARCUS JUNIANUS JUSTINUS). *Epitome historiarum Philippicarum Pompei Trogi*. Ed. Otto Seel. Leipzig, 1935.

JUSTINIAN. See *Codex Iustinianus*.

[JUVENAL] (DECIMUS JUNIUS JUVENALIS). *Juvenal and Persius*. Ed. and tr. G. G. Ramsay. LCL, 1918.

KEIL, HEINRICH. *Grammatici Latini*. Hildesheim, 1867 (repr. 1961). 8 vols. (*Diomedis Artis Grammaticae Libri III* in Vol. 1, pp. 299–529.)

KERÉNYI, CARL. *The Gods of the Greeks*. Tr. Norman Cameron. New York and London, 1951.

——. *The Heroes of the Greeks*. Tr. H. J. Rose. London, 1959.

——. *The Religion of the Greeks and Romans*. Tr. Christopher Holme. London, 1962.

KOCK, THEODOR (ed.). *Comicorum Atticorum Fragmenta*. Leipzig, 1880–88. 3 vols. (Cratinus, Vol. 1).

LACTANTIUS, LUCIUS CAECILIUS FIRMIANUS. *Divinae Institutiones*. In: *PL*, Vol. 6, cols. 111–822.

——. *See also* MARTINI.

LEOPARDI, GIACOMO. *Poems*. Ed. and tr. Geoffrey L. Bickersteth. Cambridge, 1923.

LIVY [TITUS LIVIUS]. [*History of Rome*.] Ed. and tr. B. O. Foster, F. G. Moore, and others. LCL, 1919–59. 14 vols.

LONGINUS, PSEUDO-. *On the Sublime.* In: Aristotle, *The Poetics: "Longinus," On the Sublime.* Ed. and tr. W. Hamilton Fyfe. LCL, 1928.

LUCAN (MARCUS ANNAEUS LUCANUS). *The Civil War (Pharsalia).* Ed. and tr. J. D. Duff. LCL, 1928.

LUCIAN. [*Works.*] Ed. and tr. A. M. Harmon, K. Kilburn, and M. D. Macleod. LCL, 1913–41. 8 vols. ("The Dance" [*De Saltatio*] in Vol. 5.)

LYCOPHRON. *Cassandra* [*Alexandra*]. Ed. Gottfried Kinkel. Leipzig, 1880. (Includes the Scholia.)

Lyra Graeca. Ed. and tr. J. M. Edmonds. LCL, 1922–27. 3 vols.

MALALAS, JOANNES. *Chronographia.* In: *PG*, Vol. 97, cols, 65–718.

MARTIANUS CAPELLA. *De Nuptiis Philologiae et Mercurii.* Ed. Adolf Dick. Leipzig, 1925.

MARTINI. *Lactanti Carmen de Ave Phoenix.* Lüneburg, 1825.

MELA, POMPONIUS. *Chronographia.* Ed. Karl Frick. Leipzig, 1880.

MENANDER. [*The Fragments.*] Ed. and tr. F. C. Allinson. LCL, 1921.

MULLACH, F. W. A. (ed.). *Fragmenta Philosophorum Graecorum.* Paris, 1870–81. 3 vols.

MÜLLER, CARL and THEODOR (ed.). *Fragmenta Historicorum Graecorum.* Paris, 1841–84. 5 vols.

MÜLLER, KARL OTFRIED. *Die Etrusker.* 2nd edn., Stuttgart, 1877. 2 vols.

NICOLAUS OF DAMASCUS. *Fragmenta.* In: *FHG*, Vol. 3, pp. 343–463.

NIETZSCHE, FRIEDRICH. *The Birth of Tragedy.* Tr. William A. Haussmann. Edinburgh and London, 1909.

———. *Thus Spake Zarathustra.* Tr. Thomas Common. London, 1932.

NONNUS. *Dionysiaca.* Ed. and tr. W. H. D. Rouse. LCL, 1940. 3 vols.

OVID (PUBLIUS OVIDIUS NASO). *The Art of Love and Other Poems.* Ed. and tr. J. H. Mozley, LCL, 1929. (*Ibis*, pp. 252–30.)

———. *Fasti.* Ed. and tr. Sir James George Frazer. LCL, 1931.

———. *Metamorphoses.* Ed. and tr. F. J. Miller. LCL, 1916. 2 vols.

PAULUS. In: *Corpus Juris Civilis* (q.v.), Vol. 1.

PAUSANIAS. *Description of Greece.* Ed. and tr. W. H. S. Jones and H. A. Ormerod. LCL, 1918–35. 5 vols.

PHANOCLES. See POWELL, JOHN UNDERSHELL.

PHILOSTRATUS. *Heroicus.* In: *Flavii Philostrati Opera.* Ed. C. L. Kayser. Leipzig, 1870–71. 2 vols. (Vol. 2, pp. 128–219.)

———. *Imagines.* Ed. and tr. Arthur Fairbanks. LCL, 1931.

———. *Life of Apollonius of Tyana.* Ed. and tr. F. C. Conybeare. LCL, 1912. 2 vols.

PHOTIUS. *Lexicon.* Ed. Gottfried Hermann. Leipzig, 1808.

Physiologus. Ed. F. Sbordone. Milan, 1936.

PINDAR. *Odes.* Ed. and tr. Sir J. E. Sandys. LCL, 1915.

——. *Odes.* Tr. Richmond Lattimore. Chicago, 1947.

——. *Scholia.* See: *Pindari Carmina.* Ed. C. Gottlieb Heyne. Göttingen, 1798. 2 vols.

PLATO. *The Dialogues.* Tr. Benjamin Jowett. New York, 1937. 2 vols. (Vol. 1: *Symposium.*)

——. *Euthyphro Apology Crito Phaedo Phaedrus.* Ed. and tr. H. N. Fowler. LCL, 1914.

——. *The Laws.* Ed. and tr. R. G. Bury. LCL, 1926. 2 vols.

——. *Lysis, Symposium, Gorgias.* Ed. and tr. W. R. M. Lamb. LCL, 1925.

——. *The Republic.* Ed. and tr. Paul Shorey. LCL, 1930–35. 2 vols.

——. *Timaeus Cleitophon Critia Menexenus Epistles.* Ed. and tr. R. G. Bury. LCL, 1929.

PLAUTUS. [*Works.*] Ed. and tr. Paul Nixon. LCL, 1916–38. 5 vols. (Vol. 1: *Captivi* [The Captives]; Vol. 2: *Cistellaria* [The Casket Comedy].)

PLINY (GAIUS PLINIUS SECUNDUS). *Natural History.* Ed. and tr. H. Rackham and others. LCL, 1938–42. 11 vols.

PLUTARCH. *The Parallel Lives.* Ed. and tr. B. Perrin. LCL, 1914–26. 11 vols. (Vol. 1: Romulus, Solon, Lycurgus; Vol. 4: Alcibiades; Vol. 7: Caesar; Vol. 9: Marius.)

——. *Moralia.* Ed. and tr. F. C. Babbitt and others. LCL, 1927– . 15 vols. (Vol. 2: *Consolatio ad Apollonium* [Letter of Consolation to Apollonius], *Coniugalia praecepta* [Advice to Bride and Groom]; Vol. 3: *Mulierum virtutes* [Bravery of Women]; Vol. 4: *Quaestiones Romanae* [Roman Questions], *Quaestiones Graecae* [Greek Questions]; Vol. 5: *De Iside et Osiride* [Isis and Osiris], *De defectu oraculorum* [Obsolescence of Oracles]; Vol. 6: *De tranquillitate animi* [Tranquillity of Mind]; Vol. 7: *De genio Socratis* [Sign of Socrates]; Vol. 8–9: *Quaestionem convivialium* [Table-Talk]; Vol. 9: *Amatorius* [Dialogue on Love]; Vol. 11: *De placitis philosophorum* [On the Opinions Accepted by the Philosophers]; Vol. 12: *De facie quae in orbe lunae apparet* [Concerning the Face Which Appears in the Orb of the Moon]; Vol. 13: *De communibus notitiis adversus Stoicos* [On Common Moral Notions against the Stoics].)

POLYBIUS. [*History.*] Ed. and tr. W. R. Paton. LCL, 1922–27. 6 vols.

POMPONIUS MELA. See MELA.

POWELL, JOHN UNDERSHELL. *Collectanea Alexandrina*. Oxford, 1925.

PROPERTIUS. [*Works*.] Ed. and tr. H. E. Butler. LCL, 1912.

PRYCE, F. N. *Catalogue of Sculpture in the Department of Greek and Roman Antiquities in the British Museum*. London, 1928–31. 2 parts. (Part I.)

PYTHAINETOS. In: *FHG* (q.v.), Vol. 4.

REINACH, SALOMON. *Répertoire de reliefs grecs et romains*. Paris, 1909–12. 3 vols.

SAPPHO. In: *Lyra Graeca*, Vol. 1.

SCHEFOLD, KARL. *Die Bildnisse der antiken Dichter, Redner und Denker*. Basel, 1943.

SCHWAB, GUSTAV BENJAMIN. *Die schönsten Sagen des klassischen Altertums*. Stuttgart, 1838–39. 2 vols.

SERVIUS. (*Servii grammatici qui feruntur*) *Commentarii*. Ed. Georg Thilo and Hermann Hagen. Leipzig, 1881–87. 3 vols. (Vols. 1–2: *Aeneid;* Vol. 3: *Bucolics, Georgics*.)

SEXTUS EMPIRICUS. [*Pyrrhoneioi hypotyposeis*.] Ed. and tr. R. G. Bury. LCL, 1933–36. 4 vols.

SIMONIDES. In: *Lyra Graeca*, Vol. 2.

SOLINUS, GAIUS JULIUS. *Collectanea Rerum Memorabilium*. Ed. Theodor Mommsen. Berlin, 1864.

SOPHOCLES. *Oedipus at Colonus*. Tr. Robert Fitzgerald. New York, 1941. Reprinted in series of Complete Greek Tragedies, Chicago, 1954.

SPARTIANUS, AELIUS. *Caracalla*. In: *Scriptores Historiae Augustae*, ed. and tr. D. Magie. LCL, 1953. 3 vols. (Vol. 2, pp. 2–31.)

STACKELBERG, OTTO MAGNUS VON. *Der Apollotempel zu Bassae in Arcadien*. Rome, 1826.

STOBAEUS, JOANNES. *Florilegium*. Ed. August Meineke. Leipzig, 1855–56. 3 vols.

STRABO. *Geography*. Ed. and tr. H. L. Jones. LCL, 1917–32. 8 vols.

SUETONIUS. *Lives of the Caesars*. Ed. and tr. J. C. Rolfe. LCL, 1914. (Vol. 1: *The Deified Julius*.)

SUIDAS. *Lexicon*. Ed. Ada Adler. (Lexicographi Graeci.) Leipzig, 1928–38. 5 vols.

TACITUS, CORNELIUS. *Dialogus, Agricola, and Germania*. Ed. and tr. William Peterson and Maurice Hutton. LCL, 1914.

———. *Histories and Annals*. Ed. and tr. Clifford H. Moore and John Jackson. LCL, 1925–51. 4 vols.

TERTULLIAN (A. SEPTIMIUS FLORENS TERTULLIANUS). *Apology, De spectaculis*. Ed. and tr. T. R. Glover. LCL, 1931.

Tzetzes, Joannes. *Variarum Historiarum Liber.* In: *Lycophronis Chalcidensis Alexandra . . . adjectus quoque est Joannis Tzetzae Variarum Historiarum Liber.* Basel, 1546.

Ulpian (Domitius Ulpianus). *Digestae.* In: *Corpus Juris Civilis* (q.v.), Vol. 1.

Varro, Marcus Terentius. [Cato and] Varro, *De re rustica.* Ed. and tr. W. D. Hooper and H. B. Ash. LCL, 1934.

Virgil (Publius Virgilius Maro). [*Works.*] Ed. and tr. H. R. Fairclough. LCL, 1916–18. 2 vols. (Vol. 1: *Georgics;* Vols. 1–2: *Aeneid.*)

———. *The Georgics.* Tr. Cecil Day Lewis. London, 1940.

Westermarck, Edward. *The History of Human Marriage.* London, 1891. 5th edn., London, 1921. 3 vols.

Winckelmann, Johann Joachim. *Werke.* Ed. C. L. Fernow. Dresden and Berlin, 1808–25. 11 vols.

Winter, Franz (ed.). *Kunstgeschichte in Bildern.* Leipzig, 1910–27. 13 parts.

Xenophon. *Hellenica, Anabasis, Symposium.* Ed. and tr. C. L. Brownson and O. J. Todd. LCL, 1918–22. 3 vols. (Vols. 2–3: *Anabasis;* Vol. 3: *Symposium.*)

INDEXES

General Index

Arnim, Bettina von (née Brentano), *xxxv*

Arnim, Ludwig Achim von, *xxxv*

Bachofen, Carl, *xxxiv*

Bachofen, Johann Jakob, *xliif, liff, liv*, 3; his contribution, *xi, xii, xxiiif, xxv*ff, *xxxiii, xliiif, liif, lv, lvi*f; influences on, *xxxv, xxxvi, xxxvii, xl*f, 3, 10f; his method, *xxxviii*ff; studies, *xxxiv*, 3ff, 6, 9, 15; theory, *xiii*f, *xv, xvi, xvii, xviii, xix*f, *xxi, xxii, xxx*f, *xxxii, xlv, xlvi, xlvii, xlviii, l*, 16; visits: to Greece, 17, 21; to Italy and Rome, *xxviii, li*, 6, 10, 12, 13ff, 21

Bachofen, Louise Elizabeth (née Burckhardt), *xxxiv, liii*

Bachofen, Valeria (née Merian), *xxxiv*

Bastian, Adolf, *lii*

Bernoulli, C. A., *xl*n

Blackstone, William, 7

Blume, Friedrich, 10

Borgia, Cesare, *xxi*

Braun, Emil, 21, 249

Brentano, Bettina, *see* Arnim, Bettina von

Brentano, Clemens, *xxxv*

Brentano, Kunigunde, *see* Savigny, Kunigunde

Bulfinch, Thomas, *xxv*f

Burckhardt, Jakob, *xx, xxi*f, *xxxiv*

Bursian, Conrad, 113n

Campana, Giovanni Pietro, 21, 22, 39, 52, 59, 61, 62f, 164

Conestabile (della Staffa), Gian Carlo, 212

Creuzer, Friedrich, 250, 253

Curtius, Ernst, *lii*

Darwin, Charles, *xxx, xxxvii*f

Eiseley, Loren, *xxx*n

Engels, Friedrich, *liif*

Erasmus, Desiderius, *xlii*

Evans, Arthur, *lv*

Fellows, Charles, 251

Fernow, Carl Ludwig, 10

Frazer, James G., *xlix, liv, lvi*

Freud, Sigmund, *lv*f

Frobenius, Leo, *lv, lvi*

Garibaldi, Giuseppe, *xxxvi*, 14f

George, Stefan, *xxv*

Giraud-Teulon, Alexis, *li, liii*

Gobineau, Joseph Arthur, Comte de, *xxi*

Goethe, Christiane von, *xxxv*

Goethe, J. W. von, *xxxv, xxxvii, xlii*, 44

Graves, Robert, 126, 131

Grimm, Jacob and Wilhelm, *xxxiv, xxxv, xxxvi, xxxvii*

Harrison, Jane, *lv*

Hastings, James, *xxxi*

Hegel, Georg Wilhelm Friedrich, *xix, xxii, xlii, xlvi, xlvii*
Heine, Heinrich, *liii*
Helbig, Wolfgang, 28n, 250
Hobbes, Thomas, *xix*
Hofmannsthal, Hugo von, *xxvii*
Huschke, Philipp Eduard, 16

Iroquois Indians, *xxxiii*

Jensen, Adolf, *lv*
Jung, C. G., *xxiif, xxvi*

Kierkegaard, Sören, *xlii, xliii, lvii*
Klages, Ludwig, *lvi*
Koppers, Wilhelm, *lv*

Lafitau, Reverend Joseph François, *xxxiii*
Leakey, L. S. B., *xxx*
Leopardi, Count Giacomo, 144, 252
Locke, John, *xix*
Lowie, Robert H., *xliii*

McLennan, J. F., *xliii, li*
Malinowski, Bronislaw, *xxix, xxx*n, *xxxi*
Marett, R. R. *xliii*
Martini, 253
Marx, Karl, *xlvi, liif*
Marx, Rudolf, *xxxvii*n, *liin*
Mexico, *lvi*
Meyer-Ochsner, Heinrich, *xxxvii, li*
Micali, Giuseppe, 212
Middlemore, S. G. C., *xxii*n
Mommsen, Theodor, *xli, xliii*, 13n
Morgan, Lewis Henry, *xxxiii, xlii, lii*
Mühlenbruch, Christian Friedrich, 4, 5
Mullach, F. W. A., 248
Müller, Karl Otfried, 218, 255
Müller, Theodor, 248

Napoleon Bonaparte, *xxxvi*
Niebuhr, Barthold Georg, 13n
Nietzsche, Friedrich Wilhelm, *xx, xxi, xxii, xxxiv, xlii, xliii, xlvi, li, lvii*
Noël des Vergers, Joseph M. A., 212

Palmer, Leonard R., *lv*n
Pardessus, Jean Marie, 6
Pastoret, Pierre, 6
Pawnee Indians, *xxxiii*
Petrarch, xlii
Pius IX, Pope, 14

Rilke, Rainer Maria, *xxvii*
Rivers, W. H. R., *xxxi*
Rossi, Count Pellegrino, *xxxvi*, 6, 14
Rousseau, Jean Jacques, *xix*
Ruskin, John, *xii*
Ruspi, Carlo, 25n

Savigny, Friedrich Karl von, *xxvii, xxxiv, xxxv, xxxvi, xxxvii, lvii*, 3, 9
Savigny, Kunigunde (née Brentano), *xxxv*
Schelling, Friedrich Wilhelm, 16n
Schmidt, Wilhelm, *lv*
Schopenhauer, Arthur, *xx*
Schurtz, Heinrich, *liii*f
Sedgwick, Adam, *xxx*
Sioux Indians, *xxxiii*
Stachelberg, Otto Magnus von, 251

Ventris, Michael, *lv*

Wagner, Richard, *xlvi*
Westermarck, Edward, *xviii*
White, Leslie A., *liin*
Winckelmann, Johann Joachim, 10

Zuñi Indians, *xxxiii*

Glossarial Index

CLASSICAL AND LEGENDARY SUBJECTS

Abylles (people living near present-day Ceuta in Morocco) 143

Acanthus (city of Egypt) 55, 60, 62

Acca Larentia (in Roman legend counseled by Heracles to give herself to the first man she should meet; she did so, on his death inherited his wealth, and willed it to the Roman people) 138, 217

Acheron (river in Hades, sometimes standing for Hades itself) 27, 59, 62

Achilles (Greek hero of the Trojan War, child of Peleus and Thetis) 13, 42, 44, 45, 52, 63, 64, 124, 130, 133, 174, 177, 231

Actor, sons of, *see* Moliones

Adriatic Sea, 229

Aeacid (descendant of Aeacus, a son of Zeus and tutelary god of Aegina, who helped build the walls of Troy) 233

aediles (Roman administrative magistrates who supervised public buildings, public order, and the State games) 193

Aegeus (legendary king of Athens, father of Theseus) 157

Aegids (descendants of Aegeus, *q.v.*) 183, 184

Aeginetans (inhabitants of Aegina, an island in the Saronic Gulf, colonized from Epidaurus, *q.v.*) 165–69, 182, 230n

Aelian (Claudius Aelianus; fl. ca. A.D. 200; Roman author) 135, 234n, 249

Aeneads (descendants of Aeneas, *q.v.*) 99, 233

Aeneas (Trojan prince, son of Anchises and Aphrodite; after Trojan War sailed for Italy, but was shipwrecked on the coast of Carthage, where he met Dido, *q.v.*; became the ancestor of the Roman people) 227–30, 232

Aeolians (Greek people inhabiting northwest Asia Minor, in the Trojan region, and the island of Lesbos) 90, 103, 201, 202, 204, 206, 207

Aeschylus (525–456 B.C.; Greek tragic poet) 12, 110, 145, 158, 161, 162, 163, 173, 183, 193, 249, 252, 253, 254

Aetolians (people of Aetolia, in central Greece) 71

Africa: Amazonism in, 105, 153, 154; Aphroditic stage in, *xlvii*; telluric-Demetrian development of, *xlvi*, 89, 103, 108, 200

Agamemnon (Greek leader in the Trojan War who, on his return, was slain by his adulterous wife Clytaemnestra; later avenged by their son Orestes) 158, 184

Agathocles (ruler of Syracuse in Sicily, 317–289 B.C., warred against Carthage) 231

agathodaemon (the "good genius" of an individual) 62, 164

Agathyrsi (a people living near the present-day river Mures in Hungary and Romania) 145

Agrippa, Marcus Vipsanius (63 B.C.–A.D. 14; Roman military commander and friend of the Emperor Augustus) 31

Ahriman (principle of evil in the Zoroastrian religion) 190

Aides Aïdoneus (Greek god of the underworld; another form of Hades, *q.v.*) 127

Ajax (called "the Locrian" to distinguish him from another "Telamonian" Ajax; Greek hero of the Trojan War who defiled Cassandra, daughter of the Trojan king Priam, and was drowned for impiety against Poseidon, or Neptune) 86

Alba Longa (town in Latium, near Rome; destroyed by the Romans ca. 600 B.C.) 42, 229ff, 231, 237n

Albinus, Aulus Postumius, 31

Alcaeus (Greek lyric poet of Lesbos; b. ca. 620 B.C.) 83n, 154, 263

Alcibiades (ca. 450–405 B.C.; Athenian politician and pupil of Socrates) 138

Alcmaeon (in Greek legend slew his mother, Eriphyle, at the bidding of his father, Amphiaraus, and was punished by madness) 110

Aleian meadow (probably in Cilicia; cf. Herodotus 6.95) 124, 125

Alexander (name often given in Homer's *Iliad* to Paris, son of Priam and Hecuba; his abduction of Helen, wife of Menelaus, gave rise to the Trojan War) 138

Alexander the Great (356–323 B.C.; king of Macedon) 117, 197–200, 231, 233

Alexander Severus, Marcus Aurelius (Roman emperor, A.D. 222–235) 234n

Alexandria, 199, 235

GLOSSARIAL INDEX

or Liber, hence her Roman name, Libera; sometimes identified
with Aphrodite) 57, 177

Arion (legendary poet and musician of Lesbos, said to have been
saved from drowning by a music-loving dolphin) 202

Aristophanes (Greek comic poet, 455–375 B.C.) 103, 158, 254

Aristotle (384–322 B.C.; Greek philosopher) *xl*, 16, 65, 84, 139, 140,
146, 151, 170, 171, 187, 249, 250, 251, 252, 253, 254

Arnobius (ca. A.D. 305; Christian apologist) 252

Arrian (Flavius Arrianus, ca. A.D. 95–175; Greek author) 199

Artemis (Greek goddess = Roman Diana, sister of Apollo; protector
of wild animals and of virginity, and of the Amazons) 131, 139

Ascanius (son of Aeneas, whom he accompanied to Italy; founder of
Alba Longa) 228

Asia, *xlvi*, 22, 89, 154, 162, 200, 223, 229; Amazonism in, 105f;
hetaeric tradition of, *xlvii*, 99, 215, 216, 217, 218f, 220, 222,
224f, 227, 228, 230, 231, 232, 233, 234, 235, 236, 237, 239,
240; matriarchy in, *xlvii, xlix*, 99f, 103, 108, 117, 158

Asia Minor, *xliv, lv*, 130, 153, 171

Aso (a queen of Ethiopia, mentioned by Plutarch, *De Is. et Os.*,
13 . 356) 181

Assyria/Assyrians, 17, 215–22, 226, 228, 233

Atalanta (daughter of Schoeneus (in other versions, of Iasus), fleet
runner who challenged suitors to race with her and suffer death
if defeated; at length outrun by Melanion, or Hippomenes, to
whom Aphrodite gave three golden apples, which he used to
distract Atalanta during the race) 97, 181n, 191

Atarantes (a people of Libya) 142

Athenaeus (fl. A.D. 230; Greek author) 251, 252, 253

Athene (Greek goddess = Roman Minerva; born from the head of
Zeus; alternative or additional name, Pallas; patroness of Athens; female warrior and virgin) 58f, 75, 110f, 124, 144, 150,
158, 160ff, 165, 169

Athens, 53n, 57n, 121, 157, 161, 182, 194, 231; Apollonian principle
in, *xlv*, 74, 75f, 111, 159, 161f, 170; position of women in,
xviii, 157f, 165f, 168f

Atossa, 108n

Attica (the Greek territory of which Athens was capital) 53n, 89, 90,
96, 103, 111, 158, 162, 166, 169, 171, 182

Augiles (a people of Libya living west of the Ammonium) 136, 138,
142

Augustine, St. (Aurelius Augustinus, A.D. 354–430, bishop of Hippo) 157, 253

Augustus, Gaius Julius Caesar Octavianus (originally Gaius Octavius, 63 B.C.–A.D. 14; first Roman emperor) 39, 100, 118, 233n, 234

Aulus Gellius, *see* Gellius, Aulus

Aurelian (b. A.D. 212?; Roman emperor, 270–275), 234

Aurora (Roman equivalent of Eos, Greek goddess of dawn and youth) 124f

Ausians (African tribe living near the river and lake Tritonis, now the Chott Djerid in Tunis) 135, 140

Autolycus (figure in Xenophon's *Symposium*) 204

Auxesia (Cretan fertility goddess) 165, 166, 167, 169, 170

Aventine (one of Rome's seven hills, site of a temple of Diana) 36, 195

Babylonia/Babylonians, 136, 220, 234

Bacchus (alternative name for Dionysus, *q.v.*)

Balearic Islands, 136, 138, 142

Bassae (town in Arcadia, site of a famous temple of Apollo) 130

Battiads (rulers of Cyrene in 6th cent. B.C., named after its founder, Battus I) 183

Bebrycians (a people of Bithynia, *q.v.*) 198

Bel, or Baal (Semitic (Assyrian and Babylonian) god whom the Greeks identified with Heracles) *l*, 218, 222, 226, 236

Bellerophon (legendary Greek hero, son of Poseidon (or of Glaucus, king of Corinth); unjustly accused of attempting to seduce Anteia, *q.v.*; sent to Lycia, where in the service of its king he overcame first the Chimaera, *q.v.*, and afterward the Amazons; later, hated by the gods, wandered homeless in the Aleian meadow) *xlviii*, 84, 105f, 122f, 124, 125, 126ff, 129, 130, 131, 143f, 151, 162

Berenice II (queen of Egypt) 96n

Bithynia (territory in northern Asia Minor, on Black Sea coast) 144

Boeotia (Greek territory northwest of Athens, centered on Thebes) 38, 53n, 182

Bona Dea (Roman earth goddess, identified with Fauna, Maia, and Ops; object of festivals in May, June, and December) 164, 193

Bovillae (town in Latium, northwest of Rome) 225, 236

Brutus, Marcus Junius (ca. 78–42 B.C.; one of the murderers of Julius Caesar) 233

Byzantium, 235

Cadmeans (descendants of Cadmus) 182

Cadmus (legendary Greek hero, slayer of a dragon from whose teeth sprang up armed men, ancestors of the Thebans) 180

Caesar, Gaius Julius (ca. 102–44 B.C., Roman general and dictator) 56, 102, 233f

Caieta (nurse of Aeneas, buried at a town of the same name, the modern Gaeta in Campania near Naples) 228

Calamus (friend of Carpus; the latter drowned after a swimming match that Calamus had let him win; the comrades were changed to a rush and to fruit respectively, the meanings of the names) 97, 191

Callias (a character in Xenophon's *Symposium*) 204

Callisthenes, pseudo- (probably 3rd cent. A.D.; author of a fabulous history of Alexander the Great) 199

Calypso (daughter of Atlas, a nymph on whose island Odysseus was shipwrecked) *xviii*

Camillus, Marcus Furius (4th cent. B.C.; Roman general, defended Rome against the Gauls) 237n

Camisa (wife and sister of Janus, *q.v.*) 139

Campagna di Roma (region surrounding Rome) 13

Campania (district of south central Italy) 229

Candace (general name for the queens of Ethiopia, especially applied to the queen of Meroë who unsuccessfully invaded Egypt in 22 B.C.; the name is also given to a mythical Indian queen who figures in a late legend of Alexander the Great) 100, 117, 118, 191, 197, 198f, 200, 233, 234

Candaules (son of the legendary Indian Candace) 198

Cantabri (people of northwest Spain, conquered by Augustus) 71

Capua (city of Campania, absorbed into Roman territory in 4th cent. B.C.) 231

Caria/Carians (region, and its people, of southwest Asia Minor, south of Lydia and west of Lycia) 71, 81, 121, 151, 166, 171, 215

Carnea (festival in honor of Apollo, celebrated in Sparta and Doric Greece in August/September) 183

Carpus, *see* Calamus

Carrhae (now Haran) 113n

Carthage, *xlviii*, 227, 231f, 234, 235

Caspian Sea, 141

Cassandra, *see* Philonoë

Cassiodorus, Flavius Magnus Aurelius (ca. A.D. 487–583; late Roman Christian historian and scholar) 33, 38

Cinyras (Cypriot culture-hero who killed himself on finding that he had committed incest with his daughter Smyrna) 125

Circe (legendary sorceress of the island of Aeaea, who changed the companions of Ulysses (Odysseus) into swine and with whom he remained for a year; favoring winds enabled Aeneas to avoid her island) *xviii*, 228

Civilis, Julius (erroneously Claudius; led a partly successful revolt of the German tribe of the Batavians against Rome in A.D. 69–70) 235

Clearchus of Soli (3rd cent. B.C.; pupil of Aristotle's, author of miscellaneous works, only fragments of which were preserved by Athenaeus and other writers) 104, 141, 203, 255

Cleitae (the Amazonian queens of the city of Cleite in Italy, founded by Cleite, foster mother of Penthesilea; the city was destroyed by the Crotonians) 108

Cleopatra (the name of several queens of Egypt in the Ptolemaic period, from 193 B.C., especially Cleopatra VII, 68–30 B.C., mother of a son by Julius Caesar and beloved of Mark Antony) *xlviii, xlix*, 100, 228, 233, 234

Clytaemnestra (wife of Agamemnon, adulterous consort of his cousin Aegistheus; murdered Agamemnon on his return from Trojan War and was in turn slain by her son Orestes) 104, 158, 159, 161, 173, 185

Cocytus (tributary of Acheron, *q.v.*) 27

Colonus (hill north of Athens, place of Oedipus' death) 182

Colophon (ancient Ionian city in Lydia, Asia Minor) 53n

Consus (Roman deity of agriculture and good counsel, sometimes identified with Neptune, or Poseidon) 35, 36, 37

Corinth/Corinthians, 42, 123, 130, 131, 162, 166, 170, 231

Corneto (Etruscan town northwest of Rome; today Tarquinia) 12, 39

Cratinus (ca. 520–ca. 423 B.C.; Greek comic poet whose works, save for some fragments, are lost) 54

Creon (father of Glauce and brother of Iocasta; King of Thebes after the death of Iocasta's husband Laius, but surrendered the crown to Oedipus; ruled once more after the death of Oedipus' sons, Eteocles and Polynices) 181

Crete, *xliv*, 177; customs in, 79, 121, 133, 151, 157n, 168, 179, 203; excavations at, *xxviii, lv*

Creusa (daughter of Priam, king of Troy, and first wife of Aeneas) 228

Cronus, or Kronos (Titan, father of Zeus, Poseidon, Hera, Demeter, and other gods; = Roman god Saturn; castrated his father,

way for his brother, who then attacked with six companions (the "Seven against Thebes"); in single combat the brothers killed each other) 27, 28, 187

Eteonus (Boeotian town on the border of Attica, in one account the burial place of Oedipus) 182

Ethiopia/Ethiopians, 135f, 137, 141, 146, 181, 199

Etruria (area of Italy northwest of Rome, home of the Etruscans, roughly equivalent to the modern Tuscany) 12, 212, 213, 217

Etruscans, *xlviii, xlix,* 28, 38, 99, 136, 141, 211, 212, 213, 214, 215, 217, 218, 229, 230, 231, 237n, 238, 242n

Euboea (island in the Aegean Sea northeast of Attica and Boeotia) 38

Eumenides, *see* Erinyes

Euneus (son of Jason and Hypsipyle) 173, 176

Euphrates, *see* Mesopotamia; Tigris and Euphrates rivers

Euripides (Greek tragic poet, ca. 480–406 B.C.) *xx,* 110, 115, 249, 250, 254

Europe, *xliv,* 108, 162, 231, 232, 233, 237, 238, 244

Eurotas (principal river of Laconia, flowing by Sparta) 170

Eurytus and Cteatus, *see* Moliones

Eustathius (archbishop of Thessalonica, latter half of 12th cent. A.D.; author of an extensive commentary on *Iliad* and *Odyssey*) 72, 73, 86, 203, 255

Fatua, *see* Fauna

Fauna, or Fatua (Roman fertility and woodland goddess, identified with Bona Dea) 144, 193

Flaccus, Quintus Fulvius, 31

flamines (sing. flamen; body of fifteen priests in Rome, each assigned a major god; their wives, the *flaminicae,* assisted them and were essential to the performance of their duties) 226, 227, 228, 229, 238

Flavians (the three Roman emperors Vespasian, 69–79; Titus, 79–81; and Domitian, 81–96) 234f

Flora (Roman fertility goddess of flowering plants and gardens, of Sabine origin; her festival, April 28–May 1, the Floralia, was celebrated with extreme licentiousness) 217, 227, 225

Floralia, 221, 225

Fortuna (Roman goddess of good fortune, called Praenestine from her temple at Praeneste, southeast of Rome; as Fortuna Muliebris she was specially honored as protector of women; also called

Isis (Egyptian mother goddess, sister and wife of Osiris and mother of Horus; recovered the body of Osiris when he had been slain by his evil brother Typhon, or Set) 27, 60, 77, 89, 117, 118, 138, 178f, 185f, 228

Ismene (daughter of Oedipus and sister of Antigone) 183

Italy, 22, 232, 195; Amazonism in, 106, 153; mother right in, *xlvi*, *xlix*, 89, 201; Oriental influence, 211, 215, 218, 219, 220f, 223, 226, 227, 228, 229, 230, 232, 234, 235, 236; *see also* Etruscans; Rome; Tanaquil

Ixion (punished by Zeus for an attempt on Hera by being bound in the underworld to a perpetually turning wheel) 51, 62

Janus (ancient Roman god of doors and beginnings) 139, 206

Jason (leader of the Argonaut expedition, during which he stopped at Lemnos and begat two sons by Hypsipyle; later married Glauce) 173, 176, 181

Jehovah, 234

Jericho (ancient Palestinian city) 41

Jerusalem, 234, 235

John the Baptist, 139

Josephus, Flavius (A.D. 37–ca. 100; Jewish historian who wrote in Greek) 250

Jugurtha (king of Numidia in Africa, defeated and captured by the Roman general Sulla in 105 B.C.) 233

Julia Maesa (hereditary priestess of the Emesan sun god Elagabalus and grandmother of the emperor who adopted that name) 234n

Julia Mamaea (daughter of Julia Maesa and mother of the Roman emperor Alexander Severus) 234

Julian, *see* Julianus

Julians (Roman patrician gens of which Julius Caesar and Augustus were members) 233, 235

Julianus, Salvius (2nd cent. A.D.; Roman jurist, author of *Digestae* and other legal compilations) 132, 251

Julius Valerius, *see* Valerius, Julius

Juno (Roman goddess, spouse of Jupiter = the Greek Hera, *q.v.*) 99

Juno Moneta (an aspect of Juno, worshiped as giver of good counsel; the word "money" is derived from her name because her temple on the Capitoline Hill became the Roman mint) 195

Jupiter (principal Roman god, originally of the sky = the Greek Zeus; at Anxur he was worshiped in the form of a beardless boy) 36

Justin (Marcus Junianus Justinus, 3rd cent. A.D. or later; Roman historian, compiler of an abridgment of the universal history of Trogus Pompeius) 199, 253

Justinian (Flavius Petrus Sabbatius Justinianus, Emperor of the East, A.D. 527–565; codifier of the Roman law) 4, 118

Juvenal (Decimus Junius Juvenalis, A.D. 60?–140; Roman satirist) 32, 33, 249

Kore, *see* Demeter; Persephone
Kronos, *see* Cronus

Labdacids (descendants of Labdacus, the father of Laius, *q.v.*) 180, 182, 185

Lacedaemonians (inhabitants of Lacedaemon, or Sparta) 142, 153, 171, 182

Laconia (country of southern Peloponnesus, chief town Sparta) 151, 182

Lactantius Firmianus, Lucius Caecilius (ca. A.D. 250–ca. 317; Christian orator and writer) 249, 253

Lada, 155

Ladon (hundred-headed dragon or serpent who guarded the golden apples of the Hesperides) 180

Laius (son of Labdacus, husband of Iocasta and father of Oedipus, by whom he was slain) 181, 182, 183, 184, 203

Lala, 155

Lamia (her children by Zeus were slain by Hera; in revenge she became a vampire, destroying the children of others) 167

Laodamia (daughter of Acastus and wife of Protesilaus; when the latter was killed in the Trojan War, her grief was such that the gods allowed him to return briefly, at the end which time she killed herself) 48n

Laodamia (daughter of Bellerophon and mother of Sarpedon by Zeus) 72, 73, 74, 125

Laophontes (alternative name of Bellerophon, *q.v.*) 126

Laothoe, 133

Lara, 155

coast of the extreme toe of Italy were known as the Epizephyrian Locrians) 136, 152, 201; Epizephyrian, 71, 86, 99, 103, 108; Ozolian, 153, 175

Longinus, Dionysius Cassius (3rd cent. A.D.; Greek philosopher, long credited with a treatise *On the Sublime*, now generally assigned to an unknown but earlier author) 41, 250

Lubentina ("willing one"; epithet applied to Venus as goddess of sensual pleasure) 138

Lucan (Marcus Annaeus Lucanus, A D. 39–65; Roman poet) 254

Lucian(us) (2nd cent. A.D.; Greek writer of satirical dialogues) 144, 252

Luna (Greek Selene; personification of the moon as a deity) 45, 46, 113n, 115, 148, 178, 179, 192

Lunus (name given to the moon as a masculine personification or to the sun as husband of the moon) 45, 46, 113n, 148, 177, 179, 192

Lycaon (son of Priam, king of Troy, by Laothoë) 133

Lycia/Lycians (country and people of the southwest coast of Asia Minor) 17, 84, 105f, 126f, 157; and Amazonism, 84, 105f, 122f, 124, 131, 143, 150, 162 (*see also* Bellerophon); and mother right, xxviii, xxxiii, xlv, 70, 72, 78, 88, 96, 103, 106, 107, 108, 121, 122, 123, 124, 125, 128, 129, 141, 151f, 154ff, 158

Lycophron (Greek poet, 285–247 B.C.; author of a poem called *Cassandra,* or *Alexandra,* which, with the scholia upon it by Isaac and John Tzetzes, is of considerable importance for mythological studies) 130, 231, 251, 255

Lycurgus (7th cent. B.C.?; legendary Spartan lawgiver) 142n, 151, 170

Lycus (son of Pandion, legendary founder of Lycia) 121, 157

Lydia/Lydians (country and people of western Asia Minor, in the area surrounding Sardis) 41, 141f, 215, 216, 217, 218, 219

Macedonia, 197, 198, 231

Magna Mater, *see* Great Mother

Malalas, Ioannes (ca. 491–578; Byzantine chronographer) 255

Manlius Capitolinus, Marcus (Roman consul, 392 B.C.; held the Capitol against the Gauls) 194

Mantinea (town in Arcadia) 90

Nymphis of Heraclea (ca. 250 B.C.; author of a work on Alexander the Great, now lost) 122

Oceanus (river supposed by the Greeks to surround the flat earth, personified as one of the Titans and begetter of all other rivers and seas) 123, 149

Ocnus (legendary figure punished in Hades by having to twist a rope of straw that was continually consumed by an ass) *xv*, 22, 26, 51, 52, 53, 54, 55, 56, 58, 59, 61ff, 64, 65, 127

Ocrisia, 225*n*

Octavian, *see* Augustus

Oedipodeum, 182

Oedipus (son of Laius, king of Thebes, and his wife Iocasta; unwittingly slew his father and lay with his mother; on discovering what he had done, he blinded himself, was deposed, and eventually died at Colonus under Theseus' protection) *xlviii*, 62, 179, 180, 181ff, 184, 185, 187

Oedipus, sons of, *see* Eteocles

Ogygian (relating to Ogyges, legendary king of Thebes, or to the flood which inundated Boeotia during his reign) 164

Olympian gods (the dynasty of gods supposed to dwell under the rule of Zeus (Rom. Jupiter) on Mount Olympus, on the borders of Thessaly) 129, 159, 162, 163, 186

Olympias (d. 316 B.C.; wife of Philip II of Macedon and mother of Alexander the Great) 198

Omphale (queen of Lydia, who purchased Heracles as a slave, made him her lover, and exchanged garments with him) 104, 142, 216, 217, 218, 223, 224, 226, 227, 228

Ops (Roman goddess of plenty and agricultural wealth, identified with Rhea or sometimes with Diana) 195

Orestes (son of Agamemnon and Clytaemnestra; avenged his father by slaying his mother, for which he was tormented by the Erinyes) *xlviii*, 110, 118, 158f, 160, 161, 162, 163, 184, 185, 188, 233

Orpheus (legendary Thracian poet and musician, husband of Eurydice; his name became associated with a mystery cult which taught transmigration of souls) 26, 29, 48, 49, 58, 62, 63, 90, 103, 112, 202, 203, 204, 205, 206

Osiris (Egyptian deity, husband and brother of Isis, god of death and resurrection, representing the masculine principle of reproduction) 59f, 89, 138, 178f

ovatio (a minor and less impressive form of *triumphus, q.v.*) 194
Ovid (Publius Ovidius Naso, (43 B.C.–A.D. 18?; Roman poet) 125,
203, 250, 251, 254, 255
Ozolae, *see* Locrians

Palestine, *xliv*
Palinurus (pilot of Aeneas' ship who fell into the sea and was carried
to land, where he was murdered) 228
Pallas, *see* Athene
Palmyra (city-state in Syria under Roman protection, destroyed by the
Emperor Aurelian, A.D. 272) 234
Pandion (father of Lycus, *q.v.*) 121, 157
Pandora (woman fashioned from clay by the gods and presented to
Epimetheus, brother of Prometheus; released the ills and afflic-
tions which beset mankind) 138, 174
Paris, *see* Alexander
Parthenopaeus (son of Meleager and Atalanta, one of the "Seven
against Thebes") 181n
Pasiphaë (wife of Minos, King of Crete, who fell in love with a bull
and gave birth to a monster known as the Minotaur) *xxviii*
Paul, St., 146
Paulus, Julius (fl. ca. A.D. 200; Roman jurist) 133, 252
Pausanias (2nd cent. A.D.; Greek geographer) 53, 54, 180, 233, 250,
252, 253, 254, 255, 256
Pegasus (winged horse of the hero Bellerophon, who sprang from the
blood of the Gorgon Medusa) 122, 124f
Pelasgians (the traditional inhabitants of Greece before the arrival of
the Greek peoples) 71, 87, 90, 91, 110f, 171, 201
Pelopids (the descendants of Pelops) 177
Pelops (ancestor of Agamemnon and Menelaus, secured the hand of
Hippodamia by using a trick to win a chariot race) 177, 183,
203
Penelope (wife of Ulysses or Odysseus; during her husband's absence,
put off rival suitors by insisting that she must finish a weaving
task, and unraveled at night what she had woven by day) *xviii*,
26
Penia (want, or penury) 131, 138, 192
Penthesilea (queen of the Amazons and their leader in the Trojan
War; slain by Achilles) 13, 130, 174
Periander (tyrant of Corinth, 625–585 B.C.) 170
Persephone (daughter of Demeter, *q.v.*) 139

Polybius (ca. 204–122 B.C.; Greek historian of Rome) 71, 86, 241, 251

Polybus (king of Corinth, foster father of Oedipus) 182

Polygnotus (celebrated Greek painter of 5th cent. B.C., who decorated public buildings at Athens and Delphi) 53, 54, 63n, 64

Polynices, *see* Eteocles

Pompey (Gnaeus Pompeius Magnus, 106–48 B.C.; Roman general who conquered much of the East for Rome) 151, 233

pontifices (sing. pontifex; Roman priests administering religious cults) 226

Porsena, Lars (Etruscan king of Clusium in late 6th cent. B.C., who traditionally attacked Rome in the interest of its exiled king Tarquinius Superbus, but withdrew after taking hostages; actually he seems to have occupied the city for a time) 230

Porus (an Indian king defeated by Alexander the Great, who was afterward restored to his dominions) 197, 198

Poseidon (Greek god of the sea and of horses = Neptune; built the walls of Troy, and on being cheated of payment, sent a sea monster to ravage the country; represents brute masculine strength) *lv*, 41, 63, 114, 122, 123, 124, 125, 126, 127, 128, 132, 144n, 177n, 180, 203

Posidonius (ca. 135–ca. 50 B.C.; Greek Stoic philosopher and historian who wrote on Pompey's wars) 151

Praeneste (town southeast of Rome, today Palestrina) 238

praetors (Roman magistrates concerned with the administration of justice and of the provinces) 193

Priam (king of Troy at the time of the Trojan War) 133

Priapus (Greek god of fertility and generation, usually represented by an erect phallus) 139, 164

Proetus (king of Argos, husband of Sthenoboea, or Anteia, who, believing his wife's accusations, plotted Bellerophon's death) 131

Prometheus (a Titan who gave fire to man; in punishment Zeus chained him to a rock and sent an eagle to devour his liver each day) 110

Propertius, Sextus (b. ca. 51 B.C.; Roman poet) 54, 250

Protesilaus, *see* Laodamia

psoloeis (male mourners at a ritual in Orchomenus, Boeotia) 175

Psyche (personification of the soul, loved by Eros (= Amor, Cupid), who visited her by night until in curiosity she used a lamp to look on him; he escaped, and she went in search of him;

Scyros (small island in the Aegean where Achilles' mother hid him to prevent his going to the Trojan War) 42

Scythia/Scythians (country and its people to the north of the Black Sea, between the Don and the Carpathians) 105, 134, 144f, 146, 152, 153

Scythius, or Scyphius (the first horse, which arose from the seed of Poseidon) 144

Segetia (Roman goddess of sowing) 35

Seia (Roman goddess of sowing) 35

Selene (Greek moon goddess = Roman Luna) 206

Semiramis (legendary Assyrian queen, wife of Ninus) 227

Semo Sancus (Sabine god, identified with the Roman Dius Fidius, whose temple stood on the Quirinal; presided over oaths) 218, 223, 239

Servius Marius (or Maurus) Honoratus (4th cent. A.D.; Roman grammarian, author of extensive comment on Virgil) 54n, 192n, 250

Servius Tullius (legendary sixth king of Rome, successor of Tarquinius Priscus; son of the slave Ocrisia, he was brought up by Tanaquil) *xlix*, 194, 213f, 219, 220, 221, 222f, 225n, 230, 238, 243

Sesonchosis (king of Egypt mentioned by Julius Valerius, probably Sheshonk I, ca. 950 B.C.) 199

Sextus Empiricus (3rd cent. A.D.; Greek physician who wrote on philosophical questions) 136, 252

Sibyl (name given to various women endowed with prophecy, especially the Cumaean Sibyl, consulted by Aeneas) 144

Silenus (a satyr, attendant on and tutor of Dionysus) 27

Simonides of Ceos (556–467 B.C.; Greek lyric poet) 83, 154, 251

Sinope (Greek city on south coast of Black Sea, whence cult of Sarapis was carried to Egypt by Ptolemy I) 117

Sintians (ancient inhabitants of Lemnos) 175

Sipylus (mountain in Lydia) 155

Sisyphus (king of Corinth, grandfather of Bellerophon; punished in Hades by having continually to push uphill a huge rock which invariably rolled down again) 51, 123, 127

Socrates, 70, 90f, 204, 206

Socrates (painter referred to by Pliny, *Natural History* 35 . 40 . 137) *xv*

Sol (the sun, as a Roman god equated with Greek Helios, later identified with Apollo) 36, 114, 192